The Ancestral Trail

Copyright Frank Graves 1990
Published by Frajil Publishing

The Ancestral Trail

Book One

Long Ago & Far Away

The Ancient World

Copyright Frank Graves 1990
Published by Frajil Publishing

First Published by Marshall Cavendish Ltd. 1992
Website: www.theancestraltrail.com
Copyright Frank Graves 1990
ISBN 978-1-873133-12-5

Book Kindly Edited by Allan Gauci

The Ancestral Trail Trilogy
Book One
Long Ago & Far Away

The Ancient World Odyssey

Since the beginning of time, creatures of the air, land and water have lived in peace in the Ancestral World. Landsmen, common beasts, birds and fishes have dwelt in harmony with insects, reptiles and mythical beasts. Ruled with fairness and wisdom by the Council of Guardians, they have known neither suffering nor the ravages of war. Now an evil spirit has come to this land and is laying waste to all that is good. The Forces of Evil have gained ground fast and many of these peaceful creatures have been killed or have fallen under the Evil One's power.

The Life Force of the Ancestral World is almost at an end.

The Ancestral Trail Trilogy

Book One - The Ancient World

Long Ago & Far Away

PROLOGUE

When he who is the Chosen One
Shall tread upon the Ancient Path
And battle there to overcome
The Forces of the Dark
Then shall the Seven be restored
And evil banished from this world

If you had asked Richard whether he believed in ghosts, witches, ancestral myths or dream people before he went on his trip to the wicked woodland, he would probably have given you a very strange answer because he neither believed nor disbelieved in things that went bump in the night. He was not of a nervous disposition, nor had he ever really been frightened by ghosts, the supernatural or, any of the other strange myriad creations and superstitions like some of his more nervous friends and relatives. But... 'That was before he had his unscheduled spectral nightmare'.

Ask the same question now and you'll get a resounding, "'Yes, I know for certain that they really do exist.'"

You could ask, why this shift in his position?

It all came about one evening when Richard, or 'Mutant', as he was commonly referred to by friends and family alike, mainly due to the very different colouring in both eyes, was happily returning from a shopping errand on his new mountain bike, he was in no hurry that afternoon, but on a sudden whim, came away from the road to the practice jumps through some of his favourite forest trails. One of which led him to stop at what had once been his favourite haunt, where the great old tree named 'Eternity', had thrived for centuries. This was the first really clear day because over the last week, the great forest had been battered and decimated by storms; this included the old tree that had been blown over by these record high winds sweeping across the whole district. The toppled tree had now left a very large crater in the ground. In no time at all, quite a few local people had benefited by the summer storms in various ways, the great old tree itself, had been quickly sliced up and removed by a local furniture maker while the rest of its timber, rapidly got spirited away through locals to be used as firewood. It was a heartfelt departure for Richard and his friends as all that remained behind now was the tree's root ball in combination with spindly sand filled roots and a very large crater. During the previous week there had again been further really heavy thunderstorms in the area that left the crater looking more like a big fishpond than anything else. The enormous tree's twisted and knurled washed roots stretching into the air like some huge spiked hair arrangement.

Richard wheeled his bike across to examine what still remained of the fallen tree; his thinking was that the upended root ball looked for all the world like a giant spider climbing up to the heavens, because the tentacle-like root system was so much more obvious stretched out of the ground, washed clean by those later heavy downpours. Richard noticed that the water level was only a small way off the lip of what had been that crater but somehow, now would become fair game among his various friends to be their newest swimming hole after school.

"Wait until I tell them, this is going to be great." he whispered to himself as he began sizing up various theme park type options in his mind's eye; every now and again he could even see tadpoles darting back and forth below the water,

"Whoa! We could string a rope slide from that tree," his gaze travelled from a large branch of a neighbouring tree down to the root ball, it was then, that something caught his eye. It was partially hidden although clearly visible with one end sticking out from in among the now washed coils. He could see what looked for the world, like a very old metal box.

"Maybe it holds gold, or rubies, or... Gotta get it out of there before anyone else arrives to claim it as theirs."

Richard moved quickly, noting that although the container seemed very old at distance, it showed slight signs of what he presumed was rust. He even made out some sort of strange golden coloured motifs dotting the container; his mind automatically presumed that with those, it was bound to be buried treasure of some kind. It wasn't obvious to Richard that anybody had visited this site since the last storm passed through, he quickly decided that this box was going to be all his.

Richard moved around the clear blue pond, scrambling over the back of the heavy rooting system making sure he could reach his new found treasure without then toppling into the water; he began levering the old box until it finally dislodged from its muddy stickiness. Grasping it firmly, it wasn't heavy, he scrambled back down to ground level and established that the catch came away quite easily; he slowly but tenderly opened the valuable find.

Inside, was just an old rag that perhaps hid something else? Richard reached out and stroked the cloth, encountering something firm that hardness assured him that it was hiding something. Gingerly taking the utmost care, Richard carefully lifted the newfound bundle onto the ground before cautiously undoing the knot to release his newly acquired treasure.

"Whoa!"

His first sighting was of all sorts of unordinary and wonderful looking inscriptions printed throughout the inside of this cloth. More importantly, there were also two further items nestling inside their folds. The larger item being a shimmering helmet; made from what appeared to be beaten silver, Richard immediately realised that the seven golden discs surrounding it meant that his, was a very special find. Each disc contained differing writing and abnormal insignias dotted around their circular edges. Beside the helmet was what Richard then thought was a woman's amulet, it too, was intricately designed with similar peculiar motifs and symbols. He picked up the bracelet to examine it more carefully,

"Must be hieroglyphics or something," he convinced himself. There was no catch on the bracelet, but as he easily slipped it onto his arm to get a better look at it, it somehow seemed to tighten down to exactly the right size for his wrist.

"Wha?" he tried removing it, but found that he could not get it back over his hand; no matter how hard he tried to detach the amulet, it was solidly stuck fast around his arm.

"Naah! Must be some form of trick bangle?" He questioned, as he searched for a hidden release mechanism. Not able to work it out, Richard finally gave up and turned his attention back to the cloth, it did not take long for him to realise that in fact it wasn't any old rag, it was more like some sort of cloak; he carefully lifted the helmet out of its position within the material and placed it on the ground to examine it further. He lifted the cloak to the sunlight and inspected the fabulously designed imprinted gold insignias braided into the material that also had an attached cape; the shawl itself contained no sleeves or sleeve holes. Richard drew himself up to his full height and in one quick swishing movement, pulled the cloak around his shoulders.

"How cool is this?" Richard found himself using the pond as his personal mirror; looking down into the water, he noticed that the material had come alive. Checking the cloak several times, he felt that something strange was happening, he double-checked, looking down at the cloth, all he saw was lovely fabric. However, checking his reflection in the pool, what he saw was the material magically shimmering and dancing even though the pool was dead calm.

"Strange or even stranger," he questioned. "Maybe just a trick of the light I suppose. I reckon this must have been some kind of king's outfit, wonder what it's doing here?" His attention turned back to the helmet once again, Richard slowly lifted it from its current position to examine the glorious find, he then made an on the spot decision. Richard did not realise it just then, that his impetuousness was somehow going to change his life forever.

"Wicked! Perhaps it is a Viking's helmet from a bygone era, or even possibly belonged to some kind of ancient tribal magician, who knows? Imagine, now it's all mine, perhaps this lot is going to make me so, so rich." He drooled softly.

Savouring the few daydreams, he climbed back to the highest point of the large root ball and then slowly but very deliberately, almost ritualistically, like some ancient king performing his own coronation, raised the beautifully crafted headgear high into the air above his head.

"I now crown myself... King Palooka of Anywhere." Richard chanted, "Ta-Ta-Taaaann-tarrraaa-Taaaaa and may my reign be a long and happy one, Ta-Ta-Taaaann-tarrraaa-Taaaaa ".

He then lowered the helmet slowly until it sat firmly on his head.

That's when everything kicked off for Richard

One minute, he stood on top of the root system trying on the fabulous helmet, but next, the sodden ground gave way to send him plummeting towards the bluish coloured liquid below. He landed with an almighty splash in the water-filled hole.

"Wha..." That was the only word he managed to splutter plunging deep below the now discoloured water, Richard never even saw the dunking coming as he hit the water and took off through an imaginary red blur at a speed that seemed to release him from its grip in seconds; allowing him to come up to take a large breath. His brain instantly panicked, instead of the root ball, there was a strange looking mountain with a zigzag waterfall in the distance, and this place had a completely different feel and look, his spinning brain could not perceive this sudden upheaval, the fall had sent him into an illusionary fantasy world.

"No, no, no, this can't be happening!" The feeling of utter panic struck out at his already strained nerve ends, Richard's great difficulty was to comprehend everything in absolute detail, understanding that this water was no longer his water hole, but instead, the liquid colouring had now become a tinkling fluorescent red. He let out a terrific wail of despair at the huge ever-watchful mountain; his frustrating scream achieved nothing but to bounce desperate echoes of irritation and fear around the sheer walls of the ravine. It appeared as if nobody was even listening to his plight, or at least, that's what Richard thought as his head began reeling and he quickly passed into unconsciousness.

"W-What happened?"

Richard slowly lifted his bruised and painful head off the ground, it felt as if there were a flight of migrating swallows passing through his senses; the feeling came and went in reeling formation as he desperately tried to understand what was happening.

"Ugggh!" Looking up, he nearly swallowed his tongue, Richard shook his head sharply to clear the foggy mists still surrounding his confused brain, but still; he couldn't believe his eyes. There, perhaps only in his mind's eye, a longhaired old man with a white beard that reached almost to the ground, was leaning closely over the top of him. Richard began blinking rapidly, he was certain that his brain was clear and for sure, this was no ordinary old man, at that very moment his confused common sense couldn't quite understand what it was that now confronted him. His eyesight it seemed was playing tricks, for he was now seeing this hunched figure looking more like some kind of oversized, puffed up, grotesque chameleon. Its bulbous eyes, the wide mouth, the v- shaped head topped with what looked like a small wreath of flowers draped across it then trailed lazily down its back, hooking onto the spindly branches of an old tree.

"Arrgh!" Richard shook his head; blinking several times again to make sure that it wasn't just his usually overworked imagination simply playing peculiar tricks.

"W-wha..."

The larger than life beast was still hovering over him. He wondered if 'this thing' had been sent to seek revenge for the time he had teased their neighbour's pet frog with a stick.

"I didn't mean it," he whispered, desperately hoping this would not annoy this much-distorted beast that now confronted him.

The thing leaned forward closely, Richard suddenly felt its hot putrid breath stroking his cheek, he turned his head away, hoping that whatever it was going to do to him wouldn't take too long or be seriously painful. In this befuddled state, he then had another stupefied moment, he saw a short boy with strange pig-like appearance, dressed in ancient leather clothing and whatever this boy was, he held a bow in one hand. The illusionary boy ashamedly turned away so that Richard could no longer observe its face, strapped to his back was a quiver filled with strange looking arrows but, in that fleeting observation second, Richard made out that the pig-like boy's clothes were also dripping wet.

"What do you want? Who... who are you..." Richard managed to splutter.

"For some time we have been expecting someone to arrive, my name is Golan; I am the 'Guardian of the Ancestral Woodland'." The thing licked at its thin lips. "You've now ventured to our sacred world as was foretold; you must quickly learn the trail of ancestors." The old man's voice, unlike the rest of its mangled and harsh looking body, was tenderly soft and lilting in texture.

"I...I want to go home."

The huge monstrosity pushed its wide mouth right up to Richard's face and pulled its thinly plated lips back over the buckled teeth, for just a split moment Richard presumed that he saw what looked like two sharp red pinpricks of some death ray where the beast's bulging eyes should have been.

"Okay, okay!"

"You cannot return to your world, at least, not until you've accomplished all of the tasks that will be given."

Richard wasn't really in any position to argue with the huge chameleon-like monster.

"W-what tasks?"

"Follow me; it is unsafe to remain here."

"W-What if... I don't want to carry out these tasks or come with you?"

"Oh well, it's your choice, you stay here and become like me. In our world, time as you know it is very different, so your stay could be extremely long or quite a short one, it's all about how you conduct yourself. You must make up your mind quickly; this can be a very dangerous place, especially if you don't know the terrain or some of the inhabitants."

Richard shuddered; he couldn't imagine himself looking like 'that', he desperately tried to remove the helmet still stuck fast to his head.

"You will not be able to remove those items just yet, they are still controlled by all seven Pods of Life," said Golan.

"W-what?"

"It's a long story, come, I will help you to remove it but, not here. Those seven gold emblems on that head covering have been activated by the Pods of Life and the helmet chose to 'bring you' to the 'Ancestral City'. That was a 'great honour'. Once removed, you won't be able to put it back on your head until such time that all 'Pods of Life' are safely restored to their rightful place."

"Great, so how do you activate these so called, 'Pods of Life'?"

"Later, now follow us, don't get lost, because there are some really nasty things in 'this world'." The beast moved away fluidly, half-hopping, half gliding forward. Instantly the strange looking pig-like boy with the bow and arrow diligently fell into step close behind Golan. Richard, not wanting to be left alone in these strange surroundings, quickly made a decision to join the group. They made their way deep into the surrounding woodland.

"Better the devil you know and all that, this is crazy, what am I doing here?" He mumbled this under his breath reluctantly moving in behind the strange pair. Golan stopped, turned and studied the young man; it was as if he had clearly heard Richard's comment. "Fool!" Suddenly his colouring changed to puce and a long red flaming tongue whipped out of the chameleon's broad mouth to crack like a bullwhip against a tree near Richard, he immediately dived flat to the ground. "Thoughts like that are not very helpful to your well being," said Golan. "Consider this journey as your most exciting adventure."

The peculiar little band arrived at a large clearing, the sun blazed down through an open canopy in the trees above and straight onto a sparkling centre circle. Richard immediately recognised that this was where his captors held court because; it looked just like that sort of animistic place. The beast called Golan sat down on the central bed of shining white stones; some decorated with moss, and then wriggled until he was comfortable. For the first time since encountering the thing, Richard noticed that there seemed to be a very faint aura that surrounded Golan's whole frame, perhaps it was just his imagination or possibly, the way the dazzling light from above caught the ogre shaped monstrosity, Golan now looked somewhat more magisterial and strangely had imperceptibly changed colour to a more silvery sheen. The large beast cleared his fat jowls by opening and shutting the great mouth in preparation to deliberate with Richard.

"Now child, what be your name?"

"R-Richard, but some friends call me M-Mutant, I don't know why really."

"Well master Richard, we Guardians were expecting someone, uh, different... Sort of well... uh, bigger and more warrior-like somehow..." Golan paused. "You 'are' a bit scrawny, but then again, who am I to question the powers that be? The prophecy was someone that could see both good and evil would come to help us in this time of need."

"I can't tell right from wrong, let alone good from evil. Naah! You have the wrong bloke, now could you kindly return me to my home if you please." Richard whispered.

"Your eyes tell me you are the one... each bear different colouring, one will locate good, the other will find evil. A long time ago, the prophecies foretold of our present predicament, it also foretold your coming, these prophecies are never incorrect."

"Oh yeah! Just because my eyes are different, there's no need to take the..." He came up short from saying what he really wanted to say because Richard wasn't quite sure just then, how far his rebellious boundaries would be acceptable in this world, so just left any niceties for the moment.

"The grey eye sees the dark side of life, the green eye sees good. Only you can weigh the balance."

"Whaa? That's nonsense." Richard retorted.

"Anyway, things change and now you're in our world and you are going to have to learn the ancient ways."

"What do you mean, 'ancient ways'?"

"Humans like you, call them myths. It goes far beyond the conjuring up of phantoms and it's through these tales, that the minds of all people confront the mystery of the universe. Unfortunately for you, you will have to learn these first and only then, you 'may' be allowed back into your own world. Never fear, this boy will initially be your guide and mentor, that coat you wear is the 'Cape of Darnell' but remember, use it with care because each time that you lift the cape over your head you will become totally invisible to the outside world. However, you can only use it seven times, once for each pod then it will no longer retain its power. You must understand this well, it has only seven lives, so do not waste those lives."

"W-What if... I don't want to learn these myths?"

Golan stopped talking, suddenly its long crimson tongue shot out and slapped against a nearby tree sounding very much like the loud report of a rifle shot. Richard jumped; it was so unexpected that it caught him completely off guard. Golan was busily chewing something but was now assured of Richard's full attention as he continued with his story.

"First thing, we need you to help us, my powers have weakened considerably since the war and I am frail and will be unable to make the trip, it needs someone young and strong blooded to achieve this journey." The pompous wizard continued.

"Me help 'you'? ...How?"

"This place is the original universe garden; you notice that we are seated beside the 'Tree of Life'. Once upon a time all life started in this very spot; this tree has always been the beating heart of the universe, it sheds seven jewelled pods every few decades of 'your' time. The seven pods represent seven facets of goodness, which then regenerate the tree and hence the whole universe. Since time began, this has always taken place, although not anymore because somebody has stolen six of the newly formed pods. The responsibility of looking after these pods was always entrusted to our special Ancestral Guardians. Each representative of a pod has now gone missing, as have six of the seven pods. It is our task, now yours, to help by your following the 'Ancestral Trail'. We all have but a short point in time to find the six pods, and also to save the Guardians because we must place them back in their rightful position before we can conclude the Great Ceremony of Aght."

"What happens if they're not replaced?"

"Death and destruction throughout this world and throughout the universe and in time terms, it means that the world will die again. We must not let that happen! You will find that the world out there," he swept his arm in a wide arc, "is already dying because evil is on the rise."

"What do you want me to do?"

"There was a great war between good and evil which was not won nor lost, it is ongoing and I'm afraid we now slowly lose this battle against the evil forces, I must remain here to be a central focus, and you accompany the boy into the Ancestral World. He is called Orkan and he too, has a quest to follow. He understands this world and will show you some of the trees and animals out there. He's been there before and he too has a duty to try to help rescue the Guardians. Each creature you meet will have different stories to relate, some modern, some old, you must learn to listen carefully to them. That way, we'll be able to find out just who have stolen the Pods of Life from here and where the Guardians have disappeared to but you must be very careful. More advice, as you travel, find a common thread, that way, you'll begin to understand our ways more quickly. Now you have to go with him," Golan pointed to the pig-like boy.

"Remember to be vigilant while out there, not everything will be as it first appears. Not all creatures will be good, those you least expect, could be your worst enemies, while others will aid you in your quest. Your task is to quickly understand and judge which is which, you have to, the very life of those around you will constantly depend on your decisions."

"Can't I rather go home?" Richard murmured softly.

"You most certainly cannot. But before you go you must again energise your amulet with the last remaining pod, guard that bracelet with your very life, if it is lost the universe and everything within it are doomed to failure and evil will have prevailed," Golan's rolled up tongue shot out and skilfully picked a sparkling white pod from the branches high above their heads, then delivered it delicately to Richard's feet. The pod began to shimmer, glowing purple colour as did Richard's amulet and helmet at the same time.

"Now you are able to remove the sacred Helmet of Roshta leave it with me, no doubt you may have need of it sometime in the future."

Richard removed the helmet and set it down against the big tree.

"I repeat, you can now remove it so at no time are you to lose that amulet. Keep it safe at all times, it's very special and it will constantly activate one of the emblems on your helmet, in that way I will give you limited guidance. If you still have it on your person, you'll return it to us at the end of your journey. If you should lose it or, give it away, you'll never leave this place alive. That bracelet will remain your main safeguard, if you need help, trust the amulet; it's your key to survival and our only link via the Helmet of Roshta. Guard it well, from this moment; you hold the universe and every living thing's future in your hands."

"Neat. It's like a two-way radio. Talking about that, what about my stereo and my torch, I think they're ruined. Who's going to pay for them? They cost a lot of money, you know?"

Richard asked. Golan didn't even seem to take any notice as he continued.

"All things from this wood are very sacred; I want you to try to understand our world by collecting from its life. Any little information or article you may be offered from the various places or inhabitants you visit, could give you vital clues as to where those pods and the other Guardians may be hidden. Now go, I'll await your return but remember, you must be strong and live up to the ancient prophesies at all times, because our time is fast running out, so don't waste it, we have but twenty six days to succeed otherwise, all will be lost."

"What happens if I don't succeed?"

"We will all eventually die terrible deaths; like all condemned men, my last meal before my own death will be you, because you will have failed us all."

Richard began shuddering uncontrollably.

"One last thing, be careful, the thieves amongst us are cunning, they may give you false pods as well as false clues, do not be deceived because these evil people have pods that look identical to that one," He pointed to the pod from the tree. "If you should open a false one of those to check, you will most certainly die. Make sure you have the real ones, hold the pod against that amulet you now wear, it will soon identify the real pods and it will help you to weed out the evil pods as well as your discovering which the real ones are."

With that, the extraordinary beast lay itself down on its bed of shining stones and immediately faded and disappeared, now Richard felt at his most alone since arriving in this place and that, scared him. Just before Golan faded completely, Richard thought that he saw a gentle, kindly old man and not the weird looking beast.

"What a mess," Richard thought aloud; bending forward he picked up the pod with its blood red stem. To his surprise, he found it wasn't a real flower pod, but more like some sort of a heavy gemstone that now pulsed with warmth to his touch.

He gently laid it alongside the helmet. Carefully and slowly he prised open the pod, a bright shining light emanated from inside, it was almost like looking into the past through a fast moving video. He closed the pod and the light was gone.

"Wow, how cool, you and me going to guard each other my little pod friend. No wonder they stole the others."

He removed his cloak and carefully placed it inside a plastic bag taken from his shoulder bag and then packed the delicate package back into his shoulder bag alongside his slightly damaged stereo.

"Okay! I'm ready for my adventure." Richard called to the pig-like guide.

They moved quickly, with Richard following in the short boy's tracks along a narrow path; but he could not help noticing that they were now moving deeper into the dark forest in the opposite direction from which they had entered that magical clearing

"One little, two little, three little bottles," he sang softly to himself trying to get up enough courage to continue moving forward behind the funny looking guide. "Pull yourself together," he chastised himself "Me and my big trap. I've always wanted to save the world, well now that I've been asked to do just that, all I want to do is go home. What a mess?"

The pig-like boy paid no heed to his ramblings and simply kept moving forward in the same direction, absolute fear had overtaken Richard's mind, flipping from one idiotic suggestion to another. He panicked and turned quickly to get away from these frightful surroundings to try to retrace his steps.

That's when it happened... He hadn't even seen the sleeping body propped against a tree as he fell headlong over something.

"Yow!"

In an instant the body on the ground came alive and instantly shot upright, all Richard saw was the glint of what could have been a knife being raised towards his throat. At almost the same time the now alive body, suddenly lurched forward face down right next to Richard, The pig-like boy was now towering above both of them, sword in hand.

"Gghhh! Gghhh! You touch him; you have me to deal with." The pig-like kicked out at Richard's assailant's foot.

"He kicked me, I was only resting, what was I supposed to do? One minute asleep, next being attacked?"

"Gghhh! Gghhh! He made a mistake, simply tripped over your body, who are you anyway, and what are you doing here?"

"I am Melek the Librarian," His attacker sat up, Richard was totally surprised to see that Melek was really dwarfish in appearance but, before he could say anything more, Melek turned his face to him and gasped, he had suddenly noticed Richard's eyes and instantly recognised him as the Chosen One.

"You... you are," excitedly, Melek rolled over and began undoing a large book from off his back. "This is known as the Book of Prophecies and it foretells the coming of Forta Electsimis, it is you, I recognised you immediately because your grey eye sees the dark side of life and the green eye sees good, you are the one sent to save us all, are you not?"

"How can I be this Forta eh... whatever?" Richard stammered.

"Gghhh! Gghhh! He means Forta Electsimis. It means the Strong Chosen One. Orkan giggled. "Golan also suggested something similar, but look at him, this weakling is no warrior, so how can this be so foretold?" The pig-like character scoffed.

"Our destiny is always foretold in this Book of Prophecies, how it does this, nobody knows. The only problem is that it is written in riddle that most people cannot interpret." The girl replied. "I was the 'Seshet or Scribe' and also the keeper of many sacred scrolls but of them all, this book was most important and that's why I stole it before it could be used by the Evil One after that war."

"War? W-what war?" Richard demanded

"Gghhh! Golan carefully omitted to tell you that there was the first great battle and that's how the Guardians and the Pods were lost to us." Orkan snorted.

"Okay, so we have a war, people missing, pods missing, me being kidnapped, an Evil One, a pig and a female scribe leading me to fight an unknown enemy, a book that tells fortunes... have I missed anything out so far?"

The dwarfish looking Melek removed the large strapped book off his back and began paging through it.

"Now that you have stated it so clearly, I can see it is exactly what the Book of Prophecies had prophesied. Let me read the last prophecy, maybe it will answer your question, the riddle will give us a clue that this manuscript does foretell the future?"

"Let me see." Richard tried to read words that the scribe was pointing at, "Nope cannot read that, what language is it written in? You are going to have to give me a crash course in those funny hieroglyphic looking things and their meanings" Melek lifted the book and read the script.

*"When he who is the Chosen One
Shall tread upon the Ancient Path*

And battle there to overcome
The Forces of the Dark
Then shall the Seven be restored
And evil banished from this world."

"Don't you see? It just has to be you? The book of prophecies must know the truth, if only we could understand the rest of it.

In the distance they heard clapping sounds, like thousands of wings flapping in the wind, the noise suddenly moving from all directions towards them. The pig-like boy stopped and sniffed wildly at the air.

"Gghhh! Danger." The boy snorted.

"What is that sound?"

"Gghhh! We're in 'BIG' trouble "Gghhh!

The Wicked Water Beast

On the First Day...

Should evil e'er the Victor be,
And darkness fall upon the land,
A Chosen One from far will come
Who sees in dark and light.
On the first day, herein points the way.
To cross the river he follows the flow.
From air and water dangers.
Safety lies in earth below.
At path's end lies the slender way,
A hidden weakness saves the day.

"What is it?" Richard shouted.

"Grapfrits!"

"Grapefruits?"

"Gghhh! No, Grapfrits! Nasty swarming flying things, let's just hope they don't come this way."

"Follow me, they have very bad eyesight but use their smelling organs to locate their prey. They came through the forest some time back and I found a safe hiding place." Melek quickly strapped the book to his back. Even with wearing a long white flowing robe, he raced away with Orkan in close pursuit. Richard tried his very best to keep up with the fleeing pair but, rounding a dark forested bend, realised that he could no any longer see them.

"Hey! Wait for me!" he screamed, he was becoming more and more terrified by the ever-closing sound of flapping wings.

"We are here!" Shouted Melek from somewhere in the dark forest canopy but, before Richard could move towards the caller, whirring sound of thousands of simultaneous beating wings seemed so close, Richard made up his mind immediately. Now that he had made his dramatic decision, there was now no chance of going back. He whipped off his shoulder bag and hurriedly extracted the cloak that he threw around his body before pulling the cape over his head. To his utter surprise, he found he could clearly see everything in front of him but, now knew for sure that his trouble was about to begin as the first of the flying creatures swarmed out of the tree line and straight towards his insecure position. Richard edged to his left and a little closer to a bush, just to manoeuvre himself out of the main body of the swarm's direct flight path.

"Oh dear, I'm dead," he whispered despairingly to himself.

The main group of the really ugly crab-like flying creatures swooped and dived left and right like a flock of swallows hunting prey, as quickly as they had appeared, so they swept past as if he wasn't there. Some of what Richard could only presume were making up the rear guard, swerved directly towards him. It was too late to do anything and as if on cue, the buzzing intensified and the whole area again became filled with what Richard thought looked like very ugly, thorny, flying crab-like oranges. The small prickly beasts slowed and began circling around the area once more. Richard could now clearly see the nasal spikes on these flying orange beasts, their closeness showed that the spikes tended to be more like sharpened knives protruding directly from their mouths. One attack from these hunting monsters meant it had all be over for him and his companions. One curious Grapfrit in particular began hovering closer towards Richard. Feeling very exposed, Richard drew a deep breath, seeing the thing at close quarters hovering right before his face, its swelling mouth pumping wildly, and to his horror saw a long needle-like probe extend directly in his direction. Somehow, it seemed to know he was around somewhere but could not locate him. The pointed spike missed Richard's ear by fractions, causing his head to whip side in a nervous reaction, at that moment, all he wanted to do was to cough. He strained to hold the tickle at the back of his throat; his will to live by not coughing was overpowering, it saved his life. Suddenly the Grapfrits gathered into a group and as if given some unknown command, hurtled off through the forest and out of sight.

"They must have got the Chosen One; he's not anywhere out there, we better let Golan know the bad news." Richard heard Melek shout.

Richard did not move, he was still shaking like a leaf, trying to recover from the Grapfrit ordeal.

"Gghhh! If they killed him there should be bones where they fed on his marrow. If they did get him then we are in big trouble, Gghhh! Golan will never forgive me." Orkan walked into view, he was following the narrow path, Richard waited until his pig-like companion was almost level with him.

"BOO!" Orkan dived to the ground, scrambled around on all fours for an instant before coming up smartly, sword ready to strike. Richard laughed so hard that the cough finally emerged and Richard chocked as he whipped back the cape to reveal his hiding place.

"That was not very humorous," said Orkan sheathing his sword. "We thought that the Grapfrits had got you." Richard was still giggling loudly when Melek appeared.

"It would not have been so funny if they had located you, they are truly nasty. In seconds they would have eaten all the soft tissue from off of your entire being, then using those proboscis spike things, drilled into your bones and sucked out all your marrow which would then be delivered back to their queen Grapfrit. We 'must stick together' next time."

"Sorry guys, just could not resist that Orkan." Richard declared. "I thought they had found me, but obviously this cape really does work." He removed his tunic and placed it into his shoulder bag. Looking upwards he whispered, "Thank you Golan, I will never doubt you again."

Orkan chuckled loudly, "Gghhh! You are just very lucky; I could have killed you. Gghhh! Gghhh!"

There's a clearing and spring water around that corner," Melek pointed in the direction the Grapfrits had just taken, "let's stop there because and we can see what the book can reveal," Melek said as he turned and made his way back the way he had just come from.

"Book? Who believes in them, they are just some put together words, right?" Richard followed the scribe.

"Gghhh! Don't be so flippant, this is a different world, there's myth, magic and as you've already seen for yourself, there are monsters. Take heed of what the librarian says, it will hold you in good stead."

They arrived at a small clear spring that gently jetted cool water from its sandy base and at last there was sunshine from what looked like an eye that beamed down into this clearing. Richard had to blink for a few seconds to adjust his vision to the sudden brightness.

For the first time he could now have a good look at his male companion in the light, he was very pretty with almost autumn coloured, very shortly cropped hair, fine features showing that there was possibly good breeding and his clothes were toga-like with a long, but loose fitting Egyptian or Greek style dress tied at the waist with what looked like a golden rope.

"How can you move so quickly in that? Richard pointed to the long robe.

"Magic and a lot of practice," he said with a naughty smile. Melek removed the large book and placed it against a tree stump then beckoned the boy to draw nearer.

"Now let's see what the next prophecy records." He turned over several pages of the big book and pointed to the text.

"Not even Guardians could understand these riddles, what do you make of this next rhyme?"

Richard tried reading it but, it was laid out in some ancient script form that he had never seen before, many of the strange words could be made out if they were a lot clearer, but most of the words were totally illegible Among them were some lovely sketches, mainly animals or beasts bordered the script.

"Hmmm let's see shall we?" Melek waved his hand across the page.

"Whaaa!" Suddenly the whole border began moving around and the script started to change. Richard thought it looked like something he had once seen in a movie, just then everything moved back into place.

"Ahhh, does that text make more sense to you now?" Melek asked, all Richard could do was nod as he read the text aloud.

> Should evil e'er the Victor be,
> And darkness fall upon the land,
> A Chosen One from far will come
> Who sees in dark and light.
> On the first day, herein points the way.
> To cross the river he follows the flow.
> From air and water dangers.
> Safety lies in earth below.
> At path's end lies the slender way,
> A hidden weakness saves the day.

"I understand the dark and light portion, that's how I first recognised you as the Chosen One, but the rest makes very difficult reading. What do you think?" Melek requested.

"Baloney is what I think; you can read anything you want into those words." Richard replied. "I think we better move to safety, that distant buzzing seems to be louder again, it sounds like they could move back in this direction."

Melek closed the book and strapped it onto his back again. Richard lay flat on his stomach and took a deep gulp of the ice-cold water before taking a plastic bottle from his bag and filling it. "Not going to take any chances," he replaced the bottle.

"Do not simply reject these prophecies out of hand," Melek said.

"At this moment, I'm more concerned about reality of a swarm than words of a book, wherever that swarm of Grapefruits are; it's more than likely they are going to head back this way." Just then the familiar buzz of wings drifted through the forest again

"Gghhh! Grapfrits are returning, let's hide." Orkan suddenly pushed his way past Richard. "C'mon! Follow the river, it's our only chance. Weeeooee!" The pig-like boy moved quickly, followed closely by Melek who wasn't hanging about for his new companion. Richard didn't need second invitations this time, he raced as fast as his long weary legs would carry him. Keeping up with the fleeing couple wasn't easy, the three jinxed and darted around a series of bushes and trees with difficulty, trying to follow the stream. At one stage Richard even overtook Melek when they heard the spinning Grapfrits approaching and sounding like ten thousand hedge trimmers carving their way through the dense undergrowth close behind them somewhere, obviously hunting at full speed.

"Gghhh! River!" Both Richard and the pig-like boy shot straight over the top of a ridge, into mid-air, the long drop carrying them down, down into the swirling blue waters below some rapids. "Help, I can't swim!" The pig-like boy shouted as they fell.

Melek had seen them hurtle into space and veered right towards a large tree.

As Richard and Orkan hit the water, Richard stretched out and grabbed the boy's hand as the two were sucked below the churning water. The powerful force instantly catapulted them like a two torpedoes below its depths. Desperately, hanging on to his companion's half trotter, half hand the rushing river bounced them down over a slimy stairway of cascading rocks and into a large pool where the mid-stream current wasn't quite as strong.

"Whoa!" Spluttering they surfaced, Richard immediately tried taking stock of their position.

"Where's Melek?"

"Gghhh! Who cares, I think they might have got his this time."

Meanwhile, Melek found what he thought was a cave at the base of the large tree, it was dark, he knew that hidden in here he would be safe. He felt around the dampened walls, his hand touched a straggly guide rope. Carefully he followed it along the dark oozing passage, without warning and it being too dark he had to feel his way along when the floor just dropped away, he clung onto the rope for all his life's worth..

Further downstream and with Grapfrits headed their way, Richard noticed they had drifted towards some tall water-reeds situated just off to the side in what was a becalmed inlet. Richard checked seeing a dense crop of brown coloured grass plastered across the far side bank. The river current slowly began guiding them back towards the central current and the short brown grass bank. Richard immediately decided that the reeds would offer them better protection and hiding from the menacing Grapfrits. Orkan wasn't helping much as Richard assisted him stay afloat. Richard's eyes constantly searched the skies checking to see if the Grapfrits had followed them. For the moment, their surprising underwater journey had quickly taken them away from the flying beasts, but Richard knew that it wouldn't be too long before the flying oranges possibly figured out where they were.

"What would have happened if I hadn't learned to swim?" Exhausted as he was, he knew that the small recessed inlet was his chance; he was tiring quickly and with Orkan's extra weight to drag along, Richard knew if they didn't get to the land soon, there was the danger of them both drowning. Close to collapse, he put his head down and pumped both legs and arms in one last huge effort to get out of the mainstream and reach the calmer water and reeds that he had seen from mid river.

"Whew!" Richard took in a deep breath and lifted his bobbing head to the heavens. "Safety, at last," he puffed, they reached the green moss covered inlet, the pig-like boy snorted loudly and was also close to collapse. There was only a short distance to traverse and safety of a small-pebbled beach; that lay at the far side of this calm water stretch. Richard didn't like the idea of them having to swim through a thick slime coating the still water ahead. Looking towards land he fully understood they could not return back up the hill and that they also had no choice but to get across the slime to reach the narrow beach skirted by steeply sloped jagged rocks forming a boundary both left and right of that becalmed beach.

"The reeds for now... That's our best chance."

Richard half pulled his unhelpful companion to the shallows until they could both stand comfortably. By reaching the cover of the reeds, his inspiration knew no bounds, he perceived a brilliant idea that he had seen on television somewhere. He snapped off two reeds, checked to see if they were hollow through the centre, finding they were unfilled. After several attempts, he quickly managed to convince his companion that the reeds would make temporary but ideal snorkels, only just in time.

Above the roar of the water they heard the clapping sound heading in their direction. "Quickly in among the reeds, just place the reed in your mouth and duck below the water."

"Wheeeooee!"

"Shut up you stupid fool. What are you trying to do, get us both killed?"

They somehow camouflaged themselves below the waterline among the reeds. Richard found that it was not as easy as he had thought it would be, trying to breathe through the small reeds they had very little option, from below the water Richard heard the flapping sound reaching fever pitch as they passed overhead. It took a time without end before the buzzing slowly faded when the searching Grapfrits moved further on down the river searching for prey.

After several minutes Richard surfaced to find the boy already standing and gazing in the direction that the Grapfrits had taken.

"Gghhh! That was clever; we tricked them, didn't we?"

"Do you think they'll be back?"

The boy pulled his lips together.

"Don't know."

"Let's wait awhile just to make sure."

"Okay."

"What's your name again?"

"My real name is Orkan but obviously people around here tend to call me Orkan, I've got used to the name and I quite like it."

"I understand what you are going through, because I too, have a similar problem to you. I was born with the name Richard, yet friends always insist on calling me mutant, the reason is that I have different coloured eyes. I hate that name with a passion." Richard complained bitterly,

"You called them friends? They cannot be that if they know you hate the name." Orkan offered.

"Golan said you had a quest. What did he mean?"

"Gghhh! As you will have undoubtedly noticed, I am slowly changing into a pig. I am a normal person from a similar world to yours I believe, but my friends and I were exploring some caves and suddenly this evil thing called Sundra kidnapped us. He brought us to this place and we all started turning into pigs. Fortunately I escaped to the mountains, now I am trying to find my way back there to help them escape as well. The main problem is that my brain is continually switching away from its human thoughts and then I can't help acting a little like a pig. There's nothing I can do about it, only because I helped the good folk during the battle, did Golan then promise that if I help you to restore the pods of life to the Tree of Life, then the combined power would be strong enough to be able to change us back to humans again. That's why we must find the pods; it's our only way back home. Golan said that I was between a pig and a man so let it be known that my name was to be Orkan until we had managed to retrieve the pods when I would get back my original name, everybody uses Orkan, so that is my name while here."

Richard had earlier noticed a large raw scar on the boys arm.

"What happened there?"

"Gghhh! During the battle I was trapped by three soldiers, I was lucky enough to escape alive. Many common beasts died that day, even more were captured and like those that went before, will all steadily fall under the Evil One's power or be killed off."

"I don't think that those flying knives are coming back. Okay Orkan, so where do we start?"

"Gghhh! A good beginning will be to get back to land."

"Well, we can't go that way," Richard said pointing to mid-stream "We'll have to make for the shore. Ugh! I don't fancy swimming through that, but we have no other choice." Richard had been taught the lifesaving method of swimming; he took a firm hold of the nervous Orkan's shoulders and started out towards the pebble beach finding the going like trying to swim through exceedingly thick soup. The thought of reaching land and safety urged him forward and when he was no more than four body lengths from the shore, suddenly the water around him started bubbling, exhausted and fed up he nearly made the mistake of stopping to see what was happening.

"Now what?" Richard became alarmed at this sudden occurrence; it felt as if there was something wriggling beneath the water. "What the...?" Richard jerked his hand upwards as he realised that the green slimy substance had come alive and was now creeping across the water and trying to move under the touch of his hand. "There's something alive down there."

Both became very alarmed with this new twist, pulling like a superhuman track athlete, he first tried to leap away onto the riverbank but the green slush held firm. He was so close to the shore but, for all it mattered, he could have been a million miles away.

"Wheeeooee!" Orkan pulled himself free from Richard's grip and forced his way onto the sloping beach. Whatever was holding Richard, hadn't managed to restrain Orkan from exiting the water, to Richard's surprise, instead of helping him his companion raced away to safety behind one of the jagged beachside rocks.

"Wait Orkan! Help me!" It was too late; Richard was left alone to face the danger by himself. Still struggling desperately he turned and faced the moving moss, Richard stopped struggling, instantly transfixed at what he could now see taking place in among the green moss. It had suddenly come alive, moving, swelling and heaving like some huge living being. He was certain that his eyes weren't deceiving him, something had caught his attention on the far side of the green pool near the silvery stream. Whatever it was, now stirred to generate a large ripple on that side of the calmer green water. Richard struggled frantically to extricate himself from the substance and reach the small-pebbled beach. It was useless he was stuck fast, all he could do at that particular moment was observe the parting moss moving in his position. The centre of the silent pool began bubbling like a huge boiling cauldron, it suddenly seemed as if the pool was like some form of massive Jacuzzi, the turbulent surface erupted with white tumultuous bubbles, from somewhere below the water's depths rose the ugliest beast that Richard could have imagined.

"Whoa!"

The first part of the creature to emerge was the top of its head; silvery coloured, thick horrific scales covered its crown with thousands of layered mirrors that all reflected the morning sun. In that fleeting moment, a strange thought crossed Richard's mind that it had been almost dark when he initially set off on his bicycle journey, yet here, it was mid-morning. Huge saucer-like black eyes showed themselves above the water line, followed by immense bull type nostrils that began snorting blue water in all directions. As the rest of its head started appearing above the water the extensive mouth appeared to be smiling at him with gigantic fangs that protruded in all directions from out of the massive head. This mirror infected beast continued to rise up slowly, showing a body that resembled of some kind of gigantic snake. Richard froze stiff when he saw the beast's horrific looking enormous hooked claws, they resembled the fearsome talons of a gigantic eagle; the slimy torso moved upward very slowly, the moment seemed to take forever as the huge body extracted itself from within a torrent of falling water. The thing somehow reminded Richard of a massive steam engine he had once seen pulling out of a station. It too, had this same way of gasping, snorting and wheezing as it prepared to pull away from the platform. The commotion and racket being caused by this dreadful thing was deafening as it finally reached its zenith height.

"A-A-A... w-w-water beast," Richard gasped.

In his mind, the thing looked like an imagined macabre green dragon extracting itself from the water to eat him. Instead of breathing fire, this apparition blew white and green mist in all directions as if to orientate itself. This he instinctively knew was some type of killing machine. He desperately wanted to run away, but his feet and body were held fast so that he couldn't move and what little strength he had, had now deserted him. Somehow he felt as though his legs, which could now touch ground were like two wooden poles planted into the muddy ground.

"Who's disturbing my sleep?" Richard opened his mouth to speak, but found that no matter how hard he tried, nothing emerged. All he could think of was that he was going to be eaten alive by this terrifying scaly water monster.

"Aha! It's not often that I have such a beautiful young man come to provide dinner. Feel the fear because you have transgressed my domain. What are you doing here?"

Richard stuttered and stammered something and found that whatever it was that he was trying to say just didn't come out of his open mouth at all; his gibberish mumblings were so illegible that it somehow reminded him of someone being underwater trying to hold a decent conversation. The more he tried to speak, the more garbled his words seemed become, it was as if he was trying to communicate in some weird Martian language.

"Come on; say something or your life will end right now because I prefer conversation before eating," said the thing.

"My name is R-R-Richard," he finally stuttered. There, he had managed to get his name out and only because he couldn't imagine anything more horrific than this freak monster that was now confronting him. This thing petrified him because he didn't want to contemplate the thought of his small body sliding down that thing's throat.

"What are you doing in my water?"

"N-n-n. N-n-nothing."

Somehow the thing seemed genuinely interested in Richard, it was somehow weighing up the shivering human to see whether he would make a good meal.

"Do you know who I am?"

"N-n-noo."

"I'm Sumar, the Moss Beast." The thing didn't actually talk as such; it seemed more to croon its words, almost as if it was trying to sing to Richard. "You have not told me that you are the Chosen One. The Evil One will reward me handsomely for capturing you." Suddenly it became very angry, instantly it reeled around and moved with mind blurring speed towards the bank where Richard was standing. Richard, although terrified, stood his ground, if Sumar was going to kill him, it was going to be now. The thing carried its huge bulk through the water like a gigantic ocean liner creating a broad wave as it moved straight towards him, then stopped within inches of the frightened boy. A huge rush of water like a bow-wave around the front of a ship created a heavy backwash that raced forward sending Richard tumbling up and onto the pebble beach.

"Wheeeooeee! Wheeeooeee!"

Before Richard could gain his senses this terrible sound broke the relative silence and continued to echo around the ravine walls. He shut his eyes tightly expecting the worst to happen to him at any second. Spa-lash. splosh, splash, the sound of something hitting the water made Richard open his eyes to see what Sumar was about to do to him.

"Gghhh! Get away from here! Go away! Gghhh!"

Richard suddenly understood what was happening. Orkan was standing with his back to Richard throwing rocks at Sumar to protect the half-dazed boy lying against the granite wall. From his prone position, Richard watched

Sumar's reactions from between the boy's spread legs. The huge beast in the water was flailing its body from side to side in what seemed like utter frustration at having lost its prey.

"Gghhh! C'mon get up!

Richard somehow found the strength to scramble to his feet seeing the beast suddenly stop moving to again start moving towards them, he grabbed Orkan's arm and tugged him up the side of the cliff and more importantly away from their immediate danger.

"Let's get out of here before it attacks us again!"

But it was too late for the beast had anticipated their move and was now dragging itself towards them.

"Come on, you are trapped, there is no escape."

"Orkan, the rope."

A golden coloured rope suddenly dropped from the cliff above. Richard weighed up their chances; he saw that the beast was now moving on land towards them, there was no choice. The two scrambled up the rope, whoever was behind this pulled the rope upwards very slowly, they used any footholds they could against the cliff face clambering away from danger. The beast raised itself then lunged high again and again with its massive talons but each time the two were just out of reach. Sumar gave a despairing roar as the two concentrated on getting to the top.

"Melek! …It's you, we thought those Grapfrits had killed you off. Here you are and you saved our lives, without your rope we were as good as dead." Richard hugged the librarian, who pulled away somewhat embarrassed.

"You see, you should have listened to the words of the book, I found an underground tunnel which led me down here, it had not been used for a long time. You were lucky because some of the walls had broken down over time, but I found this golden rope."

"Wow! Talk about luck."

"Luck has 'nothing' to do with it; it was prophesied by the Book of Prophecies, was it not? When I heard the screams from below and saw what was about to happen to you, I just knew what I had to do."

"Melek come here let me give you a hug."

The dwarfish scribel turned and moved away, Richard looked at Orkan and shrugged as he then realised that something about him was now somewhat different, he had changed out of his long robe and was now in a short white leather huntsman's suit not unlike the one that Orkan was wearing.

"What? He saved us, why shouldn't I give him a hug?" said the bemused Richard.

Orkan simply shook his head forlornly. Melek collected up the rope and handed it to Richard.

"It weighs nothing, it's so light?"

"It will help us again I think."

"Gghhh! You carry it, I have enough with my bow and my sword, Melek carries the book, your turn to carry something besides that strange bag of yours." Melek took the rope and wound it around his waist. There was a distant buzzing noise.

"Oh-oh, are you thinking what I'm thinking? Let's get away."

The three raced upwards along the path, it lead them straight back into the forest, they moved quickly, darting and twisting until Orkan stopped.

"Gghhh! Welcome to the 'Ancestral Forest', it's good to be with someone that's normal when you enter this place."

"W-what do you mean? Why is this part called the ancestral forest?"

"Gghhh! I've been in here before. We must tread carefully."

"What's in this forest?"

"Apart from ancestral and cultural spirits of the forests, there are nature spirits, which inhabit rivers, mountains and all trees; all of these spiritual beings are to be found here which are known in your world as Gods and Devils. There are those who will seek to harm us, we must be very careful." They sat down and chatted, Richard was surprised at how deep and grown up Orkan's voice sounded. Richard decided that Orkan wasn't a boy but in true fact was a fully-grown adult. What he hadn't noticed before were that Orkan's muscles were firm, powerful and fully formed, this was not the body of a teenager. He was standing confidently, his brown coloured ill-fitting wet tunic made from some form of sacking, otherwise no other clothing covered him except for the small quiver of strange looking arrows strapped across his back, a short bow in his hand and a short sword attached to a thick belt.

"What happens now?" Richard asked.

"Gghhh!" We should follow the line of the river."

The main thing that intrigued Richard was that the young man's pointed and jutting ears ran almost the full length of his head from top to bottom. He wondered how he had come to be in such an uninviting place; there was more to his explanation than Orkan had let on earlier.

"I'm not..." A sweet sound of singing came drifting along the river.

"Quiet." Richard placed his finger to his lips. "Can you hear that?"

"Gghhh! What could that be?" snorted Orkan.

"What do you think it is?" Melek was obviously very nervous, "maybe we should first consult the book? Everything that the prophecy predicted has already come to pass. Tunnels, rope, water beast and Grapfrits, they were all forecast by the book weren't they?"

"Gghhh! Danger."

"Why do you keep snorting like that?"

"I can't help it. It just happens."

The singing grew louder and clearer.

"It sounds like an angelic choir of some sort, let's go and find out who's making that beautiful sound."

"No. It's bound to be something nasty."

"We've got to search everywhere Golan said."

"He did not."

"Are you coming or what?"

"No, there's nothing good down there."

Orkan's stubbornness was going to be hard to get along with, thought Richard.

"Well, I'm going."

He lifted his bag and began walking in the direction of the singing voices. Reaching a thick clump of bushes, kneeled down to see whether he was close enough to ascertain who was singing. Suddenly he heard the rustle of bushes slightly to his left.

"What the... Possibly another beastie, I had better hide in this bush." The bushes to his left rustled again, Richard's taught nerves caused him to jump and spin around to face whatever it was rustling the bushes, he was undecided whether to move away or stay. His brain suddenly reeled and screamed as he felt himself being knocked over sideways.

The Man-Eating Maidens

On the Second Day...

Rock conceals and grass deceives
But Heroes win the day.
An arrow gold behind the leaves
Shows the brave the way.
Peril, water, death await.
Avoid the tempting hand.
Purple eyes that have no fate
Twice arrive but not too late
To pluck from death the shining Grail
And lead them to another place.

Richard's eyes scanned the dense bush for signs of what could have made the noise; possibly it was watching him from some nearby hiding place and was waiting to pounce. Shikatic, shikatic, the rustle of dry leaves being trodden underfoot somewhere to his left forced the boy to sink deeper into his unsafe hiding place. His ears strained to catch the slightest sound now, but all he could hear was the rippling of water and the gentle singing sounds being carried on the wind. Maybe it just a bird or rabbit scratching for food in the undergrowth thought Richard. After what he had been through so far, he wasn't prepared to move and give away his hiding place until he was sure what was out there. Shikatic, shikatic, there it was again, but much closer this time. Richard crouched as low as he could go but the sound drew ever nearer to his hiding spot, the bushes suddenly parted and there stood Melek.

"You are no good at hiding yourself, you must learn from Orkan, he can hide anywhere, he becomes almost invisible when he wants to." Melek removed the book and seated himself.

"Now my young friend, it's time to see what is next in store for us," he opened the book. "Ah-ha!"

"I do not so like Ah-ha, that way it sounds like trouble but go on, what does it say?"

Rock conceals and grass deceives
But Heroes win the day.
An arrow gold behind the leaves

Shows the brave the way.
Peril, water, death await.
Avoid the tempting hand.
Purple eyes that have no fate
Twice arrive but not too late
To pluck from death the shining Grail
And lead them to another place.

"What does that mean? It's all gobbledygook." Richard said.

"I don't know either but so far the book has got it right, hmm, 'have no fate' I somehow think means someone is going to die?"

Richard lifted the book that he could now understand and mused over the riddle, absentmindedly he turned the open book over.

"Wait, what's that? There seems to be a sparkle there," she pointed at the middle of the book. "I've never seen that before." Melek gently moved his hand across the spine of the book. He moved his hand up and down in a rocking motion until very carefully extracting what looked for all the world to Richard like a thin bladed golden letter opener except that inlaid into the blade was some sort of dust covered glass or stone.

"Wow! What do you think it is?" He took the thing from Melek.

"I really could not say, but whatever it is it has been hidden in here for a very long time. "

Then as Richard slowly began to move the knife around the stone in the blade seemed to come to life and change its coloured spectrum dependent on the direction Richard pointed. Suddenly Melek gasped.

"I think it might even be the ancient Espial Diviner, it's one of the oldest treasures that even the guardians had deemed been lost centuries ago."

"A wotsits diviner? What does that mean?"

"Legend has it that the Espial Diviner will guide you to your heart's desire, it is supposed to be the ultimate path finder to your dreams. You notice it only began working when you touched it, you have the power within your grasp that is... If it truly is what I think it is you have somehow, made it find you because you are the Chosen One, don't you see?"

Richard moved it in a large arc, the colouration spanned from a strong red through to a gentle blue when he pointed it in the direction of the singing.

"You see, it glows strongest where the wailing is, so must we head in that direction?

"Gghhh! Help! Help me!"

"Orkan?"

Richard and Melek raced toward the voice, it had come from the direction of a huge old log.

"Where are you?"

"Help me somebody!" I am near an old tree."

"There, we're close," Richard peered over the top to see Orkan lying spread-eagled on the ground and covered with literally thousands of what could only be described as blood red coloured earthworms.

"Uggh Gghhh!"

"Be careful where you tread, once one attacks, they all attack. Try to reach my sword."

Richard gingerly leaned over the log, he didn't need being attacked by worms and waited for an opportune moment, Melek grabbed his feet to make sure Richard didn't slip and with one swift movement, he extracted the sword together with a few worms. Melek instantly used the letter opener thing as a knife slicing through the few that Richard had collected.

"Whew, got it. Now what?"

"Quickly before they suffocate me, cut me loose."

Being careful not to harm Orkan, Richard set about cutting through the moving mass because each cut meant the worms released a foul smell.

"Smells like a sewerage farm," Richard declared

It took a little while but finally, Orkan was able to wriggle clear and dived to safety over the fallen log. For a while all three removed the remnants of the red worms.

"What were those?"

"Gghhh! Gghhh! Don't know but, I sat down and next thing they had swarmed over me."

"They are a distant relative of leeches, much longer and they would have sucked you dry." Melek said sort of innocently.

"Gghhh! Gghhh!" Orkan snorted as Richard's friend disappeared walking on all fours and sniffing at the ground. "Orkan, what are you doing?"

"Couldn't let you go near the river maidens because I've seen what they're capable of. Quiet, I can still hear them."

"What river maidens?" Richard demanded urgently.

By now, Richard was sure that it had to be something terrible, nothing that he had had encountered in this world so far resembled 'anything' that he had ever seen before. Knowing something of the terrain and what it represented, Orkan carefully knelt behind some bushes indicating to the others to join him before very deliberately parting the branches so that they could have a good look at the river maidens without fear of them being seen.

"Gosh. They're beautiful," Richard whispered, he was instantly in love with all five girls. There, seated along the banks of the river, sunning themselves, five lovely young girls busily tended to each other, it was almost like something from a painting, their bodies glistened against the faint sunlight being thrown down from overhead. Richard presumed that they had all been swimming in the river and were now drying themselves on the warmed rocks while out of the water.

"Water is evil," stated Orkan in hushed tones.

"Like Sumar?" Richard enquired. "Sumar's in all water, not only in the mountain pool."

"You mean it could be here as well?"

"Maybe not here, but then again, it could be."

He wondered why they weren't afraid of Sumar. Surely, living in this dangerous place, they should know of the terrible thing that lurked in the waters around them.

"Let's go and talk to them and warn them of Sumar," he said enthusiastically, relieved to see other humans in this bedevilled place. Richard decided to become their knight; he would be able to rescue them from danger.

"C'mon, we must go to their rescue."

"No. Stay where you are."

Orkan grabbed at Richard's arm and urgently pulled him down behind the bush again. "Let me go, we must warn them."

Orkan was far stronger than his short body conveyed; in one movement he wrestled Richard to the ground and rolled him onto his back.

"You listen to me, or else I'm going to leave you here on your own. Do you understand?" Orkan was upset. Again, there was that look of concern on the young man's pig-like chiselled features. Richard rolled over and started getting to his knees. Golan had said that he must be careful. Could his guide be lying to him? Richard thought back to the way Orkan had run away and almost left him to fend for himself against the Grapfrits. He decided not to take any more chances until he was certain what role his guide played in this whole affair, had Golan been offering a warning when he had said something about not taking anything at face value? Could this just be a dangerous bit of deception from his guide? Richard wasn't sure what was going on, he had to make decisions on his own from now on; he glanced back towards the direction of the water then at his companion.

"No," he thought, "these were only five pretty young girls and, they were in terrible danger." He looked quizzically at the short man, his face pulled in disagreement showing resolution to help these young maidens now seated on the riverbank.

"You may or may not be a chosen one but you are also very stubborn and foolhardy, I can offer advice and sometimes guide you so, before you go barging into something you know nothing of, stay where you are. Watch carefully, they are not what you think they are. In this wood, you never accept anything as being what it seems at first." There was that ominous warning again, Richard thought.

"Wheeeooee!" Richard almost jumped out his skin.

"Will you stop doing that? It scares me stupid." Orkan waited, suddenly the girls became highly agitated and then, like one person, all five dived back into the river and started splashing and shrieking very loudly again.

"What's happening to them?" Richard asked urgently.

"Look over there," Orkan pointed at the far bank where they would have swam if the Grapfrits hadn't have been chasing them, Richard couldn't see anything as he looked at the brown grass growing on the far side of the river bank. His eyes strained hard in the semi-darkness of their position to see what Orkan was pointing at. Suddenly he saw some form of movement; it wasn't entirely clear to him what it was that was moving over on the far side bank it seemed as if the racket that the maidens were making had awakened something against that bank, it started moving. As whatever it was, rose to enter the water, Richard suddenly caught his breath.

"Gghhh! Gghhh! Wait, do you see him?"

"Yep, look at his clothes, they're strange," the thing turned towards the screams, "Look at his face."

"Leopardman," whispered Melek.

It looked like any human man dressed in some form of ancient peasant cloak except; he had purple skin and strange yellow and black cat-like eyes.

"Help us please kind sir. We're stuck fast to the bottom of the stream and something's tickling and pinching us. Please come here and help us to get out of the water." She held out her arms invitingly to try to get him to respond to her plea.

"What will you give me in return for helping you?" The girls giggled and one of them yelped as if something had pinched her.

"Please help us!" One of the girls implored.

"We'll become your personal servants if you manage to get us out of this place."

"All of you?" A cruel smile formed on the man's mouth and his eyes seemed to widen in anticipation.

"Yes, yes. Please help us." The leopard offered his hand and suddenly his face contorted with horror as the maidens pulled him into the water.

"Look... Tolosh, there are many of them."

Richard's eyes searched the grass, there in full view was a hairy little man no bigger than an average sized doll, the most striking thing about it was that when it opened its mouth wide and yawned, its head seemed to open up like a divided apple being split in two halves. Richard could see that each half contained nothing but a series of jagged fangs that looked like those in a shark's mouth that he had once seen in a museum. The teeth were all pointed and razor sharp, something like those found on a carpentry saw, one bite from that mouth would probably be enough to rip an enormous hole into anything that the little creature wanted to make a meal of.

"You see. Gghhh!, there are more dangerous things than Sumar in these waters."

"What is 'that'?" asked Richard, "and what about those poor girls swimming out there? Aren't they in serious trouble?"

"That is a Tolosh, don't move, just keep on watching the river bank." The little figure walked into the water and disappeared below the surface like a tiny monstrous submarine Richard's attention was drawn back to the far bank. Suddenly the grass seemed to come alive as hundreds of little men got to their feet, yawned, scratched themselves and entered the water in similar fashion almost like an otter family would do. Richard trembled at the thought of these little beasties lurking below the normally calm water. When they were all gone, he could see that what had looked like grass, were only the hairs of these little men who had all been sleeping against the river bank that was now nothing but a wall of brown mud.

"W-W-What's going to happen to those girls now?"

"Nothing."

"What do mean, 'nothing'? Did you see those teeth on those beasts? I'm going to help them."

"No don't!"

Again Orkan grabbed Richard and pulled him to the ground.

"The river maidens only enter the water when they think they're going to be fed, it's a cleverly laid plan, that leopard man is finished don't be fooled by the young girls, they're only Tolosh in disguise and if you try to go to their rescue, which is what they want, then you'll also be eaten alive by those Tolosh below the surface."

Richard got up and nearly retched, the water by now was blood red, there was a feeding frenzy happening the savagery of the Tolosh was beyond Richard's comprehension. In less than a minute, what had been the leopard man was stripped to the bone. These little monsters then snapping the left over bones with their saw like teeth, Richard stood there mortified.

As quickly as it had begun so there was stillness and the clumps of grass started to reappear on the muddy banks once again. The five young girls had seemed to have disappeared; Richard started to move forward before both Melek and Orkan grabbed him.

"The girls are gone; you said they would be safe."

"Listen... The girls are Tolosh, go near them and you will suffer the same fate." Richard and Orkan were so wrapped up in their own argument that they hadn't seen that someone else was now approaching the riverbank.

"Help us please kind sir. We're stuck fast to the bottom of the stream, and something's tickling and pinching us. Please come here and help us to get out of the water." Again, she held out her arms invitingly to try to get him to respond to her plea.

"Oh no. Gghhh!. Another leopard man we cannot let him face the Tolosh."

Richard didn't care now and broke away from the others, shouting at the top of his voice he charged towards where the leopard man was about to meet his maker. Orkan and Melek raced behind Richard, all three were screaming different things, the man swung around to face the intruders.

"What's the problem?" The man had a very distinctive drawl as he asked the question

"Tolosh, they're not maidens, they're Tolosh." Richard noticed the man's eyes; he immediately remembered something from the book of prophecies.

"Tolosh? What are Tolosh?"

"You go near them and you're dead! They've just eaten another leopard man like you, he fell into their trap and all that's left of him are some bones below the water. They are like Piranha, they attack on mass and it was horrible."

"That must have been Rasitta; he was ahead of me and was a great fighter."

He moved forward to Richard, then without warning had a long blade knife held against the boy's throat.

"I am Maerkat, now who did you say you were?"

"He is a Chosen One, you must let him go." Melek insisted.

"Oh really? Who says he's even going to live any longer?"

Richard felt the knife push harder against his windpipe and even felt a trickle of blood.

"I saved you from them didn't I? A-ask yourself why." Richard stammered.

Suddenly Orkan shot forward sword drawn and pointed right between the leopard man's eyes

"Gghhh! harm the boy, you're dead and I will personally feed you to the Tolosh."

Maerkat glared at Orkan even though not attempting to lower the knife. Melek stepped forward.

"If you want to kill anybody as revenge for your friend, then take me, for the boy has been set a task by Golan, Keeper and guardian of the Life Force. He is possibly the 'only one' that can overcome the Evil One so, spare him and take me."

"Hmm," Maerkat sneered. "Perhaps I do owe him my life. I am a man of honour so this boy's life is spared and I will help you. Where are you bound?"

"Our mission is to locate all Life-Force pods, here..." Richard dug into his bag and removed the pod that Golan had given him.

"Have you perhaps encountered anything that look like crystal flower pods while on your travels?" Richard held the amulet up towards the sun, suddenly all the background pleading and wailing subsided, it was instantly very quiet and all attention was then instantly concentrated back on the maidens and the water.

"We can help you," spluttered one of the girls, "there is just such a trinket below these waters, all you have to do is dive for it." She held out her arms invitingly to try to get one of them to come to the water. Orkan turned to Richard and smiled.

"You see, if we were unsuspecting travellers like that last gent, we would have immediately jumped in to try to get the pod. Their friends would make a meal of us. They're extremely cunning little people, you must understand, they rely on the fact that anybody passing this way will be gullible enough to listen to them."

Richard breathed a huge sigh of relief, considering himself lucky that he had Orkan with him as a guide, his brain was confused because he wasn't sure how he was going to navigate himself around all these dangerous pitfalls. Could he trust the guide even though at the time, he hadn't been warned about Sumar? Orkan had more than made up for his actions now.

"We're not going to come near you because you're the Tolosh and you'll not be feasting on us today. Anyway you are liars, I do not believe that one of these lies below those waters, and you lie to us to get us to your trap?" As Richard taunted and the maidens became more hysterical, jumping up and down frantically continually imploring for help by screaming even louder in an attempt to entice the two into the water, Orkan could see that the grass was once again beginning to slide into the water.

"Come!" Orkan started pulling Richard back toward the bushes the maidens realised that their food could be disappearing.

"We will show you the crystal flower pod, I'll get it for you, but you will have to take it from me as I cannot move from the water while my feet are stuck fast."

Richard muttered under his breath to his comrades.

"Show me the pod first, then I will enter the water to collect it from you." He took three steps to his right and nearer the enemy as one maiden ducked below the water and out of sight Richard looked across the water and could only see muddy banks at the far side, he shuddered to think what lay below this calm looking pond.

"C'mon they are just wasting our time." They moved out of sight of the maidens and into the forest, ducking down and creeping back behind a bush where they could observe the young girls and the river. They waited and watched, as the little hairy men began climbing from the water to again lie down against the mud bank, making that side of the river look as if it was covered with brown grass once again. Likewise, the maidens stopped their shrieking and extracted themselves from the water to settle and wait for their next unsuspecting victim. Suddenly the maiden that had disappeared resurfaced.

"Here it is, I have the pod, where are they? Yoo-hoo! I have your pod, come and get it."

"Before long some of these will become man-eating fish that swim all the way to the sea where they grow up to become gigantic sharks that eat everything they can find."

"You mean this is the breeding ground where all the fierce sharks originate?"

"Not all sharks, only those large ones that circulate the planet, fearing nothing or no one. These Tolosh here, represent all of the man-eating fish of the world."

"Like the great white shark?"

"Yes if that is a man-eater, this is the start of life for all the man-eating fish that go to the sea, some turn into shark-like beasts, while others become vicious small fish that hunt in packs. Whatever they become in the outside world, they are totally unafraid of man. It is as if they were set on this earth to destroy man in their waters, they're simply swimming carnivorous animals but out of the water they're helpless. From here, the balance of nature is constantly maintained, now what do we do to get that pod?"

"Mearkat, Melek, you stay here and watch to see what happens, any problems give us a signal. Follow me!" Without waiting, Orkan quickly sprinted through the opening in the bush and raced towards the Tolosh girls.

"Don't..." but it was too late to stop him. Richard thought that his pig brain must have taken over again and gave chase watching his companion hurtle towards the maidens and in one movement Melek's rope whipped through the air wrapping itself around the maiden's wrist. He gave one sharp tug and the pod flew from her hand just as Richard dived like a goalkeeper to take the pod before it dropped back into the water next to the bank.

"Got it!"

But as he looked up he could see the water beginning to bubble a few feet away, he quickly rolled away just in time to prevent the many clawed hands trying to reach him and pull him into their domain.

"Gghhh! Too close for comfort, let's get outta here."

"I don't believe it," laughed Richard. "It's changing into a big fish."

Orkan reeled in his rope with the thrashing maiden still fixed to it, he pulled her onto the bank, slowly the fight seemed to leave her as she began to metamorphosis back into a real grass type Tolosh once again. The transformation continued until the creature looked as if it was about to die, the young girl had been tall and slim, but now as a Tolosh, was now hairy, short and dumpy.

"Here, a present for you, now let's cook the fish and eat it."

"What? I couldn't eat something that a few moments ago was a young maiden, I'm not a cannibal you know."

"But this isn't a woman. Gghhh! See, this is a river fish that will swim to the ocean and maybe turn into a shark. Gghhh! They taste very good when cooked I've heard. If they don't turn to sharks when they reach the sea, then next year they'll come back here to die and become food for the Tolosh anyway. So what's the difference? Either we eat it now or it becomes fodder for those creatures. Life in the wild isn't easy you know, it's a constant cycle, birth generates life and then comes death."

"All the same, I'm not eating 'that', let's get away from the water, there are too many awful beasties in it."

"Wait. Remember, they've just eaten and she is probably carrying an entire load of new spawn that won't turn to fish if she doesn't live."

"You're right," Richard turned towards the river and the remaining young maidens.

"This Tolosh will die if not allowed back into the water, we want something from you."

"Someone that you've eaten must have been carrying this pod." Another Tolosh on the far bank stood up and before their very eyes, started changing into a beautiful young maiden. The Tolosh grew tall and its hair fell away from its body like a tree shedding its leaves in autumn. Its saw-toothed mouth drew back and with a loud 'Plop', fell into the water revealing yet another beautiful river maiden replacing the one that was on the bank, she moved into the river and joined the others.

"It was a female that had the body of a beetle, very hard shell but not as nice tasting as this last one."

"Trufor?" Melek blurted out. "It must have been her; she is the only Guardian that it could have been."

Orkan yanked the rope sideways and it came away, the Tolosh maiden struggled for quite some time flipping and flopping along the ground to make it back into the water. It should not have bothered because as it made it back, the Tolosh pounced on it in a wild scramble and devoured the thing in seconds.

"I would never have believed this. Oh, why did I have to come to this place?" Richard looked up to the heavens and shook his fist in anger, "They call 'me a Mutant' " back home? Guys, if only you could be here and see this. 'Everybody is a Mutant here."

Richard now realised that he had a lot to learn before being allowed to leave the woodland as he opened his bag, extracted a plastic bag and gently tucked the pod of life into the bag.

"Do you think that there's much further to go? This place is terrible, it gives me the creeps and I'm bushed."

"Just remember what we saw at this place today, you have it in your power to upset the balance of nature, but you didn't," Melek said. "One day if the world keeps using the rivers as they are now, then these types of wonderful things will die before reaching the safety of the sea. That way, the Tolosh won't go to the sea and the rivers will become far more dangerous for everyone."

"I hope not. Anyway, after what I've seen today, you would never catch me in a river again."

"Why not. There are far more dangerous things floating in the rivers today."

"Like what?"

"C'mon we've still have a long way to go." Orkan moved off and Richard followed him while the others fell in behind, the sight of the hostile Tolosh attack meant that very little was said,

"Two down and five to go," this encounter had made up his mind that he was now more determined to find the missing pods and guardians.

They moved up a long winding path that took them high over a long open valley spreading way below them. As they reached the top, Richard noticed that the forest reached the very edge of the long ridge to their right. No sooner were they away from the ridge and into the heavy undergrowth when

Orkan grabbed Richard and yanked him roughly into the centre of a thick bush.

"Orkan!"

"Shut up," hissed the guide placing his hand firmly over his companion's mouth. Richard then heard the sound. It was a steady rhythmic thumping sound ahead of them.

"T-they're coming this way. Gghhh! If they see us, we're dead meat, not a sound from any of you. Gghhh! Do you understand?" Richard could see that Orkan was terrified, what terrible thing could possibly scare his companion who had already thrown stones at Sumar and grabbed hold of a live Tolosh he thought. This had to be the worst yet, his fast moving brain cried out and for the first time he knew the meaning of 'Super-Fear'...

Baal - He Who Mounts The Clouds

On the Third Day...

Beware the silken ways
By evil spinner spun.
Yellow orbs that hasten days
Destroy when serpent comes
Some may perish, some feel pain
Tribulations not in vain
Three will tread these paths again
To save the precious one.

The sound moving toward them sounded very much like that of many soldiers marching in step.

"I think it could be a troop of Cozards," whispered Orkan.

Whatever these Cozards were, they had scared the wits out of his pig-faced companion; Richard could feel Orkan's body actually shaking from fear of the beasts heading quickly in their direction. Both lay face downwards, not daring to look up at the approaching unknown horrendous foe, rage, fear, and excitement all coursed through Richard's veins as the steady thumping moved to within inches of the bush alongside the pathway, then stopped. Richard felt Orkan automatically stiffen, had these Cozards detected them? Richard felt his whole body break into a profusion of sweat as they both lay waiting for whatever it was, to do what it was going to do followed by the sound that both of them dreaded most, it was the rustle of leaves as they both realised that the bush around them was being parted. Nothing for it but to look up and see what this particular enemy looked like before it attacked them. Richard suddenly made up his mind that he wasn't going to just lay face downwards to be attacked as he moved his head he felt Orkan's strange trotter like hand trying to restrain his curiosity by keeping him looking at the ground. Tearing Orkan's hand away he turned to face his assailant but what met his eyes instantly made him wish that he had remained ignorant of their attacker. He however, was determined not to lie down and be eaten by this huge black and hairy monster, Richard jumped to his feet and back peddled as fast as his legs would carry him, the thing just watched the petrified boy as he half fell, half tumbled backward through the bush, something in the back of Richard's brain told him to stay and try to protect his still prone companion but his brain screamed for him to run away. His eyes came to rest on a dead branch which he quickly lifted above his head in what he considered looked like a threatening pose.

"Move away from my friend," Richard summoned up all the courage he could muster as he challenged the creature. The thing, gazing down on his companions was an enormous ugly spider with twelve hairy legs as opposed to the eight that Richard was used to; this was definitely no ordinary bathroom variety type spider. Richard eyed the two yellow pincers at its mouth and noticed that they seemed to be drooling in anticipation of a meal. The other thing that struck him quite forcibly was that the spider wasn't black as he had first assumed, but was striped with different colours like a psychedelic rainbow. It must have been his immediate panic that made him first presume that it was black, he decided. "My, my. What a temper you have young man."

"I warn you, if you don't move away I'm going to flatten you with this stick."

"Are you now?"

"D-don't think you scare me. I've destroyed many of you sort before," challenged Richard. The 'many' that he was referring to were those that crept up the plughole and into their bath at home. None of them were this big though, but Richard wasn't about to reveal this to the beast at this stage.

"Oh, you have, have you?"

"Yes. So you had better move back." Richard moved forward so that he was just out of reach of the beast, he valiantly waved the wooden branch towards the spider. "Certainly." The spider didn't walk as such, but seemed to hop back a step.

"Now, does that suit you? You cannot get away from me even if I took a hundred steps backwards I would still be able to annihilate you and your friends."

"Orkan! Get over here." Orkan looked up cautiously toward the spider and in one movement caused through panic was suddenly standing behind Richard.

"Weeeooee! Gghhh! What's that?" Richard's confidence wasn't really growing in leaps and bounds as he realised that he had not got the better of this particular beast and that it wasn't going to attack them immediately but did intend to tease them for a while before doing what it was going to do.

"It's ¬only¬ a large spider," he said unconfidently. "Admittedly, it's big as far as spiders go, but still only a spider." The thing suddenly became agitated and shuffled and hopped around seemingly as if the ground beneath its many feet had become red hot.

"I'm not just any spider. I'm Baal, the spectral spirit spider that renews water life and travels through the universe replenishing the liquid givers of life."

"Huh!" Richard was unimpressed. "I suppose you can fly as well?"

"Go now!" Maerkat cried, jumping to his feet, sword drawn. "Orkan, get them away to safety." Melek raced towards them as Orkan hustled Richard back through the thorn bushes and supposedly out of harm's way for a moment.

Maerkat swung his sword in an arc that was a silver blur that travelled almost faster than the eye could follow. Again and again he sliced at the almost tree trunk like legs of the spider's front legs. The creature reared up whistling and screeching with agony as the bushes where seconds before had been an opening snapped back closed. Maerkat had managed to sever two of the beast's talons that now lay twitching on the ground, the large spider retreated quickly while the leopard man turned and scrambled through the bushes to rejoin the others.

"That was Baal!" He panted. I've come across him before, he's quick and very deadly and I only managed to cut off two of his legs but, that won't slow him much because he'll soon grow two more in their place. Our only chance is the trees, if he should catch up to us in this clearing we're done for. Follow me!"

Maerkat darted lithely ahead of them around the bushes and into the forest, twisting and turning in an intricate maze that would have bamboozled any pursuer, stopping several times to allow the others to catch up. Puffing and panting, no sooner had they reached him and he was off again looking like a dappled spectre amidst the heavy foliage.

"How could the guardians have lost the war when it had forces like Maerkat?" Richard panted.

"I think we have travelled enough," Orkan suggested. Maerkat stopped and looked back, there seemed to be an instinctive rapport between these two soldiers.

"We must be wary, Baal will not give up the chase so easily though." Maerkat listened intently, sniffed the air then went down on all fours placing his ear to the ground; there was utter silence, not even the normal forest sounds of birds and crickets were to be heard. "You're right, first let's find our bearings and get away from this area." Maerkat indicated for the others to be seated as he cleaned off the dripping mess from his sword and replaced it into its scabbard.

"Here take this and see what direction we should follow." Melek handed Richard the Espial Diviner

"I will check the next riddle." Melek took the Book of Prophecies off his back.

"Who knows, it's been sort of right so far, maybe it will help us this time." Richard said rather sarcastically.

Melek gave him a disapproving glance as he opened the book.

Beware the silken ways
By evil spinner spun.
Yellow orbs that hasten days
Destroy when serpent comes
Some may perish, some feel pain
Tribulations not in vain
Three will tread these paths again
To save the precious one

Richard listened but was more intent with his little plaything, moving it back and forth watching the colours change, the most obvious direction was indicated when the stone turned almost golden. It seemed to be trying to convey their direction but all it seemed to Richard was that it pointed directly toward thick and thorny brushwood.

"It's that way then, let's test your theory Melek."

"It's not 'my' theory, ye of little faith. It's your destiny being foretold."

The group moved towards the thorn bushes, Richard noticed an array of honey dripping and luscious looking berries adorned the plants.

"I'm hungry." He stretched out to pick one, "they look as if they're ripe."

Maerkat's hand shot out and pulled Richard's arm away.

"Never touch those; it's the Killer Sunrise bush. One touch and you're dead, they may look delicious but each berry contains an aging poison that will pack the rest of your life into less than half a minute. For a few seconds you will gain the most incredible strength and then as quickly you'll just shrivel and die a most foul death. I know, because some of my comrades once fell to that plants deadly poison, one minute they were young fighting soldiers, the next they were bare bones on the ground, the affect is almost instant."

Maerkat drew his sword and began clearing a pathway making sure that he never touched any of the thorny plants or its enticing fruit while cautiously, his companions followed the new path also making certain not to make any contact with the lethal berries. They reached a clearing and Richard's heart sank because the Espial Diviner had led them straight into a trap, this was clearly Baal's lair.

"Melek, that toy has led us straight to Baal, look at those, those are spider cocoons and I'll bet I know who the owner of this establishment might be."

"Don't understand it." The young scribe shook his head.

Maerkat was so frustrated that as he walked around the hanging cocoons he slit them open only to reveal Baal's prey inside, there were animals, people, and even fish inside; this definitely was a hunter's storage area. One of the cocoons emptied its contents onto the ground, bones snapped as the morbid remains scattered, Orkan saw the glint and picked up a beautiful badge from the ground.

"The Mighty Mulkat, he was a fine warrior and landsman," sighed Maerkat recognising the trinket. "He had the fiercest of tempers and the reddest hair you've ever come across. This was his family's insignia, handed down over many generations and was supposed to bear magical powers. He tried explaining them to me at a festival but, I was too sleepy to listen, I wish I had paid attention."

Orkan flicked the ring to Richard.

"You better take it, perhaps with your so-called magical powers it may do something for you, it didn't do him much good though, did it?"

Richard simply fixed the badge to his shirt, suddenly a high-pitched whistle, everybody instantly knew what it meant as the huge spider broke cover of the bushes and surged into the clearing.

"This time measly creatures," Baal wheezed, "you will not escape!"

"The bushes! Back the way we came."

Maerkat's reaction was lightning fast, the others had no chance of moving.

"Did you think it was that easy to escape old Baal?" the spider screeched.

The three were suddenly trapped as Baal began to feed a sticky silk at all of them simultaneously. The more they struggled the tighter the substance seemed to constrict them. Out of the corner of his eye, Richard noticed that Maerkat was making his way back, surely the thing would see him.

"Hey Baal," Richard shouted trying to keep the things attention focused on himself. "You think you can keep us like those others?"

All Baal's many eyes swivelled toward Richard; this allowed Maerkat to move out of sight and around the back of the beast. His sword raised, he sank it deep into the hind legs, again and again he hacked until the spider's heavily weighted body had nothing behind to hold it up properly and it sank slowly to the ground. Maerkat then jumped onto its back and repeatedly sliced into the soft upper hairy flesh, green slimy stink laden liquid gushing like a fountain from the cavities caused by the sharp sword, but, Baal was tough, he was a survivor like Maerkat although his concentration was now no longer fixed on the three being wrapped with his sticky solution. Orkan had somehow managed to get to his knife and quickly slit through the web, in no time at all he had set his two companions free just in time as the huge spider retracted what legs remained forming himself into a ball and rolled over several times as Maerkat jumped to safety.

"Quickly we must help him." Orkan drew his sword.

"Get away! Save yourselves, I'll take my chances!"

Orkan was undecided, when Melek grabbed his arm and tried to lead him away.

"Gghhh! We can't just leave him?"

"Yes we can," Melek replied. "First rule of war, don't waste lives unnecessarily, remember that and now, respect his wishes. Go!" He then gave Richard the same treatment, Orkan looked back once again, there was a questioning expression on his face.

"Run!" Maerkat shouted. "If you don't you'll waste everything, get the boy to safety. I can look after myself."

The distraction was enough for Ball to pounce, its pincers sank deep into Maerkat and the leopard man coughed a deep gash oozed blood and in the grasp of the enemy he seemed to go limp. Orkan watched in despair as Baal although very weak and supposedly dying himself, tried to lift the nearly unconscious Maerkat to its mouth. With one last superhuman effort Maerkat struck out and his flaying sword seemed to pierce each and every eye of Baal before he became limp.

Orkan turned, he raced after his companions, and there was nothing more he could do here and Maerkat had been right, Golan had given him the task of keeping Richard safe. As he ran he heard first the deep despairing wail behind him that was then surprisingly followed by a high pitched whistle, this was repeated several times. Orkan and his companions met up and moved deeper into the forest but unbeknown to them this constant whistling had also roused another creature. The thing moved quietly through the undergrowth following the heat trace of what had harmed its master; it must now find and destroy this enemy of Baal. It was Melek that first heard the rustling of Lotan's approach..

"What's that?"

They all stopped to listen; the crackling of dried leaves beneath the thick body was the only sound to give away Lotan's position. Like a flash, something dropped down out of the overhanging branches and in a sudden blur encircled Richard. It, like Baal was multi-coloured, and strong as it began squeezing the boy with the grip of a huge coil of rope.

"Yowee!" Richard screamed as he quickly realised what it was.

"Weeeooee!" Orkan squealed. "O-Orkan it's a s-s-snake," gasped Richard. Its head turned to face its two victims. Both of them gasped for this was no ordinary snake. It looked like the reptile was suffering from a severe bout of mumps. It seemed to have several weirdly shaped bumps protruding from various places around the area where its neck should have been. Now, as its ugly head with its hypnotic eyes moved slowly to and from before them, Melek could clearly make out that the bumps were only contained around the head and didn't extend further down the snake's slippery body.

"Sssiiss, sssiiss." The forked tongue moved rapidly in and out of its wide mouth as it sensed and tested the air and its trussed victim, Richard tried to move but found it absolutely impossible, like a huge python or boa constrictor, the thing had him trapped tightly within its powerful coils and could take its time before making a meal of him.

Suddenly Orkan had one of his ideas.

"Gghhh! We've got to help him, split up, it cannot then get both of us then. Any ideas?"

"The rhyme, yellow orbs...?"

"Of course." Orkan panted before Melek could complete the sentence.

"Yellow orbs that hasten days. It must mean those berries that Maerkat said aged his people. Only problem is I don't have any."

"Yes there is a bush of them just over there."

The two quickly moved off to find it leaving Richard to think he was being left to die, he gasped, not daring to take his eyes from the weaving reptile's head as it swayed slowly back and forth over him. Richard had always been petrified of possibly meeting a snake, that was, ever since he had read Rudyard Kipling's version of Rikki-Tikki-Tavi the mongoose, who had confronted a vile King Cobra. From then, until now, the snake had always represented the most evil thing alive; he now knew that there were far more dangerous things lurking here than the snake, but that still didn't help him from retaining his absolute rigid fear and horror of any form of slithering reptile.

"I-I'm sorry. I didn't mean to undermine your status as a spirit."

"C-can you speak?" Richard asked.

"Yes's," the snake hissed its reply without even moving its mouth as it continued to rock back and forth and Richard felt its grip tighten ever so slightly.

"W-what're you going to do to me?" Richard requested, hopeful that the thing was only fooling around.

"Don't rush me; I'm thinking whether between you and your runaway friends, whether together you'll make up a decent meal."

That was it, Richard felt the blood actively draining from his face and his legs begin to wobble as he thought of himself sliding down this things throat. Richard wondered whether to offer Loan a pod in exchange for their lives. There was no way he could be able to reach his rucksack while he was so tightly trussed up by Loan.

Orkan meanwhile had taken an arrow and spiked three of the poisonous berries simultaneously onto it. He then withdrew his sword and carefully stripped a few of the toxic berries off the bush onto the ground. He knelt and gently lifted them one by one on the end of his sword into a small leather pocket the side of his quiver.

"Must remember they are stored in there, they could be useful now, back to the snake." Melek followed the soldier.

"Hope this works."

As they drew near they could hear that Richard was now desperately gasping for breath. Lotan swayed back and forth, there was almost pleasure in its eyes when Orkan raised his bow with the lethal arrow and pointed it straight at him.

"Sssss one chance is all you have, arrows normally just bounce off me, that is, if the hit me at all."

"The mouth, go for the mouth, its vulnerable there." Melek urged.

Orkan slowly drew back the bow but the snake's head was weaving in anticipation.

"Hey! Hey!" Melek drew his knife and raced to one side of the huge reptile, it turned being distracted by this new attacker and that gave Orkan the opportunity he was waiting for.

He released the arrow and it flew straight right into the back of the huge snake's throat. The huge beast shook its head violently trying to dislodge this tiny object from within its throat and Richard suddenly noticed that the six strange bumps seemed to be swelling like boils trying to explode outward from around Lotan's head.

"Gghhh! Get away Melek!"

The two raced to safety before turning to see what effect the arrow might have. Lotan reared up, dwarfing his two enemies into insignificance as he just seemed to be expanding and expanding, the ripples moved from the reptile's head and along the length of its long body, around the coils where the unfortunate Richard was now being squeezed even more tightly before its eyes seemed to bulge and pop out.

"SIISSSS! SIISSSS!

Its furious thrashing felled bushes and trees like matchsticks while Richard was hurled onto the ground with Lotan's tail slashing wildly just above his body. The power was awesome to behold as both Orkan and Melek stumbled backwards to avoid this monster trying to reach them. Lotan suddenly stopped its thrashing from above their position the snake gazed down as if about to attack then they were amazed as Lotan's skin simply wrinkled into folds, the face instantly bagged and even the wide mouth, with rotting gums spewing saliva overtook the reptile in seconds. Melek raced around the beast to Richard.

"Are you all right?"

"Just about, what happened? I thought that I was done for." Richard was anxiously scrambling about in his bag for something.

"Orkan saved the day once again."

"Oh no! The pods gone. My bag must have opened when that thing was thrashing about; Golan's going to kill me."

Lotan just seemed to fall to ground and go through his last death throes, twitching ever so slightly now and again.

The three began hunting around the clearing for the pod; it was Melek that first spotted it.

"It's there." Melek pointed to the other side of the clearing near to where Richard was standing. "Get it and let's get out of this place."

Richard turned and saw the glowing pod but rather than see danger he suddenly had the feeling it was there.

"Move away from me Melek, get Orkan, I fear that we are not yet quite done yet."

Melek did not hesitate and raced towards Orkan and the bush moved near Richard to reveal a very injured, but very dangerous Baal equidistant from the pod. Richard knew he had very little chance if he made a dash to retrieve it, then again he knew that they could not go on without it. His two companions watched the stalemate situation in horror, finally Orkan made up their minds for them

"Richard, run! Get away, Baal will kill you too, we'll have to return, you at least have an amulet... Leave it!"

Richard moved like the wind and all three tried making their escape.

"So predictable," Richard heard Baal's tortured voice behind him.

"Well, at least we know that other people are also searching the forest." Richard pulled back and moved across and placed his hand on Orkan's shoulder.

"Thanks for your help. We'll make a good team. Baal is too injured at the moment to chase us very far; perhaps you're right, live to fight another day and all that?"

"Gghhh!" Orkan looked slightly embarrassed.

"Weeeooee! Richard shouted at Orkan whose nervous laughs were intermittently dotted with deep snorting as the little group left the area safe in the knowledge that two of their enemies were now dead and very injured.

"I think that we've dealt with those two for the moment and they won't be back in a hurry," said Richard.

"I'm going to keep this badge for good luck it almost willed me not to be stupid. Come my friends, we've still got to find the guardians or the pods."

They moved along cautiously because the light of day was fading and in case Baal made a miraculous recovery and lying in wait they knew they had to be on guard. Richard saw Orkan lean forward and raise his trotter-like hand to his ear as if straining to listen for some noise. He turned to Richard and shook his head to indicate that there was something in the pathway ahead of them...

"Not more trouble, is it never going to stop? What is it now?" Richard shook violently.

The Enchantress Illusion

On the Fourth Day...

An acrid laid devolves to stone.
The sorceress is now full-grown.
A sickle's strike one mighty felled.
By burning letters, evil quelled.
One orb purple, one orb blue,
Night light helps release the True.
Survive the fight, regain the prize.
Beyond the height a fine surprise.

"Gghhh! Gghhh!" Orkan sniffed at the air.

The pebbled path was absolutely clear ahead of them. Richard listened and could hear the crunching sound of someone moving in his direction. Without warning came an almost audible sound of something shuffling on the stone path.

"W-where's that sound coming from? Perhaps there's another path on the other side of these hedges." The group moved quickly up a gentle mound as Orkan continued to goad them from behind, Richard pulled up sharply when he reached the top and turned to the others, but Orkan, dragging Melek simply barrelled him over the ridge.

"Don't stop, it could be Baal." Orkan urged.

They had no choice as soft earth fell away underfoot and once over the edge, having little or no hope of clambering back as they slithered almost helplessly downwards between the bank of straggly trees and bushes.

. Propelled by Orkan's energy the group finally made it to the bottom, all were breathless but at least Richard felt that they were now safe from whatever was up there.

"Whew! I need a rest, let's make camp right here."

"Gghhh! I don't think so. Can you smell it?"

"What?"

"It smells like, er, roses."

"Of course it does, we're in a forest, aren't we? Only I don't think its rose petals."

"No, it's not from the flower garden. It's here; from around us somewhere, I do not think we are out of harm's way just yet."

"Oh no?" Melek said quietly. "Then you had better explain that phenomenon." He pointed to the heavens.

Above them, could clearly be seen that the stars were now hidden by what looked like ten equally spaced moons, their radiance was very eerie casting unnatural shadows over this landscape. Orkan kneeled down and sniffed at the ground, standing up his eyes searched for clues.

"Gghhh! over there," pointing to what in this light looked like old style temple buildings in the distance. "We might find someone to help us."

As they approached the area they noticed that this place was more like a walled city than something that had been randomly built, two gigantic stone pillars greeted them at what seemed like the main entrance. Nervously they moved to the gateway and peered in to what at first glance looked like a smooth avenue of white houses slashed at intervals by a series of darkened alleyways, but for a city this place had a very silent quality, nothing or nobody seemed to stir in what Richard could make out of this ghostly town.

"Perhaps they are all asleep?" Melek whispered.

They moved forward very gingerly into the open courtyard laid out beyond the huge pillars, all senses now eagerly strained to pick up the slightest sound or movement but, the only sounds were of their own breathing and the crunching of their own deliberate footsteps on what was now a loosely pebbled roadway. Richard quickly realised that everything was made of stone, even the beautiful statuettes that dotted this courtyard.

"Gghhh! something is not right, look at those figures, it seems as if they had all been moving in different directions, look at the horror etched on their faces, it's as if they were all frozen in time at the same moment?" Orkan's voice seemed to shiver slightly. "I think this is supposed to represent part of the battle, whoever constructed these is either a brilliant sculptor or we have something to fear right here, keep your wits about you."

They kept moving across the large courtyard examining the wonderfully laid out statues of what seemed like mainly warrior birds in full battle outfits just frozen in action. There were also some strange looking huge insects in various poses and also dressed in battle gear.

"Maybe this place could be Petropola," Melek announced proudly. "I have heard many stories; this was thought to be a mythical place where the queen that rules is called Mirrah. If the stories are true then we are in great danger, because Mirrah is powerful and evil, it is said that with the aid of a sickle she can turn people to stone."

"That explains the decoration, these figures are just too lifelike to have been carved by anyone, Melek's theory seems to be the logical one. C-Can we please get out of here?" Richard nervously enquired.

"Time to consult the Book of Prophesies, maybe it will give a clue as to where we are really heading." Melek removed the book and laid it flat on the pebbles.

"Those moons provide enough light to be able to make out the next part." He turned the pages until he found the verse that most applied to their environment.

An acrid laid devolves to stone.
The sorceress is now full-grown.
A sickle's strike one mighty felled.
By burning letters, evil quelled.
One orb purple, one orb blue,
Night light helps release the True.
Survive the fight, regain the prize.
Beyond the height a fine surprise.

"These silly rhymes... what do they really mean? All I can understand is that we are going to have a fight and possibly, those words indicate that we might win, the rest is pure nonsense." Orkan offered an opinion.

"The sorceress must mean Mirrah, I don't want to meet her, let's all turn around and leave before she arrives." Richard was petrified but didn't want the others to know. "Then again, we could find a pod here, that line about a prize?"

"Gghhh! Look!" Orkan pointed towards the far side of the courtyard. Just then, there was the faintest of sounds ahead of them, the noise of crunching underfoot but, they could see nothing. The sound of footsteps moved closer to the group.

"Orkan, there's somebody else here."

"Then where are they?"

"I don't know ...I can just feel its presence. P-Orkan let's move, there's something evil stalking us." Orkan beckoned to them to follow him along the pathway.

"Crunch, crunch."

The only sound on the pathway was that of loose stone being trodden underfoot. Orkan suddenly stopped dead still, the others did the same.

"Crunch, crunch."

"Oh, oh, you're right. There's something or someone following us."

"Cough, cough."

"What was ¬that¬? Did you cough?" Richard enquired, knowing full well that it wasn't Orkan or Melek.

"Did you see me cough?" Orkan opened his arms in helpless gesture, "Of course you didn't."

"Then you explain a fresh air cough."

"Who's there?" Orkan demanded drawing his sword. "Come out and show yourself at once."

Nothing moved except for the faintest of breezes. "Whatever it is, it is not about to show itself." Melek offered.

Richard moved to the side of the pathway to where there was loose sand at the base of the hedge. He scooped up a handful and moved back to Orkan, whispering something.

"Right."

The two turned and remaining in-step with each other, took exactly six paces along the path and then stopped simultaneously.

"Crunch, crunch." Then silence.

"There!" Orkan pointed to a spot near where he was standing. Richard hurled the fine misty sand at the spot, to their amazement an outline of a human figure formed in fresh air.

"'Yes'! Got you!" Richard shouted as he punched out into the air to show his glee.

"Cough, cough, cough."

The thing bent forward and raised its hand to its mouth as it suddenly went into a deep coughing spasm. The more it coughed the more visible the thing became.

"Oh, oh, if it's who I think it is, we're in 'big' trouble," said the now worried Orkan.

"W-who is it?" Suddenly Richard's brief elation simmered to coolness. The outline now revealed that whoever it was, was also wearing some form of toga like garment, whatever it was; now began to identify itself because the thing stopped coughing and took a step in their direction.

"Very clever ruse young man, you could have blinded me but I am protected."

"Well, it wasn't very clever of you to creep around and scare us like that, was it?"

Panicking, Orkan pulled his snout like nose up to indicate to Richard to shut up because this obviously wasn't the sort of person that was used to being talked back at.

"'Whaaat'? You dare have the gall to tell me what to do in my own garden."

The thing reached out to some unseen object there was a bright flash and in front of them stood a tall red-headed woman, long dark robes and golden serpent bracelets that seemed alive in the dancing light. This seemingly young maiden who had deep purple eyes and hair that almost reached her feet seemed to float just above the ground. Richard drew in a large breath.

"Goodness, you're beautiful, you see, she's not a witch?"

The young girl stared at him for a moment and then, like some sort of chameleon, the violent purple of her eyes turned to softest blue.

"You're not from here, are you?"

"No, how did you know?"

"That's fortunate for you, everybody knows me. I'm Mirrah, the oracle, and you have entered my garden at your own peril."

The girl stunned Richard with her beauty, she had to be the most perfect person he had ever encountered there was almost a dream quality to everything about her. His mouth hung open as he gaped at this slim enchantress.

"B-b-b." Richard drew a breath and tried to speak again. "B-b-b," it was no use, no matter how he tried this awful stuttering sound was the only thing that came forth.

"What's the matter with your friend?" Mirrah directed the question to Melek.

"I think he could be in love." Melek replied.

"B-b-but," Richard, at this point decided it was no use and shut up.

"So, the young man has fallen under the spell of my beauty, strange though, normally it takes longer than that for my power to react unless I use this of course, then it's instant."

Mirrah thrust forward took a pair of gold mirrors from within her robe; she gazed lovingly into them and with a sweep brushed back her hair.

"What about you? Do you think I'm attractive?" She directed the question to Orkan.

"Oh yes. But then again, I'm not human, so I wouldn't rightly know how 'they' measure beauty."

He indicated toward Richard and Melek with a nod of his head.

"I see, now what are you doing in my garden? I was foretold of your arrival; apparently you are on a mission why has that brought you here?"

"We're trying to find the seven pods of life and the guardians that have gone missing. You haven't seen any of them, have you?" Richard blurted out without being able to stop himself, it was at that moment that he suddenly noticed that Mirrah wore winged sandals as the young girl had recoiled ever so slightly to his question, but the recovery was not fast enough to hide the fact from the astute Orkan.

"I don't think so, but you're welcome to look through the rest of this square but, I think you will find what you seek in my special garden."

Beckoning for them to follow, she turned and almost glided her way along the path towards the structures at the far end. The group followed passing by the many elaborate stone people at war.

"I have heard stories whether true or not of her luring people into her garden only to turn them to stone, do you think it's going to be our fate?" Melek whispered.

"Running is no longer an option, she has winged feet." Richard replied, his brain was racing knowing that he must somehow get them out of what now seemed an impossible situation. They moved around a corner.

"What does Mirrah do?" Richard enquired loudly. Orkan looked at the back of the girl ahead and as if to gain approval, turned back to Richard.

""Gghhh! Mirrah is one of the greatest oracles here; she knows a great many things." Orkan played along.

"A combination of beauty and brains, how is it such a young girl know so much?"

"For an eternity Mirrah has used those tools she carries to extract information from travellers passing through her garden and nobody can resist her beauty and those tools. The sickle is the powerful sickle of 'Hades', from the abode of departed spirits and it supposedly can also make her invisible. The golden sickle that she carries can change people into something different and the winged sandals make sure she never gets caught out."

"You said eternity? Surely not."

"Oh yes, she's as old as the planet itself."

"Whaaat? I don't believe you." Richard turned at looked at him disbelievingly."

"Her age and looks never alter."

"Enough!" Mirrah spat out. "You say another word about me and I'll turn you to stone." Orkan made a sign to indicate that he had buttoned his lip.

"Right, you want to see if any of the guardians are here? Well, go ahead search, here is my special garden."

The group followed along the path to her garden and as they rounded the corner Richard drew in a long breath, for in the strange light of the moons, before them lay the most cared for, luscious garden with a large river meandering through the middle. The whole place was covered with bright green lawn, an abundance of multi-coloured flowers and dotted around the garden were all sorts of perfectly proportioned statues. "This is fantastic. Look there's the mountain with the zigzag waterfall. Richard pointed to the distant blue mountain he could only just make out the fluorescent line of the falling waterfall. For the first time he realised how much ground they had covered. He turned to Orkan and saw the pensive look on his face; he wasn't interested in the mountain.

"Something wrong?"

"Doesn't it strike you as odd?"

"What?"

"Such a perfect garden situated right in the middle of such chaotic surroundings. You've seen some of the nasty things that live beyond those hedges, why don't they invade this place?"

"I don't know. Why?"

"Have a careful look at the statues. If what I've heard is true, Mirrah only invites people into the garden to turn them into stone, nobody who comes in here ever leaves." Melek whispered. Richard felt his knees weaken.

"W-what?"

"That's right. Keep walking and keep admiring her garden and you mustn't say anything to offend her. Do you understand?"

"Yes, but how're we going to get out of here?"

"We need time to think. Keep moving and continue paying her compliments, the only thing that may save us is her vanity."

"Her vanity?"

"Yes, she's also supposed to be the vainest person in the world. "

You saved yourself from being turned to stone just now by pretending to fall in love with her."

"I wasn't pretending, I think that she is the most beautiful person that I've ever seen."

"Good, keep that thought in mind and you may be able to use it against her if we're lucky." Mirrah floated on ahead, she seemed mesmerised by her own garden for a short while.

"Everything's too ideal, not a blade of grass or an ornament out of place."

"J-just like you, er, ...i-it's really the most perfect, ...and, ...the most beautiful thing that er, garden ...I've ever seen. W-who does the gardening?"

Mirrah burst into frantic laughter.

"Ha, ha, you know little pig, I like your friend, he's amusing."

"What was funny about 'that'?" Again she went into peals of laughter.

"I'm the only person here."

"Then you do the gardening?"

"You fool, didn't your fat friend tell you about me?"

"No, should he have?"

"There's nothing that I don't know. It was I that that initiated speech, it was me that created all alphabets; it was me that created language so that all people were able to communicate with each other. The world would be nowhere without Mirrah."

Really?" Richard turned to Orkan with a sarcastic smile etched on his face.

"Orkan you should have told me about this fantastic young lady, wait until I tell my friends about my meeting with the cleverest person in the world, they'll all be gutted that they weren't sent on this mission." He turned back to see Mirrah again looking at herself in her golden mirrors. "May we look at some of the statues in your garden?" Without looking away from her mirror she waved them away.

"Go on, I'll be keeping an eye on you from here." The trio walked around the garden pretending to be examining the statues while trying to work out how to get away. Mirrah blocked the only exit from the garden.

"Perhaps we could sneak through the hedge," offered Richard.

"Not a good idea. We don't want to upset her because she would know immediately and we would be brought back to face her wroth. No, we've got to think up a plan." Suddenly Orkan stopped in front of one of the most imposing statues in the whole place. "Oh no!"

"What?"

"Look at the statue here, it's one of the guardians and he's been turned to stone."

"Nonsense," scoffed Richard.

The statue was that of a tall man with big, slanted eyes in full battle regalia, the figure reminded Richard of a huge eagle except this one held on firmly to a mace raised as if to strike the defiant giant earwig in front of it. Richard started to reach forward towards the statue.

"Don't touch it!" Melek yelled.

"You never know what could happen to you we must handle this matter delicately."

"Are you sure it's a guardian?"

"I think this is 'Juroot' he's – or rather was – the Guardian of Birds and Truth. What to do now?"

"We contact Golan, he'll know."

"Brilliant." Richard went into his bag and extracted the amulet given to him by Golan, feeling the instant warm sensation of the thing in his hand.

"Give her the badge." Golan's voice just seemed to float into Richard's thoughts.

They continued around the garden while preparing a plan, when they arrived back at the entrance to the garden they found Mirrah still admiring herself in her golden mirrors. "That was so educational," said Richard.

"But, I think I had rather see some statues changed, you're a little bit behind the times."

The deep purple eyes reappeared and Richard hoped that Mirrah wouldn't act too hastily for him to be able to put his plan into action.

"Behind times?" Two purple rays seem to spring from her eyes, Richard and Orkan trembled.

"My friends and I have travelled far to find you." Melek said, "The Evil One sent us to give a present to enhance your beauty even further and to increase your powers."

"A present? It's been a long time since anyone gave me anything, normally I have to take it." Mirrah replied.

Richard quickly unclipped Mulkat's badge and held it out to Mirrah.

"Ahh, it matches the colour of my hair" Mirrah let out a sigh tinged with satisfaction. She tucked the mirrors and sickle under her arm and stretched out her hand. Richard noticed that her hand, unlike the rest of her body was strangely withered and clawed. So much so that she struggled to fasten the ornament onto her own robe, then looked hard and long at the three.

"I-it only adds to your beauty." Richard sighed.

"I have made my decision, in exchange for this present I am going to give all of you the immortality you crave in among my special collection of statues." Mirrah raised her sickle.

Richard glanced at his companions, there were exchanges of pure desperation on all of the faces, their plan had backfired as the gliding figure slowly moved nearer, Melek was the first to notice the smouldering on Mirrah's robe. Mulkat's badge began glowing and emanating deep red hot onto the surrounding cloth, suddenly the mysterious gold rim began to crackle and spat out across Mirrah's breast that instantly seemed to formulate into molten drops of metal spraying across the front of its wearer. Mirrah dropped sickle and mirrors as she frantically tried to beat out the burning agony as well as trying to rip the pendent off of herself.

"Gghhh! we must get her tools. " Orkan dived forward and scooped the mirrors and sickle backwards to Richard, but was not fast enough in his retreat and even with her intense agony she was still moving forward, eyes stared at the group in intense hatred then Richard saw her for what she really was. She now looked like a bitter witch as her features took the look of a haggard old lady before she snatched back her hand to protect her features but, the spitting metal was now so bright and intense that she could not shield herself or her looks from the three.

"Gghhh! she's got me, get away, save you, and flee!" Orkan screamed

In this light it looked as if her bracelets writhed on her arm as if they had come alive when she tried to protect her face from the molten onslaught. The flashing heat spread wider and reached out towards her arms, momentarily distracted; she whipped sideways causing Orkan to stumble but she did not release her tight grip.

"She's really a witch." Richard screamed.

"I'm not seeing my friend die like Maerkat did." He lunged forward with the sickle but, Mirrah tried to parry the blow and it glanced off her free arm. The effect of this was that Orkan was suddenly released as Richard again swung the sickle and this time, felt it sink home into her chest.

"Gghhh! Get away." Orkan screeched. Richard seeing his friend now clear, pulled back, sickle still in hand as the torched Mirrah seemed to freeze into stone but at the same time was burning fiercely. The acrid smell of sulphur suddenly filled the air causing the trio to withdraw to safety and watch the helpless blazing effigy. Slowly the whole being of Mirrah just seemed to sink down and collapse into an ember pile of bright flame and putrid smelling smoke.

"Wow! We did it; another evil one loses a scalp?" Richard enquired nervously.

Once the smoke cleared they were surprised to that Mirrah had dissolved into a black mound of hard lava, Richard felt that his legs were designed of soft cotton wool, he slowly sank to his knees. "Man! That was a close call."

"You did well my warrior friend, for a moment back there I didn't think your ruse would work, especially when she grabbed hold of Orkan. Do you realise that if she had maintained her grip when you attacked her, that Orkan would have also been turned to stone? We have all been extremely fortunate today."

"Gghhh! that was a very brave thing to do Richard, you should have left me, next time do not be so foolhardy."

"That's all the thanks I get? Oh well, I suppose it's your way of saying thank you?"

Orkan simply grunted. All three were now seated; Richard was examining the sickle and mirrors.

"The riddle said something about a purple orb and a blue orb, do you suppose it could have meant these two mirrors?"

"It was believed that only Mirrah could free her captured guests, the sickle is for turning people to stone, maybe the mirrors are meant to release the people except they are not purple or blue. Even with moving them around, the reflection of the moons shows up as white in them." Melek offered.

"But the Book of Prophesies must have it right, we cannot see it though."

"Perhaps the moons change colour somehow?"

"Gghhh! let's see what happens tomorrow, but for now we must rest. I will stand guard over you and then Melek and you young man can watch over us until the dawn. That's when we will make a decision; also we can keep an eye on those moons?"

The night passed off without any further incidence, Melek woke Richard and then instantly curled up and in seconds was fast asleep. With Mirrah having been reduced to a hard lump the whole place had lost that menacing feel and with the others asleep, Richard became bored very quickly. For a while he used the sickle as his sword in a pretend battle against unseen foes and of course he won every fight by vanquishing his enemy. He picked up the mirrors and could clearly see himself on two fronts, but as he spoke to the mirrors, he noticed that their clear hue becoming darker in tone. Richard tilted one of them so that it caught one of the moons, and it didn't take long to register that the oncoming dawn light was changing, the once reflected white moon was beginning to have its rainbow effect on the moon's colouring.

"Get up!" Richard screamed loudly. "Quick! It's about to happen and we must save Juroot."

Both companions were instantly awake, Melek struggling to fix the large book to his back. Above them, the moons seemed to be reacting violently to the arriving daylight as distant rays began filtering through, the moons began to fade and change colour. Richard handed Orkan one mirror.

"Juroot!"

They raced across to the magnificent statue, and then adjusted reflections until blue and purple light beams merged on the giant birds face, the effect was instantaneous. The mirrors shook as two bolts of pure energy shot out of each mirror creating an audible ripping sound through the quiet morning air, the crescendo of a loud thunder when both streaks hit Juroot's features almost sent both of them reeling backwards.

"Whoohee!" Orkan shouted and then almost as quickly recognised that Richard was in danger. He grabbed the boy and yanked him backwards.

"The mace!"

In Juroot's hands the mace began to shake and the blow was about to fall just where Richard had been standing, it all seemed to take a split second before the huge mace buried itself into the ground that sent stone shrapnel flying in all directions and just missing Richard's outstretched leg. Like autumn leaves falling from a tree, the grey stone flakes fell to the ground and seemed to dissolve like melting ice. Juroot blinked then his gaze fixed with deadly intent onto Richard.

"Oh-oh! Is he mad at me?"

"So the prophecy was correct," he exclaimed. "There is one that sees in dark and light." His features softened ever so slightly, "you have done well today." Removing a dagger from his belt he handed it to Richard.

"Take this, it will serve you well, now, tell me what is happening on the outside."

The three told the giant guardian everything they knew to be happening, he said nothing but constantly nodded approval of their exploits to date, but when told of their leaving a pod with Baal, spoke for the first time.

"You must return, if even one pod is lost to evil forces everything you achieve from now will be in vain. Do not worry, at least you know where the pod is, and by your acquiring that sickle you now have the will and power to help you to overcome Baal."

There was a sudden movement to the side, Juroot's mace was instantly up in the air and it flashed down straight at Richard. The heavy blow missed him by fractions; again it was lifted and dropped.

"Whoa!"

Richard turned; close behind laid a dying giant earwig or beetle that had lain at Juroot's feet when he was still a statue.

"Sorry about that, some of the moonbeams must have reached it and reversed the spell." Juroot said. "There are more of its kind out there, so be careful, be on your guard because they are superb fighters." Juroot rose, took the mirrors from Orkan and Richard and began walking around the garden stopping to catch the moonbeams onto those he recognised as his compatriots.

"I will have to spend time here releasing the forces of good each morning when the time and moons are in their correct position." As Juroot released each of them in turn, the bird soldier stepped forward and saluted the leader. As he continued his work the guardian explained their capture and the rise of the Evil One.

"It started slowly, then became worse. People started disappearing, at first it was only one or two, but then whole villages started to go missing and what remained behind was carnage with poisoned wells and entire populations going missing. It became a form of destroy and lay waste to everything type tactic."

"Couldn't it be halted?" Richard asked.

"No, it soon became evident to us that the whole fabric of our Ancestral World was being eroded by this unseen force. Guardians were dispatched to find out what was happening but they too went missing, I was the third to leave the security of the Tree of Life and as you now know, I did not return. That means that there are others in my same position, you have freed me, you still have much to do and very little time to do so, that is why it is imperative to get hold of that pod from Baal." Juroot raised his mace in salute and farewell as the little group set off towards the city gates.

By the time they again climbed the steep hill and reached Baal's forest, it was mid-morning, sweat poured off Melek.

"I must rest; these books get heavier by the step."

"Books?" Orkan asked. "I thought you only stole one book?"

"Ahh! Well there was a book about monsters and magic, it is but a small book."

"Ghhh, get rid of it then."

"No! It too, may even help us to solve our quest. Books have that effect, nothing then a word that helps you." Melek gave a smug grin as he extracted the small book from a hidden pocket within his robes. The pages were parched and worn and the cover had gold leaf inscription. Richard took the book, the title was clear it read, 'Morbane's Book of Monsters and Magic'.

"How do you think this might help us?"

"Morbane was the oldest and wisest of our scribes and magicians and had travelled the Ancestral World extensively writing about monsters and beasts and their magical powers he had encountered on the way. It was from this book that I somehow knew, or at least must have learned of Mirrah and of Sumar." Melek said, proud of the knowledge that he had contributed to their fortunes thus far.

"Okay, keep it, but you carry it, right?"

Melek nodded and replaced the book back into the hidden pocket in his robes, while Richard extracted something from his bag. He handed both companions a hard boiled sweet.

"Suck them."

The delight and taste was very evident on both faces.

"Ghhh! How sweet these coloured stones are, are they magical?"

"Nah! Something I brought from my world." Richard simply giggled aloud.

After the short recovery break they set off and soon found themselves passing the spot where Lotan had fallen, the skeletal remnants were still where the huge snake had had its demise but it also amazed Richard as to how quickly the large carcass had been stripped clear to the bare bone.

As they moved towards the clearing, they heard the now familiar shrill followed by the trampling bush crushing sound.

"You two distract him, I will try the Maerkat trick and circle round behind." Richard melted into the undergrowth.

The two readied themselves for Baal's frontal and sticky attack to come lancing towards them but instead, the creature rapidly appeared before the two and seemed to be dragging its hind quarters where its back legs had not re-grown as yet. The huge spider reared up to attack and from the corner of Orkan's eye he caught sight of movement to the right of the creature now towering way above them with an almost unbalanced motion. Having its back legs still missing meant it was not as manoeuvrable as it was when they first met the giant insect but, it still moved fast enough even with this harboured vulnerability.

"Ghhh, we meet again Baal."

Instinctively but, too late Baal realised that Richard was missing, it swung to its side following Orkan's gaze as Richard rushed in to be faced by the beast's soft underbelly. He knew he had only this one chance to succeed as he raced below the mountainous spider, drawing back the sickle and with all his strength lodged it into the weak underside where Baal tentacles could not reach him just yet.

"Ghhh, get away!"

Richard continued his directional run as hard as could fully realising that as soon as he had passed the spider then the thing would see him and attack, he just hoped his speed would catch the thing off guard long enough for him to escape the deadly pincers.

"Ghhh, its working!"

Having cleared the beast Richard raced through some brush and circled back towards his companions, what met his eyes was a surprise, both were now racing in his direction but, above them he could clearly see the teetering stone form of Baal, the only problem was that the giant monster was about to fall and it was going to come crashing down on top of them. Richard almost skidded to a stop, turned and raced as hard as he could back into the thorny brushwood.

Baal fell flat on its face burying the sickle beneath it, after the commotion the forest area seemed strangely silent. The three waited for some time in order to be sure that Baal did not move.

"We should now call this place Spider Mountain? Stone? Spider? Oh forget it." Richard was still very nervous.

"No, it is a good name for this place now." Melek agreed.

"Pity he fell on the sickle, it would have been a handy tool to have. Right, let's find the pod."

"You must use this." Melek handed Richard the direction finder. Richard rotated it until it glowed golden.

"That way."

In the silence they forged their way through the cobweb wood until they reached Baal's cocoon filled larder again, it had been tidied up since their last encounter with Baal and the clusters of silken bundles were again neatly hanging in regular lines. Orkan immediately set about stripping them open delicately using his knife to slit them lengthways, bodies, beasts and fish were exposed.

"There, that's the one!" Melek insisted.

Orkan opened the web and the pod fell out, Richard cupped the valuable prize in his hands, it was strangely alive and warm.

"Yup! It's a good one this. Think it's time to move on?" He commented as he placed it into his bag.

"Ghhh, kill them!" Orkan suddenly started stomping the ground.

Richard immediately saw what had got Orkan so riled up; there were three or four spiders that he had dislodged from one web now trying to make the safety of the surrounding brushwood. Richard grabbed his knife that Juroot had given him and raced to help his companion, the little things were perfectly formed miniatures of Baal.

"Do you think we got them all?"

"Don't know, they took me by surprise. I hope we did, another Baal would be a catastrophe."

"If any did escape, it will take time for them to develop; maybe we will have completed what it is we are supposed to do before then?"

Orkan tugged at Richard.

"C'mon let's get out of this place."

They moved down a path into the forest leading up to a ledge from where they could see the valley spread out below. Panting, they sat down to catch their breath.

"That's a beautiful view, where are we?"

They were all standing on the edge of a precipice as Melek pointed out a spot almost on the horizon across the other side of the valley. Richard could just make out the shape of the zigzag waterfall.

"Wow! We have travelled a long way." No sooner were the words out of his mouth when there was a loud crack and suddenly all three were launched into mid-air and falling rapidly.

Richard's mind moved into super-panic mode once again...

The Flying Beasts of Detonation

On the Fifth Day...

A flight through air to withered land.
Beware the storm, the desert spanned.
A bone-filled grave awaits the brave
But hidden bounties save.
Within dark earth a lonely night
From skyborne spite at dreadful cost
A hard-won treasure now is lost.

Wind roared in their ears as they sped faster and faster to their oncoming misty fate way below when all of a sudden Richard saw the huge shadow pass across the cliff wall. The next thing he knew was that he felt was a thump and an iron grip like steel bands around his chest, looking down he saw huge yellowed horny fingers encircling his rib-cage. To his right he could see that both of his companions hanging limply within a similar giant fist. The immediate thought before his vision doubled and passing out that sprang to mind was, that they had been saved from a horrible bone breaking death only to be taken in mid fall by something huge.

"Oh no, here we go again," thought Richard.

Richard awoke with Orkan shaking him hard.

"Wha..."

"Ghhh he's alive!" Orkan stated, the relief in his voice, quite evident.

Groggily Richard got to his feet; Melek offered the boy a sip of water.

"Where are we? What happened?"

"We are on a ledge, there is a path leading from here down there. Whatever happened, we were saved, Orkan thinks it was by a bird of some description." Melek offered. "Be careful there's a long sheer drop over the edge of that rock just over there and you don't want to fall."

"Not fall again you mean?"

"Look down into the valley. From here, hopefully we are relatively safe from harm but who knows from what. See that path leads down to the valley but we will be exposed to aerial attack the whole way down because we've left the cover of the forest."

Richard gazed from their high vantage point across what seemed like outstretched moors way below.

"I can't see anything to worry about. There's just rolling marshland and grass in the distance."

"Exactly but your eyes deceive you, that's desert. In olden times, that same area would have been awash with beautiful sun covered plains filled with people, animals and lovely cornfields. But that was before the great battle but now look at it, bleak, cold and barren."

"How did these things happen? What do you think happened to change it?"

Orkan held his fingers to his lips and then pointed toward the distant hills.

"Gghhh! The Evil One and the battle caused this and I've been here before... I think."

"So?"

"Keep your eyes peeled for Oganga."

"Who's Oganga?"

"Oganga is a Guardian of the Air but, I do not know whether he survived all I do know is that his cave is somewhere over in those blue hills. Oganga, the spirit of birds watches and waits but I wonder if he made it through the last battle."

Richard's eye caught sight of slight movements on the plains and he suddenly realised that there were no ordinary human people moving around on the distance plains. That must be part of the 'real' world stretching way out below them, he thought, his heart skipped a beat, if only he could move forward and possibly not attract their attention somehow, then maybe he and his companions could escape this terrible place. The only problem as Richard saw it, was that they were now standing near a straight incline and by the time those tiny specks had managed to reach him by any roundabout route, anything could have happened. He shook his head and turned back to Orkan.

"The spirit of birds, what's that mean?"

"Look! What's that?" Orkan pointed towards a seemingly large bird-like shadow soaring on the air currents well below their elevated position across the valley, Richard could only just make out the giant shadow was skilfully gliding in circles across the plain and towards their position.

"Weeeooee!"

"Orkan!"

"I can't help it. It's this silly pig brain that takes over. Now I've done it, haven't I?"

Richard looked back towards the shadow that had changed direction and was now heading directly towards the ridge where they were now carefully stationed on this precarious ledge. The shadow remained well below their line of vision when it disappeared from their view beneath the edge of the ravine.

"Where's it gone?"

Like a prop-engine plane revving up, a sudden loud ear-shattering whirring sound filled the air all around the two, Richard jumped, the clatter although a lot louder reminded Richard of the time he had tied a ruler to a length of string and whirled it over his head. The frightful din lifted in intensity so that both Richard and Orkan had to cover their ears. Whirr, whirr, whirr, the deafening sound seemed to envelope them from every direction.

"What is it?" Richard screamed at the unhearing Orkan.

Then, suddenly Richard understood as the noise abated and the enormous creature appeared, hovered and set itself down on the rock at the edge of the ravine. It shuffled until it got close to the edge and could comfortably scan the whole valley floor. Richard wasn't absolutely sure but, as Oganga folded its gigantic wings against its back, they seemed to form into a large shell. Looking at the creature from the back, it suddenly seemed like a gigantic flying tortoise.

"Who's your friend, Orkan?" The voice seemed to float softly on the wind.

"You saw us then, Oganga? My friend is called Richard and he's helping us to try to find the missing guardians, we're trying to follow the ancestral trail and find the stolen pods from the tree of life."

"Don't be afraid I know who you all are, my name is Oganga and I am a friend. Like your companions I escaped from the final battle and have been searching for survivors." Oganga paused, then added sadly, "There are not many of us left behind."

"There are more than you think," Orkan broke in, "We have just come from the City of Stone and Juroot is free."

"I know, I have recently seen him," Oganga said, "But he and his troops were in trouble and fighting for their lives."

"W-What?" Richard was both horrified and terrified; "It all seemed fine when we left him."

"You must be the Chosen One?"

"Yes. He's been given the wisdom to see everything and was chosen by the helmet." Melek offered.

"That is good. Juroot urged me to search for you as your mission is more important than his, luckily for you I heeded his words otherwise you would now be spattered on the valley floor."

"Yes, thank you for saving us," Richard mumbled, his companions followed with their gratitude.

"Now I must take you to the valley floor"

The 'thing' turned its head right around like an owl might do and Richard could see that its head was narrow and pointed, yet reminded him somehow of a chameleon he had once seen. Its strange eyes protruded sideways from its head like two big tennis balls that moved independently from each other so that it was looking forward with one eye and backward with the other. Richard looked towards Orkan who was violently shaking his head to let him know that it wasn't a good idea and he was in danger if he accepted.

"No thank you. I prefer to have both feet on terra firma."

"Orkan, you are teaching the boy well, Richard, never take anything you see or anything you're offered here for granted."

This repetitive statement from these strange beings was becoming monotonous Richard thought as he tried recalling how many times he had heard this warning today.

"Let me tell you why I'm the spirit of the birds, my particular guardian is Juroot, would you like to hear more?"

"Yes please."

Oganga spread its wings and settled again, Richard couldn't get over the fact that the thing looked like a flying mixture of a tortoise and chameleon.

"When man first came from below and settled in the valley, they had two yearly celebrations, the first being to pay homage to Sahamay for producing rain during their harvest season and providing bountiful crops. This commemoration was called Oshipe. The head of the household would dress up and gather the first ripe harvest. Together with his family, he would offer their thanks to Sahamay. The father or family head would pass a small portion to each member, saying loudly, 'Eat of the rich harvest that Sahamay has provided for us this season.' The Oshipe was practised regularly and it was taboo to reap the new crop until this ceremony had been carried out. If any family didn't comply, it was taken as a form of greed and the population sometimes suffered extreme famine during the next year.

"How were they found out if they didn't carry out the Oshipe?"

Richard was inquisitive, now starting to relax he didn't feel so alien amongst these strange creatures, this Oganga thing wasn't as frightening as some of the others that he had already encountered during the last few days.

"I watched over them and could see everything what went on, their actions were reported to the various spirits who took appropriate steps. From high up in the sky you'll be surprised what goes on without those below realising they are being watched."

"You're nothing but a tell-tale then." The creature sucked in deeply and shook its body as Richard felt Orkan rap his hand showing his displeasure.

"Watch out, don't upset him," Orkan whispered urgently. The beast opened its mouth and shot out its long red forked tongue in their direction, it looked for the entire world like a fire-whip as it crackled and sparked tiny daggers of flame around it.

"Golan number two. W-What I really mean is..." he hesitated while trying to find the right words to say. "You are the one that sees all and knows all and reports back to the other guardians. Right?"

Richard saw Oganga visibly relax and draw in his long tongue once again.

"Motor mouth," he accused himself softly.

"I'm not here to betray others, I have a duty to carry out and if people don't obey nature's rules, then they suffer."

"What is the other ceremony you mentioned?"

Richard wanted to get Oganga's thoughts away from his unfortunate slip of the tongue.

"That was known as Omatla. It was a celebration that closes the old season and calls in the new one. The chief of every village would appoint five old men to act as the Sekango or men who called for Sahamay to produce rain and in the early morning they would march east to greet the rising sun. Each carried a hollow stick that he swung around his head to make a loud whistling noise, the whining made by them was like that of a large bird calling to tell everyone of their arrival and when they all did this in unison, it sounded like a flock of large birds approaching to the corn fields. No one was allowed to come out or even see if it was the Omatla or the birds."

"Why not?" Richard conjured up the picture of the strange event with a few old men waving sticks and everybody in hiding.

"Well, if it wasn't the Omatla and in fact a real flock of birds then they would have been scared away by the sight of people, on that one day only, people were supposed to let the birds feast freely, if it was the Omatla, they would seize any small livestock or children and carry them away with them. Children and beasts were supposed to be indoors and not outside for the Omatla, animals such as young sheep, goats or even fowls that roamed freely through the village were always seized. It was a sign of bad fortune when people heard the sound of beating wings and those in their houses would dance around as if the rain was falling on them. This livestock and children were then all gathered together and that night slaughtered in preparation of a great feast, which all villagers shared."

"You mean the people ate the children, that's cannibalism. It's disgusting."

"Not really, everybody knew what was expected of them, and therefore, parents tried to keep their young inside, the only ones outside were those that wouldn't listen. Sometimes the Omatla would take pity and trade the children for one of the family's beasts then again, sometimes they would not and the children were slaughtered along with the stray beasts. At the feast everybody would always leave small portions on the ground for the birds to eat the following morning. Those families that didn't heed the ceremony by coming from their houses or not leaving small livestock outside for the Omatla, and then ate the food without leaving something for the birds suffered great famine the next year. Those that paid attention and celebrated the feast correctly, had abundant harvests."

"So, why are the moors so barren now?"

"What was realised was when the new chief came to power he was a disciple of the evil one and stopped the ceremony by not appointing the Omatla, that year the entire region had famine and people were dying every day. Huge evil vultures started appearing from nowhere and began attacking the people, they have a powerful leader called Boltor, which spurs them on, this made life unbearable in the valley. Those villagers that were not tortured or converted decided to leave this area to find better ground. As they moved away, they told everyone that the region was haunted by evil spirits who destroyed their crops, nobody dared come here after that and the valley has remained uninhabited ever since."

"What about me, I didn't know the story and I'm here."

"Oh yes, but you and others like you are only temporary visitors to this place. That's why all the ancestral spirits are gathered here and won't allow anybody to settle here."

"What if somebody did try to settle around here?"

"They wouldn't last very long before they moved off, you have found out that there are both good and bad spirits in all areas. You've probably seen some of them already? In fact you met Mirrah, how would you like to live here and have the bad spirits captured anyone who tried to settle here?"

"So, your work to watch the valley isn't very difficult because you don't have many people to attend to."

"My friends of the air keep me informed. I'm here, I'm everywhere, whenever people plant food, there are traditional ceremonies that take place. If they omit giving thanks, then their ground endures a bad year."

"What sort of ceremonies?"

"From your world you've seen festivals of dancing around the villages, haven't you?

That is simply one form of celebration that was very similar to dances around this world; this ritual has a common theme of fertility through death and rebirth. These moors are now extended to all parts of the Universe, this becoming a barren land will eventually affect all living creatures."

Richard said, "I'm beginning to see that this Evil One must be defeated."

"Are you sure you wouldn't like to fly with me Richard?"

"No thanks."

"Then I must go back to see whether I can help Juroot."

Oganga shuffled once and with that, the huge wings spread as Oganga dropped off the rock and disappeared from sight, Richard watched to see the huge winged creature soar out across the valley but it just never reappeared in view.

"Where did he go?"

"Who knows? He's a tricky one that, if he wants you to see him then you do, if he doesn't then you won't. Perhaps he is in a cave below us or turned himself invisible, with the people of the skies, you never know what will happen next. Come now, we must proceed."

Richard shuddered slightly, birds tended to be everywhere, were they all reporting back here he thought to himself? Could they really be unseen spies in the sky?

"Spooky, an eye from above is very disconcerting?" he commented idly.

Suddenly there was a loud whooshing sound and before either of them could do anything Oganga swooped in and grabbed the three companions in its large taloned feet.

"Weeeooee!" Orkan screeched. Richard felt themselves being hoisted as the deafening whirring sound of Oganga's tortoise like wings beat the air and lifted them off the ground and into the skies above the gigantic drop of the ravine. He looked down and felt his head start swimming.

"Orkan! What's Oganga doing?"

"Gghhh! Gghhh! I don't know!" He screamed at his distressed companion.

Like a falling stone, Oganga suddenly dived towards the valley floor, all screamed as they felt their senses reeling with the instant falling sensation. Richard was sure that he had left everything but his body behind, and anyway, his stomach was fast lurching up and into his mouth. His face was being contorted and pulled in all directions as the gravitational forces reacted to the sudden downwards movement. Suddenly the giant bird levelled out above the valley floor and slowed to a hover. The noise from its wings now down to a gentle slopping type of sound.

"Oganga! What are you doing to us?" Richard shouted. Oganga suddenly dropped them onto the ground before landing right next to them.

"I forgot to tell you that today is the Omatla ceremony and you should have been inside, now the Sekango will find you and you'll possibly become part of the celebration."

"Gghhh! You mean we'll be slaughtered and eaten tonight."

"It depends." Richard felt the hairs on the back of his scalp rising. His brain raced as his eyes searched for some form of escape, suddenly he had an idea. He quickly removed the amulet from his rucksack, opened it and thrust his hand through the ring.

"Golan, Golan, Are you there?"

He felt the amulet start pulsing and suddenly a flash shot from his hand, there was now a ray of light stretching outwards from the thing that looked like an invisible screen against the sheer rock face. Golan magically appeared in what Richard could only think was an extraordinary vision on the cragged rock.

"How did you do that?" Oganga asked. "Golan, Oganga is going to give us to the ceremony of Omatla."

"So?"

"We're going to be killed and eaten."

"Oh, that's a great pity. You were doing so well."

"Can't you help us?"

"No. I can give you some advice though. Possibly Oganga will accept something in return for your lives."

"What?"

"What have you got?" Richard thought about it. The only things of any real value were the pods of life, the magic rope and the pathfinder.

"Oganga, this is one of the pods of life, its magical powers can do anything," Richard held out his arm and moved straight towards the bird spirit, Richard could see that Oganga wasn't sure of its powers, having seen the vision appear from Richard's fist. Oganga lifted into the air and hovered above the frightened companions, a little too afraid to settle in case the boy did have some unknown power in his fist, but the ceremony had to be adhered to. For a long time neither moved from their position, finally Orkan broke the impasse.

"Gghhh! You said that sometimes a trade would save the children? Why don't we make a trade for our lives?"

"Like what?" Oganga enquired. "You take us back to where you found us at the top of the cliff and we'll give you the magical pod in return for sparing our lives."

"What?" asked Richard. "No way."

Orkan leaned towards Richard.

"Don't forget, Oganga has to get agreement from Juroot who will side with us, no harm will befall the pod anyway it will be safe with Oganga and we can always try to get it back later like we did with Baal. If we're dead Oganga will simply take the pod to Golan?

"You're right."

"I cannot take you back, those are my orders, you however, have to retrieve the pod from Baal or Enlil but, I will help ease your path forward. Keep that pod, you have need of it." Oganga had momentarily considered the extended fist and then instead suggested that he move ahead of the group to scout the area for them. Oganga gently lifted off and the three moved off in the same direction. With Oganga keeping watch above, some time later they stopped to rest from the searing heat, Melek opened the Book of Prophesies and read out the next text.

> *A flight through air to withered land.*
> *Beware the storm, the desert spanned.*
> *A bone-filled grave awaits the brave*
> *But hidden bounties save.*
> *Within dark earth a lonely night*
> *From skyborne spite at dreadful cost*
> *A hard-won treasure now is lost.*

"A hard-won treasure lost? Could that be a pod I wonder, we are going to have to be on our guard."

Across the desert the wind suddenly seemed to pick up and sand seemed to float all around obscuring the mountains on both sides. It was Orkan that first saw the swirling red dust devil coming from a long way off across the barren wasteland and it was heading directly in their direction.

"What's that?" Melek screamed.

"A desert twister, the worst kind."

It was flinging up sand, stones and rocks in its path, at centre stage was an ominous black funnel of a tornado like a huge rope joining earth and sky as it snaked like a giant whiplash towards them.

"We've got to get under cover somewhere otherwise we're going to be sucked into that churning mass." Richard screamed.

"Ghhh. But where?"

"Over there, behind that boulder, there's a small gully, it's our only chance."

The race was on; Richard dived into the indentation in the ground just as the swirling mass reached them, with both Orkan and Melek in close order landing on top of him. A blast of seething hot air and stinging sand tore angrily at the group and then, the deafening roar as the eye of the tornado passed over their humble hiding place with such force that it lifted both Orkan and Melek right off Richard's back. In a flash they had both disappeared as if snatched by a gigantic hand and then Richard found himself being lifted and bounced across the land as if caught by a huge wave. Eventually the grip of the strong wind released itself and Richard came to earth with a huge bump in a depression filled with skeletons – he guessed that this must have been the scene of one of the terrible battles that everybody had talked of. Shaking to clear the dust from himself, his eyes searched the area for his companions, he saw Orkan in the distance.

"Whew! He made it, how much more of this terrible place can I endure?"

Still very shaken, he collected his things and started making his way down the gully before he saw the familiar figure of the wise young librarian approaching from the other side of Orkan.

"We're very lucky, it was only down to your quick reaction that we're not all inside that whirlwind." Orkan said pointing to the distant tornado. Also, that wind bringing us to this place is also somewhat fortuitous, see the cactus; at least we can wet our lips."

Orkan hacked the outer skin revealing a soft white pulp inner portion that he delicately cut out. Grabbing a handful he held it above his head and opened his mouth while squeezing the pulp, which gave up its liquid.

"Ahh! That is sooo good, here you try some."

As both Richard and Melek began drinking of the soft nectar, they heard the familiar whirring sound; it was Oganga hurtling towards them. The giant bird set itself down amid a flurry of sand.

"At last! I have been searching everywhere for you, that storm caught me by surprise, I thought it had got you."

"Nope, we're made of sterner stuff than any old windstorm can throw at us." Richard joked.

"I was up above those hills, I have found some of my compatriots hiding while trying to rest up there, currently they are not in good shape,

I fear some of them won't make it through the night. However, one told me a story that a Life-Force pod is hidden in a mountain lair that is guarded by Enlil and her mate Erna."

"Then we must go there. Now!" Richard demanded.

"It will not be easy, Enlil keeps evil slaves and Erna is sadistic, they will not let a pod disappear from their hideout, you can be sure of that."

"That no longer matters, we must at least try to recover a pod, if this Enlil character has it, we have to retrieve it?"

"Enlil's den is in those mountains, I will take you up there." Again Oganga seized them in his massive talons and soared high into the air, rising in circles on the hot desert wind. Then when Oganga had judged that the altitude was correct he banked and shot towards the mountainous horizon, Richard watched in awe as they neared the dark peaks gliding softly and with skilful elegance between jagged peaks. Suddenly Oganga dived down over the saddle-strewn hills, a raucous screeching filling the air about the place seemingly bouncing off the sheer faces of the mountainsides.

"Sky troopers! We must land, these vultures don't even wait for dead prey, they kill anything they can, we have to lose them."

For all his skill and strength Oganga was unable to lose his new trackers, the weight of his cargo slowing him sufficiently for them to keep pace.

"I'm going to have to drop you off, when I do, hide away otherwise they will have you. Brace yourselves!" Oganga swooped over a ridge and like bombs being released he aimed his precious cargo straight at a scree-laden slope.

The group bounced, tumbled and sprawled harmlessly across the loose stones as Oganga reeled high into the sky and catching the following pack off guard with the sudden change in flight pattern. The three quickly found themselves up on their feet.

"Over there, behind that large outcrop!" Melek shouted urgently.

The three had no sooner got behind cover when several of the chasing pack passed their vantage point and swooped in an upward arc trying to follow the now climbing Oganga. From this position they watched as Oganga circled from above then dived, picking off one of his followers after another. In all this aerial combat, it was Orkan that pointed to a new unnoticed arriving group headed by a bird almost as large as Oganga.

"Boltor! Just when Oganga was doing so well." Melek was concerned.

"Boltor?" Richard asked.

"Bird of Thunder, he attacks with thunderbolts but I think there are too many for Oganga to fight on his own, he will have to flee, we're in real trouble now."

Just then, a wing of larger birds seemed to fill the air from below where the companions were hiding, they instantly began attacking the smaller vulture types following behind Boltor.

"Must be Oganga's friends, at least it evens up the fight a bit." Orkan commented sort of matter of factly.

Boltor seemed to fire several bolts of blue sparking lightning from its huge talons towards the attacking wing, most of them managed to dodge the oncoming bolts except for one that took a full blast. Richard thought that it looked just like a downed fighter plane he had seen on television, smoke billowing from its feathers it left a trail as it fell into the gorge below. This had immediately alerted the majestic Oganga, high above who swooped down faster than an arrow.

Boltor only realised at the last second that he was about to be attacked from above and almost as fast as a blink, flipped himself over backwards, his talons, like some incessant machine gun firing bolts of lightning trace, But Oganga had arrived too quickly for this move to be effective, in a flash he had embedded his huge talons into Boltor's breast and the two huge birds still locked in a death struggle plummeted down towards the gorge and out of sight from the three companions. Above them, the vulture like creatures were fleeing for all their worth with Oganga's troops in hot pursuit. The three waited for a while, the whole area was suddenly quiet and calm before Orkan broke this silence.

"Look, there's a cave small, let's rest in there."

The opening was hardly visible to Richard, but Orkan moved into the narrow crack and then called for the others to follow. Inside the narrow opening the cave opened up.

"Ghhh, I'll take first watch, you two need the rest."

They did not need any prompting and were soon fast asleep against the back wall. Soon Orkan settled down and began softly sharpening his sword against a rock.

"Before the sun, behind the moon, the days like thunder run. By month end the time is up and all evil will be done."

Orkan jumped, and then settled again, Melek had been talking in his sleep, he turned and gazed at the wizened young scribe, these words meant nothing to him. He stretched out and wondered just how long he should let his companions rest, thoughts of that day floated through his brain.

"Ghhh, w-wha..."

Orkan came awake with a start, he had fallen asleep, slowly he gathered up his sword and moved to the entrance of the den and was surprised to realise it was early morning already. He woke the others and once up, revealed Melek's little rhyme.

"What do you think it means?" He snorted.

"Possibly just some ramblings I must have read somewhere." Melek offered.

"It sounds like one of those prophesies from the book. The important thing now is the quest, we have got to try to track down this Enlil character, wonder what happened to Oganga?"

"Ghhh. No sign of life out there."

The trio stepped into the daylight onto the hillside. All around the area lay the signs of the fierce battle, large feathers still littering the ground. The morning light gave off a baleful shade of red as Richard walked round looking for any signs of their bird allies, it was strange, there were no signs of any bodies below that he could see.

"We must climb upwards, there is no way down from here, I think we should rope up together."

There were no arguments and they did just that with Richard in the lead, Orkan and Melek bringing up the tail they began their slow climb. The rope was invaluable as they helped each other ever upwards through difficult stretches. They reached what they thought was the summit only to find a steep drop down to yet another valley below.

"At least it's green down there, what a contrast view. Look left, the valley is a parched desert, look right and the valley in filled with forest, how strange." Melek said.

"Maybe all the farmers settled in that valley, that's why it's so green? Anyway somewhere around here we will find this Enlil character, the choice is simple, desert or forest?" Richard asked.

"Ghhh, let's go, I've had enough of sandstorms."

Slowly but surely they began making their way down the mountainside towards the inviting greenery. The three were inching along a narrow ledge when Melek lost his footing, he scrambled for a handhold but it was in vain. He was now suspended over a sheer drop, the others tried steadying him but he was in total panic swinging like a pendulum back and forth against the cliff.

"Hold still, we will pull you up." Richard shouted, the rope having again showed its worth, Making sure they both had steady purchase, little by little they dragged the outward facing and terrified librarian towards the crest of the ledge. Just as he reached it, Orkan stretched out and grabbed the small-framed girl by the clothing on the back of his neck. Melek got such a fright that he literally spun in mid air, there was a snapping sound as the Book of Prophesies suddenly began tumbling away down the mountain; spinning and bouncing in high arching leaps. They heard the thud, but nobody could even begin to guess how far down the cliff it had travelled.

"The straps must have chafed against the rock face when you pulled me to safety. The book was correct; it most definitely is a Treasure Lost?"

Cozards – Meeting the Flying Killers

On the Sixth Day...

Marching, flying - death at hand?
The brave must fear them both.
Hark the words in ruined land
Of wise and ancient growth.
Wings that weapons cannot quell
Will catch them unaware.
Chosen's choice of touch will tell
And lead them safe to open air.

How the group managed to survive the perilous descent down the steep slopes of the mountainside Richard never knew but, descending it with much pain involved they did, making slow but steady headway. Rope burns; pummelled feet from negotiating sharp rocks and aching bodies saw them reach the level above the tree-line where strange-looking giant groundsels and giant heathers randomly started appearing. On the upper reaches of the timberline, straggly trees began to replace grey rock and all the while their eyes strained for some sight or trace of the big book that had been lost.

"Ghhh, there is that it?"

Orkan pointed across the trees to a stunted and spindly looking tree standing on its own. They saw the familiar, leather-bound shape resting unevenly in among the spreading boughs.

They were excited and overjoyed as they made their way across to the gnarled and weather beaten tree. Orkan scrambled up the mangled trunk until he managed to draw level with the book and then being as careful as he could took hold of one of the straps.

"I've got it!" he shouted triumphantly as he gently prised the valuable treasure from the tree's knarred upper branches.

A few seconds later he was on the ground, the three companions were so ecstatic that they almost did a funny little dance around the big book that they thought they thought had been lost to them.

"We think we had better check the next prophecy?" Richard offered, Melek and Orkan examined and repaired the leather thongs holding the book.

"You're right." Melek opened the book and began reading the riddle.

Marching, flying - death at hand?
The brave must fear them both.
Hark the words in ruined land
Of wise and ancient growth.
Wings that weapons cannot quell
Will catch them unaware.
Chosen's choice of touch will tell
And lead them safe to open air.

"I don't like the sound of this one, it bodes evil." Richard admitted. "Still, it says we'll be safe in the end, or at least, that's what I think it's telling us?"

"You see, maybe you are beginning to understand the word of the book." Melek commented. "It is becoming clear to you, I still do not comprehend the rhymes."

"Ghhh. Me neither."

After a short break they continued their downward climb towards the forested valley basin, once in among the trees Richard noticed a sound he had not heard for a while, it was a gentle rustling that quivered from wind playing among leaves in the canopy above them. Moving further down the incline into the forest Richard could not help notice that the foliage seemed to be dead or dying, it was very unusual, as if something or someone had been poisoning the ground because it seemed that the lower reaches of the once-green foliage was shrivelling, while higher up the trees maintained their greenness.

"You noticed it too?" Melek said. "It's as if a poisoned mist had seeped through the forest, killing all before it, birds up there are making their noises but the forest floor is bereft of any visible life."

"Ghhh! Methinks Enlil had a hand in this destruction, this is how the Evil One would like the whole land to be, dead, dying or in his power."

Then the distant sound seemed to take on a definite rhythmic beat, very much like the sound of marching feet and brisk shouts coming towards their direction.

"Ghhh! Over there," Orkan led them to a wide crack in an old tree, it made a perfect hiding place as they crammed themselves in through the opening.

"Gghhh! Cozards are coming."

"Cozards? What are these Cozards that can cause so much fear?" Richard enquired,

Orkan's hand immediately clasped itself over Richard's mouth.

They huddled closely together as the sound of a steady thumping march made its way in their direction and increased in volume. Orkan still had his hand over Richard's mouth. From his viewpoint Richard could only just observe the trail into the forest, then he saw them for the first time. Like soldiers, they marched in some form of goose-step straight towards them. Because of Orkan's hand over his mouth, Richard gagged as he tried to suck in breath, but the firm grasp wasn't eased. The first thing Richard noticed about them were their strange legs. These were thin and covered with what seemed to be hard scaly plates rising to the knee, very much like those he seen on fighting bantam cockerels. After this initial impression, he saw that their feet were shaped more like two heavy clubs which accounted for the thumping as the marched together in unison. Each foot had two grotesque, and razor sharp spiked toes protruding forward from the bulbous base. There were another two spikes high up on the back of each heel. Richard was horrified; those legs with their armour plating could only be used for fighting.

"Grapfrits with knives and now this, was this place filled with beasties that only wanted to slice up anything and everything here?" Richard's fast moving brain questioned as the Cozards bore down heading directly towards their position. "One kick from those knifed feet would rip any opponent apart and cause considerable damage," whispered Richard to himself.

Above the knees the rest of their short framed bodies were also beyond belief to the young man's eyes, their bare upper bodies and arms were exactly like a human form covered with armour, but the head was unlike anything Richard could have previously imagined. It was no wonder that Orkan kept his hand tightly over Richard's mouth, if he hadn't, the young man was sure he would have given away their hiding place to the oncoming Cozards. Their faces were their only vulnerability and shaped like that of a large snapping turtle, except for the mouth which had a pointed beak lined with sharp teeth, making them look something like a group of ancient marching pterodactyls. They approached and quickly passed by the tree without looking either left or right, Richard wishing the ground would swallow them. From the back, he could see they each had tails that swelled to form a heavy club-head. Like the feet of the beasts, this part was obviously also used for fighting and only once the group were out of sight did Orkan take his hand from the boy's mouth.

"Sorry about that, but if you had given us away... The Cozards are the meanest people in this forest. They're bullies of the worst sort, for fun, they like to use those knife-like feet to strip skin from any lone victim around here, they are always to be found in groups, never alone. They won't tackle anything bigger or stronger than themselves, but the three of us certainly wouldn't be any kind of match for them."

Richard moved forward slowly.

"A-Any chance of the Duke of York's men marching up the hill returning this way?"

"No. Gghhh! They're very stupid, they march around like that all the time and normally you hear them long before you see them. It's only when they're not on the move and anything bungles into them, those problems arise."

"Where are they going?"

"They're 'strange', marching around the forest looking for defenceless people who they can kill and eat and that's the only time they sit down and that, is when you can make a mistake and bump into them. They will march to the cliff face before realising they cannot proceed further, then they will more than likely march down that hill again. You must always remain on guard and be acutely aware of the wood and its changing sounds, come let's move on, we've still got far to travel."

They moved down the trail and Richard could see where the Cozards had trampled straight through the forest with their heavy clubbed feet. Orkan suddenly pointed to a large and strange tree that seemed to be bent, broken and seemingly dead up to about half way up. It looked for all the world as if some high wind had blown the top half over and the leafy section, now strewn across the ground was entwined with thick vines and creepers which seemed to grow in among all the once splendid branches.

"This was probably the wisest tree in the forest." said Melek.

Richard's gaze moved along the trunk and came to rest on the cluster of foliage on the ground, the heavily veined shoots spreading in all directions looked for the entire world like a mass of intertwined grey and green snakes. Richard shuddered at the thought, he hated slimy things at the best of times, but any snake had to be the worst of all.

"I need another short break, I did not rest for long last night." Orkan suggested and he and Melek made themselves comfortable. "You take first watch; a short nap is all I need."

Both companions were almost instantly asleep as Richard settled himself among the creepers against the old tree...

"Wish I could drop off like that." Richard mused.

When he finally decided to move on he woke Orkan. As he did so behind all the greenery and grey undergrowth he suddenly saw a flash of whiteness like somebody moving inside the thick and entangled vines.

"What's that?"

It was only when Richard had a closer look that he was sure that he saw movement from within the creepers.

"Gghhh! What's 'what'?" asked Orkan.

"Something moved in between the vines of that creeper. It could have been a rabbit because it was white...I think."

Richard peered intensely through the darkness and into the undergrowth to try and see what had attracted his attention. He was fast becoming a nervous wreck with all these strange beasts lurking in this wood.

"Hello Orkan, you sleep and leave your friend to stand watch over you, not very clever," came the deep voice from within.

Without waiting, Richard spun around and in panic felt his feet moving like a pair of pistons in a motor; they moved so fast that he was sure he could almost smell burning rubber from the soles of his shoes. The thing that struck him as strange, was that no matter how hard he was trying to run, his body wasn't moving at all, looking down at his gyrating legs his heart skipped a beat as he saw that a vine had wrapped itself around his middle and was the reason for not being able to get away. He had never been the most fearless person but, this forest, he was sure, had been put here to create havoc to his reasoning. What the heck was happening and how could a vine grow around his middle so quickly.

"H-Help me Orkan!" The little man just smiled and didn't move at all, Richard felt trapped, perhaps Orkan wasn't meant to be friendly, maybe he was trying to help the forest creatures to make the most horrible things happen to him.

"Relax. It's only the Green Man. This isn't the first time that he's played a trick on you."

The green man, what was the short pig talking about, the 'green man' was somebody that sold vegetables in their town, this had to be something nasty, thought Richard, his mind racing in utter panic. Somehow he had to loosen himself. "Let me go!" Richard demanded desperately as he tried slipping from the Green Man's clutches.

"Only if you behave reasonably towards me and stop that infernal racket."

"W-w-what?" As if a whistle had blown for a half time break, Richard stopped struggling and took in a deep breath, he was exhausted and whatever the Green Man was, it was a lot stronger than him.

"P-P-Please don't hurt me."

"Nobody said anything about hurting you. There, you are free again," came the deep throated voice. Richard stood dead still as he watched the vine loosen itself from around his midriff and start coiling its way, like a big worm back towards the central undergrowth.

"Let me introduce you to Richard, he's taking the ancestral trail and trying to help the guardian recover the pods of life and we're trying to find the guardians. Have you seen any of them?"

Orkan was...sort of matter-of-factly about Richard's mission, as if nothing had even happened. With sudden awareness, Richard realised that Orkan knew what was going to happen because of the twinkle in his eyes, and his broad smile that seemed to stretch to the bottom tips of his strangely elongated ears.

"I'm very pleased to be able to meet you in person Richard; my associates have told me much of your arrival in this place." Leaning forward at the waist, Richard again peered even harder into the dense bush undergrowth to try to make out who, or what, was addressing him.

Suddenly he stood straight up. In among the trailing vines was a grotesque face of a really old man protruding from the old tree; no body, just a face etched into ancient bark was now talking to him. The green face seemed swollen, twisted and puffed up and vines seemed to be flowing outward from within its mouth. It reminded Richard of something he had seen on a church wall somewhere. Could it be a gargoyle, he wondered. The distorted face seemed to be trapped like a prisoner behind bars of the tentacled vine.

"Beware the Cozards and the Killer Bees, they are in this area,"

Richard then noticed a face sketched in the tree's bark is smiling at him, a face that appeared friendly as the tree then began speaking again, and explaining that it must pass on a warning gleaned from its associates. The old tree warns the three about the Cozards, as well as enemy flying squads that are on the lookout for anything that moves in this area because the Evil One had started alerting his teams to be on the lookout for this interloper.

"W-Which associates."

"The trees of course, you talk to us regularly and think we don't know what's going on. Well, we understand everything. I could tell you exactly where and what you've been up to today if I wanted to. From this position all plants are linked together underground by an intricate root network. That's how everything is communicated among us. If something happens anywhere in the country, the nearest tree, bush and even grass passes the message to the next plant and so on, and in a very short time, the message reaches me here. Richard's mind boggled, plants talking to each other through a complicated network of roots. He had heard of talking to plants, but this was ridiculous. "You know that I'm the one of the oldest of all things in this forest?"

"No, not really."

"Many, many years ago I had my head cut off by one of the knights of the then round table?"

"Really?"

"Oh yes, it should demonstrate to you that trees and plants were here long before anything else arrived to start the destruction of this world. One of our kind even gave birth to all living creatures. What did they immediately do, they used us as firewood. What do you think of that?"

Richard was still transfixed by the sight of the curious face. He became aware of the Green Man's feeling and could gauge the strength of its emotion. As the face was speaking, so vines seemed to spew in great lengths from the thing's hideous green mouth. The more emotional the statement the faster the greenery seemed to eject across the ground from its twisted orifice.

"Mankind has always chopped down trees for their firewood, not many people realise that plants are really living things or have they ever really spoken to a live tree before. You must agree, it's quite something to suddenly meet up with a tree that actually talks back. Why don't all plants communicate with humans?" Richard enquired.

"They did once. But humans became so superior that anything that opposed them, was immediately attacked and killed. The best thing for us plants to do was to shut up and only talk to each other by developing a language of our own so as to protect ourselves from man."

"What sort of language?"

"When it's very quiet, just listen. You'll hear what sounds like a creaking noise, that's us talking to each other and if you listen long and carefully enough, it won't take long to understand what we're saying to each other. Mind you, it will be like learning a foreign language, you have to start talking back to the plants and that's the only way to understand what is being said."

"But people don't realise that you too, are capable of speaking and that's the reason they treat you so badly."

"We don't mind being used. However, man is now going over the top and quickly destroying us in vast quantities and very soon they will pay the price for all the harm that they're causing."

"How?"

"By cutting back huge forests, if you think about it, we used to spread our limbs everywhere, and now look. This place is becoming a huge barren wasteland today, but once upon a time those very same areas were abundantly covered with vast forests. All that is left of us is the coal and oil under the ground, out residue where we once shed our leaves in gigantic quantities over time. Then man arrived on the scene, and began to rule the world. Very quickly, the huge tracts of land that are still covered with gigantic trees are going to become these barren deserts as well and weather patterns are going to change, people are going to starve, develop unknown diseases and it will all come from cutting us down."

"Can't anything be done about this?"

"Alas, no. Human beings and animals will have to learn the hard way before they do something about it. We provide clean air and a balance to nature, mess about with it and then dire consequences are bound to follow. Many forests are simply dying from pollution floating through the air and landing on us. Like you humans, trees also suffer from pain and disease."

"Can't anything be done at all?"

"Oh yes, there's still time, but that's why you are here in order to try to help good push back evil and that will hopefully return the universe to its former glory, there maybe a chance to turn back time but not much, but as I said, there is still a chance for everyone to make it happen. If we fail, at first there will be gentle warnings, warmer weather patterns, thinner air and brighter sunlight, forests dying all over the world, these are just some of the indicators. If we and man miss this chance to recognise or repel these, then it won't be long before we and the universe too, will die."

"What's your role in all this?"

"I'm the spirit of everything botanical and as I said before, I was here long before man, beasts or insects."

Richard was now completely spellbound, fascinated by the long streams of greenery pouring from the twisted mouth as it continued to speak. What his mother had said about man destroying the environment was now only beginning to make sense. Perhaps he had been a bit harsh, in future he would take notice of what 'some' grown-ups had to offer.

"If your kind and evil don't take heed of what is happening around us, they will kill me and if I die off, then so do all plants and trees. Here, I suggest you take these on the rest of your journey."

As if by magic, a long vine coiled and snaked towards Richard, stopping just short of where he stood. On a broad leaf at the end were seven small pebble shaped seeds. Richard took hold of them.

"You now hold seven seeds of life, guard them well because those represent the seven points of life and you will need them before your entire journey is at an end. If anything ever happens to mankind, as we know it, and it manages to destroy me, then plant those seeds together in a circle around you somewhere near underground water. The whole cycle of life will start at that point again."

"What do you mean start again?"

"I'm not the first, the world has suffered this same fate eight times before and each time, man destroys his world and himself leaving a long time for all the planets to go through a change and all of life starts again from the beginning. Some people will escape and live underground and revert back to being like apes. One day when the seven seeds start growing again and the planet becomes a forest, then, and only then will man come to the surface again. If you'd need them then you must plant those seeds before going into hiding below the ground."

"I'm not sure I know what you're talking about."

"You will know when the time comes. In the meantime, you have been given the task of trying to maintain life by finding the pods of life. Make sure you carry out my request if you should not succeed with your given quest."

"When will all of this happen?"

"In your lifetime if your people don't learn from their mistakes. Remember, guard those well and one day they will help you in return. You've been chosen for a reason and if man destroys me, I'll need a wise and compassionate successor for the new world. Therefore, Richard learn well. Try to understand what you're seeing while on the ancestral trail. It may take several visits, but one day, you'll understand."

Richard could feel the short hairs on the back of his neck rising as this kindly face presented something he wasn't quite sure of. He looked around towards Orkan, partly for reassurance. The little man just smiled knowingly.

"Why me?"

"I asked the same question a long time ago and was given this answer. 'That destiny is for us to know and you to find out'."

"But what does it all mean?" Richard was so baffled and perplexed by now, he just didn't know what to think.

"One day you'll understand because I know you're the Chosen One and you must heed my advice as we don't have much time left." The voice from within the vines seemed to be gasping for breath. "Watch out for the Cozards."

"We've seen them already," Richard said with an air of confidence.

"Be always on your guard." The tree went on. "There are eyes and ears everywhere now and enemy flying squads are on the lookout for anything that moves or may threaten the Evil One."

"Ghhh! You mean Grapfrits?" Orkan interjected. "We've dealt with them before."

"No, no," the tree's voice had weakened, "Others that are dangerous with deadly stings."

"Stings? Like wasps?"

"Yes, remember my warning. Now go and complete your task and please find the rest of the guardians. You carry me with you and one day you'll possibly hand over to someone else, that's how it all works."

"He must mean Grapfrits." Orkan suggested.

"Take care." The old tree murmured. "They are quicker and more deadly than you can imagine."

"Well at least that explains the 'wings that weapons cannot quell' part of the rhyme?" Richard said. "At least now we are forewarned."

Richard felt a tug at his clothes and turned to see Orkan indicating that their time with the Green Man was finished. Reluctantly, he turned back to bid farewell to the strange face, seemingly trapped behind the foliage. The Green Man's tentacled vines were all around and suddenly Richard realised that the branches had been carefully pick pocketing him as he spoke. He found that his rucksack had been opened without his knowledge.

"Wha..." he couldn't believe that the Green Man would steal anything." P-perhaps we'll meet again?" For the first time since their meeting, he saw what he thought could have been a hint of a smile appearing on the twisted mouth.

"Perhaps. Just remember, life is what you want it to be. Talk to the trees, I'll be listening."

After waking Melek and thanking the old tree the companions started off down the hill, remaining deep in thought, other than Juroot and Oganga, this had been the first friendly thing they had encountered since entering the place.

"Orkan. What did you mean by telling him that the guardian had sent me on this quest?"

"Oh... did I say that? What I meant was... uh, you are seeking the pods and the guardians. Come let's move."

Orkan was up to something, Richard could just sense it because his answer had been too glib and now he was walking quickly so that the boy wouldn't be able to ask him anything at the moment.

"I'll talk to you later about it, you're not going to fob me off that easily," Richard whispered crossly under his breath. He was determined to know the truth. Orkan had lied, Richard felt even more uncertain of his companion.

"I'm going to have to keep an eye on ¬you¬, my piggy friend" he muttered, as they moved, Richard lifted his rucksack from his back to close it again. He peered inside.

"Orkan! Stop, wait. I think that The Green Man's stolen a pod from my bag. I'm going back." Orkan just kept moving.

"Orkan!" His companion didn't take any notice of Richard's shouting. "Orkan!" Richard found himself screaming this time. Left alone by his little guide presented a problem. Should he go back or catch up to Orkan. For a moment he didn't know what to do so he sat down exactly where he stood. It was then that he realised just how tired he was.

"Hell!" Richard didn't normally swear, but this was one of those occasions that he felt it was the thing to do. His head buzzed from exhaustion and he shook it to get rid of the sound. It didn't go away, in fact the noise was growing and Richard realised that the sound wasn't coming from within his head. Worse still were his companions now racing up the hill towards him followed in the distance by what looked like a black hand but, Richard soon realised was a huge swarm of bees.

"Oh no! Not again," he said as he quickly searched for somewhere to hide.

From afar, the bees looked a dark, smoky mass, but already the first scouts were edging nearer to his friends and Richard could make out that they were much larger than ordinary bees, more like oversized bats, he turned and raced back up the hill.

"Killer bees! They are what the tree was warning us about." Richard shouted.

"Ghhh. No water to hide us this time." Orkan cried.

They broke clear of the timberline; ahead lay only a landscape of the soaring mountain and scars of recent landslides. Using loose stone debris as a natural staircase like mountain goats they raced upwards but were fast running out of options when bellowing echoed to their left.

"Cozards! Does frying pan to fire mean anything to anybody?" Richard panted.

Richard was close to panic, a swarm of killer bees behind, the Cozards to their left and a sheer rock face ahead when he blinked, there seemingly etched into the rock was an outline that looked just like Golan's face.

"A message! Follow me."

"Ghhh! Message?"

"Look! A crevice in the rock."

The leader of the Cozards had broken clear of his troop and was almost upon them as they reached the narrow split in the rock. Melek had trouble squeezing into the gap, Richard had even more trouble and the lone Cozard was only a short way from them.

"I'll hold him up!" screamed Orkan turning to face the attacker.

The storm trooper's parrot like mouth curled back in an awful grin as he swung his heavy axe towards Orkan. Watching from the narrow gap in the rock face, Richard and Melek watched in horror as Orkan jerked his body backwards and slipped falling backwards as he did so. The blow missed, but the Cozard quickly flung himself towards Orkan, weapon again raised for a fatal blow, suddenly the attacker raised his hand to his neck giving Orkan just enough time to pull back his legs and kick out at the distracted soldier. The hard trotter like hoof hit its mark straight into the Cozard's chest sending the storm trooper backwards over the ridge towards the oncoming troops. Orkan jumped up and squeezed himself through the gap.

"He had me at his mercy, why did he stop?"

"The bees, one of the scouts stung him on the neck." Melek replied.

"Look! The swarm are attacking the Cozards."

The bees starved of prey in the forest, had sensed far richer pickings from the band of newcomers than from the small trio they had been targeting.

"Those bees carry the sign of the Evil One; it can't get any better for us because evil verses have no scruples." Melek said.

The Cozards with their total precision had immediately formed a tight ring to fend off the large bees but, it was of no use, the bees surged in like water finding cracks and squirming through the weakness points. Gaps appeared in the Cozard's shield wall first as the bees seemed to have the upper hand then the Cozards seemed to fight back strongly, they were well matched.

"When this battle is over, the victors will come looking for us." Melek reminded his friends.

"You're right, we won't escape out there" Richard replied. "Let's see if this cave leads anywhere."

To their surprise they found it lead into a dark, domed chamber that was open enough to stand upright in and in the dim light from the crevice Richard spotted a dark hole near the back.

"That could lead somewhere, it's our only chance." Without waiting, he instantly began to crawl through the small dark hole, the others followed but before long it opened up so that Richard could again just about stand upright. Afraid of what lay behind him he moved as quickly as he could and suddenly bumped up against a rock with his shoulder.

"Oh-oh!"

The sound was deafening, he realised too late that he had triggered a rock fall, the ground below their feet simply seemed to give way as they were hurled downward; rubble, dust, rock and debris all brought together. When it had all settled and Richard regained consciousness he tried to move but not being able to, his immediate thought was that he had been trapped under the rock fall.

"Orkan! Melek I'm trapped!" he screamed.

"Ghhh! So are we all, but the rubble does not trap you, we're all bound by ropes. There's somebody or something down here with us.

"W-What?"

Just then Richard heard a sound echoing down a tunnel somewhere, it sounded for all the world like voices and those voices really sounded as if they were heading towards their position.

"Help!" Richard screamed, his voice seemed to bounce around the cavern walls.

"Quiet you idiot, we don't know whether they be friend or foe," grunted Orkan knowing full well that Richard's shouts would have already alerted others

The Twins and the Cannibal Leader

On the Seventh Day...

Captives bound, caged underground.
Release is found in length around.
A magic beam by evil seen.
Enemies will rise from below,
And dark waters carry the foe.
Prisoner's plight beyond the stern,
Now the slithering monsters turn.
A new deep opens 'ere the burn.

Richard found the uneasy truss was hurting and every time he moved the sharp edges of the stalagmite rocks that he was roped to seemed to dig a little deeper into his back.

"Orkan help! Haven't you got anything that can free us?"

"Nothing that I can think of and I just cannot move," came the swift reply.

The three companions sat uncomfortably as they listened to the voices getting closer and closer.

"Ahhh! See how they squirm but, the ropes hold them fast," says the leader. "My name is Zock." Suddenly a squat dwarf appeared from the gloomy cave followed by a crowd of smaller dwarfs that all seemed somewhat slightly nervous and seemingly tended to hang back.

"You are my prisoners Ha-Ha!"

Orkan noticed that his captor now held Juroot's dagger in his hand who suddenly made a lunging movement towards Richard, then jovially stood back and made a great belly laugh at his captive's obvious unease.

"This knife will set you free from your bonds but, do not attempt to escape in any way, you are my captives." Zock quickly used the sharp blade to cut free the three companions,

"Thank you Mister Zock," Richard offered, hoping that these could possibly be friendly people but then immediately Zock grabbed Richard and shoved him roughly towards his companions.

"Bring them to the food-hall," he ordered.

The rest of the short grinning dwarves hurry to obey their leader by surrounding the three companions, others carry some of Orkan's weapons then playfully swung them around in mock attack, hopefully more to scare the three than to actually do any damage.

"Hurry up! Get them moving, we celebrate tonight." With that command, Zock headed off down a darkened passageway leaving his men to push, pull and jab at their captives as they too were herded off through a maze of passages.

"I'm not happy with this situation," Melek declared only to find that he promptly has something sharp dug into his rear end.

With only hands still tied, the trio are forced to march through a maze of intricate caverns while they constantly keep a watching brief on the rag-tag group for weaknesses in order to find a possible escape from the playful dwarves wielding their own weapons. As they round a corner, the now triumphant Zock steps from the shadows and leads his band even deeper into his mountain lair,

"Who are these guys?" Richard asks his friends "are they good or evil?"

Melek explains that they were once his people, but now they're firmly under the control of the Evil One and he believes have even possibly turned to cannibalism. He adds that the dwarfs are more than likely taking them to the pot. "I think we are due to suffer a horrible death if we do not escape, thank goodness they have not taken the Book of Prophesies away with them, I think they are only interested in any form of weapon so did not see the book as being useful to their cause."

The trio and their captors finally emerge into a vast, domed cavern at which near the centre of the cavern stood a magnificent totem pole adorned with faces of wicked glee and savagery. Richard could not but notice that all around the cavern were giant cooking pots, some are bubbling at full blast with lifeless limbs floating inside their sickening stews. To his horror he then recognises the unmistakable smell he had earlier detected as freshly slaughtered meat; it was both rank and salty.

"Watch how they all seem to salute that totem; I wonder what significance it holds for these people? The totem was wonderfully carved with all manner of heads, some human, some animal and some very strange and macabre heads.

Orkan had also noticed that every time one of them passed it they touched it then hit their heart with a fist in soldier like salute. "Perhaps we could use that to make good our escape, they all seem to fear what the totem stands for.

"Keep that thought." Richard replied

They were pushed nearer to a precipice to see what their fate would entail, below was a very large circular pit and at its heart was an enormous bubbling cook pot with what were unmistakably body remains gently boiling away in the stinking stew; first an arm would raise to the top of the boiling soup then disappear, followed by a leg and then even a partially cooked head appeared for but a moment.

"Arrghhh Gross," was all Richard could offer as he felt his stomach heave.

The whole pot was surrounded by what looked like cave exits, but on closer inspection of these darkened areas Richard suddenly realised that they all contained what looked for all the world like cages almost hidden just inside their entrances.

"Oh-oh! We better try to get away and fast, anybody got any ideas? Try not to show any fear." He was given an unceremonious sharp poke in the rear for daring to speak.

Above the pot in the centre hung a large wooden latticed cage with a trailing rope from it to a large rock near to group, a few of the little men were releasing the rope and Richard realised with some shock that their fate was going to be sealed as he watched the men begin hauling on the rope bringing the cage towards their position.

"Your chariot awaits," Zock chuckled loudly and was duly applauded by his compatriots as the three were roughly bundled into the cage. .

"Gghhh! This is not good, we are trapped so what do we do now?"

"The Book of Prophesies," said Melek. "It still contains a hidden item and could be used as a knife, but more importantly the words may give us some inspiration?" He removed the book, laid it on the floor while swiftly backhanding its spinal content to Richard so that those watching didn't see the slick move.

> *Captives bound, caged underground.*
> *Release is found in length around.*
> *A magic beam by evil seen.*
> *Enemies will rise from below,*
> *And dark waters carry the foe.*
> *Prisoner's plight beyond the stern,*
> *Now the slithering monsters turn.*
> *A new deep opens 'ere the burn.*

"The first line makes sense, the second does not, what do think it means by 'Magic Beam?' I don't see any beams in here." Melek said just as Orkan slumped to the floor but Richard put his arm around Melek's waist as if to console his to the watchful onlookers.

"The rope,' found in length around' the book said, it must mean the rope around your waist, that's our way out of here?"

"We need weapons not rope," a distraught Orkan muttered. "See, they have left them down there on that rock but we are trapped in here, what good is a rope?

"Rope? Slipknot? We have a chance to get them back," Melek understood where Richard's thinking was heading, as Orkan quickly got to his feet.

"Good idea, we have but one attempt worth taking, if we miss, we end up as stew? They are going to anyway so let's go for it?"

"It will be my duty, I know how this golden rope works," Melek moved to the edge of the cage and in one underarm movement flung the rope in a long arc towards the weapons and it landed almost perfectly around the pommel of Orkan's sword. He gave the rope a swift jerk to tighten it then slowly pulled it towards the cage.

"That's better." Orkan reached out and retrieved the sword, "now what's next, have we got anything else we can use?"

"The pod...for some reason they did not take my bag, if they did, they probably thought there was no weapons in there." He searched and found his torch. "Voilà the Magic Beam!" He checked it to see if it still worked, it did.

"Gghhh! What is that?"

"The Book of Prophesies is correct yet again. This is my magical beam and has a laser light now, we at least stand a fighting chance, Melek, use your rope to slip the lock and be ready to shake up old Zock, he won't be expecting us to fight back so, surprise is on our side right now." Richard outlined his plan as Melek skilfully unlocked the cage by hooking the slipknot around the handle and drawing it back.

Meanwhile in an adjoining passage Zock and his men were holding court and there was discontent because except for the leader everyone was nervous of eating the unknown one because they felt it could bring them bad fortune. It was all about Richard, they fully recognised that the other two were from their world so they could go into the pot but not the strange one. Eventually Zock conceded by agreeing to cook Melek and Orkan and leave Richard as their prisoner for a while until they could decide his fate.

"Right, we cook the two now and leave the strange one until I have instruction what must be done with him, the great totem will tell us. Come let's start," with all in agreement he led his people back towards the brood-hall as drums struck up a frantic pounding that filled and echoed throughout the underground passages and halls.

Entering the great hall once again he gave the orders. "Bring the two for the eating ceremony and you," he pointed at Richard, "stay where you are."

His people pulled the suspended cage towards the edge and once near enough one of them jumped across the void to open the cage door. Just then, Orkan gave the gate a swift kick sending Zock's man hurtling down into the thick soup below. After the initial scream it was all over in a flash, the dwarf's head appeared for seconds still trying to scream and then he just disappeared below the stewing liquid.

Orkan moved to the gate, ready to jump and fight at any given moment.

"Ha! You no longer have surprise on your side but I will admit that was very clever. Now. Seize them," Zock roared.

Richard placed his arm through the bar and switched on the torch pointing the laser-like beam straight at Zock's face. Pure pandemonium broke out as they saw what looked to them like some sort of powerful beam of red light coming directly from the strange one's hand.

"Arrgh!" Zock threw up his hands to protect his eyes and fell backwards dropping Juroot's dagger in the process while the others scrambled, pushed and pulled trying to trample each other to death in an effort to get away from this unknown death ray. Orkan did not need a second invitation as he leaped across the void and retrieved the dagger, his sword swinging through several arcs cutting some of the followers down. In seconds, the great hall had cleared itself of the dwarves and the few injured ones either tried dragging themselves away or were dead.

"Gghhh! Gghhh! Anyone see what happened to Zock?"

"Last I saw was him crawling on all fours that way." Melek pointed towards a tunnel on the left." Let's move because they will regroup and there are too many for us to fight, we have scared them but vengeance is what they will be seeking and believe me, they are not stupid."

Orkan led the way down a main tunnel and shortly they came across a slightly wounded dwarf, Orkan had no mercy for the man as he pushed him ahead of them along the torch lined passageway.

"Listen"

Lone drum sound started and was quickly followed by others joining in, it triggered something in their prisoner who seemed to be getting up courage and turned to try to escape but, Richard simply flicked the switch of his torch and the dwarf stopped the struggle.

"Look its Golan." As he had swooped, the beam across one of the many tunnel exits ahead Richard had seen a silhouette of what seemed like the chameleon-like guardian at that entrance, "we must go down that way, Golan was there and it's his way of guiding us out of here." With the drums now again beating at full tempo they all knew that Zock would soon be on their trail. As they made their way down the darkened tunnel the air began losing the smell of cooking to become fresh and cool.

"Water, it's a lake," Richard swept the torch across the surface of the water, it was calm but on the sloping sand he saw something that made his heart flip with delight, "boats, now that's our way out of here." What they saw was an array of boats, rafts and put together pontoons on the shoreline..

"Gghhh! Better to sink them then we cannot be followed." Orkan raced to the first boat stabbed his sword into the rotting timber and it went through like butter. Racing from one to another like a demented jumping bean he continued thrusting the sword into each boat bottom.

"Orkan it's time to leave," the constant drumming was now becoming much louder, "Zock's guys are coming." Richard urged.

"Remember the riddle?" Melek said calmly, "it mentioned monsters and every time we have been near water monsters have appeared? Could they be lying in wait in these waters but, what choice do we have, Zock behind, monsters ahead?"

"The unknown is the better bet, which boat is undamaged?" Richard queried. "Let's get out of here."

Gghhh! This one." Orkan pointed to the best looking of the raggle taggle fleet, I purposely left it because it seemed the best boat here." They clambered aboard and Orkan after tossing his captive into the stern gave the boat a hearty shove as he jumped in. At first it was a little wobbly but soon they got a rhythm going and moved away from the shores with both Richard and Orkan pulling together. It was not long before they had covered a fair distance from the shore when Richard saw the first torchlight appear from one of the tunnels.

"Oh-oh! Here they come, row faster they won't be able to catch us because we have enough distance between us. Anyway, they won't be able to see us in this darkness." Richard could only just make out shapes moving along the shoreline by the flickering torches. Then one dwarf moved away from the group to a tunnel entrance and began drumming in what sounded like a coded message, stopped beating, several hard beats, stopped beating, several more hard beats and in short time more torches filtered out of the tunnels onto the beach.

"I told you they weren't stupid, they know which way we are headed," Melek was seated in the bow, "they will come after us, Zock needs vengeance and we have undermined his leadership. He won't give up chasing us."

"Gghhh! Or he will die in the attempt? I need but one face to face go with him." Orkan retorted. "Gghhh! What's happening? It's getting harder to move?"

"It's almost as if we are trying to row through syrup," Both were now straining fiercely at the oars but they had slowed down to a crawl when there was a sudden bump and the little craft came to a halt. "What caused that? Can you see anything Melek?"

"Too dark." The small boat started wobbling then the sound of scraping against the hull from the underside. "Something's moving in the water, maybe we've met our monster as the riddle stated we would?"

"Here, use this torch, only problem is it lights up so we can see what is down there but will also tell Zock where we are, what do you think?"

"Gghhh! I would rather face my enemy if I can see him, the sudden lurch of the craft made up their minds instantly. Melek took the torch, he had seen how Richard used it on Zock and began fiddling with the button until suddenly a broad beam of light filled the surround, Melek stumbled backward in panic and up against Orkan. "It's not one monster, there are 'many monsters.' We need something they have teeth like the Tolosh." Orkan and Richard shipped their oars and turned to face their new enemy.

"They are there." Zock saw the light in the distance, "follow me, this time we will get them." He scrambled into a flat-bottomed boat and without waiting for the rest started heading towards where he could see the white beam flash. He knew these waters well and the dangers that existed within them so taking a breather he lit a candle mounted on a skull at the front of his boat then did the same to one at the back. The rest of the dwarves were battling to catch up to their leader who was again on the move.

"What is that?" Richard could see the movement below water, when one of the shadowy forms broke the surface, teeth first; it snapped its razor sharp jaws against the side of the boat and held on for a few seconds, its red eyes staring directly at the three companions and their captive. There was no doubt in Richard's mind what this thing wanted to do with them as a cold chill ran the full length of his frame. "Looks like some sort of enormous eel."

"Weeeooo!"

Orkan's sword flashed through the air striking the thing's top jaw that flew upwards and landed with a plop in the water. Suddenly the attacking thing became the target for the other monsters as the water began heaving with huge bodies each trying to get their bit of food. Richard looked back at the shoreline and could see that Zock's boat was already a lot closer to their current position and gaining on them very quickly.

"Orkan we need to distract those things again, it's not going to be long before Zock reaches us." Richard grabbed the oars and tried rowing, the boat was moving because in among the ensuing melee of the below water monster group becoming locked together in their combat for food they had made a temporary pathway for the boat to move freely again.

"Gghhh! You're right," before Richard or Melek could react or say anything Orkan heaved their now screaming dwarf captive high above his head and tossed him into the waters behind their boat and just in front of the fast approaching Zock's boat. With all the kicking and screaming the eel-like monsters quickly moved towards them leaving the passageway clear for the companions to take the oars and row as hard as they could towards a sunlit opening and shoreline.

"Zock is battling to get through those beasts and putting up a brave fight," said Melek who could just see what was now behind them. He won't give up though.

They reached the shore and as they got out of the boat Orkan used his trusty sword to stab several holes into the bottom of the boat. "We don't want them to use this anymore do we?"

"You're nuts! What if we need it again?" Richard was furious because of his companion's individual actions without first consulting his companions. "Now there is no going back, you must at least speak to us when you decide to take any action."

"Gghhh! I saved us by throwing the dwarf to the monsters, we do not have time to have a conference when in battle, my decision was the right one." He was clearly upset and stormed off in the direction of the sunlit hole.

"Orkan wait! Sorry," but the damage had been done and there was no stopping by the pig-like warrior.

"Words have wings, once they have left your mouth they can never return, said Melek almost apologetically."He will calm down shortly, I think we should follow him because our strength lies in being a unit together?" Melek handed the torch back to Richard.

"You're so right, me and my big mouth." He put the torch back in his bag then jumped up. "Cannot find the pod, must have dropped it somewhere.

"We will find it but first let's find out where the soldier has gone, we need his fighting skills."

They trudged up the beach until they reached the sunlit entrance where they overlooked a small valley surrounded by sheer cliff faces and saw below them a totally different world, it was filled with trees, plants and greenery. It was not very large in extent but the whole place was a suntrap and exceptional calm and serene.

"Wow! Look at that, what a difference from Zock's underground mess, this is like heaven." Richard spotted Orkan in the far distance reaching the end of the path leading to the bottom. He tried shouting but it made no impact as Orkan disappeared into the foliage on the valley floor.

"A 'new deep' could mean this place?" Melek said, "We should follow him because we are not complete without him. We will have to also keep our guard, Zock will come again and as we have already seen, not all beautiful places are safe?"

"Let's go find Orkan." The two set off downwards along the winding path. Reaching the base they moved cautiously but quickly along the well-trodden pathway until they came upon a much wider track. They stopped behind a bush to gain their bearings; Richard could not see his friend anywhere.

"Nothing," he said, the thought as he wondered was whether his companion had now deserted them, then came a slight rustling sound from somewhere behind them. "Zock! Follow me." The sound was moving closer; Richard went into mode and raced blindly through the undergrowth.

"This way!" He heard his seeming distant voice shouting. It seemed to give him renewed strength and pull at his exhausted body but then he tripped and broke clear of the thick bushes, lurching full length onto his stomach into what seemed to be a large clearing.

"No place to hide, I'm done for." Just then he heard a sound that filled his very soul with dread as the buzzing sound increased in intensity, Richard was like a trapped hare, as he scrambled around searching the open space for somewhere to conceal himself. Suddenly he froze. A swirling, twisting, bubbling black mass suddenly swept from the writhing thick foliage into the opening. Richard seemed mesmerised, when something or someone suddenly grabbed him and flung him to the ground.

"Ouch!"

"Shut up and don't move a muscle if you value your life," whispered a voice just loud enough for Richard to hear over the deafening roar moving directly towards their position.

"Uumff."

The weight on top of him was pinning him so tightly to the ground that he could hardly breathe properly. He could only watch in anticipation as the noisy, swirling mass enveloped the area and now a deafening roar as he felt whatever it was flicking against his exposed parts. For a moment, everything dimmed and Richard thought he had seen his last, he shut his eyes tightly, as quickly as it had arrived, so it was gone and all he could hear was the receding sound of the black mass.

"Uumff," He tried to move. The weight was still there.

"Wait, they haven't gone far enough."

They waited for what to Richard seemed an eternity; whatever was pinning him down suddenly removed its weight.

"All clear, you can get up now."

Richard spun onto his back expecting to see Orkan, but to his surprise, he saw a brown skinned standing over him, hand outstretched to give him a hand up.

"W-who are you?"

"My name is Metie, who're you and what are you doing here?"

Richard took the handsome man's hand and as he stood up he realised that the man's skin felt ultra soft and wet to the touch, he pulled back his hand and for the first time had a close look at the man's face. It was patterned with what seemed to be delicately fashioned shimmering brown scales similar to a fish.

"What was 'that'?"

"It was only a swarm of killer bees," he said casually. "If you had run or done something stupid, they would have attacked you but, fortunately my sister and I were here and I saw you."

"T-thanks. My name is Richard and I was searching for my friend Orkan when they came along."

Richard suddenly felt very hungry and tired. Keeping up with Orkan had been hard going and he asked if he would be able to rest up for a moment after that harrowing experience.

"Yes, let's sit down and I'll get some water and fresh mushrooms to eat before you continue on your way."

Richard was almost about to sit against a strange looking tree when Metie screamed loudly at him.

"Not against 'that' tree!"

"Why not?"

"In this valley you must become aware of anything and everything around you, take a good look." Metie moved away and Richard followed away to his side, turning to look at the old fossilized trunk with its two leg-like branches sprouting from the top. There was a large hole in one side of the old tree when suddenly Richard realised that the tree looked just like the body of a person stuck upside down in the ground.

"Ah, you can see it now. Can't you? That was once Zurl, a great philosopher of the people hereabouts." Just then, Melek appeared, slightly out of breath. Richard made the introductions

"I have heard of you Melek of the Sauge, my people say you have become a great philosopher, however with the war, I had not heard anything from the outside world." The two gave each other a strange salute.

"What was that about?"

"Metie was the tribal leader before the war, I remember my father talking for long hours with him when I was but a child. The evil one destroyed those days, Zock fell under his influence but I presume that you are still fighting evil?" He turned to Metie.

"Of course I am, see there is your father." He pointed at the strange tree.

"Why did the swarm not attack you?" He asked with a slightly suspicious tone in the voice.

"I realise you may not trust me but your friend was just very lucky to have fallen right next to Zurl and the reason I say lucky is that swarm moved away so quickly because a swarm is here already and that tree indicates to those of us who live here that nasty people and things move about within this area. Everyone but me think that tree happened to be a nasty cannibal once and the hole in its body reminds us of his sticky end, but I knew him he was never a cannibal but his offspring is."

"What do you mean? Was 'that' once a real person and your father?"

"He was, a long time ago, here let me show you why you were so lucky, had you fallen anywhere else you would now be dead" Metie bent down and picked up a stone about the size of a small egg. He extracted a beautifully intricate diamond studded sling from his belt and placed the stone into the broadened thongs at one end. He swung it round several times and then suddenly the stone shot out and thumped hard into the strange tree. The sound of the hollow tree echoed through the forest like a deep cannon shot. From within a loud buzzing sound rose as a black spiralling plume poured out high into the open sky above it.

"Stand still, don't move." The swirling column rose out of the tree and then slowly descended back into the tree.

"You see."

Richard saw a movement to his left and was surprised to see another Metie entering the clearing. Only after studying the form for a second did he realise that the person had long hair and was a woman.

"Ahh, Mockie ...come and meet Richard and Melek."

Like Metie, she was dressed in a loose brown robe that almost touched the ground. Richard couldn't help noticing that she carried a diamond-studded lasso tucked into her belt.

"Richard, this is my twin sister." Richard lifted his hand in salute from some distance away before he could blink; she had whipped out the lasso sending one end of the sparkling rope soaring over his hand. She gave it a hard yank throwing Richard off balance and sprawling to the ground at her feet.

"Who sent you here?" She demanded sharply.

"G-Golan did." With a flick of her wrist the lasso seemed to jump back into her belt as if by magic.

"Oh that is a good thing"

"He's searching for someone called Orkan."

"Y-yes, he's my guide. I-I, er... lost him on the trail, what am I going to do? This is a terrible place; it's full of nasty things."

She now leaned forward; He could see that her skin was covered with hundreds of shiny scales that now looked like slivers of brown diamonds. It was that, that gave both of their skins the effervescent glowing sheen.

"So, you two think we're nasty, are we?"

"No! But, there are a lot of other creepy things around here."

"Stop bullying him Mockie. Shall we eat?" Metie called.

"Afterwards, I'll go and find your friend, someone passed me a little way back, I do not know what they looked like but, I will bring this person to you."

"That's fine by me, I'm starved."

"You and Metie talk while I also gather some food." Richard sat and watched his newfound fish-like friend picking mushrooms, berries from trees and digging for roots. After a short while he gathered them and made his way to them. Richard wasn't sure what to say to Mockie, mainly because she scared him.

"There, that'll make a grand feast." Mockie piled together a few twigs and sticks and then took the sling and looking up to see where the sun was, used one of the diamonds as a magnifying glass. Very soon Richard noticed a thin trail of smoke from one of the dry twigs. Once the fire had flared up and died down, Metie scraped the hot ash aside and placed the goodies he had collected in the centre.

"Just like a scout," Richard commented.

"What's a scout?"

"Oh, just something from my world."

"He is the Chosen One and that's why Golan sent him to try to retrieve the pods and guardians

"Umm." Metie scooped the cooked food onto the makeshift plate made from the bark of a tree. He set it down. "Here eat."

Richard was only prepared to try the mushrooms. "Umm, that's good," Richard said surprised at the flavour. He extracted his water bottle and passed it to his two companions who both rejected it. Richard thought the reason was that the bottle looked foreign to them so he took a long swig and replaced it.

"Now, this friend of yours, what does he look like?"

Richard described Orkan and where he had last seen him.

"You stay here Mockie, I'll find this Orkan."

He turned to Richard, "Make sure you stay here no matter what happens, do you understand?"

"Don't worry, I won't move." Richard watched Metie disappear into the foliage, and duly realised just how tired he was but even so, felt a little unsafe and exposed sitting in the centre of the clearing like this.

"I'm very tired; I'm just going to lie down over there." Mockie simply nodded and pointed to the forest's edge at an overhanging branch which would give him enough cover to see all in the clearing yet allow him to be hidden from sight.

"Rest there, I will keep watch until they return."

Richard lay down and as soon as his head hit the ground he was almost instantly asleep.

"Metie! Help, ...help!" Richard suddenly came awake as his confused brain tried to come to terms with what was happening. His eyes searched the clearing and then he saw it.

"W-wha..."The ugliest little dwarf with an enormous head was busily shoving Mockie into a large bag. Richard froze. The 'thing' had a head almost twice as big as its body. It seemed to be slobbering as vile green mucus dripped from both corners of its huge mouth. Zock had taken a completely different appearance in this sunlight,

"Hey you!" Richard screamed, knowing he had to try to help Mockie.

The startled dwarf glanced up as Richard scrambled from his hiding place and grabbed at a broken stick. Zock was in two minds as Richard without thinking raced across the open ground swinging the stick around his head and screaming like a wild banshee.

"Let her go!" With one hand the thing lifted the bag onto his back and turned to face the oncoming boy but at the sight of the screaming boy seemed to unnerve the monster and Zock fled into the undergrowth.

"Now what?" Richard wasn't certain whether to follow Zock into the dense undergrowth. He stopped to listen, he then heard Zock racing away with Mockie.

"Metie!" Richard shouted as loud as he could, feeling utterly helpless, he sat down right where he was because he just wanted to cry. Suddenly he heard crashing though the undergrowth.

"Zock's returning, probably with his tribe this time," Richard searched the area; Melek was nowhere to be seen he quickly decided to face the thing as it emerged from the greenery. Bush and twigs were being trampled underfoot right in front of him but yet he couldn't see anything.

"Right, it's you and me, ugly man!" He screamed as a blur shot from the forest edge. "Richard! What's happened?" The lance like stick stopped just short of Richard's heart. "Mockie's been spirited away by an ugly dwarf called Zock."

"Whooeee!"

"Orkan?"

"Yes, I found him looking for you when I heard your scream." Orkan appeared and Richard threw himself at his companion.

"Piggy, I missed you." Orkan looked at Metie and then shrugged his shoulders.

"Never call me Piggy, do you understand?"

"I'm just so happy to see you again."

"Sorry to have to break up your reunion, but where is Mockie?"

Richard told Metie everything he had seen. Metie listened intently.

"Right, we must move quickly, his name was Zock the Scavenger and one of the most terrible of all cannibals."

"Gghhh! We know."

"Where is he taking her?"

"Well, maybe to his underground lair, I'm not sure." We'll help you, won't we Orkan?" Orkan smiled knowingly at Richard. It somehow reminded him of his father's smile when he used to tell his bedtime fairy stories.

"Gghhh!, of course we will."

"I'm sorry Metie, I should have stayed awake, do you think she'll be all right."

"Oh yes, this isn't the first time he's tried to steal Mockie."

"No, ...what happened?"

"He has an obsession to eat Mockie. He's tried several times to trick Mockie by pretending that he was me. But, each time she recognised his gruff voice no matter how hard he tried to disguise it." Richard collected his things, including his stick and the three set off while Metie completed the story.

Metie stopped and reached inside his cloak and pulled out a bag.

"A swarm of wild bees." He pointed to an old tree stump. "We're going to need them." Metie placed the bag over the opening.

"Hit the bark with your stick Richard."

Richard gave the dead wood a resounding smack. Suddenly there was a violent buzzing and the bees flew into the bag that Metie closed and tied.

"Come on."

"Metie followed the trail toward Zock on the edge of what was a shallow lake where they had come from a little earlier but this time Metie led them along the shoreline until they reached a ramshackle old house. Metie signalled Orkan and Richard to stay hidden while he sneaked in through the back door while Zock was busily attending to the fire in which he was going to cook Mockie. Metie quickly placed the pouch with the bees into the bag that contained his sister.

"What is he going to do against Zock?" said Richard. .

"Gghhh! Shhh," Orkan held his finger to his mouth. They saw a movement to the right; it was the twins working their way towards them. "Metie here!" Richard indicated their position behind a rock and the couple took up position next to Orkan and Richard. "Any problems?" Orkan enquired.

"No, we were lucky."

"I'm glad to see you're safe Mockie." For the first time since they had met each other, she gave Richard a somewhat tentative smile.

Inside the house Zock eagerly moved the bag to a position next to his fire. For some time he waited for the blaze to increase until it was time to place Mockie into his pot of boiling water. He opened the bag next to the fire and instead of the expected young maiden; he encountered the bees that were so mad at being placed next to the heat that they attacked the first person that they came across. The whole room swarmed with bees.

"Serves you right you cannibal thing," shouted Richard as the dwarf ran screaming from the house followed by a swirling black mass. Zock fled in terror with the bees close on his heels. Never before had he encountered a swarm of bees as cross as this but in panic his brain worked out that his attackers didn't like water. He raced to the lake and dived in. The bees kept on stinging, and he was in such a state, that he panicked and dived into the shallow water head first and stuck fast in the mud. The swarm didn't go away and kept on attacking him. They stung him very badly as his funny short body writhed in pain. Suddenly all was silent; Zock was quite dead when the bees started eating away at his stomach leaving a big hole where the bees now made their new home in the void.

"That's horrible." Richard was shaking as he watched the macabre scene unfold before their eyes.

"Old Zock is just like that tree in the clearing.

"C'mon Richard, we've still got a long way to go, and you need to learn much more on this trail." "So have we." Mockie said. She leaned forward and planted a kiss on Richard's chin

"Here, I don't know if this will help you, I found it in Zock's house." She pressed something into the young man's hand.

"Look Orkan, it's the pod of life, Zock must have stolen it from me."

"Come Mockie, they must press on, with Zock dead perhaps we can get the rest of the tribe together and hope we meet up again. Good luck with the rest of your quest."

"Wait, how do we get out of here?"

"There is no way out of the sacred valley because of the sheer cliff face except heading across the lake or, there is that tunnel, I am not sure where it leads but nobody uses it because of missing people."

"We have no choice then? No boat equals, no monsters or cannibal dwarves, we have to see what lies down that path and whatever it might be, it can be no worse than anything we have faced so far?"

Metie and Mockie moved off leaving Orkan and Richard alone once again.

"Melek we must find him first?"

"Gghhh! Right let's go back for him," as they began to retrace their steps they saw the familiar librarian talking to Metie and Mockie at the entrance to the valley. They saluted each other and he came in their direction.

"What happened to you?"

"When you fell asleep I went and visited my father, I had read that there was a way to release him from his present position by stuffing the tree with a special brew of herbs, it takes a long time but he will eventually return to this world as the man he was. I did not know what had happened to you so came here in case Zock had seized you. Metie told me what happened and what course you were planning."

"There is no alternative if we are to find the guardians or the pods?" Richard stated.

The three headed off in the direction of the tunnel that Metie had pointed out

"The story is that everyone who enters that tunnel never returns. That could be ominous or it could be good, let's hope we are lucky and it takes us to a nice place?"

"Knowing our luck, it's not going to be good." Orkan interjected. "I'm not scared but nothing good lives under the ground."

Imprisoned Man and Beast

On the Eighth Day...

Cross the gap without mishap,
An arrow saves the day.
Find the side but Chosen falls,
Save him fast! Then at last
From blazing fires comes the glow.
And then you know that air reveals,
The pod to feel, and Evil steals
The beasts to meet the blow.

"Metie and Mockie are such good people; do you think that they will succeed in converting the dwarfs from their evil ways? Richard asked as they trudged towards the tunnel opening.

"They have special powers worthy of becoming guardians and have escaped the war with the evil one, it will not be easy for them but I believe that they will overcome the tribe because Zock no longer acts as the tribe's mouthpiece and influence. Let's hope I'm right in my assumption." Melek stopped and lifted the Book of Prophesies off his back and opened it "Before we enter that tunnel I think we should check what fate awaits us in there, don't you?"

"I'm going to fill my water bottle in case we need refreshment and there is none in these." Richard hastily made his way to the fearful water's edge and checked that none of the eel-like monsters were lurking before he filled the container. He saw the pod given to him by Mockie and then simply acting on a hunch he placed it in the centre of the amulet. "Just as I thought, a fake pod but I'll keep it just in case." When he got back to his companions Melek showed him the riddle he had found.

Cross the gap without mishap,
An arrow saves the day.
Find the side but Chosen falls,
Save him fast! Then at last
From blazing fires comes the glow.
And then you know that air reveals,
The pod to feel, and Evil steals

The beasts to meet the blow.

"Don't like that bit about Chosen falls? Does that mean I am going to trip or worse still, am I going to die?"

"Gghhh! Not if I have anything to do with it. Come, we must move on."

"Just one more thing, the pod Mockie gave me is a fake, can we trust them now or is that tunnel that Metie told us about, simply another evil trap?"

"She said she found it in Zock's house didn't she? That makes far more sense to me because he was in league with evil, so for the moment let's give them both the benefit of the doubt and see what happens." Melek closed the book and strapped it onto his back.

The tunnel was not as dark as they expected it to be; from somewhere sunlight seemed to filter in at periodic intervals on their journey, as they rounded a bend Orkan grabbed both of them.

"Careful, do not take another step." In front of them was a gaping fissure, "methinks this is a conveniently placed trap. Round a bend and straight down into a chasm if you missed a step? Now how are we going to get across?"

Richard extracted his torch and shone it down into the hole, there seemed to be no bottom to it or at least nothing showed up beyond the powerful beam.

"That hole is deep, thank goodness you acted and did not take my advice and try to discuss the matter, anybody falling down there has no chance of surviving."

"In battle you have to sometimes use your intuition and initiative." Orkan smiled, "so I'm again free to act on my own am I?" All three laughed.

"Let's see how good you are with your bow and arrow? Do you think you could fire over that clamp?" Richard pointed the torch to a point on the wall beyond the ravine, "More difficult could you do that with Melek's rope tied to one end? If you can do it with a single shot, I promise that I will never use the name Orkan, Piggy or anything similar to you again"

"Gghhh! Only one way to find out." Orkan released his bow, withdrew an arrow, held it in front of his eyes checking the shaft for straightness and then held out his trotter-like hand to Melek.

"No, I will fasten the rope to your arrow." He delicately wrapped it around the shaft twice before looping it back and tying it. "There, now it won't slip." He held fast to the other end of the rope as he stepped back.

Orkan gave it a swift tug and it didn't budge. "Good!" His position ready, he took careful aim, a deep breath then fired. The arrow flew high into the air then in a long arc descended and wrapped itself around the clamp. Melek heaved on the line to ensure that it was firmly secure.

"Gghhh! The name is Orkan from now on I believe." He was very pleased with his achievement and Richard could only stare at the rope in amazement.

"You win, you go first."

"Why me?"

"Because you're the heaviest and if that rope loosens, the two of us can take your weight but, with you on that side it gives us all a chance to cross and also help to insure any slip-ups"

While Richard and Melek pulled on the rope to give it the required tension Orkan made his way across the deep gorge across without any mishap Melek followed suit and except for a slight wobble when he thought he felt the book was loosening he too, made it safely across. They then both egged Richard on not knowing that this was mentally his worst nightmare. He stared at his hands around the golden rope, they felt wet and clammy and were white from the tightness of his grip as panic gripped him he knew he could not do this. Then he heard the noise of running footsteps coming from around the bend behind him, he simply lifted his feet and swung out over the black hole as he braced himself for the impact that he knew was coming.

He had escaped just in time as several members of Zock's tribe hurtled round the bend and suddenly pandemonium broke out as the first half dozen unable to stop in time careered over the side and into the black darkness. Richard could hear their screams as they travelled downwards bouncing from rock to rock until there was silence. One dwarf took aim and hurled his spear towards the dangling Richard; it slammed into the stone face next to him.

"Oh-OH!" Hand over hand Richard begun scrambling up the rock face using anything he could for a foothold while both Orkan and Melek pulled as hard as they could while keeping an eye on the enraged dwarves on the other side of the chasm. As Richard was almost at the point of safety there was a sudden lurch of the rope.

"Whaa!"

"Gghhh! The brackets dislodging."

Richard began scrambling and the dwarves saw their chance as they hurled whatever they could at their somewhat helpless enemy. A club hit him squarely in the back but did not dislodge him because fortunately his bag took most of the impact but he knew full well had that blow been a little higher and caught his head he too would now be a casualty of the deep gorge. The blow only served to strengthen his will to survive and very quickly with the aid of his companions managed to reach the top and almost dived across the floor to safety with all sorts of debris still landing around them, Richard rolled onto his back and saw Melek flick his wrist and the rope magically came away from the now dangling clamp. Orkan grabbed the back of Richard's tunic and hauled him away from the edge towards the safety of the continuing tunnel and out of range of the missiles raining across the chasm.

"Stop! Stop! Melek shouted.

"Gghhh! Never! No time for talk, we have to get away from here, those little devils are 'really' determined to get us."

"Look there Richard, isn't that..."He was pointing at a spot a little way from Richard's body. In his prone position he turned his head and immediately recognised the ball-like crystal for what it was. "Is it really another pod? Richard reached out and grabbed at it

"Orkan Stop Let me go." Richard struggled hard to free himself but the pig-like boy's grip was like a vice and he just kept dragging his companion away from the danger area. Finally around a bend he stopped and sat down against the wall.

"What was that all about?" Orkan enquired sort of matter of factly.

"Look," he held up the sparkling ball-like crystal, "we nearly missed it because you would not listen.

"Good for you we have the crystal back but you and Melek would have been of little use to our quest if you had been injured back there. Our safety must be paramount, and as you have found out, we have been fortunate enough to survive an attack and come away with a pod."

"Orkan, your logic astounds me sometimes. This is not a game, our duty is to find the guardians and the pods of life."

"We cannot find them if we are injured or dead, can we?"

"You did well back there, the Chosen One is alive and I think we have had a marvellous day as a combined group, don't you?" Melek said fastening the golden rope around his middle once more. "We all played our parts, no more Zock, Metie and Mockie will soon control those people because they are now leaderless."

"All right, I admit that as a team we work well together and each have our own strengths, next time I will truly try." Orkan pushed himself to his feet and in a single movement lifted Richard onto his. "We must keep moving, I still don't trust those little cannibals back there."

They trudged along this tunnel for a long time, stopping only for something to eat and drink. Much later they reached a fork where it split

"I think we may have to use the Path Finder to guide us?"

Melek removed the big book and slipped the crystal dagger from its hiding place and handed it to Richard who swung it in a wide arc.

"That way," he pointed the direction of their travel as he handed the magical instrument back to the librarian who quickly stowed it safely and followed after his companions. They moved through several now changing areas, colours of the walls became streaked between red, brown and yellow while the path was becoming trickier to walk along and also loose underfoot dotted with jagged shards and pebbles. After navigating this pathway for a short while it evened out slightly.

"Aargh! What's that terrible smell? There's something 'very rotten' ahead Orkan immediately withdrew his sword and moved far more cautiously until exiting the tunnel onto a wide ledge overlooking an enormous cavern below. The whole area was bathed in a shadowy red, almost deep orange colouration given off by the combination of red and yellow rock formation filling the whole subterranean area below their position. A wide and winding track crossed the valley floor in a zigzag line and in the distance they could make out what in the haze seemed to be some form of citadel. Except for the pathway all the ground as far as they could see had been dug out like a monstrous gigantic moat.

Underground dwellers seem to love sheer faces don't they?

"Gghhh! As I told you before, nothing good lives under the ground. We must be ready for trouble in this place." They moved down and along the path, the smell becoming more and more putrid with each step.

"Rotten Eggs, that's it. That smell coming up from the bowels of the earth is hydrogen sulphide? I learned that in science." Richard looked at his companions who both shook their heads. "Sulphur?" Again just blank stares. "I bet there's a volcano of some sort in this area, that's the smell it would make, we better tread very carefully, if you feel the ground tremor then we get away from here but fast. All right?" Both shrugged and nodded approval but Richard could tell that what he had said did not really mean anything to his companions.

"I think that castle must be Enlil's fortress." Melek said, "It has that feel about it but, we cannot go back and must press on because the book said the 'air reveals' and that it certainly has done, which means we are still on the right path forward no matter what confronts us now."

"I thought somebody called it Enlil's Dungeon? Doesn't look like that to me, looks more like a haunted castle from here, maybe this Enlil character is really Dracula." Richard laughed at his own joke until he realized the two were staring blankly at him. "Just my little joke."

Nearing the tall structure Richard saw that there was a ribbon of smoke rising from what he had first thought of as the building and the truth suddenly dawned on him that the whole area was in fact a live volcano and that the plume indicated that it was still very much an active volcano. Somehow while the carved out stonework around was to make it seem like a building of sorts it was in fact a live volcano on the inside.

"Wow! That must have taken a lot of manpower to achieve."

"What? Orkan asked.

"This place was once a lava bed of sulphur, once filled with pumice, ash and magna or red hot rock and now look at it, the whole place has been sculptured, shaped and trimmed by some kind of workforce. This area didn't just happen, it has been carefully constructed from the original lava flow and 'that work' would have needed a 'lot of workers' in order to dig out and carve these structures. Even that building ahead was shaped into a castle, it was once head of the volcano spout and that column of smoke is what is creating the foul smell in this place. Inside those walls we will find an active volcano but if this is Enlil's realm then we are facing a monumental task and possibly our scariest nightmare all rolled into one."

"The book stated 'pods to feel' so we must proceed, no matter how difficult the task may seem, the book has always been correct?" Melek said quietly.

"I know, I know but being forewarned is being forearmed and this will be no pushover, we must expect the worst once we cross that threshold." They kept trudging on until almost reaching the outer walls of the castle. Richard saw the end of the trail and guarding entry was a magnificent old world huge set of steel gates.

"Gghhh! Big trouble. Can you see them? Orkan pointed to either side of the great gate but Richard had been so entranced by the beauty of the designs on the gate that he had missed the two guarding dogs partially hidden in the shadows.

"Whoa! They're so... er, so huge? How the heck are we ever going to get past them?" Richard was truly afraid because on both sides of that magnificent gate were what looked like the twin hounds of hell. Each was tethered to the castle wall by a heavy and lengthy steel chain that was fixed at the other end to broad steel spiked collars but now, the two broad barrel chested dogs simply sat baring massive white bladed fangs that automatically indicated pure savagery and death should those ever be used.

"I thought my neighbour's Great Dane was huge, he's a pup compared to the size of those two." He joked nervously falling in behind Orkan just in case. Getting ever nearer he could now see that their eyes were just two pinpricks of black surrounded by large blood red pupils and that, simply added to the boy's discomfort. "Definitely these two would make Romulus and Remus seem like tame kittens." He quipped apprehensively as the two beasts slowly rose to their feet and quietly moved forward menacingly to the end of their chained restraints and straight into the pathway in order to face their oncoming visitors.

"I don't like them, they're not going to allow us through and even so how do we handle them and at the same time manage those enormous gates? Possibly there's another way in?" As they moved much closer the two huge animals began snarling pawing at the air as they strained forward towards the new comers.

"I'll keep them occupied, you two attempt to slip past and try to open one of those gates. The trick is to draw that securing bolt then work quickly, we won't have much time before these two realise what is going on and you do not want to be trapped between the gate and them if they do?" Richard studied the gate with its massively long sword that acted as the main bolt.

"Right, we're ready." Orkan slipped his sword of its scabbard then moved to his right as close to the edge of the path as he dared and then took two steps forward. The pair of howling beasts quickly moved to cover his move and raged forward almost to within biting distance of Orkan and straining so hard to reach him that their chains now so tight that they made strange twanging sounds. Richard was mentally convinced that if this continued the bolts in the walls holding the two would become like the clamp before and pull out of their secure positions, he knew that they had to act quickly so grabbing Melek by the arm they raced to the great gate.

"The bolt first!" Orkan shouted as he struck out and nicked the lip of the nearest dog. Blood, foam and spittle pouring from the raging beast's mouth made it look even more terrifying as he ducked, dived and darted so closely in front of them that he could smell their foul-smelling breath. He knew that if he couldn't hold their attention for long enough his companions would not stand a chance of escaping them. "Hurry!"

Richard and Melek managed to drag the sword-like bolt back and then summoning up all the strength and fear began trying to drag one of the gates open but, it seemed to be stuck in position. With one last effort the huge door began to inch open, this was all the two needed and from somewhere their combined and renewed will gave them the last ounce of energy to force open the gate enough to pass through.

"Wait here." Richard took one look around the door, weighed up the situation and then raced across to join his friend.

"Gghhh! What are you doing imbecile?"

"You are going to have to trust me on this one, get ready you have to join Melek while I take care of these two."

"Gghhh! But..."

"Get going and watch for the signal," Richard commanded.

Orkan moved to his left and watched as the two beasts also moved apart each one now covering one of the two companions.

"Ready? Richard drew Juroot's dagger and threw it at the hound directly in front of him, it hit the mark and suddenly there was a spurt of blood that only seemed to incense the creature further and send it into full blown rage, In an instant the other dog was across the void trying to reach Richard leaving the path clear for Orkan to be able to sprint to the gate.

Richard pulled the tunic cape over himself, he felt as though quite visible to the beasts but knew that this had worked before also a short way in front of him the two dogs were now shocked into silence. Both large beasts were stunned, there was an enemy, then he just disappeared into nowhere now they were confused and sniffing at the ground in circles. Richard moved before the beasts could pick up his scent and raced to the gate to join the others.

"Gghhh! Help me shut this gate." Outside the two huge beasts suddenly picked up Richard's scent trail and realised where their enemy had gone and came bounding towards the three all now pushing the gate closed. Just in time Orkan slammed the inner sword bolt shut when there was an enormous clang as the two animals hit the other side of the steel gate at full tilt. Safe from the outside beasts the companions turned and for the first time they could take in the inside of the building.

"Wow! What a difference from the outside, just look at all those columns and beams?" They were staring straight into what looked like a huge open cathedral with amazingly sculptured columns and finely carved stone beams, each containing its own separate ornate central motif statuesque beast. Amazed, they slowly moved through inspecting the line of exquisite and intricate carvings until they reached the centre of the hall where there was a huge circular column that Richard told them was the smoke stack for the volcano. At the other end of the great hall they came across a winding staircase leading down into what to them seemed like the bowels of the earth.

"Gghhh! There's no way back for us so we have no option but to go forward and find the next pod?" Orkan drew his sword and led the way, the further down they went the hotter it became and they began to hear the distant soulful cries and wailing. "There is much pain in those cries, whoever those people are we must try to help them somehow?"

The further down they moved the woeful voices got louder while the heat was now almost unbearable and then they were at the bottom of the long stairway. They moved through a narrow arched doorway and straight into the back of an untidy rock pile that hid the door from the huge cavern that lay beyond. The three peered around the high mound in the centre of the cave; a large sulphurous, bubbling hole heaved and popped spitting out molten rock.

"Gghhh! Enlil's slaves, hundreds of them, I had heard rumours of people disappearing, I'll wager these are the disappeared."

Richard had never experienced such mournful wailing in his life. All sorts of questions flooded through his brain such as what sort of dreadful beast could be powerful enough to keep all these slaves under its jurisdiction and make these souls cry out and moan so mournfully?

"Look over there, it's Enlil and Erma." Melek pointed to a smoky spot somewhere beyond the bubbling mass. All around the seething cauldron differing moaning creatures formed a chain that shuffled along the narrow winding pathway hauling heavy logs to feed the central flaming mass. "They're all in some sort of trance as well as pain, that's why they are obedient."

"It's more like they are in a type of hypnotic or drugged trance, now I can see why people fear Enlil. He has complete control of their minds. Wonder how he gets them into this state?"

Were these vicious monsters capable of some sort of hypnotic influence or ready to pounce as soon as the group showed themselves? He moved up close behind his companion.

"Orkan, I think we are going to need that bow and arrow to do its work again" Richard whispered as the loud groans continued in the background and the group moved away from their hiding place and out into the open area falling in among the zombie like slaves all leading them closer to the centre and as the haze continued drifting, Melek again pointed out the two enormous bat-like creatures perched high above the central bubbling pit.

"Look to the top of that pile of bones in front of them, if it is what I think it might be, then we have found another pod, the book has found it for us?"

Richard's eyes scanned the area in front of the two flying beasts and then he saw what he had seen, on top of a massive pile of scattered but interlocked bones was his sparkling prize.

"Any suggestions? How are we going to get up there? Sooner or later, they will pick us out among this lot and then we are in big trouble." Suddenly he felt a sharp tug at his tunic, turning slightly he saw a definite drifting formation of Golan outlined within the smoke. Richard felt a chill pass down his spine. "Of course, the cape is a perfect disguise, Orkan you two stay hidden as long as you can or at least until I can get a lot closer to Enlil and Erma then use your trusty bow and arrow to try to dislodge that stack of bones so that the pod drops down. Surprise is our only element."

"Gghhh! It is a long way but I will try, those two have the power to immobilise everyone somehow, I will make a plan because we have only one chance so you too remain hidden from them." Just then Melek moved very close to Richard.

"Will that cape hide both of us? You will need my roping skill to capture that pod when the time comes."

"Don't know but it's worth a try." Richard pulled the cape over them. Orkan can you see Melek?"

"You are both hidden from view, wish I also had that protection, remember that bats sense things by echo location so you two must be careful, use signals and do not even whisper to each other as you get closer. Now go!"

The two shuffled away awkwardly at first but soon fell into a rhythmical step being careful not to disturb any of the workers or snagging the cape against the timbers they were dragging towards the central fire. The two passed by the bubbling cauldron and made their way to the foot of the two pillars. The two giant bats were now directly above their position and no matter how many times Richard and Melek moved in order to get a clear view of the pod they found it almost impossible to see it for the huge stack of interlocked bone structure built like a massive nest. They could not move backwards to gain a line of sight because the edge of the bubbling cauldron was at their backs nor could they move left or right as this would allow them a view of only one of their enemy so this was to be the best position for the moment and then trust everything to what happened next. Richard extracted the torch and flashed it in Orkan's general direction. They did not see the arrow's flight until it had passed the cauldron and was almost directly overhead.

"Oh no it's too high." Richard had broken Orkan's cardinal rule and spoken, above them Enlil and Erna suddenly stiffened in confusion and immediately began to spread their gigantic wings in preparation of an attack. The arrow had then rammed straight into the stem of a thin white chalk column near the roof of the cavern that split apart and as it did so in turn, smashed into and loosened a giant upside down crown of stalactites hanging directly above the two giant bat-like creatures. The chain of fast moving events took over as stone spear stalactites began raining downward and onto those in their pathway below. Melek was the first to have the foresight at what the consequences might be and quickly dragged Richard towards the cliff wall directly under the perching stones used by Enlil and Erna in order to try to protect himself from the onslaught of falling debris about to arrive.

"Whaaa!" Again Richard had broken Orkan's golden rule of keeping his mouth shut.

Above their position Enlil and Erna tried to escape but it was too late, their spread wings and bodies were suddenly pierced through by these falling stone spears, one particular stalactite catching a necklace worn by Enlil and snapping it loose it fell. The missile attack was so strong that the pair in total panic, and with their bodies and wings badly damaged, flew straight over in trying to get away from this constant barrage; but as the heavy weights took their toll on them, they dived headlong into the boiling cauldron and for a very short time seemed to calling for help and then were gone.

"Whoa! Another evil destroyed?" The debris field from the carnage was almost at an end; it formed a large semi-circle and now was reduced to only the lighter material fragments such as small bones, feathers and a necklace dropping down from above their heads. "Wait! What's that? Richard tossed back the cape and took a step forward only to be held back by Melek.

"Wait until we're sure that it's over." With that warning, a round flickering crystal fell to the ground and started rolling towards the central inferno. Richard tugged to free himself in order to stop it from disappearing forever. Melek held him fast and suddenly there was an almighty crash overhead and the main crown crashed down teetering on the edge of the cauldron yet stopping the pod from rolling any further, Melek released Richard and with a deft flick of his wrist the golden rope shot out and looped around the pod. Concentrating on the pod and not wanting it to escape, he slowly began reeling in the object while Richard stretched out his arm and collected up Enlil's fallen necklace. The thing began to flicker then glow brightly and Richard began walking towards the lip of the fiery cauldron, his arms now hanging limply by his side, one hand loosely holding Enlil's necklace. Melek looked up and saw the boy as he pocketed the retrieved pod.

"Now all of this is 'MINE!' You slaves are all 'MINE!' This empire is all 'MINE!' Nobody shall take it away from me!" his demented ravings screamed to the unseeing, uncaring mass of bodies before him.

"Oh no you don't!" Melek shouted as the golden rope snaked out again, this time ripping the necklace from Richard's grasp. With another flick of the wrist the rope and necklace shot out over the centre of cauldron and Melek whipped it back, the necklace dropping like a stone. As it hit the boiling liquid the whole place began to shake furiously. Before settling down again, Richard turned and looked at Melek, the demented look gone from his eyes.

"What? That must been some sort of aftershock, I think the volcano could be getting ready to blow, we better get out of here." They headed off to find their companions; noticing that on their way towards him that all the beasts were acting strangely; tossing their bundles away, shouting, not wailing and this unnerved the pair,

"Told you I would come up with a plan, what did you think of that shot?" Orkan boasted.

"No time to talk now, make for the stairway." Richard in the lead they headed for the tunnel and the pile of rocks concealing the entrance.

"They're starting to follow us." Melek looked back in concern as an enormous bear turned and began moving in their direction. "Run!" They followed the winding track along which many beasts seemed to be acting differently. They covered the distance quickly but now behind them and following the bear's lead, it was becoming a moving mass of bodies in their wake. They reached the stairway and simply raced as fast as they could upwards and towards what they knew was the huge cathedral in the hope of finding an escape route that they had possibly missed on their way into hell hole. They could make out voices shouting below.

"Gghhh! They're still following us; I think they could be seeking revenge for what we have just done to their masters? Orkan puffed as they spilled out of the tunnel back into the ornate hall "Look for an escape route, there must be one somewhere because Enlil captured these people from outside and brought them here somehow, he would route he used to get to the outside, let's find it." They half walked, half jogged towards the large gateway at the other end, also knowing full well what lay beyond it.

"They're coming!" Melek shouted as he saw the hall begin filling with an assortment of wild beasts pouring from the void in increasing numbers from way down the back of the hall. "There are just too many of them to fight, we don't stand a chance." The little group reached the huge steel gate and realised they were now trapped and turned to face the vast tide of beasts moving down the hall towards them.

"Gghhh! At least I will take a few down before the kill me." Orkan drew his trusty sword and then kissed it. "Be true." Richard unsheathed Juroot's dagger.

"Need to tell you this first, your arrow missed the bats and was too high," he nervously joked patting his companion on the shoulder.

"Gghhh! That was my plan, one arrow, two foes, one would have come for me, that's why I shot at the column, I knew that the soft chalk because would not withstand the force of my arrow and would fall onto that stalactite crown above their heads and it did."

"Really? You meant that to happen that way?

"Well, I wasn't quite sure that it would turn out the way it did but then again they were slow leaving their pedestals and that was their downfall."

"The Chosen One also played his part, if he hadn't of shouted and momentarily distracted them, they would have possibly had time to make good their escape, you both worked in unison." Melek angelically declared as he flicked his golden rope towards the approaching beasts led by the bear-like creature. They all stopped short a little way in front of the small band, each seemingly stretching their heads to gain a better view of the small group.

"Gghhh! We will fight to the death if you take another step" Neither group dared to move a muscle for fear of activating the fight but both sides were ready even though none of the large group seemed to have anything but timber clubs. The bear turned his back on the gateway and held his arm aloft, the muttering instantly stopped.

"The warrior is Golan's assistant." A loud cheer rose from the group as he turned to face Orkan. "I somehow knew that we would be rescued from Enlil and today you have achieved that for us all." Huge cheers again erupted. "I am Sarkel from the forests near the Tree of Life. I have seen you accompany Golan through our woods. When Enlil's curse was suddenly lifted from us, I thought that it might be you and that's why we followed you. We are your friends and of no threat to you, in fact if there is any way we can assist you, please just ask."

"Gghhh! You are correct, I am Orkan and we are on a quest to locate the missing guardians and the pods of life."

"Enlil had a pod of life that he never let out of his sight; he kept it on top of a pile of our friend's bones to demonstrate what was to happen to us all." The crowd murmured their disapproval.

"You mean this one?" Melek took it from his tunic and held it aloft, there was an audible gasp from the ever growing group." No my friends, we wrested this away from your captors and also destroyed Enlil's magic necklace." The crowd cheered loudly.

"That necklace was pure evil, it was what Enlil used to put us all into some form of trance, he just had to wave it once and we somehow became helpless slaves of his, Erna was the worst though, she enjoyed our predicament and would kill in the most horrific ways possible, at least Enlil did not kill for fun. Good riddance to them both and now we can return."

"The world outside as you knew it has changed, there has been a battle between good and evil. Many of your family would have been involved and may no longer be there, you said the word return? Is there any way to that except through this gate? Do you know what lies beyond?"

"The hounds of hell on the other side, but do not mind them, we can tame them and in answer to your second question, there is only one way to the outside world that is through a small door in the middle of the building and a stairway to the top."

"We saw no doorway when we examined it." Richard chipped in. The bear turned and looked at him but suddenly there was a murmur as a great big horned beast pushed its way to the front of the crowd. It made a wild grab for Orkan and lifted him up into the air while making a very loud bellowing noise. He then gently placed Orkan on the ground.

"Gghhh! Do not be afraid, we have at least achieved one of our tasks successfully for this is Broon, leader of the Common Beasts and one of the missing Guardians." Orkan stated proudly. "This is the librarian and that is..." Broon slapped Orkan on the back and turned to his followers.

"See this boy's eyes they are different colours, he is the Chosen One that we have been waiting so long for." The large animal hoisted Richard into the air in order that everyone, including those all stationed down the long hall could see what Richard looked like. "If there is to be another battle, we will need to prepare ourselves for it, down here. We are now safe from all enemies, we have the heat, we have the steel and between us we do not yet have the weapons to fight but with all that material available we can make the required weapons. Who is going to help to fight this evil spreading through our land like a plague?" As one voice, everyone screamed their allegiance as Broon hoisted Richard onto his shoulders and began heading back towards the centre of this great hall. Sarkel the bear-like beast did exactly the same by swooping a protesting Orkan onto his shoulder to follow Broon through the multitude and a Centaur like beast did the same to Melek, the whole place was now like some sort of festive street party as the beasts hooted, hollered and cheered the parade moving down the centre. On arrival at the centrally beautiful decorated stone column, the three were led to what seemed like just another panel surrounding this monstrous beast filled, larger than life realistic sculptures.

"This hidden door takes you into the volcano smokestack and there is a stairway that winds its way around it all the way to the top of the mountain and is the route out of here and to our outside world," said Broon as he grabbed hold of a carved tongue of one of the smaller decorative statues and pushed it into the mouth.

"A hidden door? No wonder we couldn't find an escape route, that's brilliant. Richard moved forward and was not surprised at how warm it was as he looked up at the stairway heading upwards. "Wow! That must have taken years to carve out?" What he could see took his breath away for inside the column was another central column with the carved out stairway leading upwards and the walls on both sides of the stairwell were the most intricate designs of life.

"It has taken an extremely long time and cost many, many lives within our Beast Community. We shall not dwell upon that though, evil is dead so let's be festive." In no time whatsoever music began to be heard, the beasts began dancing their own dances others served up food to the travellers like hard boiled eggs, fruit, milk and even mead.

"Where does all this food come from?" Richard enquired having had the first decent meal since his arrival.

"It's from Enlil and Erna's private hoard. That's why the central fires must all be kept burning, heat is sent to the underground gardens, aviaries and crèches, to them life was cheap and Enlil was developing and generating his own slave community because on each raiding party there were less and less beasts to capture out there. His main problem was the fuel required, they had denuded the mountain and surrounding forests so was experimenting with huge forested pits built in alongside the volcano where you rescued us all today.

"I'm so tired, there is going to be a lot of noise in here, do you think we could sleep in there?" He pointed to the bottom of the stairway.

"Gghhh! Speak for yourself young man Melek and I are not about to let this opportunity go to waste are we Melek? It's been so long since we had the chance to enjoy a moment like this." Melek simply shrugged his shoulders at Richard as Orkan pulled his away towards the dancing crowd.

"You rest now," said Broon closing the panel and suddenly the noise was shut out as the panel closed, there was some light filtering down from above somewhere as Richard used his bag as his pillow. He lay down and for a while took in the wall characters and the last thing he remembered was them seemingly detaching themselves from the walls above him.

Man Eating Plant of Death

On the Ninth Day...

The growth, the fumes,
Beware the foe. The hungry fire
Never tires. See - it boils.
The flame. The soil.
Death believes in leather leaves.
Foes explode. The brave are slowed.
Danger waits where water flows.

"Whaaa?" Richard's startled awakening was due to his night of haunting nightmares because there were several beast faces now situated and surrounding him, the nearest being the one with huge horns. An automatic reaction kicked in as he fumbled to find Juroot's dagger.

"You slept soundly young man." Richard blinked several times as he began to realise that it was Broon gently shaking him.

"Broon? I had some terrific nightmares."

"After all you have been through lately it is little wondering but it is time to move, let us go and wake your friends." Richard arose and followed Broon and his associates back to the main hall where they found Orkan and Melek still asleep.

"Your companions will not be very clear headed today, too much mead and dancing I fear." Broon quipped. Once everybody was up and had some light refreshment, Sarkel the bear appeared and whispered in Broon's ear. "It would seem that certain members of our kind wish to present you with a token of their gratitude." Broon then declared loudly so that all could hear, then he waved.

Three Orang-utan looking animals made their way through the assembled crowd and each took up positions in front of the three companions. Each then held out a mail-linked shirt as Broon stepped forward and lifted it over each of them in turn.

"Wow! How cool is this?" Richard gently touched the silver vest it was so light and pliable to the touch because it had the consistency of gossamer. "Thank you so much."

"Our people made these while you slept but, do not be deceived, they're made of finest spun metal that will withstand all weapons. We felt that it is small reward for what you did to release us and those will hopefully help you along the way with your continued quest. In the meantime we will use this place to quickly prepare ourselves into an unseen fighting force and then like Juroot and some of the bird forces, we too will make our way back to Golan and the Ancestral City.

"Sounds very much like that is our invitation here is to now leave." Melek whispered to the others. Broon and Sarkel walked them to the stairway's entrance then bid them farewell with rough salutes.

"We'll meet again before this is all over I'm sure. Go safely and good fortune to you all." With that, they both retreated and the large panel was closed behind them.

"Gghhh! What festivities and methinks it's going to be a long day, we perhaps overdid that lovely mead a little," an overhung Orkan said, rubbing his head all the while as they made their way up the long circular stairway to the top of the volcano funnel.

Once they reached the top of the rim they had an unbridled view stretching out a long way. Below them the entire volcanic mountain slopes seemed almost devoid of any vegetation, while the immediate surrounding areas were covered with greenery.

"See, that's what is left of the Ancestral City." Melek pointed towards what to Richard looked like a grey mass far in the distance. "Our travels have brought us a long way don't you think?" They started off down the path finding themselves passing by brittle, charcoal- tree stumps and had almost reached the base when there was an eruption of sound to their left that immediate sent shivers through all of their bodies. It was the noise of beating on shields, barked orders and fierce yells that they already knew very well and was coming from not that far away.

"Gghhh! This way." Without waiting Orkan shot off their path and scurried straight towards the nearest cover, slipping and sliding in the muddy eroded soil as he raced headlong downward. The other two followed as best they could and Richard even stopped twice to assist Melek when he went tumbling past him but they made it to the sheltered area behind some rocks.

"Gghhh! Over there!" Orkan pointed to what was a ferocious battle. "Cozards verses Grapfrits, not your usual fight, evil against evil."

The Cozards had used their battle formation by forming a tight box behind their shields and were making serious inroads against the swarm of attacking Grapfrits. "If we try to make the forest it might just attract their attention? Let them fight and when they are distracted we can decide whether to risk the rest of the open ground."

Spiky flying balls probed and prodded at the Cozard's tight defence occasionally one would make it through under the shield and suddenly from underneath a huge bellow would be let out as the Cozard was attacked. His companions simply pushed each lone Cozard out of their ranks to face the Grapfrits alone and quickly drew their shields closed.

Each time a lone Cozard was hoisted away from the group the Grapfrits then concentrated an aggressive attack latching onto the now defenceless prey, their razor sharp needle noses digging into the flesh around the face that fell in like a punctured balloon. At the same time shields opened slightly as long swords flashed cutting some of the low flying Grapfrits neatly in half.

"Uggh! That's disgusting." Richard said as he watched the carnage between the forces play out. There did not seem to be any winners as Cozards fell and were attacked on masse and had their blood sucked out of them while hacked and bits of Grapfrits kept hitting the open ground and flapping about like headless chickens in the midst of this violent struggle. "Think I'm going to be sick, they are all busy, we should not even be here, let's make a run for it."

Orkan nodded, the three moved away towards the safety of the forest still quite a way below where they found themselves slipping and sliding down the bare mountainside.

"What do you think those could be?" Richard pointed toward several bronze-tinted mounds with what seemed like massive clams above and runners that had all been pushed up between the charred and dead stumps of cut down timber.

"Gghhh! Never seen anything like that before, they look like some kind of leather plant but let's be careful."

The slope of the hill meant that they could not head left because of the battle that side, and to their right there was a deep trench of washed away soil erosion that would be almost impossible to negotiate, the loose and inclined sand behind them meant no going back that way. The only option was to keep heading towards the humps between them and the safety of the forest but as they got nearer Richard's throat tightened as he realised that these were plants but very different from anything he had ever seen before. The whole area between them and the forested safety seemed to be pockmarked with larger necked flowers trimmed with saw-like teeth and lots of tentacle type above ground root systems spreading outwardly away in all directions from their base.

"I have a bad feeling about those weeds, isn't there 'any way' we can skirt around them?" Melek asked. "We should have stayed on that path."

"Gghhh!" They're just plants, I will cut them to pieces." Orkan drew his sword and moved forward slowly with the others close behind. There are signs of combat about these strange looking plants, look at that one over there, if my eyes do not deceive me there's a set of beast's claws between those tooth-like jaws, what say you?

"I think it's time to check with the Book of Prophesies before we take another step. Melek declared unstrapping the big book. "Perhaps it will reveal something about the plants to us before we go barging in simply thinking that they are not dangerous foes." He read out the riddle.

> *The growth, the fumes,*
> *Beware the foe. The hungry fire*
> *Never tires. See - it boils.*
> *The flame. The soil.*
> *Death believes in leather leaves.*
> *Foes explode. The brave are slowed.*
> *Danger waits where water flows.*

"Hmmm, leather leaves must mean these plants but that is not much of a clue? What really worries me is that there are bones scattered everywhere." Rather than watching the big plants, Richard's eyes scanned carefully through the piles of debris surrounding each plant, He was paying attention to the tendrils in particular. "Doesn't that look like a Cozard's helmet? I'm certain that could even be that Cozard's armour, those snake like roots are moving I think. See that brown oozing stuff coming out from the armour? I think those roots are still somehow feeding from that Cozard. Ugh!" Richard withdrew Juroot's dagger just in case. "I think these plants are alive and could be feeding their roots that could even be their own macabre offspring. Watch out for the roots, those are the true huntsmen here, I reckon they are the dangerous ones and it's not these large flowers."

"Gghhh! I think there is something in what you think, I just do not trust any flowers that seem to have teeth and house a jaw, that one to the right has something's tail dangling from the mouth. We must find our way through this maze somehow, let one of them even try anything, this blade will have them prostate with one cut.

Just then an odd cat-like beast with spotted fur scuttled across in front of them, it stopped near the Cozard's armour and turned to inspect the trio with huge saucer shaped eyes. Richard could not help noticing that as it did so that there seemed to be a slight flurry of movement from the tendrils behind the animal's back.

The first root that touched it gave it such a fright that it half jumped toward the open mouth of one of the flowers. It turned and again inspected the group; its whole body was quivering with fear and anxiety. Richard looked at Orkan who simply shook his shoulders.

"That thing is too nervous to be in league with the Evil One."

Suddenly the plant threw back its flower head sending the strange looking animal to the inside of its mouth and its leathered jaws clamped partially closed like the bars of a prison gate. To Richard it looked something like a large bird swallowing a fish. Before his companions could prevent him, Melek sprang forward and raced towards the plant's stem and managed to jump up to grab its helpless victim by the tail, he tried dragging it out but found that the grip of the powerful jaws were just too powerful. Richard looked at Orkan, who simply shrugged, then Richard made his decision to help him, he turned and looked towards the plant and was horrified to see Melek clambering up and over the plant's partly closed jaws.

"Melek! No! It's some kind of trap, get out of there." But, it was already too late as he raced to the plant and grabbed his by the feet but the plant had already got a firm grip of his upper body.

"Help Orkan!" Richard screamed at the top of his voice as the plant began to go into its bucking motion again.

"Wheeooee! Wheeooee!" Richard felt the extra weight of Orkan

Whatever this plant was now it carried them easily dipping and bucking and soaring upwards towards the sky in an effort to shake off the pair of hangers on as well as to suck Melek deeper into its mouth bowl. Richard felt Orkan's release then the plant came to a standstill and the boy turned his head to see Orkan hacking his way through several tendrils that had crept up on both of them. There was a muffled scream from within the bowl by Melek almost drowned out by the fizzing, hissing sounds as Orkan easily carved away a path through the active roots trying to attack them.

"Quickly help me, these flowers are flesh-eaters, they are just like enormous Venus fly-traps that I once saw in a science lesson.

"This is not science, this is reality my friend." Orkan was wildly hacking at the plant's stem that was defending itself by releasing some sort of toxic gas towards the pig-like boy each time his sword found its mark.

It dawned on Richard that his action was almost futile by his hanging onto Melek's feet this way, the plant was just too powerful, he tried stabbing into the things mouth with Juroot's dagger but, the plant reacted in turn by defending itself and squirting forth a foul smelling gaseous liquid out of its punctured orifice while trying to repel its attacker.

Richard let go of Melek's legs, he heard his plaintive yelp from inside the bowl but he had a plan.

"Orkan leave that and help me collect anything that will burn."

"What for?"

"Trust me just this once, we're losing this battle and I think I know how to combat this thing by science." Orkan stopped his battering and quickly moved across the path he had made collecting up twigs and leaves. "Here, we need that stuff piled up right against this thing." The two quickly placed their motley collection of debris against the flower's stem.

"Fire! We need to light this stuff." Orkan picked up a flint rock and placed his sword deep into the tinder dry stuff they had just collected. Richard looked up and saw that Melek's legs had already moved a little deeper in towards the back of the plant's feed-bowl. His muted cries could hardly be heard any more

"Hurry, that thing is beginning to devour Melek."

Orkan struck his sword with the flint and a shower of sparks fell directly on to the dried tinder, he did this several times then kneeled and blew hard into the glowing mass, the flame automatically took hold and began lapping up the stem of the giant plant.

"Stand back." Orkan grabbed his sword and moved away as Richard withdrew Juroot's dagger once again. "Just hope this does what I think it will." Several quick motions of stabbing through the rising flames brought the desired result; the plant defended itself by hissing out its gaseous protection.

"Yeah! All right! Who's da daddy!" Instead of harming its attacker the protective gas ignited with huge ferocity that it was as if somebody had discharged an incendiary bomb in their midst. It blasted a huge gaping hole out of the side of the plan's stem, which in turn leaked a liquid that began burning ferociously. The plant's flower flopped forward and opened its powerful jaws. Orkan immediately jumped up and dragged Melek out of the things flesh-bowl mouth and away to the comparative safety of his pathway.

"Ugh! They stared as the bewildered librarian unstrapped the book from his back and began inspecting the sodden acid covered book carefully; he looked at his companions and said nonchalantly, "That chain mail vest actually seems to work." His face was covered with huge blood red circular welts almost as if he had been attacked by a swarm of giant mosquitoes. Each ring red on the outer rim with what looked like a puss filled brown central dot.

"Gghhh! Any longer and you would have been turned to soup I think"

"The little beast, did that also escape?"

"I'm afraid not or I haven't seen it. Are you OK?" Richard placed a comforting hand on his shoulder. "Let me have a look if the beast can be rescued." Richard saw that the raging fire had taken firm hold and was burning fiercely and that the plant was leaning over at a precarious angle, the head almost pointing to the ground in front of them.

"Gghhh! Too dangerous to try and get inside that plant." With that Orkan gently drew Richard away from the about to topple plant. Then it happened, the fire and blast had created a hole in the stem just too large for the heavy flower head to carry on standing and like a tree being felled, it simply flopped down, bounced once or twice and the deed was done, it was officially now deceased. On the ground in front of them the now harmless plant laid there, its vile mouth open by the force at which it had hit the ground, releasing some of its slimy content. Richard saw the movement and walked to the slimy patch and thrust his hands into it. He lifted out a weak, dripping, spotted cat-like feline out of the mess and laid it on the ground next to Melek.

"It's almost dead."

From somewhere Melek produced a cloth and wiped the muck from its battered body. Another gas explosion from below their feet seemed to immediately rock them all back to the present. The raging fire was now descending downwards and into the base of the plant, looking around they noticed that a ring of creeping tendrils had also begun hissing and some were now sprouting small fiery nozzles. Just then, there was another huge explosion from the next flowering giant.

"Oh-oh! We have got to get away from here. Now! I forgot about the root system. It must all be linked together somehow and this place will shortly become one gigantic fireball." The second big explosion also seemed to revive the little beast and sent the dripping feline scurrying away. It stopped, turned and as to thank them nodded its head from side to side then headed off up the hill towards the volcano. "Forgot about the root system, it must all be linked together somehow and this place will shortly become one gigantic fireball."

"It will survive, I can't help feeling or wondering if that beast was sent to watch our progress and report back to Broon? Something tells me he is going back to join the beasts." Melek watched the little thing scampering up the slope as he strapped the book onto his back. "Right, I'm tired but ready."

Orkan quickly led the way down the hill along the line of the soil eroded crevice while trying to stay clear of the main flowers and chopping through any tendrils trying to block their path to safety while behind them more and more of the flowers were now exploding.

"Gghhh! How did you know that fire plan of yours would work?" Orkan hacked at yet another root.

"I didn't. When I stabbed the plant in the mouth it defended itself by squirting gas at me and it was just like a smell of petroleum, that's something we use as fuel from coal where I come from. It then triggered the idea that these plants could be using the fossilised trees as their protective defence by creating a liquid substance or a gas to protect themselves. That was my gamble and luckily it worked, what I didn't bargain on is that all these plants seemed to be linked together so this whole area will soon become a huge fire storm."

"Wisdom? Without your knowledge we would have lost this battle. I am beginning to see why they call you the Chosen One. I don't think that the Cozards or Grapfrits will be able to reach us, because they will try to investigate the noise and smoke" Orkan could see that the rivulets of fire being passed between the tendrils was moving at phenomenal pace down the area towards the forest and the explosions were now becoming more frequent in its intensity.

"Cozards!" Richard pointed to the far side of the strange flower field, his companions could make out the troop racing down the hill and in their direction ducking and diving to avoid the giant flowers where the fires had not reached. "We're too exposed up here. Faster, it's our only chance."

They moved as fast as Orkan's swinging sword would allow but also kept an eye on the fast moving Cozards. Richard then saw his ultimate nightmare start appearing in the skies beyond the ensuing Cozards. The Grapfrits were flying above the fires and smoke and were also heading towards the little group. Richard's eyes scanned the hill and the forest as he turned to look down at the deep gully below.

"There's water down there now." Further up the ravine there had been nothing but a very deep and dry soil eroded valley; but from somewhere the gully must have come into contact with a large underground spring that over time had forced soil down its valley and then silted and built up further down to create a dam of sorts. The only problem was it was a long, long way down a slippery soft and sandy sheer drop. He could see that the Grapfrits had just about caught up to the fast approaching Cozards but that their aim was not aimed at the soldiers but this was more like a race to see which team could reach the little group first.

"Fire Storm, Cozards and Grapfrits all heading for us, we don't stand a chance do we? Melek said. I think our good fortune is about to run out. Richard turned to his faithful amulet and it began to glow.

"Golan if you could help us in any way now is the time." His eyes searched for something to give them a chance to escape but there was nothing. Just then, there was a huge explosion, Richard turned and realised that the cause was that several flowers had exploded simultaneously causing the monumental eruption to balloon a mushroom cloud skywards and the best part was it had been exactly where the Cozards had been.

"Wooooeee! Down, get down!" Orkan screamed.

"It's like an Atomic Bomb." Richard dropped to his stomach using a small ridge as cover because all he saw was flaming Cozards, burning bits of them and their armour, together with bits of lurid plants that came hurtling by in every direction as the very strong hot blasted wind, caused by the explosion, streamed across the whole area and passed by them in an instant. The companions dared not move until being sure that the danger had passed, the whole area now seemed to be covered with fire and smoke accompanied by a series of loud explosions sounding off at constant intervals. Just then there was a series of clattering and clashing sounds all around the trio, Orkan jumped and began swinging his sword furiously.

"Gghhh! Grapfrits!"

Richard rolled away from Melek and onto his back and was astonished to see a sky now filled with flaming and exploding Grapfrits above their position. A loud crackling filled the air as a squadron of injured, blazing and critically damaged Grapfrits passed by overhead, their wings beating furiously in an attempt to escape the carnage all around.

"Watch out! A flaming Grapfrit came plummeting down towards the group only to have Orkan swing his sword and split the thing in two, the two halves bouncing away down the hill only serving to set the tendrils alight and within seconds passed the fire one to another

"That means trouble, when that reaches those flowers the explosions start going off, we're truly trapped now."Let's try to follow those injured Grapfrits, they will know the way out. The three jinxed, leaped and dodged their way past the active roots with the surging fires not far behind giving chase, the main problem that the same fire was also racing in from their left and there were signs that it had begun to take hold in the area directly in front of them, even the ground all over now seemed to be on fire as plants and roots spewed the foul juices everywhere. Richard again looked to his right at the gravel pit filled with water to assess their chances of remaining alive if they needed to jump from that height into it. It was too far down to even contemplate what he thought would be a suicide attempt so he simply followed Orkan and Melek, knowing full well that they were fast running out of options to survive as the fires closed in from all sides. Orkan stopped.

"Gghhh! No use." The fires and exploding plants seemed to have the upper hand and would surely engulf the trio before too long. The smoke swirled all around them and down into the large valley below so that Richard could no longer even see clear daylight anymore

"There is a way, but it will be like jumping from the pan into the fire and we may not survive."

"Gghhh! Any death is better than being burned alive and I want to die fighting, what's your idea?" Richard explained about the dam and mentioned that it could be very shallow and that it was a very long way to drop. Just then the swirling smoke spiralled and turned in the wind and Golan's face appeared in the dark haze and seemed to drop down towards where Richard knew the lake would be.

He moved between his two companions, grabbed each of their hands and stepped forward to the edge of the long drop. Behind them came yet another huge explosion of several plants, this was the biggest yet; Richard knew they only had seconds to react before the searing hot winds arrived to cook them alive.

"Jump!" Richard screamed, nobody needed a second invitation as they leapt into possible obliteration.

Witches and Wizards

On the Tenth Day...

Landing from the witches brew,
In spellbound lands of fear.
Battle nightmares, one then two,
Ending three in crystals clear.
Revoke the spell - the book will tell
Testament's beginnings see.
Add four elements, make a spell.
Say the word that sets them free.

Although somewhat protected, they fell like stones and in their mid-air plummet heard and felt the superheated force of the after-blast pass above their heads as flame, plant debris, Cozard and Grapfrit parts shot out towards the other side of the distant valley ridge. It had passed with such ferocity that it both pushed the smoke into a huge vortex while at the same time sucking up everything it could in its wake, including the three companions.

"Hang on to each tightly!" Richard screamed above the roar as they began reversing their intended direction of downwards travel and started shooting upwards and outwards towards the centre of the dam.

"Yah! Yah! Yah! Orkan screeched at each violent buffeting of the heated windstorm that they now found themselves part of. "Gghhh! Gghhh! Going down, hold on."

The fierce wind suddenly released its powerful grip and again from somewhere far behind and high on the ridge there was yet another almighty thunderous explosion. Richard looked down and in this mayhem made out a wide line of the dam's water had also been affected by this maelstrom and was still being sucked up directly towards them in a large white and angry looking hurricane type vortex.

"Hang on, we're going in" Melek's plaintive cry was the last thing the others heard as they were collected up by the force of the rising wall of water as it spun, pushed and pulled at their bodies. Richard suddenly had the thought that he now knew what it was like to be stuck inside a washing machine in full cycle spin mode as they were whirled, spun and bounced around the outer fringes of this torrent yet they were still managing to hold on to each other.

"Gghhh! Gghhh! Going down again, hold on."

As quickly as the water had risen to meet them in the wake of the powerful after blast, now it had passed and the grip between speed of the wind and rising water had been lost and the liquid vortex began slowing as it lost its power. The three dropped gently back into the wall of water then as it receded back downward, gathering speed, from his earlier encounter Richard soon understood that the column of water above them would also be like a giant stepping on an ant once they hit the dam surface, he just knew he had to escape as he felt them being sucked deeper and deeper towards the central part of this vortex. Richard kicked his legs as hard and as long as he could hoping to get himself and the others to a spot where they could at least breathe.

"Ahh! His head popped out of the wall of water and he took in the biggest breathe of air that he could then pulled with every bit of strength he could summon up to get his companions into the same position.

"Gghhh! Nothing good about water." Orkan spluttered after taking in a lifesaving gulp of the warm air.

"Aargh! Look down, we are about to die." Melek screamed as the water wall dragged them around still spinning itself and the companions furiously fast. Their heads had appeared out into the circular centre of the water walled vortex that went all the way from top to bottom and below their position they all saw a huge nothingness but a deep black void leading right down to a muddy dam bottom and the cyclone was now slowing. "No wait, we are going to be all right."

"Gghhh! Gghhh! Going down yet again, hold on everyone." As the high wind energy strength quickly dissipated, so the wall of water began to fall into itself closing up the central air column below the three companions and the whole water storm started to collapse and fall in on itself forcing everything from inside the hole through the wall to the outside. To Richard this now became like surfing a wave or sledging down a snowy mountainside as the three shot out of the wall, dropped a little way then slid on their bellies down the long slope of the disintegrating mayhem behind them.

"What a ride, can we do that again? Please?" Richard imploring laugh more out of relief than anything else. Richard tried getting his bearings but, unlike being high up with an overview of the area now by being down at water level it was far more difficult, his only point of reference being the top of the volcano. "Looks like we have lost ground backwards towards the volcano and I guess we are now only about a third of the way so let's try to reach that side. It won't be as sheer as one we've just come from. Here Melek, let me help you." Richard could see that the librarian was struggling because of the added weight of the book on his back.

"Thanks but I will manage, just don't go too fast because I won't be able to keep up if you do" Melek panted doing a sort of dog paddle. After a short stint Richard saw another wind from the last explosion rocket high above them.

"Oh-oh! You don't often get what you wish for? Another wind means another vortex, lock arms again." No sooner done than the water began churning all around their bodies then it suddenly began to rise high into the air. The group were fortunate to find themselves right at the heart of this new vortex and dropped down through the centre to hit the now almost dry stony bed of the dam.

"Ouch!" Richard looked upwards, everything was calm, no wind yet surrounding them was this huge circular wall of water stretching skywards.

"Look, a cave entrance." Melek pointed to his left and sure enough he was right, a bluish light filtering from its entrance. "Come on before that wind-wall comes tumbling down again, we will be drowned." The three raced to the entrance and once inside they could see down the long and upward crystal lined passageway.

"Gghhh! Go! Go!" Orkan took the lead and at a trot began their ascent to safety and towards a distant but much brighter lighter that they then presumed would be taking them back to the outside world once again. "Gghhh! There's something wrong ahead." Richard looked past Orkan and saw that the crystal walls at the roof suddenly seemed to be contracting inwards towards the centre and that the passageway now looked triangular in shape ahead. Looking back towards the dam exactly the same thing seemed to be occurring and the passage looked as if it was shrinking.

"The tunnel's closing up," Richard shouted. "Run!" They stumbled along chased by a gritty sounding rumble as the passage steadily squeezed shut in their wake. "This way," Richard grabbed Orkan, for there was a narrow opening to their right, and their path to the light had shut enough to figure out that something was happening ahead. Richard turned into the only opening they had come across pulling Orkan and when he looked back saw that Melek's big book had been nipped by the closing walls. He rushed back, unstrapped the book, gave him a push and twisted and bent the still sodden book until it came free. "Almost lost it and we couldn't have that, could we?" Melek smiled and strapped the book onto his back again as the entrance snapped shut completely. Richard got out his torch and scanned the place they now found themselves in.

"Gghhh! Now what?" They took quick stock of their situation, it was a cave, it was fairly dark except for the feint green glow given off by several wall crystals and there were several large boulders blocking their way and although it felt and looked drier than the passage they had just vacated, it had no exits that anyone could see just then. "There aren't any decent hiding places around here and I think we're trapped." The tunnel floor suddenly came alive. Creeping from the large stones towards them, rustling twitching, crawling; a brown messed carpet interspersed with red dotted flickers was slowly and steadily moving forward as the three moved backwards. Richard's torch showed the sea of thousands of rats before them. "Where did they come from? Never mind, we have a fight on our hands, if you still have Juroot's dagger use it." Orkan whipped out his sword and Richard the dagger.

"Orkan they are coming from behind those rocks, that must lead somewhere don't you think?" Melek queried.

"Like the roots before, I will cut a path through this mass. Follow me and do not trip up otherwise they will swarm over you and you will be finished." Orkan's soldiering temperament and training came to the fore as he jumped forward slicing and slashing at the horde of rodents with Richard and Melek following close behind and protecting his back.

"Gghhh! Never say die until you're dead, head between those two large rocks when I say so. I have rodents with a passion. Brrrr!" For every one Orkan seemed to kill, another immediately took their place and there just seemed no end to the moving mass ahead of them. By torchlight Richard suddenly noticed that each time Orkan's sword lashed out slicing through a rat, its corpse seemed to start vanishing, not all at once but slowly, until there was nothing left. Looking behind he saw that the cave floor pathway Orkan had made so far was hazy with ghostly shapes that were becoming fainter and fainter, until they popped out of existence altogether. Melek saw this same thing happening.

"The rats are just some kind of cruel illusion, remember the prophecy spoke about nightmares. I think this is what it meant. They aren't real, they are only some sort of figments of our imagination."

"Oh yes! I am slicing through my imagination all right... They're real enough to me." Richard stepped forward and stood alongside Orkan.

"He's right and there's only one way to prove it." Richard dived towards the brown furry mass that turned tail and fled back behind the rocks like a boiling wave of brown fur. "See? Melek was correct and we must learn to trust each other's judgement." Just then there was a noise behind him interspersed with strange scraping sounds. From behind the rocks and into their field of vision appeared the largest rat any of them had ever seen; it was more the size of a medium sized dog than a rat. "OK! We have a giant rat instead of many rats." Richard got to his feet; in one hand he had the torch, in the other, Juroot's dagger as he slowly backed away towards Orkan and away from the huge rodent now steadily stalking him.

"Gghhh! Don't panic. It's simply an illusion. That is a great impression of an unreal rat don't you think?" Orkan said sarcastically.

If it was an illusion, Richard thought to himself then they needed to burst it like a balloon. Lifting the dagger he flung it straight at the giant rat's blood red glowing eye, the aim was accurate in helping the dagger find its intended mark and it sunk right to the hilt. The creature showed no pain or emotion nor did it scuttle away but instead, it swelled; bigger and bigger between the rocks until its insides finally burst under the strain. Blood slopped from its now open mouth and the two enormous incisors dropped to the ground before it exploded in thick clouds of yellowing smoke.

"Yes! It was just an illusion".

The smoke began to clear and the three now found themselves in the same cave that had somehow transformed itself and was now lined entirely with glistening crystal walls. Small beads of condensation ran down the carved surfaces that added an extra dimension of light to the whole place. A magnificent tall woman dressed with flowing robes of shimmering blue stood to one side of a glowing throne of flickering prisms. She was tall, icy but looking very statuesque and somewhat extremely cold with her multi-faceted pointy headgear made from white crystalline set against almost translucent pale skin

"Whaaa? Who's that? She's gorgeous."

"You have done well to get this far," she hissed "but this is your journey's end and you will go no further."

"Who are you?" Richard asked bravely.

"I am Zibella, the all-powerful," she boomed, as she raised her hands and began to chant.

"She uses a strange language that I do not fully understand but there are some words that I do know and they sound like she is making a spell of sorts." Melek whispered quietly.

"W-wheeooee! I do not like that. I have heard tell of a witch and her curse but I thought it was Mirrah who was the witch?"

"Who, or what's that?" Richard wasn't sure in his mind what was going on as the chanting voice kept repeating.

"It's the high priestess Zibella. She scares me." Melek whispered again.

"High priestess of what?"

"As far as I know she makes spells and changes things into insects and such." Melek replied.

"You mean she's a sort of a witch?"

"Witch, ...sorceress, ...night-hag, ...chantress, take your pick, any name will do. All I know is that she's the high priestess. Her magical powers are legendary throughout the Ancestral World."

"Is she going to harm us and what did she mean by we will go no further?"

"I'm not sure, some say she does good things while others say she's all evil. All I know is that everyone fears her powers. Witches, as you call them are part of this world, but unlike the things you've seen so far, they are in all worlds."

"What do you mean?"

"Wizards and witches are shunned by most people and whenever calamity or misfortune of any kind befalls anyone, they immediately find a scapegoat and blame it on somebody whom they suspect of having some form of sorcery or magic powers. As you've already seen this world is different with its demons, spirits and ghosts, but wizards and witches take the blame for most inexplicable happenings in this world."

Richard was slightly mystified by Melek's answer.

"Adsuma! Aba Absurdo! Brutumi Fulmena! ...Here! Now! Forever!" Zibella stopped her chant and then pointed her hands toward the companions, a blue flash shot out of the end of her fingers.

"Whaaa!" The blue streak seemed to enter their bodies and Richards's legs suddenly became very heavy and sweat now poured from his forehead as streaks of cold. Blue light lanced them from Zibella's fingertips. Richard went to draw Juroot's dagger but found himself unable to move or react in any way and the cave walls seemed to be receding very quickly as if suddenly the crystal walls of this sparkling cave were growing at terrific pace.

"W-wheeooee!" Richard noted that Orkan's screech tone now sounded very high-pitched, it reminded him of the time when one of his friends had inhaled a deep breath from a helium balloon. Looking at Zibella sent cold shivers through his whole body for she and the cave weren't getting bigger, the full realisation hit him that 'they were growing smaller'.

"Help!" Melek croaked. Richard looked at his, to his utter dismay he was turning a sort of greeny yellow and becoming wartier. He then checked on Orkan, the same thing was happening to him but the thing that he also noticed immediately was that his companion had now developed... long webbed-feet!

He inspected it through unbelieving bulging eyes, his own mouth had suddenly become dry from fear as he tried to wet his lips he saw the thin black tongue lick out. It was his tongue! He blinked, and then he hopped. That strange movement took him completely by surprise landing on all fours and seeing the two frogs before him. One was busily scrambling out from beneath a large book while the other seemed to be full of anger and frustration and that's when Richard knew for sure what Zibella had meant about going no further.

"What's happened to us?" Both Melek and Orkan spoke at the same time.

"The witch has transformed us into frogs," Richard replied, forming the words with great difficulty.

"Well at least I won't be able to grunt anymore," Orkan replied almost stoically.

The entire cave was filled by a booming cackling sound and Zibella walked behind her bright crystal throne and was gone, leaving the companions in her wake all struggling to come to grips with their own predicament and sudden awkwardness. Orkan was hopping, flipping and flopping about uncontrollably and Melek was still struggling to get out from under the big book.

"Golan, please help us," Richard implored croakingly. He noticed that one panel of the crystal wall suddenly glowed brighter than the rest; in his own mind this was some sort of sign from the guardian and then the panel dimmed again to match the rest of the cave's crystals. He looked over to the struggling Melek and the large book and for no reason whatsoever, the words 'Book of Reversals' popped into his head.

Just then Melek broke free of his book and sprang forward landing on all fours directly in front of Richard.

"Can you remember the prophecy?" Richard asked his immediately,

"Of course," the Melek-toad croaked back and awkwardly began belching out the words of the riddle

> *Landing from the witches brew,*
> *In spellbound lands of fear.*
> *Battle nightmares, one then two,*
> *Ending three in crystals clear.*
> *Revoke the spell - the book will tell*
> *Testament's beginnings see.*
> *Add four elements, make a spell.*
> *Say the word that sets them free.*

Richard immediately seized on one particular line, "Testament's... Beginning... See! That must surely 'mean something'?"

"It does!" Melek gave a little hop, "Join the first letter of each line of the riddle and it makes up the word 'LIBERTAS' " Melek made another hop, "What is another word for libertas?"

In unison both Richard and Melek spoke as one, "Freedom!"

"We must locate this Book of Reversals, it's got to be in here somewhere?" Orkan had now settled down and was mastering his newly acquired status, he still showed some anger, puffing himself up to resemble himself more as a bullfrog than the more petite Melek who Richard felt was more toad-like. "We search in different directions but keep within calling distance of each other?" The three split up and moved across crystal-covered floors. It was Melek that found the book hidden behind Zibella's crystal throne hidden among several loose crystals.

"It's going to be tough getting that book out of there." Between them, they managed to lever the book from its hiding place by rolling several shards away then Orkan levered the book on one side while the other two used their powerful hind legs to push the book onto a level surface. It took a while to open the book with great difficulty then took turns flipping the pages until eventually finding the spell they were seeking. Melek read out the lines to his companions.

LIBERTAS
Glean by the Fire of Candlelight,
From Earth a crystal, sparkling bright.
Dip into well Water, a droplet lingers there,
Which turns to a bubble and rides the Air.
Your mortal self awaits the time to rebel,
Shout LIBERTAS
And break the sordid spell.

"That's what the last two lines from the Book of Prophesies was trying to tell us, it all makes sense now?" Melek gave his little excited hop.

"Maybe to you it may mean something, not to us it doesn't. Please translate," Orkan demanded angrily.

"The riddle is saying that we need to find four different elements in order to reverse the spell." Melek snapped back.

"Does that mean 'any' four elements or specific elements? As far as I can make out that riddle simply describes only three elements, Fire! …Water! …Earth Crystal! So where is the fourth element?" Richard queried.

"We are the last element, when we see the bubble, we all need to shout the word 'LIBERTAS' to break Zibella's spell. Don't you see?" Melek was becoming a little frustrated.

"Of course!" Richard replied. "The three items are all already here; the glow behind the throne is that candle that increases brightness through the crystal prisms, the heat of that candle also causes condensation that drips from the walls making a pool of water. It all makes perfect sense now, we first need that candle."

"Let's do it," the impetuous Orkan sprang towards the candle but still not in full control of his faculties or powerful back legs bounced straight into it and tipped it over. It rolled and fortunately bumped against a blue crystal shard knocking it into a small pool of water. Although accidental, the three watched as it hit the water and a perfect, rainbow-coloured bubble broke the water's surface and floated upwards.

"Shout Libertas!" Melek screamed.

"Libertas! ...Libertas!" All three shouted and as the word left each one's mouth so the spell began to simultaneously unwind and Orkan grabbed both of them out from their position under the throne. Crystal walls of the cave seemed to immediately close in at terrifying speed with a subtle noise that sounded like holes were ripped through the very air itself. Then as quickly as it had started all was quiet.

"W-wheeooee! We're back to normal," Orkan shouted with glee.

"Must collect the book, "Melek gave one of his little hops and jarred his ankle, then turned and pointed toward the front of the throne. "Zibella!" An enraged Orkan shot around to see the witch calmly relaxed in her place of authority.

"Gghhh! Turn us into frogs would you?" He made a dash for his items still lying on the cave floor and in one movement, swept up sword, bow and quiver of arrows. Turning he placed an arrow in the bow and in that microsecond to release the arrow, Zibella lifted her hand and red flame shot directly at Orkan.

"Silly Orkan!" she screeched. Orkan reacted almost as quickly spinning to his left the flame missed his head, hit the crystal wall and bounced back heading directly for the throne and Zibella who in turn caught it in the palm of her hand drawing it back and releasing it at Orkan again. Orkan had already drawn a bead on the witch and fired, when arrow and flame met in the centre, Orkan's arrow was deflected and missed Richard's ear by a hair's breadth while the deflected red flame hammered into the floor with a thunderous roar, Orkan went for a second arrow only to see Zibella changing from icy beauty to old hag, her laughter was also changing and she now gave out a haunting cackle but she was fading away.

"The Book! Get the Book!" Melek implored.

"My bag! It has the pods in it." Orkan lifted both bag and book and slung them across his shoulder and as he did so, there was a tremendous cracking sound from the floor. He spun around towards the cave that suddenly resembled crazy paving that began separating as the floor started to disintegrate around his very feet. The widening cracks then began breaking at their edges quickly becoming crevasses that tumbled and fell in on themselves. Crystal columns started teetering and falling and above the sound of the crashing shattered rock, the crumbling bedrock of crystal walls and the large falling boulders rang out the high-pitched, clear screeching of Zibella's demented laughter.

"Gghhh! Made it," Orkan skipped, jumped and hurdled across the cave reaching the throne to be with the others. "Now what?" All the while the psychotic laughter persisted ringing throughout the cave.

"She's having a joke," Richard shouted pointing out a shadowy hologram type image of Zibella that began appearing on the far side wall but instead of the icy beauty Zibella's transformation was now complete and what they saw was simply the old hag witch. Orkan handed the book to Melek then drew another arrow. "Don't waste your arrows on her Orkan, she's just an illusion."

What they witnessed was the true Zibella with thinned hair shrunk back to the scalp, her eyes were like two blood red opals, her skin gnarled, withered and drawn into hollows and even her fabulous gown had disintegrated to old rags. The cackling started disappearing as she started fading away leaving simply a shadow of grey in her wake. There was a small puff of black smoke as she disappeared completely but, the whole place was still collapsing around them.

"This way!" Richard shouted jumping over a yawning narrow chasm in the fast diminishing floor, Orkan and Melek were right behind as Richard began scrambling up a narrow gully that had been hidden from view behind the tall throne. "I think there's an opening ahead, let's hope so and that it's not also disappearing."

For a while they pulled, pushed and scraped their way through the narrowing shaft. In the rush to get out of there their arms and legs were having bits of skin removed and the tunnel seemed to be almost impassable in places but somehow they got through until they reached a split in the rock where it then widened out.

All the while the noise of crashing boulders from behind seemed to be following the three up this incline.

The Evil One's Servant

On the Eleventh Day...

Ties that bind release the one
In deepest darkest thrown.
The shortest length can longer run
By faith and faith alone.
In desert lands beneath the sun
Power of steel and weight of stone
Defy. But when the day is done
Mountain berries split the bone.

They reached to top of the incline, Richard checked to see whether there was anything but all he saw was that their escape route had led them to yet another cave. Orkan crawled up next to him helping Melek to join them. The sound behind was becoming louder with each passing second.

"Gghhh! what do we do now?"

"Well, we can't go back. There's only one thing to do, that's to move forward and be ready for trouble." They extricated themselves from the narrow opening and stood up. "We were like moles back there, if that tunnel had got..." Orkan had heard it too.

"Did you hear that and I bet its Zibella, she's tricked us, I told you that I didn't trust her." Melek whispered. Coming from somewhere much further into the cave they had clearly heard what sounded like the murmuring of voices and loud screaming from a distance away.

"Let's see who's in the cave and whether they're friendly. Let's go." Richard took the lead and the wide-eyed pig-boy was almost stuck to Richard's back as they moved slowly down the narrow passage towards the continuous blood curdling screams. No sooner had they entered the main body of the cave when from behind came a thunderous whoomping sound. All three jumped and Richard could clearly see that the area they had just exited from was caused by that split in the rock that had slammed together and tightly sealed that area.

"The cave is widening." Melek said

"Wheeoo...!" Richard immediately turned on his companion who now held both hands tightly clamped in front of his mouth.

"Shut up will you? Do you want to tell everybody that we're arriving?"

"Gghhh! It's not my fault. I can't help myself, it just happens and there's nothing I can do about it."

"Then keep your hand over your mouth. Surprise is the only element we have on our side and you're going to blow our cover if you persist with those silly shouts of yours."

Orkan looked down at his feet then up at his companions. He pretended to zip his mouth shut, "Gghhh! I can but try."

Richard felt a little sorry for the now forlorn looking pig-boy and placed his arm around his friend's shoulder. This simple action seemed to somehow strengthen their resolve to face any unseen opposition.

"Right, let's go and tackle this new enemy." They steadily moved forward round the next bend onto a lip of the place that opened up into yet another large cavern.

"Gghhh! Maybe we're back where we started is this Zibella's cave, or at least it looks like it could be a similar place" The whole place sparkled with crystalline walls around the outer perimeter but this time his soldier's eye picked out a strategic strongpoint placed in the middle of the large area. Maybe it's not but she cannot be trusted."

"Look to the left of that mound there is some sort of movement down there isn't there?" Richard couldn't quite make out what it was.

They moved cautiously down the slope towards the large central mound, Orkan with an arrow all ready to fire in case they ran into Zibella once again, he was not prepared to be caught off guard as had previously happened. Once they reached the edge of the mound they moved to the left where Richard had seen signs of movement.

"Gghhh! Hold it," Orkan raised his hand, Richard and Melek both peered around the side of Orkan's broad frame and were astonished at the sight of two almost identical pig-like men seated astride, digging their trotters into and hitting what looked like a horse down on its haunches. From this rear view position of the goings on it was not quite clear what was happening except from the yelps and groans they fully understood that the horse was suffering badly at the hands of the two.

"This could be a trick or even an illusion but what they are doing is not right" Melek whispered. From their slightly obscured position all that the companions could make out was that the poor horse was completely finished and the two were having none of it.

"Gghhh! I hate bullies, they are too busy to notice us, let's give them some of their own medicine." Orkan moved fairly sharply, racing across the open ground around the mound. Melek shot past Richard and as they reached the group Melek's hand flicked out sending the rope in lasso over the top of the two horsemen that were instantly dragged off what looked like a horse from Richard' perspective.

"Woooeee! Now pick on someone your own size," Orkan stood over them, sword having replaced his bow and arrow. By the time Richard arrived at the group Melek already had the two bullies trussed up like Christmas turkeys and Orkan was busily threatening to decapitate them.

"Wait Orkan," shouted Richard, "we need questions answered and they may be able to tell us more about this place?" He moved closer in order to get a better view of their bullying captives adding with a naughty wink, "then you can take them to task."

"Gghhh! I so want to cut them into strips, that's what these two deserve. What were you two hoping to gain by treating that poor horse so badly?" Orkan demanded roughly snatching at Melek's rope and turning their faces up.

"Woooeee!" Orkan released the rope and almost staggered back a step. "These are landsmen that come from the same place that I do." He gestured furiously toward the two on the ground. "We are soldiers, not bullies, you have no right nor have you been trained in that manner. What's wrong with the two of you?" Richard had not ever seen his compatriot lose his temper before; it was not a pretty sight as Orkan began kicking out towards the two.

Richard and Melek turned away knowing that they would not be able to interfere as Orkan, although very angry with his own people would be the only one to know what punishment had to be metered out to the couple of bullying pig-like men.

"No! It's not their fault, it is mine. Let them be, they are not to blame!" The companions turned to face the voice behind them coming from the horse now struggling to get to its feet.

"Oh wow!" Richard exclaimed realising instantly that this was not just a horse, it was half-man half-horse. "You're a Centaur aren't you?"

"Untie my companions please," The beast almost implored. Now that they could see the beast properly it was Richard that first noted the large bloody gash on the things front quarters.

"How did that happen?" Melek pointed to the nasty looking wound.

"Escaping from Klaw," came the simple reply.

Melek coiled the rope around his middle and moved across to the beast withdrawing a cloth he began dabbing and trying to clean the wound, "This needs attention and rest to heal properly."

"You are 'Orkan of the Truculents' are you not? I recognise you; you are a legend among our people." One of the bullies spoke out.

"Gghhh! On your feet you two, if you try anything I will make good my promise," Orkan was again becoming upset but Richard had not missed the question from their captives and decided that now was not the time to question his companion. Instead, he went across to Melek.

"What are you all doing here?" Richard asked the fascinating creature.

Outside there is nothing but desert and we were attacked by Klaw and his soldiers, the two on the ground are all that remain from that battle. As you can see I was wounded and they helped me escape and we found this cave but, we are all in danger because I think this is Klaw's personal dungeon. There is water but no food that we could find and I grew weaker. Those two, by beating me were trying to keep me from going to sleep and passing into oblivion. I do not think I can survive much longer without any form of nourishment. Without their help I would simply have laid down, gone to sleep and already have passed away into another life."

"Here eat some of these, they contain mountains of sugar and could help," Richard took a packet of soft sweets from his bag removed several and handed them to the centaur who gobbled them back.

"They taste very good and I'm sure will help for a short time. Thank you" the mild mannered beast offered in the hope of more.

"There, your wound has been healed," Melek stood back admiring his handiwork. Richard could only gape, the terrible gash had disappeared.

"How... How did you fix that so quickly?" He stammered.

"That special cloth had help from this," He opened the cloth to reveal a pod inside, "That's how it worked its magic, it wasn't me."

"A pod? Where did you find that one?"

"Let's just say it came from Enlil and the pod found me shall we?" Melek smiled triumphantly. "You were too preoccupied at that time to see it so I kept it safely wrapped in this cloth."

"You carry on looking after it then, do not lose it we need them all." Richard turned back to half-horse, half-man, "What's your name and where do you come from?"

"I am Chiron the eldest and wisest of the Centaurs, from the tribe of half-horse men and half-brother of Zephus. It is said that our tribe of Centaurs were spawned on Mount Pelionotto by a cloud nymph. We have never been a warring tribe so many of our kind were slaughtered during the Great Battle. Also, because we are known throughout the land to have always been great teachers, we mentored many of the great heroes of myth. We had never seen evil so did not know what was happening. Without your help that wound was incurable and unbearably painful because I think that Klaw and his army tip their weapons with hydra poison. Parts of our tribe called the Kheironetes, also known as 'skilled with the hands' as your young companion knows full well, because he bears those same skills in being able to save me as he did." Richard's mind did not miss that comment either as he realised just how important both his friends really were.

"Right that's cleared that up, you said something about a dungeon?"

Just then a heart-rending scream for help seemed to come from within the mound in the middle of the cave. They weren't absolutely sure because the sound reverberated around the walls.

"That's the third time we've heard someone scream, it might be coming from up there." The Centaur offered. "I was too weak to find out and my two companions refused to leave my side so we just don't know."

"Gghhh! That scream was a genuine cry for help. You wait here, if it is a trap then try to make your way to the Ancestral City and tell them why we did not return."

On climbing the slippery mound all three found themselves peering down into a seemingly bottomless blackness below their feet.

"Orkan, something down there strikes me as odd."

"Please don't say that."

"Look down there, there are spikes blocking the way. Hallo down there, how deep is this hole?" Richard hollered into the shaft. As they looked down they could see that the protruding spikes were sharpened then Richard also noticed that they laid out in a spiral formation.

"Those spikes form a trap, climbing down is practical because you can use them as a stairway but once down you cannot use them as a stairway to get out again." Melek offered.

"Why do we always invite trouble in this way? Hallo down there!" Richard shouted again.

"Hallo! I don't know how deep I am. Please help me." The voice floated up even as Richard was pondering their possible options.

"What are we to do?" Melek questioned. "I doubt whether your rope is long enough to reach the bottom."

"I wonder if your book might give us any clues?" Together they scanned the book.

Ties that bind release the one
In deepest darkest thrown.
The shortest length can longer run
By faith and faith alone.
In desert lands beneath the sun
Power of steel and weight of stone

Defy. But when the day is done
Mountain berries split the bone.

"That says it all, I believe it is long enough to reach the bottom. You are the smallest so Orkan and I will keep hold of the other end so if I am wrong we can pull you up again?"

"All right we may have one chance at this but please, hold on tightly." With a flick the end of the lasso rope shot over his two companions and Melek tied the other end around his waist. "Remember not to pull me back up too quickly because those spikes sharp sides are facing downwards to prevent anyone from escaping." Melek stood on the edge, shuddered and then before losing his nerve began to scramble down following the like of the intricate spiral. The whole way down he questioned whether he could help the person below or was it a trap, was the rope going to be long enough, what if he could not get back out because of the sharp downward facing blades on each spike. The only thing that allowed his to continue were the words 'faith and faith alone' he then realised that the rope had stretched and that the prophecy had been correct.

"There's his signal, let's get him out, gently now." Orkan and Richard began a slow hand over hand rope pull.

Below Melek slowly made his way around the spiralled knife sharp spikes resting periodically as he steadily moved upwards through the blackness with an unknown weight. Melek thought the climb down was difficult but this upward travel was fast sapping every ounce of energy he could muster. At last he heaved himself and his cargo over the top of the rim of the deep shaft and collapsed totally spent onto the ground.

"Oh, Thank you for saving me." The voice whispered into his ear as the two lay panting and trying to catch their breath.

Melek simply nodded as he rolled over to see what or whom he had risked his own life to get out of the hole. What he saw surprised him, for it was a very large wasp-like beast struggling to its feet, the leg slightly damaged.

"Thank you again, I am Covelette, the Guardian of Insects. Klaw, the Evil One's servant, captured me. He stole my weapons and threw me into that dreadful pit to die; thank goodness you got me out."

"We rescued another guardian," An excited Richard gave Orkan a slight bump.

"Couldn't you have flown out?" Melek panted still recovering from his climb.

Covelette then unfurled a pair of transparent, gossamer-thin wings, "Those spikes?" he said. "You cannot fly very far if your wings are torn and in ribbons. No I tried to escape by climbing but this damage to my leg was caused by those spikes and that weakened me very badly."

"Right," Melek pulled himself up and quickly coiled the rope around his middle before strapping the book onto his back. It now seemed heavier than before his rescue mission.

"Now, tell me who you are," Covelette said turning his large, glittering eyes on each of them in turn.

"Gghhh! Let's get off mound first, up here our silhouettes stand out." Orkan and Richard helped Covelette down the steep mound until they reached the weak Centaur and his two companions. Richard explained that they needed food before being able to carry on. Covelette did the most extraordinary thing by producing many blue white pellets onto the ground, much like a hen laying eggs would do.

"These are extremely nourishing and very filling," She said picking up several and handing them to each in turn. "Eat, they will sustain you." Orkan tossed his to the back of his throat, swallowed and rubbed his stomach.

"Gghhh! Delicious can I have another please?" With his approval everyone then tried the egg like pellets and soon there was a nod of approval from all. "I would suggest you share the rest amongst yourselves for when times are bad. One of these will abate your hunger for several days, that's how I managed to survive for so long. Now, even though wounded I can help you but first, I need to know who you are?"

Richard took it upon himself to explain their mission and what had transpired on their journey to date not forgetting to tell her that Juroot and Oganga were now alive. All the while Melek tended to the nasty wound on Covelette's leg.

"It's cleaned up well but it does not seem to be healing as did Chiron's wound." Melek gave Richard a quizzical look, "Perhaps the pod has lost its power?"

"No, I think that the pod you used is meant for beasts." Covelette said. "I am an insect, not a beast and therefore you need the pod that tends to insects. Unfortunately, it was taken from me by Klaw and taken to the Sand City."

"Sand City?"" Richard was intrigued.

"Yes, it lies at the far end of the desert sands and it won't be easy getting the pod back from there because Klaw will do everything in his power to stop us retrieving it but at least we must try. I will guide you to the Sand City."

"Gghhh! You three have food and water, try to get back to the Ancestral City and report to them what you have seen today. You make sure that no harm befalls Chiron as his skills will be needed, otherwise I will personally see to it that your lives are forfeit. We grow stronger as each day passes now, we need to get to this Sand City." Orkan commanded authoritatively, he pointed at Richard and Melek. "You two will carry Covelette, this will leave me free to defend us from any attacks made by Klaw. I look forward to doing battle with this bully."

"Do not wish for something you may later regret," Covelette advised unwinding a belt from around her waist and handed it to Richard. "Take this, its powers will help you when you most need them." Richard took the belt and it fitted him perfectly and as he snapped the buckle into place he felt an unexpected flow of strength pass right through his body.

"Hey! That's so cool maybe I will turn into a Supa Ranger?" Richard gently helped the wasp-like creature onto his back and was quite taken aback at just how light she seemed to be. "Let's go." He gave Chiron and his companions a sort of salute, "Be safe and let good fortune guide you." Following Covelette's guidance, he and his companions made their way through various tunnels until they eventually emerged into the open.

"Gghhh! Now that is a dry patch of desert." Orkan said as he gazed across the barren land. All they could see was a huge stretch of emptiness of sand and scrub before them being blown by a hot harsh wind, sending tangles of tumbleweed scurrying across the forlorn landscape.

"Orkan hand me your bow and arrows." Covelette commanded.

"Gghhh! Why? I never let anyone use them."

"Trust my judgement I would not ask if there was not a good reason," Covelette declared.

"You are a guardian and I will obey you but, it does not feel right." Handing the items across Richard could see that Orkan was not well pleased as he begrudgingly released his weapons to Covelette.

"Look to the distance, you can just make out the outline of a city on the horizon. We have a difficult and journey in order to reach the Sand City." Covelette said and stepped off in brisk fashion taking the lead. They trudged on wearily finding the desert with its soft sand both tiring and hard going but none of them faltered until they eventually reached the high sand dunes created by the continuous winds and could no longer see their goal.

"This is where I must leave you for a while." Covelette said spreading her wings and flapping them to raise herself above them like some form of hovering helicopter. "Keep your direction and try to stay on course and also, do not travel on any high ground because you will be seen from further away." With that she shot off.

"Wait!" Richard shouted but Covelette was already too far away to hear his plea. "She's tricked us and taken one of Orkan's weapons. What now?"

"I think she has a plan in mind. We go on and stay away from the top of the dunes." Melek said quite adamantly. They headed along the gullies and to check that they could with an occasional stop, to locate their bearings that they were still on course. Richard realised just how dangerous their situation was because every now and then their path became blocked by a sand dune so they climbed to the top and used the ridge to gain the position before diving over and getting themselves to start traversing the next gully. Several times both he and Orkan had to assist Melek when his knees began to buckle.

"You could hide an entire army here and we wouldn't be any the wiser unless we came upon them by luck? Not very much further to go," Richard stated apprehensively as they rounded yet another sand dune. At least we know what our goal is but whether we achieve it is another matter?"

Orkan halted at the bottom of the next gully and was about to speak when an ear-splitting laugh hammered at their eardrums.

"Up there!" Richard pointed to the sand ridge ahead of them and what he saw was a sight that sent his heart careering down into his boots.

"Gghhh! Klaw," Orkan said, "This is where my bow and arrow would be handy."

Silhouetted against the sky was a figure wrapped in a torn black shroud. From his horned helmet and his skull-like face to his feet, there was not a scrap of flesh to been seen? The entire creature, even the spear that he brandished aggressively above his head, looked as if it was made of bone. Klaw was living up to his reputation; he was truly a menacing sight.

"We've got to get out of this gully," Orkan cried. "Run!"

"That's right scared little rabbits, run!" Klaw's harsh rattling voice rang out contemptuously. "See where it gets you I am on your trail and you cannot escape my wrath." Suddenly his hand was full of bones, small chunks the size of knuckle joints, that he raised above his head then flung into the sand. "Nobody ever escapes my army."

"Oh-oh, trouble," Richard looked back and saw something that again almost made him freeze but he managed to overcome this fear. "Klaw's building his army." What Richard saw was Klaw's action and then watched in horror seeing a forest of skeletal-like full-grown warrior type army simply sprouting at extraordinary speed from the area where Klaw had just distributed his bony type pebbles.

To Richard's untrained eye they all seemed to be smaller versions of their raging master. Each held broad shields, carved out of bone into identical images of skulls and in the other, each clutched short, long, thin-bladed swords of bone.

"Go my children, bring me back their heads!" At Klaw's command they banged the swords against the shields in unison then started marching purposefully down the side of the sand in the direction of the companions.

"Get back up the hill!" Orkan barked, hustling the others to higher ground while keeping a weather eye on Klaw and his advancing troops. He saw Klaw's hand go back preparing to throw something amid his weird crackling evil laughter. His arm shot forward and pebbles rained towards the little group through the air and landed all around them but, these were not pebbles that landed in the sand, it was more of his fast reacting and growing army into newly grown skeletal warriors. Their only avenue of escape was back through the gully, but Klaw's bone-men were a step ahead of them and broke ranks to fan out at both ends of the gully blocking their last escape route. They were well and truly surrounded by a dead army.

"Gghhh! Nothing left but to fight our way through." Orkan swished his sword at two approaching soldiers and with a crunching sound. The headless bodies teetered a few steps then tumbled down the slope. "We have a possible chance because they're not as strong as they look. Take heart my friends." Forming a tight group with Orkan in the lead, his renewed confidence allowed him to cut a wide swath ahead of the companions. The battle raged as the knot of ferocious combat drifted along the gully Richard using Juroot's dagger, Melek, his rope, they formed a strategy of sometimes moving up the side of the dune to gain advantage all the while leaving a trail of bones in their wake. The only problem were the numbers facing them, there were just too many and as they were thinned down more pebble bones were hurled in their direction by the evil cackling Klaw from his position at the top of the ridge.

"Gghhh! My arm!" An unfortunate fluke stroke from one skeleton glanced across Orkan's arm leaving a sizable gash, but not deterred, he changed hands and continued his fight although found the going was more difficult than and not as effective as he began slowing. Melek seeing his discomfort moved to his side, his rope was doing as much damage as was Orkan's sword as he repeatedly flicked it out like a trout fisherman at work, the looped end gathering in around several soldiers at once then, with a hard yank of the rope left several skeletal heads bouncing around in the sand. His rope was very effective as he cast it out time after time. The only problem that Richard could notice was that this slip of a girl too was beginning to visibly tire.

As if on cue, the horrified watchers saw Klaw hurl more bone pebble towards the dune at the end of the gully that made a team of ghostly skeletal horses complete with soldiers appear that then moved together in unison to a point ahead of the small fighting band where they came to a halt.

Richard's eyes scanned the area looking for some way out of this gully filled with opposition intent on just one thing but, after quick assessment he understood that there was none.

With cold clarity this spectacle made Richard jump once again as this gully clearing quickly becoming filled with this repulsive-looking group of horses and riders that he immediately recognised would now constitute extra hazards. The skeleton-men were all mounted and awaiting the word from their leader to charge.

"What is happening? Richard watched as suddenly all Klaw's soldiers stopped fighting and took several backward steps leaving a wide ring between themselves and the companions.

"Gghhh! Look at Klaw, I think he is coming down to finish the job." Richard saw that the skeleton leader and several others were bounding down the side of dune, his voice now having taken on a much harsher tone than before. "He probably wants to handle the coup de grâce himself but I will fight him to the end so be ready."

Klaw muscled his way through his soldiers pushing them aside as if they were nothing but strips of paper. "You may have released the guardian from my dungeon but, I won't lose you." He screamed as he entered the open space between the little band and Klaw's troops. His speed took them all by surprise as he grabbed Melek and threw his roughly to the ground, in a second lightning fast movement he used a double-headed axe that he had collected along the way from one of his troops with such speed that with one smashing blow, he knocked Orkan's sword from his hand. He quickly pushed the deflated Orkan to the ground before turning his attention to Richard. He stared at him for a while through darkened eye sockets that revealed nothing, Richard didn't have to see anything but certainly felt waves of hate flowing towards him.

"So, it is as forecast? You are the Chosen One?" Klaw snapped at Richard as he lifted the large axe above shoulder height, "Maybe we lost a guardian but this day hasn't been wasted after all and I do not intend keeping you alive for much longer. Your life will ensure that good disappears forever." He took a step towards the now terrified Richard who was sure that this was to be his end but for some reason the belt Covelette had given him gave him strength and the lightweight vest from the beast's added confidence. He gripped Juroot's dagger tightly and slipped his hand into his pocket and found his torch.

"Right, we're all born to die someday and I suppose if it is my turn at least I won't end up a nasty, hateful skeleton like you." He suddenly hurled the dagger at Klaw who was not expecting any form of retaliation and desperately tried to avoid the missile that caught him on the cheekbone between his mangled teeth and black eye socket ripping the bone apart and leaving Klaw with a gaping hole in his face.

"You have spirit, I give you that," Klaw said taking a few of his bone pebbles into his bony hand and rubbing them across the holed cheek. As if by magic the dark hollow seemed to be mending and closing up again. But now! You die!" Just then, Richard's head began to spin wildly and became filled with a high pitched whistling noise, he became very certain this was his moment to be killed by Klaw and that he was about to meet his maker as Klaw again lifted the large axe and prepared to rain down a death blow. In one last attempt to do something, anything at all, and in a feeble endeavour to show bravery or try something different he shone his torch straight towards the evil skeleton.

The Scorpion Men

On the Twelfth Day...

Mirage city in the sand,
Out of sight but close at hand,
Hides the fairest in the land.
Corridors of staring eyes
In streets of half-forgotten sighs
Lead them to the golden prize.
Travellers fight pincered might,
Cobra's Keep a dark surprise

The whistling in his head became much, much louder only to be immediately followed by an almighty thud, crunch with some squelch thrown in; to his mind it somehow reminded Richard of the noise made when someone steps on an enormous beetle. Instead of striking out a look of astonishment seemed to pass over Klaw's features, then almost as if Richard was watching something being transacted out in slow motion, Klaw rocked forward, then backwards as the heavy axe slipped from his grasp falling into the dust without sound. Klaw swayed for a few seconds, before toppling face up into the sand where his entire body just seemed to disintegrate into smaller bones except for his now bared ribcage.

"Whaaa!" Richard could not believe his good fortune, he had come so close to death and now it was his tormenter being the one to die. "How?" He glanced towards Orkan who pointed towards the sky.

"Covelette you didn't desert us." She was hovering like a helicopter directly above his head and the gentle fluting sound that Richard had supposedly heard inside his brain now became abundantly clear, it was the sound of her fluttering wings making the noise.

"Did you really think that?" Covelette asked disappointedly as she landed next to him and folded her wings away. "I needed to get hold of a rare poison, I knew it was the only thing that could kill Klaw but, the plant does not bloom anywhere near here and that is why I left." She handed the bow and arrows to Orkan. "That served us very well." A crackling sound from along the gully filled the air as Klaw's soldiers began toppling over and also started breaking up.

"Look! They're all just dying." They watched in horror as the large force of warriors, with their leader now dead, began simply disintegrating all around them to become just lifeless bone heaps. The group watched in awe until at last the whole area had settled down to become a massive white field of crumpled white bone corpses.

"Wow! That's awesome; I 'really' thought my time had come. You saved my life, thank you."

"There is one thing I must first do," Covelette hobbled across to Klaw's ribcage where the arrow had found its mark piercing deep into the rotting mass that had been his heart, where now an evil-smelling yellow ooze was seeping into the sand. Covelette ripped the arrow from its position and tossed it to Orkan, "Be careful with that arrow it remains very poisonous at the tip, one scratch will mean sure death, keep it safe."

"Here, wrap it in this then you will know which it is," Melek handed Orkan a strip of cloth.

Wrinkling her nose against the stench, Covelette began searching Klaw's remains, even digging in among the foul soft tissue within his ribcage. At last she discovered what she was looking for, a delicate string bag containing a finely wrought blowpipe together with a bundle of needle-sharp darts. "I think we are now ready to face the Sand City, I can fly but as yet am unable to walk any distance so, will you again help me Chosen One?"

"Certainly, it would be my pleasure to carry you once again, compared to what you have done for me today it is a small task, I will never doubt the actions of an ancestral guardian again. He hoisted her onto his back and once more led the way across the expanse of sand.

"I thought deserts were always supposed to be hot, the wind has swiftly become so cold," Melek complained. Covelette sniffed at the oncoming breeze and caught the smell of electricity mixed with a hint of burned rock.

"There's going to be a desert storm, I can sense its arrival." Covelette mentioned quietly in Richard's ear. "This open area is not a good place to be in when the storm arrives." They trudged on as the light began fading, the cold wind picked up and specks of sand started to painfully blast their skin. It did not take long for the wind to rise to a howling shriek as it became a ceaseless torrent of sand and desert debris drilling straight at the little group that were ill equipped to withstand the building headwind ferocity.

"This is going to be far worse than I thought. Keep your heads down and mouths shut and do not look up because the sand blast will only scour your eyeballs in a moment." Covelette screamed trying to be heard over the noise being whipped up by the arrival of this storm. They did as ordered as they shuffled along in single file each with hand grasped to material of the one in front to avoid losing contact and becoming detached from the rest of their party. Each footstep was laboured as the ferocious wind swirled, moved and occasionally fell quiet only to come sweeping through again. Step by step like blind lepers on a pilgrimage they moved slowly towards an unseen goal, the only one seemingly to know their direction of travel was Covelette who endlessly guided Richard's unsighted advance.

"Is that it?" Richard asked the wasp-like creature during a lull in the storm as they topped a high sandy ridge. For the first time in quite a while it seemed as if the storm could be somewhat abating and blowing itself out. Ahead he saw the change in scenery, as the ridges of desert sands seemed to level out to reveal a blurry haze of what looked like at this distance a mass of yellow, sand-coloured buildings surrounded by a single high fortressed wall,

"We have reached Sand City," came the reply from the guardian.

"Then how come we didn't quite see it properly before? It's big enough to have seen it, sandstorm or no sandstorm?"

"Maybe you are seeing a mirage and it's not a city at all." Melek joked.

"No, what you thought you saw before. All those ridges going off into the distance, was really the mirage." Covelette explained, "Sand City has been here all the time. Great camouflage, wasn't it? Klaw and friends didn't want anybody finding it so created this confusing figment of imagination desert to fool us. Klaw, the sand, debris and desert wasteland were all real enough but, clever enough for most people to give up and turn away. The storm was the last obstacle to stop us, now we are through that and there it is in all its glory.

"Gghhh! Without you, none of us would have made it. You are a true guardian" This was a rare occasion that Richard had heard Orkan make a sort of apology

"We have had an arduous journey to get to the Sand City and we are all tired." Covelette looked directly at Melek. "I think that before we move on we should have a rest in the bottom of that rocky gully, now eat the pellets I gave you in Klaw's dungeon and then sleep for a while, we are going to need all the strength we can muster. I do not require much rest so will keep watch over you while you regain some of your energy." They moved to the sloping gully and Richard helped Covelette onto a small outcrop above their position where she could keep a lookout towards Sand City. Within moments, after eating the pellets, the companions fell into a deep exhaustive sleep.

Covelette dozed from time to time and when she was certain that they were all soundly asleep, manoeuvred herself off the ridge and moved to Melek's side. She coughed up a spit ball and as gently as she could, wiped the oily substance over the librarian's face that was still badly pock marked with red and brown welts before struggling back to the ridge. When she felt the time was right, flapped her wings into a drumming sound, a startled Orkan came awake in an instant, jumping up, sword already in hand before realising where he was or what had woken him.

"You are a true warrior Orkan." Covelette commented. "I noticed that you sleep in spasms, something that I too do."

"Gghhh! That is because we are different to the humans. Is it time?" Orkan asked. Covelette simply nodded and the pig-like boy proceeded to gently waken Melek then Richard. "We must get to Sand City before Klaw is missed."

Refreshed and eager the little band set off towards the featureless land below that began flattening out nearer to Sand City. On one of the last rock outcrops they halted to survey the buildings and imposing windowless walls noting that the place was only accessible through the large single gateway that was guarded.

"It's going to be difficult getting in there, which cuts out the element of surprise." Richard thoughtfully voiced.

"You are right, take a close look at the six guards, they're scorpion men and they are deadly." Covelette reflected.

"Oh-oh! Look at the size of them, their pincers are bigger than me." Richard said, horrified by the six creatures protecting the gate. "What do we do now?"

"The Book of Prophesies may give us some idea" Melek suggested taking it off and turning pages until he found the right passage.

Mirage city in the sand,
Out of sight but close at hand,
Hides the fairest in the land.
Corridors of staring eyes
In streets of half-forgotten sighs
Lead them to the golden prize.
Travellers fight pincered might,
Cobra's Keep a dark surprise

"We have to enter the city, you all wait there." She took off and using the contour of the surrounding area flew as fast as she could and just out of sight of the guards. On her way around the place she noticed that a small part of the giant wall had cracked and toppled leaving a big enough gap for them to pass through. Flying in a wide arc she returned and reported back her discovery.

"This means a longer march doesn't it? Rather that than mixing it with that lot." Richard answered everyone's thoughts. They skirted the gullies and ridges around the city, eventually arriving at a spot directly in front of the crumbling wall. "Looks perfect, did you see if there were any scorpion men inside?"

"None that I could see but we must be on our guard, I'll keep watch from here and if you hear the sound of my wing flapping change in any way it will mean danger. Now you must go first, followed by Melek and then Orkan. "May fortune be your only guide."

Richard went off making himself as small as he could by running in a crouched position until he reached the pile of fallen sandstone. He gave them a thumbs up sign before scrambling his way through the wall opening. Melek followed quickly and then it was Orkan's turn. He looked up at Covelette hovering above ready to warn of any impending danger and when she gave the signal he sprang from cover and raced full tilt until he reached the wall. Covelette then flew across and joined the group.

"Now remember, the scorpion men are terribly vicious, cleverer than the Cozards and are also a lot more intelligent. Klaw may have been a skeleton but he ruled over this city through guile and barbarous means. I don't think that they yet know of his demise so the scorpion men are still under his command." Covelette offered the group her advice "What I heard happened was that he somehow managed to change a troop of Cozards into his own special team of deadly bodyguards, they act like Cozards but can talk and reason for themselves and that is what makes them so dangerous."

"You mean they're Cozards in a different guise."

"Oh no, they simply carry out their master's bidding and if you are approached then. Keep an eye on their tails at all times, if they start vibrating, run for all your worth. I've also heard that the one thing they can't do, is move as fast as we can."

Richard shuddered. He knew that they would have to leave the safety of this place shortly and were then going to face having to run the scorpion gauntlet. He wasn't a happy young man at that particular moment.

"Right, don't show fear and remember, be arrogant." Covelette moved forward and turned the corner. Richard moved aside to let Orkan follow next and walked with Melek for a short time before slowing down slightly in order to bring up the rear.

They steadily marched in step making their way down the long stairway towards the central building at the heart of Sand City. There was a lot of activity from all sorts of downtrodden individuals and beasts as they neared the bottom of the stairway.

"Gghhh! It looks like everyone around here are nothing but slaves." Orkan whispered loud enough for the rest to hear.

At the bottom one of the scorpion guards that none of them had noticed, moved from his post to observe the group more closely.

"Gghhh! We've been spotted."

"Just keep going as if we're part of the scene down here," Richard hissed.

Covelette didn't slow her pace as she led them past the strange looking guard, Richard could now see that close up, it was really like a huge scorpion. The guard stood upright using eight powerful back legs to balance itself but more frightening, were the twin powerful pincers acting as its hands. As he passed the guard, Richard remembered Covelette's words but couldn't help himself, he turned and looked straight into the scorpions two red, burning eyes on the top of its head; also noticing another five pairs of eyes along either side of the head area. The now slightly unnerved Richard moved on, he felt very much as if he had been singled out by the guard and felt the hairs on the nape of his neck start prickling. He turned again, to look at the bulbous poison sack on the sharply pointed tail. The Scorpion Man hadn't moved as he studied them march past him and through a large grey gateway looking more like a drawbridge than anything else.

"Well done." Covelette turned right and without slowing down, walked along one of the narrow alleyways in the direction of the castle. Richard saw what looked like cat's eyes shining in the dark from within the shabby grey buildings both to his left and right; he felt them examining these strangers and it made Richard feel uncomfortable and uneasy knowing that their every movement was somehow being recorded by these silent onlookers.

"Gghhh! Can you see them? They're all around us." He whispered.

"Eerie, it has the feeling of a ghost town."

Clickity, clickity. Richard couldn't help himself turning to see a guard who had suddenly appeared in the alleyway behind them, swaying from side to side as it started up the narrow street after them.

"Keep moving no matter what. It might be nothing." Covelette didn't look either left or right as she spoke softly to Orkan. "At the next intersection, I'm going to turn right, you and Melek carry straight on and tell Richard to go left. We'll meet up at the castle, all right?"

As Orkan passed on the message to his friend he could see that the guard was fast catching up to them. "I hope this beast follows one of you, he's enough to make anyone nervous."

As they reached the crossing Covelette moved off as planned, Orkan and Melek headed straight and Richard now suddenly feeling deserted and alone, turned to his left. The eyes were still there, examining his every movement from within the dingy little hiding places.

"Oh-oh. Keep calm," He reminded himself but the urge to run was almost overwhelming. He again glanced back and saw that the following scorpion man was not following him and instead was heading in the same direction as Orkan towards the castle.

"Whoo! How nerve racking was that? He breathed a sigh of relief and quickened his pace; at the following corner he turned right and headed in the direction of the castle once again. "So far, so good."

"Hey you!" Richard didn't look and just kept walking even though in his heart of hearts he knew that voice was being directed straight at him.

"Hey you!" Richard kept walking. But then he heard the ominous sound that made his blood run cold.

Clickity, clickity, clickity, and the scorpion man was coming after him. Richard's mind screamed at him to run like mad, but he somehow knew that he had to keep moving and not show any form of panic. His paced steps increased.

"Hey you, wait! ...I want to talk to you." Richard knew the game was up he immediately felt the reassuring steel hilt of Juroot's dagger as he turned to face the ugly beast. Richard drew a large breath and sniffed the air; at close quarters the guard gave off a pungent smell of squeezed lemons, a bitterest acidic smell. Richard's brain was searching for some form of escape, all he remembered were Covelette's words to run at the first sign of trouble and now here he was, facing the enemy.

"Try and bluff it out." Richard prompted himself, as the thing scuttled up to him. "Yes, what do you want, I'm in a hurry," Richard said with some authority.

"You are headed to the castle are you not?" The scorpion rattled.

"Of course, where else would I be going?"

"Give this package to Klaw's men?" Richard sneered at the beast as he offered a small ball of a sack to the boy.

"Why don't you take it yourself?" No sooner had he said it than he knew that that reply was a mistake.

"You always treat us like this, just because we're only soldiers, you think that you can talk to us like that? One day Klaw will realise that we are his strength and not you." The thing's tail shook violently accompanied by a noise sounding like hundreds of applauding cockroaches.

"Apologies," Richard sighed and held out his hand. "I'll do it this once, but don't make a habit of it."

"Haven't I seen you before somewhere?" The Scorpion Man peered more closely at Richard.

"Do you want this delivered, or what? I'm in a hurry and haven't got time for your stupid questions." Richard turned on his heel and began walking, feeling that the hammering of his heart could give him away.

"Bureaucrats, you think you own this place. We'll show you." Again, there was the noise of the rattling cockroaches made by the guard's tail Richard increased pace wondering just how he had survived the ordeal and now began thinking of how his compatriots were doing. It didn't take too long to reach the gates of the castle.

Meanwhile Orkan and Melek were nearing the large building through a narrow alley, when they were confronted by two scorpion men blocking their path. Orkan tried pushing his way past but one of the scorpions grabbed his body in its pincer and suddenly Orkan's soldiering came out as pulled back whipping out his sword he slashed through the scorpions arm and then the other, both went flying but in that moment the other scorpion's tail shot out catching Orkan in the hip. Even Orkan's speed did not help him see the deadly poisonous coming as his body was pinned against the wall.

"Gghhh! Run, get away!" Orkan shouted as he tried hacking the huge sting now entrapping him. "Tell them what's happened." Melek raced back the way he had come turned left and further along the narrow alley a doorway opened slightly, then was opened more.

"Get inside quickly." Once inside, Melek was quickly ushered through the small house into a soft rounded vase-like nesting grey mass built like a wasp-hive. "They will already be searching for you, climb inside, don't make any sounds."

"Covelette what are you doing here?" Melek thought at first that it was the guardian he was addressing pushing her through a tiny entrance hole.

"I am not Covelette, we have been searching for her, have you seen her?" Just then there was heavy hammering from the front.

"They're here already". The wasp-like figure grabbed a shawl and a walking stick and transformed herself almost magically into an old and bent old wasp. Melek could hear raised voices a lot of banging, the clickity rattle of scorpion men moving about the place and then they were gone and all was quiet. It was too quiet, after a while Melek crept out of the hive making his way towards the front he saw items were upturned and more disturbing was that both shawl and stick were lying on the floor. Melek quickly checked around and found hanging behind the half open front door, that the scorpion men had missed, a small bag similar to the one Covelette had removed from Klaw's rotting ribcage. Inside the bag he discovered the same type of blowpipe and darts, stuffing them into his belt he peered out the front door into the now deserted alleyway. He very carefully made his way to the castle to try to meet up with Richard. When he got there he didn't find them and decided that they had probably been captured as well, He was now very much alone, needing time to think. He noticed the administrators freely coming and going from the castle. Melek slipped in among some of them and at the castle found the stairway, not even realising that at that very moment, Richard was meeting up with Covelette at the front of this big building.

"What happened?" Richard eventually found Covelette waiting for him, he explained and showed her the bag he was supposed to deliver. Further along the narrow alley Richard could see several Scorpion Men guards. "Where are Orkan and Melek?"

"I don't know, I just hope they are not doing anything to jeopardise our mission. Let's wait here for them," Covelette had picked a spot quite near the main building watch the moving crowds but also Richard could see that the place was swarming with guards and also almost human-like administrators.

"If they have been caught, as soon as he opens his mouth, they'll quickly realise that he's an outsider." Covelette said casually as Richard explained about the bag he had been given.

"What's in it?"

"I don't know, I was too afraid to ask." He loosened the string and peered into the bag. "Covelette, ...it's," he immediately looked about and lowered the tone of his voice. "It's a pod of life."

"Let's see." She almost snatched the sack from his hand and tipping it upside down the pod rolled into her hand. Her antennae moved up and down as she lovingly clutched the pod to her breast. "Yes, it's one of the real ones, I wonder what he was doing with it?"

"I think it might be a trick and somehow that scorpion could have recognised me as an outsider because finding this so easily is too good to be true, this is not just a stroke of luck, we are being watched or set up?"

Covelette gently rubbed the pod against her badly wounded leg and before Richard's eyes, he saw the nasty gash close and seal itself "It is a true pod. Here, keep it safe." She dropped the pod back into the silken bag and handed it to him and then tried walking. "See my injury has now been repaired."

"That's fabulous but I'm getting worried about the others though."

"What exactly do you mean? The scorpion man recognised you." She suddenly looked alarmed.

"He asked me if we had ever met before, but I fobbed him off."

"That's not good, they could be watching us. Come, let's try and find the palace courtyard."

"Why?"

"They're clever; sooner or later they remember things or where they saw you. You were right, the pod is a trap to get us all together somehow and then they will drag us to the courtyard. I'm afraid they may have trapped Melek and Orkan already and are trying to lure us in as well. Somehow they have put two and two together and set off the alarm. "We must move quickly." They passed through the main gate in among several other slaves, passing the watchful gaze of yet more scorpion guards.

"This way," Walking at a steady pace so as not to draw attention, they climbed the great stairs into the main building. Again, more guards as they entered the great hall of Klaw. Richard's eyes continually searched for any sign of Orkan.

"This way," she almost yanked him off his feet as she turned into a narrow passageway and up a long flight of stairs taking them to an observation gallery high above the main hall. "We will be able to see better from up here. Look for Orkan?"

"There he is!" In the middle of the courtyard below stood his little pig-like friend between four scorpions, his legs and arms were now manacled together.

"Oh-oh, he's been caught by the guards and they are going to present him to the Sand God. She moved around and then back toward Richard, "Wonder what happened to Melek."

"What is the Sand God?" Covelette simply ignored Richard's question, she was deep in thought "We must save him."

"The only way to do that is by us reaching the centre of the courtyard. We can't do anything here, an immediate plan is required otherwise your companion will never get out of here alive."

"Orkan won't tell them anything."

"He will when the Sand God starts sucking his blood."

"W-what do mean, suck his blood?"

"Look at everybody around us, they're divided into two definite types, the administrators and the Scorpion Men. I thought I explained, the way Klaw got his skeleton army was to first use people as slaves, then to change them by squirting some form of venom into their bloodstream. Don't tell me you didn't know that's the job of the Sand God?"

"Why didn't he do that to you?"

"There are those certain individuals, like myself being a guardian that his venom won't affect. He would then injure us and kill us very slowly by locking us in his dungeon and letting us die. Klaw enjoyed watching suffering and was evil to his very core."

"W-what about Orkan?"

"Let's hope he tells the Sand God everything, even that Klaw is no more before the monster sinks his fangs into your friend, that way, they will be panicked into trying to protect this city and this courtyard. Hopefully we'll be there ahead of the Sand God.

"Now, c'mon why would they protect this courtyard?"

"Because it is the ritualistic centre of Klaw's evil empire, the tree in the middle of the courtyard contains jewels and is the heart of this destructive domain. We have to destroy the tree somehow."

"But?" Richard started then thought better of it as they followed the narrow passage, checking each one of the inward facing windows. Covelette stopped, in a corner alcove was Melek busy studying Morbane's Book.

When she saw the pair she flew at them and hugged them tightly. Richard could see she had been crying, "They captured Orkan, I did not know what to do, I could not find you so I came up to gather my thoughts." She followed them down not quite knowing what to look for.

"There, we are at the courtyard." Richard looked at the timber door knowing what lay beyond.

"We'll never get past the Scorpion Men."

"Not from the ground, we won't. But, they won't be expecting a visit from the sky, will they?"

"T-the sky?"

"The golden rope, have you still got it?" Covelette asked Melek

"I have, also I have this." He extracted the small purse from his belt

"Where did you find this?" Melek quickly explained what had happened.

"These items belong to one of my sisters; you keep hold of it and use it when the time comes. Orkan will be in untold pain and therefore useless to help, we three have to do this ourselves."

Suddenly there was a great roar from the courtyard behind the door. Richard turned to a window; he could see an enormous black and yellow something entering the great courtyard from the opposite side.

"C'mon Chosen one it is time, we've got to move quickly." The noisy cheering in the courtyard came to an abrupt halt.

"Hurry!" Covelette urged. "You try to distract the scorpion men, I will try to deal with the Sand God. Without waiting she pushed open the door, stepped out into the courtyard, and flew into the air. Richard could now see the beautifully multi-coloured jewelled bush from his position.

"Move! Try to get at least four jewels." He and Melek raced into the open courtyard towards Orkan and the four scorpion men. From above, Covelette was using her blowpipe to great effect, as each dart found its target into the eyes of the scorpion men they were blinded and disorientated.

"Wheeooee!" Orkan fell to the ground in an effort to save himself from the massive pincers snapping in all directions as the scorpion men tried defending themselves from the unknown attack. This was just what Richard needed, he knew he had to stay clear and by skirting around the now bumbling scorpions, he raced towards the tree. They reached it but the jewels were high in the tree, Melek whipped out the rope and flicked a few times pulling the jewels from their positions.

"Four must I continue?"

"Get as many as you can." Richard looked up and saw a dark shadow swoop down and suddenly grab at Covelette with one of its giant talons, the squealing Orkan now being held fast in the other.

"Boltor!"

"Wheeooee! Wheeooee!" Richard looked back and saw the black shadow had missed Covelette and was making a wide turn to start heading straight down to her once again. He snatched at the jewels on the ground and stuffed them into his pocket.

"Gotcha!" He watched as the shadow again tried to capture the wasp-like Covelette then again rise high into the sky. The scorpion men, who due to their blindness were fiercely attacking and using their bulbous stings on each other, momentarily distracted Richard's attention. He held up his hands to show Covelette that he had the jewels. Suddenly there was the most terrific roar as Boltor dropped out of the sky and seized the guardian in its talon.

"Smash them!" Covelette screamed.

Suddenly Boltor seemed to stall, its wings began flapping in an uncoordinated way as it dropped down into the courtyard with a crash leaving both Orkan and Covelette tumbling and bouncing across the ground. Melek had seen the danger and used the blowpipe and poisonous wasp darts, this was now the result of his valiant quick thinking.

"The pods, you have the beast pod, see to Orkan, I will check Covelette." Richard suggested. Before long using the pods both Orkan and Covelette were up, badly shaken and feeling the effects of their ordeal but, walking again when another wasp-like figure descended from the sky and hovered above Covelette.

"Erinno! You missed all the fun," Covelette said.

"No Covelette, the fun is just about to begin, I escaped the scorpion men when they were gathered together because of the attack on the courtyard, they're on their way here now." Covelette, although feeling a little groggy, rose up high into the air.

"Melek give Erinno her blowpipe, it has already served your purpose," Melek handed over the little bag to the wasp that had saved his life and then the two lifted high into the sky just as an army of scorpion men flooded into the courtyard, their stings rattling in anxiety and scorn.

Richard, Orkan and Melek drew their weapons and prepared to make a stand. Out of the billowing clouds kicked up by their entry, evil scorpion men emerged on mass. Pincers clacking, red eyes glowing and tails ready to strike. The three were now completely surrounded.

"Aim for their eyes!" from overhead Covelette ordered. "That's their vulnerable spot." Covelette and Erinno moved fast and purposefully before the group had taken any steps towards their foe, they had their blowpipes to their lips and were spraying a fan of lethal darts at the enemy, each dart finding its intended target. Disarray and pandemonium broke out in the scorpion army ranks as they were blinded and immediately began attacking anything within reach. A stream of arrows from Orkan's bow joined lethal darts spat down from above as he pulled and re-pulled his bow with lightning speed.

"Gghhh! Running out of arrows" Orkan drew his sword and as Richard drew Juroot's dagger he touched one of the quickly forgotten crystals from the tree. He extracted them and handed them to Melek.

"These must be destroyed, try to do it now with all this confusion in front of us, Orkan and I will try to give you some time." Then Richard moved in beside his companion. "There are just too many, luckily being blinded they are killing each other."

"Gghhh! Don't be too sure, the ones with their sight intact will kill off the blinded ones and then they will kill us."

Melek fastened a jewel into his looped rope and flicked it high into the sky towards Covelette who extricated the jewel.

"Another!" Covelette shouted and then flew high above the castle watchtower and released the jewel. It fell fast and when it hit the tower exploded like a bomb, showering a fine coloured dust upwards high into the sky. Melek in the meantime had retrieved the rope placed another jewel into it and flicked it skywards to Erinno this time who did exactly the same thing, then another and another until six jewels had been smashed onto the tower. The light swirling breeze carried coloured smoke right across the city.

On the ground the battle between the scorpion men had intensified dramatically and Orkan's trained battle vision was now seemingly becoming a reality as waves of the scorpion men attacked their colleagues with unbridled ferocity as a coloured haze descended from the heavenly blast cloud.

Both Richard and Orkan could see that the battling breakthrough by the larger force killing their own was almost at an end and that they were in imminent danger of being swept away before the advancing scorpions. Through the coloured haze, Richard then saw a huge black and yellow shadow moving in behind the advancing army.

"No! No! No! It's the Sand God." Richard screamed. "When is this nightmare ever going to end?"

The Three Headed Serpent

On the Thirteenth Day...

Three heads to find the true,
Three jaws to bite them.
Six eyes to see the few,
One king to fight them.
Venom hides the golden goal,
Another prize awaits.
Released it takes a dreadful toll
On those who chance its fate.
Deep in darkest tomb,
Beware the cracks of doom.

"It is done and we have overcome the evil of Klaw's realm." Covelette and Erinno landed behind Richard and Orkan, "We are safe."

"Are you nuts? These scorpions are going to murder us all."

"No. See the crystal cloud is already at work." Before their very eyes, the scorpion men seemed to be changing back into Cozards.

"Aarggh! They are becoming Cozards again, they'll kill us anyway."

"They do not belong in this place, they will shortly leave of their own accord." Covelette said as the now changed scorpion men switched into grunting Cozards. Their leader barked several commands and the army collected up their dead, dying and wounded colleagues. "That cloud will eventually cover the entire Sand City reversing what an evil Klaw and the Sand God had achieved. Everyone here will go back to what they were and move away, back to their homes while others, like the administrators, will again start to administer this land if ever we manage to regain peace."

"I don't see the Sand God anymore? I did see him but he was partially hidden by the scorpion men when they attacked."

"He somehow escaped and could still be a threat to you. There is also still danger in the Sand City for there are those souls that will not be touched by the cloud and who still carry allegiance to Klaw. We will stay behind and gather the forces of good together and it will take time to root them out before we head back to the Ancestral City."

"What can we do to help you?" Richard asked.

"You must try and complete your mission, we are going to need every guardian and pod available, you have been given that task," Just then the leader of the Cozards barked an order. The bedraggled army banged weapons against shield and at full march started leaving the courtyard while other creatures and beasts entered the area looking dumbfounded as they aimlessly meandered around the place.

"We have much to do and not much time. You must go your way but, we are surely bound to meet again, May any accidental discoveries bring you triumph." Covelette and Erinno opened their wings and flew away.

"What now?" Melek asked

"I don't really know but somehow I sense that trouble will find us if Golan has anything to do with it. Let's get out of here first, I would like to see what is going on outside these palace walls." Richard led them back the way they had entered the sand palace.

In front of the palace the whole feeling was very different, no scorpion men, in fact there was a general air of normality tinged with liberty as people scurried around beginning to realise that there was change.

"I think you may need this," Melek handed Richard the Pathfinder. He nervously swept it from side to side, the instrument glowed gold when pointed towards a narrow alleyway to their right. After Melek had again replaced the Pathfinder into the spine of the book, the trio ducked into the narrow passageway that seemed to become tighter the further along it they travelled; they were again three blind companions in what was not a very pleasant land of experience. Reaching a small arched gate at the end of the alley, they passed through to find themselves now facing a large white and yellow square. From what they could immediately gather was that this place seemed to be filled with statues and columns.

"Brrr! Do you somehow get the feeling of déjà vu?" His companions looked blankly at Richard. "Like you have been revisiting the past?" Still there was no reply, "This has that sort of Mirrah garden experience don't you think? ...statues? ...columns? ...Juroot?

"Gghhh!" Not at all, look you only have to examine the work, the sand carvings are eroding as are some of the columns. Now, Juroot's statues were crisp and clean because they were made from real subjects?" Orkan argued

"Suppose you are right and yes, it does look a bit like a graveyard of sorts." Richard kept on moving down the line of columns, touching each as he passed them. They seemed to stretch out in a straight line and go on forever.

"Something moved over there," Melek pointed toward an area filled with crumbling sandstone statues, some new, others so weather-worn that it was difficult to make out what or who, they represented. "Did not see what it was but just caught it out of the corner of my eye. It was very quick but it was there."

"Gghhh! Maybe something is tracking us? Where exactly would you say whatever it was made the move?" Orkan enquired, sword already in his hand,

"Near or from behind that plinth," Melek pointed. Orkan led the way to a flattened plinth that held no statue. "Look, this is very strange; sand around this large podium has been flattened as if trodden down. Now take a look at all the other bases, they are different because they all have sand piles built up against them where the wind has blown it into that position. Not here?"

"Gghhh! He's right, something or someone has been using this space around here, this is not the sign of a tracker, it looks like whatever it is lives, here somewhere." Orkan's keen soldier's eye searched the area for more clues. "I get the feeling that they could be living secretly within one of these platforms, probably this one and does not want to be seen. They could even be watching us right now." Orkan searched the plinth for any irregularities by touching, pushing against every slight bump in the stone. Nothing moved, nothing gave. "This just has to be the hideout?" Orkan whispered. "I feel it in my bones."

"Wait, I think there may be something over here." Melek had moved to a ball shaped sandstone right at the edge of the plinth.

"Let me help," Richard moved across and the two began pulling and pushing the ball in unison, it was loose. "Once more, push." Even as he spoke he felt the plinth base move beneath his feet, then came the rasping clank from some underground mechanism kicking into action. One end of the large podium tilted upward while the other side down deep into a massive opening. "Orkan!" was all Richard could scream as they rapidly slid steeply downwards on the now sandy incline. Although Orkan tried jumping to safety he was too far from the edge and did not fare any better than his two companions. Their downward journey quickly ended with them all being shot off the end of the tilted plinth, and then bouncing head over heels down a soft but sandy mountain slope below the now angled podium.

"It looks like some form of chamber?" They picked themselves up, shook and dusted themselves and started scanning the place, light poured in from above so what they saw was that a large empty room, save for at the far end something half-lost in shadow, the rest of this chamber surrounded with massive ornately carved pillars interspersed with arched voids. The walls and pillars all had the same carved themed adornment that flowed through everything they could see in this light.

"Gghhh! Something tells me this is not a good place." Orkan said examining the huge reptilian open-mouthed snakes shown throughout the chamber.

"Brrr! After our experience with Lotan I know exactly what you mean." Richard's eyes travelled across the almost lifelike Hydra serpents spread across all aspects of this chamber. "All these snakes represent only one thing, this place leads us to a lair of some sort of slithering reptile. It cannot be a good omen, can it?"

"Do you still have some of those poisonous berries left Orkan?" Melek asked, he too was also very nervous.

"Gghhh! I forgot all about them and yes I do, why?" He removed his quiver and took one arrow and being very careful, spiked a couple of the extremely toxic berries. "At least if there are serpents like Lotan about, these at least, give us some sort of chance."

"Before we go any further, it would be a good idea to consult Melek's book. At least it might give some sort of a clue what is going to happen, its cryptic messages have been correct most times." Melek quickly got the book onto the floor and in the dim light finally found the riddle that applied to their present circumstances. He whispered the lines.

Three heads to find the true,
Three jaws to bite them.
Six eyes to see the few,
One king to fight them.
Venom hides the golden goal,
Another prize awaits.
Released it takes a dreadful toll
On those who chance its fate.
Deep in darkest tomb,
Beware the cracks of doom.

"Gghhh! Three heads, six eyes equal three serpents? Lotan was a single foe, but three? We have a problem on our hands and I think we should split up. Me at the back that places me in a position and ready to fire should any of them attack one of you two?" Orkan's military thinking brain had automatically kicked into gear once again.

"Good plan Orkan. We place ourselves in danger becoming the inducement bait to draw them out and attack us, while you can get away? I don't like that because it also says 'One king to fight them,' does that mean me?"

"Has Orkan ever run away?" Melek intervened.

"I suppose not, I was just voicing my thoughts, sorry Orkan, you're right. I will inspect around that large mound on the far side, something could be hiding behind it? Melek, you move around the perimeter and check inside those cave-like arches that nothing is lurking there. Here take this." Richard handed Melek his torch. "Orkan you have to make sure you can see us both at all times, and guys, call out if you see 'anything' at all suspicious. C'mon, let's do it."

Melek began skirting the boundary pillars and shone the light into each void seeing nothing but the occasional spider or rat. He moved ultra-cautiously, planning his escape with each step, pillar and opening knowing that serpents were the ultimate masters of disguise and traps. He had every reason to be nervous

Richard headed towards the untidy large pile at the far side of the room.

"Can't make out what it is." No sooner had the words left him we he heard a rasping slither sound of scale upon scales as the mound began moving, unwinding itself revealing a tail coiled around and through a snake throne.

"Oh-oh! We got trouble!" Richard's blood ran cold as three monstrous snake heads appeared from within the throne somewhere and rose high above him, hoods spreading widely casting shadows across the room. As one, three heads supported by the powerful body swayed in side-to-side motion yet, unconnected long black tongues tasted the air individually, mouths opening independently yet only a single body.

"Dragora, I have read of this mythical reptile, run away!" Melek screamed.

Richard spun and shot to his right as one of the heads tried darting him with a deadly, slender, pointed and venomous missile,

"Sssiiss! Weaklings! You cannot escape Dragora." The reptile's slow, deliberate movement unnerved Melek and as he moved to get back to Orkan. Dragora immediately reacted to his movement, three heads jerked backwards in a coiling motion, then whipped forward like lightning sending another venomous missile straight at the fleeing librarian.

"Dive Melek!" Orkan screamed loudly. He didn't hesitate as he flung himself forward.

Orkan saw his opportunity as Dragora's heads began rising back into the upright position, one mouth opened as if about to say something, Orkan fired, his aim was straight, it was true. The arrow struck the back of the throat of this reptile head.

"Gghhh! Got you" Orkan was pleased with himself as the stricken head lashed independently of the other two and let forth a high-pitched, hissing screech that echoed throughout the chamber. Even with one head now out of action, Dragora began slithering towards the companions. They heard the rustling of the serpent moving across the sand.

"Sssiiss! You will pay dearly for your actions." Even with one head writhing in agony, Dragora's three heads managed to jerk backwards in their coiling motion as they had done before. The companions now knew what was about to happen.

"Gghhh! Must reload with more berries, try to distract that thing." Orkan moved behind a pillar fully knowing that he was going to be Dragora's main target. He could hear the large reptile getting closer as he fumbled with his quiver to stab the few remain berries, he had to settle for two. Richard had shot off left and Melek right but this time, each head individually selected a different target, spitting the deadly poison dart at each of them. Richard swivelled although not quickly enough and the dart caught him full in the chest. Melek however moving, watched and waited for Dragora's head to drop in a spitting motion and again he dived full length to avoid being hit by the deadly missile.

"Gghhh! Dragora " Orkan stepped from behind the pillar and waited as the serpent's head was on the rise and then fired, the fast moving reptile attempted to sway away, Orkan saw that the arrow had not met its intended mark.

"Gghhh! Last berry, must make it count," Orkan said to himself rounding the pillar to reload. Melek pulled himself up and turned to see what had happened, two heads were writhing in pain on the big serpent but even his simple movement of standing up drew the attention of Dragora. Richard watched in horror as one of the snake's heads turned and suddenly the huge reptilian body was now moving away from him towards Melek who as far as Richard could see, he was now well and truly trapped.

"Help me!" Melek shouted, he was transfixed with nowhere to run.

"Sssiiss! You at least will die a painful death." The serpent's slithering body had surrounded his position and any possible route of escape as the head lowered to his level, its forked tongue snickered out over Melek's face testing the librarian's smell of fear. The lightning fast head struck out at him, sinking its fanged teeth deep into its prey. Luckily for Melek the gossamer mail-chain vest that Broon had given him and 'The Book of Prophesies saved him at that moment and as he struggled the binding holding the book gave way. The snake's fangs were deeply embedded in the book as it shook its head frantically to rid itself of this momentary nuisance.

Richard raced across the room and to draw Dragora's attention from Melek, he plunged Juroot's dagger deep into the snakes back through its broad main central body muscle. Richard now saw that Dragora was severely damaged, one twitching head with an arrow that was sticking through its windpipe and its tip showing out of the back, the second head was flapping loosely, Richard saw that the second arrow had entered that head through the eye orange coloured socket that was now leaking volumes of yellow pus, while the third head struggling to dislodge Melek's big book from its mouth.

"Watch out!" Orkan shouted, Richard saw the snake swivel its head at speed to see what Richard had done and suddenly its entire focus was taken up with the retreating Richard. It was still shaking its head violently from side to side and the book suddenly flew through the air. Melek immediately headed off to locate it while Richard scrambled backwards and towards the spot where Orkan had now reappeared,

"Sssiiss! We were going to leave your death until last. Your action has given me little choice but to kill you first now." Dragora moved quickly towards the backing Richard and was about to strike when there was an almighty thump as Orkan's arrow with its final berry struck the huge reptile in the mouth.

The high-pitched screaming noise filled the chamber like a wind tunnel, Dragora's three decommissioned heads now all writhing it didn't take long for the great snake to finally collapse to the ground, pulses of green slimy venom spewing from its jaws. The bedlam of the chamber was suddenly at an end except for an odd rasping crackle of breath sounded Dragora's final death throes.

"Look at the book, it's not ruined but it does have two holes where the snake sank its fangs into it. The book saved my life." Melek said, lovingly checking pages to see how much damage there was.

"Gghhh! Talking about a life being saved, I thought I saw a dart hit your chest?" Orkan enquired of Richard.

"That's right but, thankfully this saved me, Broon said it would." Richard pointed to his chain-mail vest.

"I think mine also saved me," Melek echoed without looking up from his book inspection.

"Gghhh!" Now what do we do? There is no escape route the way we entered this place and I cannot see any other exits in the room. We're stuck down here forever are we not?"

"When in doubt, use the Pathfinder." Richard said confidently. "Melek, pass it to me."

"It's not here." He saw the book spine had separated and opened. "It must have dislodged when the serpent flung away the book? It must be somewhere between where I was attacked and where the book landed. We cannot proceed without it." Melek said in a tone of impending doom.

"Then we had better find it, hadn't we? Richard commanded. "Come on it can't be that far, just hope it hasn't buried itself in this sand." The three began searching by walking abreast along the line of possible travel of the book. They carried out an initial sweep across the area and not finding it, they doubled back this time dragging their toes through the sand, just in case the Pathfinder had somehow disappeared below the sandy surface.

"Gghhh! Over here!" Orkan's excited voice brought the others running.

"Well done." Richard said, as he drew near. "We would have been lost without..."

"Gghhh! No," Orkan interrupted. "It's not the Path Finder, but look at this," He pointed to a stone grille set into floor. "Also, I'm certain that there's something moving down there." Richard looked at it, he heard a rustling noise coming from below their feet, it sounded as if thousands of scaly creatures were moving on dried leaves.

"Melek the torch, do you still have it?" Melek nodded and handed it to Richard who then peered through the grille. "It looks like a narrow stairway, but dare we investigate what's moving around down there? It could be another Dragora, or even something worse?"

"Gghhh! As far as we can see, there is no way out of this chamber is there? Perhaps those stairs will guide us out of here." Orkan drew his sword.

"Talking of that we need to find the Pathfinder, it can give direction. Melek you continue searching for it while we investigate down there for an exit."

"Good thinking but we must keep calling out to each other; I really need to know if you run into trouble. Here take your torch, you will need it more than me, there is enough light here to see the Pathfinder.

"Will do." Richard followed Orkan down the narrow steps, nearing the bottom. Orkan stopped and pointed as a tentative reptilian snout peered from around the corner.

"Oh-oh! It's another snake." Richard whispered urgently. Orkan stopped his sword blow in mid-air because whatever it was, seemed to gesture to the two as it raised a front foot and almost pointed with its clawed talon. Then it turned itself awkwardly and hauled itself around the corner and back into the darkness.

"Gghhh! That was not the action of animosity; I think it wants us to follow."

"Could it be leading us straight into some sort of trap?" Richard asked. After his encounter with Dragora, he remained a little weary.

"Gghhh! No, call it instinct; it was more frightened of us than we of him. We tread carefully though." The two moved cautiously to the foot of the stairs where the reptile had been, around the corner Richard flashed his torch across a room almost the same size as the chamber above, "Gghhh! There are so many down here." As far as they could see, the place was filled with literally hundreds of differing reptiles of all shapes and sizes, some still wearing battle attire, others wounded, all seemingly dazed by the sudden light. The large lizard that had beckoned them was in the foreground, it's beautiful incandescent hue, like a slick of oil under summer sun glimmered in the beam of light.

"My name is Apeptas, we have been here since the war, captured by Klaw."

"Klaw is no more."

"Good, what about Dragora?"

"Gghhh! We have just destroyed Dragora did you not hear us do so?" It was obvious to Orkan that there would be no escape route from this chamber.

"We are of the desert, our leader is Zard the Noble Serpent, most of our forces were captured then brought down here to rot. Dragora was Klaw's jailer in the Sand City."

"Follow us we must find a way out of this place." Richard led the way up the stairs.

"The Path Finder is found, it was firmly lodged in the mouth of that serpent." Melek excitedly waved the Pathfinder.

"We have found a huge army of lizards down there." He quickly explained what they had found and just as Apeptas dragged itself out of the hole.

"Most of Zard's soldiers were thought to have been killed during the war, they are fearsome fighters when fully armed." Melek declared as another and yet another started appearing. The chamber started filling as straight away he could see them searching for an exit. "Our numbers grow."

"Gghhh! This is good… military trained army is always very good. Apeptas, do you think your people can help us to find a way out of this place?" Orkan watched as Apeptas manoeuvred his forces around the chamber.

"Look what else I found in that snake's mouth." Melek held out an amulet to Richard who took it turned it over, Looking at the intricately honed marking on each of the differing coloured inset stones circling the bracelet.

"Nothing out of the unusual with this, I think it's just a piece of pretty jewellery?" Richard held it out to hand it back when Orkan immediately snatched it from his grasp.

"Gghhh! Let me inspect that." As they watched the amulet gave out a slight flicker of light. "I think it has somehow recognised me, you already have one and Melek has the Pathfinder to take care of, let me look after this." He looked over at Melek imploringly, he nodded his approval, he placed it on his arm and felt the amulet lure him into its dark depths, beckoning with warm promise. He looked at the dead snake that unlike Lotan that had withered, Dragora had begun swelling like a balloon being filled with water, so much so that cracks were appearing and a green slimy substance was leaking into the sand across the cavern floor, Orkan's eyes were also misting and making it difficult to see properly but, he felt somehow that he should not tell the others about it.

"The Pathfinder led us here but it seems to be different somehow, perhaps it was damaged by Dragora?" Richard showed Melek what he meant as he waved the Pathfinder towards the dead snake, it glowed gold yet, when he moved it left or right it kept changing colour. It is not pointing us in any sort of direction now, it keeps changing its colour. Why do you think that has happened?" Again he swept the Pathfinder in a complete circle and it simply alternated several colours. When he pointed skywards it showed a completely different hue to when he pointed it downwards. "I think this thing is kaput?"

"I noticed something when I was inspecting the damage to the book. It did not make any sense then but, I think it could refer to the Pathfinder." He again unstrapped the book and laid it down flat but, now found he was having great difficulty reading. "My eyes are stinging and watering so much that I am unable to read this properly." He pushed forward the book to Richard, all the while the irritant was worsening, he rubbed his eyes.

"Mine are also watering so badly I can only just make out the words." Richard battled to get through the riddle.

Across Green fields, Overland you go,
where winter solstice White brings Ice and snow.
The Grey dove flies to fresher Air,
and shuns the Yellow swamp of Wastes' despair.
When Blue eyes, to Water clear aspire,
round campsites Orange tongues will wage in Fire.
Out of Stone, the Cities cloaked in sand,
and Brown caves weave in secret, Underland.
The Silver moon shines potent magic Light,
through Black skies loom in silent dark of Night.
Golden glimmers brightest on the spear,
and leads to Good, when journey's end is near.

"That's what it must mean, the Pathfinder's arrow does indicate what lies ahead, I think we have been reading it incorrectly. It spells out what the different colours represent, green meant overland before we entered the forest. " His eyes were painful as he tried looking across the room, he could vaguely see that all the larger lizards were now stationed around the pillars in the room then, as if by unseen command, as one, they all levered themselves onto their back legs stretching their claws as high on the pillars as was possible for each to reach.

"I think that stuff leaking from Dragora is creating a gas of some sort." Suddenly he saw that the lizards were using the pillars as some sort of fireman's pole, together they dragged their claws downwards towards the base when suddenly a huge flame shot straight out from one of the pillars. In an instant the entire roof of the cavern was a fireball followed by a mighty explosion. Pillars started toppling, the floor and walls began cracking. "It's Dragora, that stuff is turning to Methane gas! This whole place is going to explode. Come on!" Richard dragged himself off the floor. "We must find a way out of here."

"Look there! I think the lizards have found an escape route." Melek said as he pulled the book onto his back once more, racing to where he had seen a tail disappearing into the ever widening cracks. One was wide enough for them to pass through.

"Orkan! Come on!" The pig-like boy seemed to be in two minds as he ran his fingers across the newly acquired amulet. Then there was another flame flash high above his head that luckily poured through the inclined opening that they slid down entering the chamber. From somewhere within his confused brain he pulled himself off the floor knowing that he had to move quickly. A sudden jolt from the floor interrupted his thinking as it felt like a huge boot had just kicked the floor from below.

"Gghhh! Wait for me!" Orkan shouted as yet another build-up of gas sparked off above his head. "The chamber's collapsing!" He screamed in panic as cracks in the floor began snaking across the floor.

"I don't think that this opening is going to be large enough." Richard was on his hands and knees looking into the pinched hole. "The lizards can crawl up that cramped space but, I don't think we can." The reptiles were scuttling past in a frenzy of panic, pawing at the sandstone crack, bumping, pushing and disappearing up into what now seemed like their only chance of possible escape. He turned and observed that Orkan suddenly had a mad, gleam to his eyes that had never been there before.

"Gghhh! Get out of my way!" Orkan pushed the other two aside and fell to the floor on his stomach began to leopard crawl through the opening. Richard was taken aback but his logically thinking brain simply passed off Orkan's strange behaviour to the stress they had all endured recently.

"If we get out of this we need to take a rest, I think this mission has become too much for Orkan to withstand. We have no alternative left, we had better try and follow him."

"His bravery is beyond question but, everyone has a snapping point, I think you could be right." Melek got on all fours, took the book from his back rolled inside what looked to Richard like a chamois cloth then, fastened the books leather thongs around his waist. "It will be easier to drag the book like a sled, this is narrow and on my back it will probably snag or tear against the passage."

"I will help and push it from behind." The two began their half crawling, half belly slide up the tunnel. Their journey was not made any easier as they scraped past jutting rocks, jostling reptiles moving much more quickly, sometimes even using the pair as stepping stones, desert sand pouring through cracks each time a fresh volley of explosive detonations sounded from behind them. Then the moment Richard had feared most, there was a sudden deep rumbling from the bowels behind and below them coupled with trembling that seemed to be shaking the entire structure.

"Move! Move! The Methane is about to blow! This is the big one." Just then something or someone bodily pulled him and Melek into a tight alcove split.

Hulkan, The Mole-Man

On the Fourteenth Day...

Follow the reptile tail
To find the hidden trail.
A monster underground!
Seek the way that height has found.
Beware the foe within,
The safety water brings
Is fine but no avail.
Eyes that fly bring new travail.

"Orkan! What's happening?" Richard panicked but as he turned and realised that it was not his companion it was Apeptas holding tightly onto them as a massive flame shot past, its trailing wake looking more like the tail of a supersonic jet fighter than anything else. A thunderous explosion leaving the whole area moving and cracking followed it.

"Come! Quickly, follow me, if we don't move now we will all become trapped. Move!" Apeptas moved very fast and the three had great difficulty keeping up as they trampled over charred remains of reptiles unlucky enough to have been caught up by the fast moving flame. Colleagues, all just having one thing in mind, were helping several others along to get away before everything came down on top of them. Fortunately the passageway became much wider the further they moved.

"There's light ahead, I think we are going to make it." Richard had spoken too soon, another more thunderous crash filled the air although this time, there was no flame to accompany the roar of the collapsing tunnel behind them. "Run!" Without being so restricted in their movement, Richard and Melek carried the book, and headed towards the light while Orkan brought up the rear. Eventually the tremors and blasts were beginning to subside, becoming fainter; the sandy floor became more peat-like loam and near the entrance turned to a thicker, dark sticky soil mixture as they made their final sprint to freedom.

"Wow! How close was that?" Richard saw that they had exited on a hillside, now covered with thousands of reptilian creatures all heading off down towards the flatland desert in the distance. "Thank you Apeptas you saved our lives, we are indebted to you."

"It is not us that need your thanks, you and your friends rescued us from certain death, it was but a small deed in repayment." Apeptas leaned forward to Richard, "Watch out for Orkan, there is something not quite right with him." The lizard whispered.

"I know, he is not right but, he will be soon."

"Now, we go to find Zard, then perhaps join forces with Juroot at the Ancestral City. I bid you farewell and continued charmed results in your quest." The big lizard turned and headed after his exhausted army down the slope.

"I'm glad to see that so many got through, they are true warriors and we are going to need all the fighting reinforcements we can get, their instinct for danger is legendary." Richard could see that Melek too, was about ready to drop just as a heavy distant rumble shook the air. They turned just in time to see sand mixed with smoke fill the area below where they were standing.

"It looks like that could be where Dragora's chamber must have been, I just hope that has not touched the good folk that remained behind in Sand City. Those explosions were each like mini atom bombs. Who would have thought it?" Richard mused as he watched the grey ball rising high into the sky in the fading light. "We must all rest now." They all slept soundly for several hours, Richard awoke to see Melek hunched over his big book.

"What's in store for us today?" Richard asked just as Orkan rolled over and yawned.

He turned and smiled at them then began reading the passage aloud.

Follow the reptile tail
To find the hidden trail.
A monster underground!
Seek the way that height has found.
Beware the foe within,
The safety water brings
Is fine but no avail.
Eyes that fly bring new travail.
Does that answer your question?"

Later that morning saw Melek up the slope, collecting berries and honey. Rounding a small ridge he could see what looked like a large pool that formed into rapids lower down; he presumed rightly that it became a waterfall beyond that. Meanwhile Richard and the sulky Orkan had found a small water spring not far away on the other side of the hill.

"Wonder why none of this water reaches the desert and correct me if I'm wrong but, you look a little out of sorts today Orkan? Anything the matter?" Richard asked.

"Gghhh! I just think you and Melek are becoming too cosy together and leaving me out of decisions." He turned his back on Richard and started heading back towards the tree where they had slept. The ground suddenly began to heave and seesaw as Richard tried to move more quickly to catch up to his companion.

"Gghhh! Hurry, let's get out of here!" Orkan shouted back over his shoulder as they heard the rhythmic thudding sound and it seemed to be under their feet

"Another explosion?" Richard shouted at his fleeing friend. The ground was rocking and bumping it was as if an earthquake was about to explode open beneath their very feet. Without warning, the ground to their left began distorting into a large bump, as a gigantic pimple of sand rose up from nowhere out of the earth. "Get hold of Melek and tell him to hang onto a tree or something."

"Gghhh! There you go again, tell Melek this, tell Melek that. You tell him." Richard could sense the anger of his reply as Orkan raced away, when suddenly the ground movement sent both companions sprawling to the ground, still heaving and bucking like a mad rodeo horse from underneath them. Noise and vibration reached a crescendo that sounded to Richard like a huge freight train was about to enter this terrible place. Richard scrambled on all fours and grabbed at a tree, trying desperately to steady himself against this fresh onslaught. He looked back towards the growing mound that was building up from the sloped ground above their position

"What do you think it is?" Richard screamed but no answer came back from Orkan.

"Whatever is making that mound must be very large." Melek had heard the noise, gathered the boy's bits and pieces then saw their predicament. He then raced across, handing Orkan his tools of the trade and was now circling downside from the growing bump of soil before realising that it now looked like a giant molehill appearing from below the recently calm and settled ground "I've got all your equipment with me."

"Stay there!" Richard let go of the tree and raced hard around this new phenomenon, diving to come up slightly above Melek's position, unfortunately he did not judge the slope too well and rolled, sending Melek flying into the bracken. "Sorry!" He noted that Melek was now limping as he helped him detach himself. "Here, let me carry the book for a while." Melek reluctantly handed the Book of Prophecies to Richard.

He turned just in time to see the tree he had been holding onto fly straight out of the ground as all of a sudden, like a gigantic pimple being burst open, the ground at the centre of the mound erupted with mud, dust and vegetation flying outwards in all direction from its core.

"Oh no. Not another horrible beast." His mind quickly returned to the Sumar who had appeared from below the water, this noise around them was just as deafening, except that the earth seemed to have become a roller-coaster ride. Richard clung on for dear life to the surrounding bracken and all he wanted to do now, was to be as far away from this violent upheaval as was humanly possible.

As suddenly as it had occurred, so the rolling, rumbling and tremendous noise stopped and the hillside was quiet once again. Richard turned to see if Orkan was safe and without harm. The pig-like soldier was busily crawling on all fours in his direction, obviously no worse for this initial encounter.

"Whew! Gghhh! Gghhh! I'm glad to see that you two are safe, 'what is that'?" He asked, a tone of sarcasm tingeing his question. Richard wasn't quite sure what to do next because his tormented mind was screaming for them to run, he just knew that his own body wouldn't have responded to the command anyway. He stayed lying flat on his stomach, his arms still tightly wrapped around the book, just in case the earth began moving again.

"Oh-oh!" The trio stared as an enormous mole-like head suddenly began to emerge out of the pile of soft and loose earth. What fascinated Richard most at first sight was the colour, dark royal blue that glistened in the morning sunlight, parting at the huge mouth lined with a beautiful set of brilliantly white spade-shaped teeth. "Whoa! It's the Sand God and he looks madder than a man with no legs in a shoe shop.

Richard now realised that those long twinned front teeth were nearly as big as they were, added to that, were the thing's two muscular stubby arms that ended with huge sharp-clawed paddle like paws.

"We thought Dragora was dangerous, those teeth and claws would rip us apart in seconds?" Richard whispered as the thing began levering itself upwards out of its mound, its body showed to its waistline. It was only then, that Richard realised just how enormous this thing really was.

"That is no Sand God, according to something I read in Morbane's Book, it is possibly a mole beast named Hulkan." Melek whipped out the book and as quietly as he could read the following lines.

When people call this mole to mind
They could never be more sincere
Hulkan be of the mightiest beast

So large, a monster, a creation to fear
With powers to transform all loam's feast
This beast is never whatever it may appear

"Gghhh! I too have heard the legend of this beast, it cannot be killed." Orkan whispered in terror. "Hulkan has no eyes to see with, but that is of little matter, although we are faster across the ground, he will still track us because Hulkan's ears act like its eyes."

"Melek is hurt and cannot run, you and I will have to draw him away down in that direction." Richard pointed down the slope. Melek, you do not move a muscle, if we make it we will meet at that bubbling spring." He pointed in the opposite direction. "Ready? Let's go." Without another word the two almost tiptoed away from the monster. Their first movement brought Hulkan's snout swinging around towards them, its nostrils immediately flared as the big beast sniffed at the air and catching the trace of fresh prey. Hulkan immediately scrabbled its huge claws through the muddy soil in their exact direction.

"Gghhh! It's coming! Run!" The two raced away down the incline, but the bracken that they had easily walked through became a nightmare of tangles as they rushed headlong downward especially for Richard who was still carrying the Book of Prophecies and slowing him even more.

"Orkan Come back! Orkan Wait!" Richard shouted expectantly. He was surprised when he saw his companion turn away and unsteadily flounder on downhill through the thickening bracken. He drew Juroot's dagger more in hope and comfort, than intention.

Melek lay in his position hardly daring to breathe while keeping an eye on the large beast at the centre of the soil bump.

"That's what the phrase 'powers to transform all loam's feast' meant." He thought to himself as he watched in amazement as the mole monster picked up clods of fresh damp earth formed them into live figures with arms, legs and heads at fantastic speed. Each time Hulkan placed the model on the ground it yawned, stretched and darted off down the hill in the direction of his two companions, all the while the building mud army would be chuckling as each of them raced away. He looked towards the spring where they were supposed to meet up and noticed there were several sizable trees growing in the that vicinity, a plan formed in his head to distract Hulkan.

"Dangerous but workable." Melek thought as he carefully eyed up the distance between his position, a particular tree he had picked out and Hulkan's locality, bearing in mind that he would have to hobble once he attempted to make any move.

Meanwhile, horrified by the sight of what he could see happening, Richard put on a magnificent burst of speed that almost allowed him to catch up with his companion. He struggled on after Orkan while the little mud figures just kept coming; they were small enough to dart beneath the bracken fronds with relative ease. The chuckling army very soon outstripped their quarry and instead of doing anything to them, began forming a large circular ring around their newly acquired captives. More and more of the chuckling mud army dolls arrived and began locking themselves into position with the others by forming a mud wall.

"Gghhh! I'll show them. Help me!" Both Orkan and Richard used sword and dagger to try to smash their way through the growing mud wall but, it was having little or no impact, as each stabbed or sliced at the wall it was like attacking the earth itself with the soft mud simply closing up and repairing itself. Hulkan's army looked impregnable as it grew in width and height.

Melek jumped up and began hobbling down the hill towards the tree he had earlier pinpointed. Immediately his sudden movement alerted Hulkan who swivelled, away from his current position and quickly tracked his direction of travel towards the opposite side of the hill. Again, he began to create mud beings and sending them off after Melek who had almost reached the tree. He used his rope around a branch to gain extra leverage and made it to the higher branches as the first of Hulkan's army came racing by not having seen his neat manoeuvre. More and more mud men passed by as Melek patiently waited and watched the fate of his companions from his perch.

"At least Hulkan's attention is now on me." Looking down to bubbling water he noticed that several following mud soldiers had accidentally landed in the spring and were slowly dissolving back to sand. He looked down the hill, seeing an almost unbroken line of reddish brown he turned to see what Hulkan was doing. "Gone, he must be heading this way or, towards Richard and Orkan. Time to go." Melek said to himself, seeing the last of the mud soldiers pass by his hiding place.

He grabbed the end of the rope and like a monkey using a vine in the jungle; he swung away from the tree and landed on the upslope of the hill. With a flick of the wrist he coiled the rope flicked it again so that most of it landed in the water, then coiled it together and headed downhill straight towards his friends. The mud men were too busy forcing themselves against each other to notice his arrival. He picked up a large branch and looped the still wet rope to one end then, began spinning it before letting go.

"Orkan! Get ready to run when I tell you." He shouted flinging a large branch over the wall. He pulled it hard and the wet rope cut through the mud like a knife through butter, he yanked even harder and the branch tore an opening out of the wall. He did this several times.

"Now Orkan!" He screamed hurling the log again and again. Orkan saw the weakness in appearing and used his sword to make cuts top to bottom that the log simply ripped through even though the mud men were trying desperately to fill.

"Gghhh! Time to leave" Both Richard and Orkan vaulted their way across the gap of entangled and fused mud men

"This way, follow me. I know how we can get away from Hulkan." Melek shouted at his companions as he hobbled back up the hill towards the point where they had spent the night.

"Gghhh! He's taking us back into the cave, it's a trap." Orkan complained, starting to slow down. "I'm not going back there."

"Don't be so silly, Melek wouldn't lead us into a trap. Think logically, why would he save us then simply take us into yet another dangerous situation? Richard was becoming annoyed with the ever un-cooperative Orkan. "Either come or wait for..." There was a familiar rumble a little way down the hill. Richard turned and saw below them that Hulkan's men were in chaos, still struggling to unform the wall and chase after their prey. "We have a head start this time, you can waste it, I trust Melek's judgement."

Melek had just about reached the point where he needed to be, fear mixed with adrenaline meant that even though he was still hobbling, he had not felt any pain.

"Hurry, I think Hulkan is about to make his entrance. Melek shouted at the squabbling pair. No sooner had Richard reached him than the recognisable ground bump started appearing right in the middle of the circular mud wall below. Orkan had suddenly decided what was in his best interests and sped up to reach them.

"Gghhh!" I'm not going back in there." He pointed to the cave entrance then turned just in time to see Hulkan's huge frame break through the bump. It took him a short while to realise that his prey had been allowed to break free.

"If he was mad last time, he is going to be livid now. What's the plan?" Richard asked urgently as Hulkan first made a piercing high-pitched whistle, then began a deep-throated wheezing noise as he began clawing at the soil dump.

"He is making more soldiers but from here they seem to be much larger than the first ones. Time to go to wherever you say we go Melek."

"I want the book back; you could have lost it back there." Melek said firmly as he helped Richard take it off his back.

"Not you as well? Orkan's been strange all morning, don't you guys trust me anymore? Richard whispered to him as he heaved the book onto Melek's back.

"Of course we trust you, are you not the Chosen One?" He was hobbling but making good time as he led them along the way he had travelled that morning. They could just see the place where Hulkan was marshalling his army. There was a noticeable difference between the newly formed group already starting up the hill towards the cave and those made earlier. The shorter ones seemed to be the faster movers. Melek led them down to the ridge and as they passed around it he said, "I noticed that while out gathering berries and honey this morning." Melek pointed towards the lake a long way down. "This path seems to lead to it.

"Gghhh! Water? Remember what happened last time we were in water? Not for me, nasty things hide in water."

"Right! I've had enough of your nonsense. You stay here and face those mud men and Hulkan, Melek and I will continue with the mission. Let's go!" Richard was absolutely livid as he and Melek set off down a narrow path that hugged the land but fell away sharply towards the lake.

"Let them go I will find another way back to the Ancestral City by myself." Orkan fondled his bracelet that seemed to come very much alive by flashing. He arrived at the ridge and as he walked around it was stopped dead in his tracks, for ahead and bounding in his direction were the mud men army in full flow.

"Weeeooo! Weeeooo! Orkan spun around and raced as hard as he could back to the narrow path. "They are coming! Weeeooo!" He screamed in terror.

"I think that this path does not reach the water, I think it bypasses the lake. Look, you can see it on the other side of the valley," Richard pointed to a winding ribbon beyond the lake. He turned to see whether Orkan had changed his mind or not, when his heart skipped several beats as he saw a sea of reddish brown pouring down from around the ridge. Still a long way behind, he had not heard Orkan's shout but instantly recognised their danger as he saw him racing down towards them and about midway between the mud men and their position.

"Run! It's our only hope," He and Melek took off as fast as his legs would allow them to run. The nearer they got to the point where the path disappeared around the bend before returning on the other side of the lake, the rockier and narrower the surface was becoming and Orkan and the mud men were gaining on them all the time.

"Hulkan is coming, I hear that sound below us somewhere." Richard shouted to the battling librarian running but also having to pick his way around the more common and jagged rocks now popping up all over their path.

"You save yourself; I cannot go any faster than I am already going. This path is getting wet and if I trip on these sharp stones, it will decree my end and Hulkan will get me." Melek shouted back.

Hulkan had become so incensed at losing his intended prey, that he had set up his army to give chase and as soon as they were all on their way, he had tunnelled like a speeding torpedo to try to head them off, knowing full well that if they reached the rocky outcrop before he did, that he would then have to go the long way around to pick them up on the other side. Underground, the rocks were becoming a problem and he knew if he tried going much further, he would hit solid rock so, in hope he turned and tunnelled hard and surged to the surface, just above the path and ahead of his chasing army. He could see the fleeing group had already passed this point, so all he could do was encourage his mud men to catch them.

"Weeeooo! Weeeooo!" Orkan was not too far from his two companions and the mud men were constantly gaining ground on him.

"Orkan is almost with us, what do we do now?" Richard shouted, as Melek was about to get to the point where the path went around the corner beside a sheer drop to the water. "We let Orkan reach us then jump into that lake."

"Why?

It's something I noticed earlier, you have to trust my judgement or it is all over for all of us."

"He's almost here, what if he doesn't want to jump?"

"You somehow make him do it, we have no second chances." Without even having to turn around, Richard could both hear and feel Orkan approaching his back, he drew as close up behind Melek as he dared, then at the moment when Orkan was directly behind, waved him past to slot in between himself and Melek.

"Gghhh! what now?" He shouted as he went past Richard.

"This!" Richard sped up grabbing the unsuspecting Orkan's arm and pulled him off balance over the sheer drop. "Jump Melek!" Looking up he saw that he was already in the air.

"Weeeooo! Weeeooo!" Orkan screamed as his stomach lurched into a triple somersault as he headed to the watery surface. Luckily the lake was sufficiently deep enough to break their fall – although it was a long enough jump, to have jarred Melek's leg even further as he hit the rocky bottom of the lakebed. They surfaced together and Richard looked up to see chaos raining down from above. As the front mud men had tried to stop on the wet path they had began slipping and sliding while the train of hard running army piled into them at speed from the back in droves. It looked almost a little lemming-like as scores started dropping down to the water from the point almost directly above the group.

"Swim! Richard grabbed Orkan and yanked him away from the spattering belly flopping mud men.

"Swim away from there, towards that side, there are rapids that way," Melek called to Richard. Every time he stopped to help Orkan, he could feel that there was a slight undercurrent pushing them towards the rapids that Melek had alluded to. Behind them, mud men were fast dissolving like butter on a hot plate, creating a complete mud bath with that part of the lake fast becoming a quicksand pit as more and more of Hulkan's army flopped into it.

"Gghhh! Cannot keep this up. Told you I hated water, didn't I?" Richard turned Orkan onto his back and began swimming life-guard style knowing full well that although they were trying for the far side bank, they were slowly, almost imperceptibly being pulled down lake towards those rapids by the undertow. From this position, he could still make out the raving figure of Hulkan who seemed to be having problems of his own.

Richard called for Melek to help, he fell back and grabbing onto Orkan's feet, kicked. Hard in long bursts until the group made it to the shallows where Orkan could look after himself.

"Right, we better move away from here, I saw that Hulkan was watching us in the water and now he has disappeared, maybe he could pop up here?" They steadily made their way up the long bank towards trees located higher up skirting the long ridge, their sodden clothes drying on their backs as they walked. Safely reaching the outskirts of cover it was Richard that again tackled Orkan about his odd behaviour. "What has happened between us and why didn't you help me against Hulkan? You ran away like a coward, companions don't do that?" Richard said crossly.

"Gghhh! I'm not sure." Orkan said looking shiftily to one side, he simply shrugged

"If we have offended you, done something wrong or you simply want to leave us, this I understand. But, up until yesterday, you were an absolute hero in my estimation but you've suddenly changed for no reason or explanation? We both helped to bring you safely across the lake, that's what companions in trouble do for each other? Orkan, there's something going on inside your head, tell us. Between us, we can try helping to put it right once again?" Richard felt relieved that he could remain calm, willing Orkan to be all right. Inwardly he felt a sense of justice as he recalled some of the good things that they had done as a team.

"Gghhh! I know, but what do you want me to say?" Again, he simply shrugged his shoulders. Richard thought back to the last time Orkan had not been acting so strangely, clearly remembering that his alteration must have occurred somewhere between releasing the dragons and following the reptiles after that first explosion. He continued racking his brain battling to complete a time line of events. A familiar drone interrupted Richard's thoughts. His companions heard it too, instantly they all broke into a headlong run, there was no need for any discussion. The three knew the sound of attacking Grapfrits all too well and were not that far away. Ducking and diving around the trees, jumping over gnarled roots, searching for cover, they knew they did not stand a chance and the fast moving Grapfrits would swarm into their midst if they couldn't find a hiding place.

A Tricky Conjuror

On the Fifteenth Day...

Flying foes are everywhere
On the ground and in the air.
Hidden from the light of day,
A place to stop, but not to stay.
Here countless dark eyes will see you,
And the burning flames will free you,
But a false friend will deceive you.
Your hidden treasure will leave you.

Behind the companions, the Grapfrits drone took on a deeper note. Richard had all but given up hope and his mind was already thinking that their only form of escape might be his cape, when ahead of them, he noticed a dark chink at the base of a very large tree that had an array of twisting, knurled and tangled roots that could possibly present them with somewhere to try to camouflage themselves.

"There!" The three made it and to their amazement found that hidden behind the maze of roots was a small door set back among the roots.

"Gghhh! Grapfrits, door... Door, Grapfrits. No contest, try it!" Richard could see that Orkan was terrified. The door was old and mildewed with surrounding timbers sagging and twisted as he pushed and pulled at it, all the while the menacing drone increased. A panicked Orkan threw himself shoulder first at the resistant door. It creaked open slowly as Orkan and Richard both heaved simultaneously until with a last shove the open was wide enough for all three to pile through to present themselves to the inner shadows. Richard was a little taken aback when he found it a simple matter to swing the door shut with comparative ease, it was as if the hinges had suddenly been oiled.

Outside, the Grapfrits buzzed their way between the tree trunks and knotted roots sensing smelling that their victims were not far ahead. Because of their poor sight, they had not seen or heard the three when they quickly disappeared through the ancient door. Excitedly, the scouting Grapfrits became somewhat agitated to indicate having located prey, like an ocean washing against a beach, the intensity travelled in waves throughout the entire moving group. They moved in among the roots with the dexterity of a frenzied colony of bats using echolocation, probing and testing everywhere to unearth their prey. The trail led them directly to the tiny door and finding nothing, even after several sloppy attempts by flying at the entryway without success, meant to them that their quarry had moved on. They picked up speed and screamed away like a meteoric shower, to continue to pursue the figments of their own imaginations.

Inside the doorway, the three waited in fear as the assault was in full flow, they waited nervously until the erratic banging slowed then stopped altogether. The three waited until the drone abated before anyone dared move a muscle. Richard let out his breath in a gasp.

"Gghhh!" Dangerous things, those Grapfrits?" Orkan breathed a sigh of agitated relief, his hand automatically moving to his wrist and the comfort of his amulet. As he rubbed the armband, he noticed that the door seemed to be shrinking slowly, the movement being slow but imperceptible. "Wonder what's in this place?" He pushed his way past the other two in order to draw their attention away from the door.

"We were lucky there," Richard said, I thought they had us. We don't need any more caves but, we better hang on for a short while just in case they double back?" It was quite dark, much darker than outside when Richard soon noticed Orkan's body was silhouetted against a distant glow emanating from deeper in the cave.

"Phew! What a stench, I think something has died in here and the cave seems to be widening. I wonder what is causing that glow ahead." Richard tugged at Orkan's clothes, "on second thoughts we don't want to hang around any longer than we need to, do we?" His voice carried and echoed against the walls.

"There's enough light here, let's have a quick look at the prophecy before moving on?" Melek whispered. He placed the book on a small stone outcrop and Richard joined him while an uninterested Orkan continued moving carefully towards the soft glare ahead. "Now, let's see what is supposed to happen next." He read out the riddle.

Flying foes are everywhere
On the ground and in the air.
Hidden from the light of day,
A place to stop, but not to stay.
Here countless dark eyes will see you,
And the burning flames will free you,
But a false friend will deceive you.
Your hidden treasure will leave you.

"The flying foes are obviously the Grapfrits, but it does not make sense because it uses the words 'On the ground and in the air', and that is not right?

"We now know who the treacherous friend could be but there isn't hard evidence?" Richard said glancing in Orkan's direction. "He couldn't even be bothered waiting for us. Something is not right?"

"The next part is also logical, it says 'A place to stop, but not to stay. Somehow, I think it's warning us of impending danger? It's time to leave."

"Orkan! Come on, we're leaving!" Richard was again surprised at how loudly his shout seemed to echo throughout the cave.

"I do not think you need to leave just yet." The harsh reply reverberated back from deep within bowels of the tree causing the two to turn and look alarmingly at each other, for the sound was definitely not that of Orkan's voice but, was more like a deep piercing shrill.

"Gghhh! I'm getting out of here." Orkan screamed, racing towards them. Richard grabbed Melek's hand as he swung the book onto his back and they raced to the door with Orkan in hot pursuit.

"The doors disappeared." Richard said in desperation just as the pig-like boy joined them. "We're trapped." Orkan looked at the black wall now facing them with sinking heart knowing that their escape was well and truly blocked, He rubbed the amulet over and over again hoping to reverse what he had done by willing the door to enlarge itself but, there was no sign of any movement. "There's no way out of here, maybe there's a way back there?"

They moved along carefully towards the faint glow and when the area began to open, the cave came to an abrupt halt opening to a cavern. Light seemed to funnel in from way above; they could even see some of the overhanging trees of the forest covering the entrance to the hole. Richard also noted that the centre of the cave floor was piled high with glowing ash and that a faint wisp of grey formed a leisurely column of smoke that rose up and into the outside world, the whole structure was intended to act like some natural chimney.

"We can't climb up that." Melek said.

"Hmm. I wonder what all this ash is doing here." Richard moved around the grey pile and stopped, his blood ran cold.

"Look at this." Both joined their companion, before them was a tall stack of bones all carefully piled up and stacked in some sort of macabre alter.

"Gghhh! Looks like someone's kitchen, I told you we shouldn't have come in here." Orkan lied.

"Be sensible about this, those Grapfrits would have hacked us to pieces, I wonder who lives here? Whoever it is, is not a friend so be ready."

"Gghhh! Believe me, we don't want to meet it; I think it must be some kind of flesh eater that cooks its victims down here. Let's get out of here."

"You're probably right. C'mon let's see if we can find a way up there, "he pointed towards the opening above them. What about trying the rope?" As Richard and Melek moved to cross the room, Orkan caught hold of his clothes.

"Too late, there's something coming down the tunnel." Orkan pointed to an opening that seemed have appeared from nowhere.

"Whoa! But, how do you know something's coming? I can't hear anything,"

"Can't you hear that scraping sound?"

"Uh-uh."

"We're trapped down here."

Orkan fixed an arrow into his golden bow while Richard looked upwards to see if they could possibly climb to the forest way above their heads. Melek pulled out the golden rope and tried several times to lasso one of the braches high above their heads without any joy.

"It's too far, downwards wouldn't be a problem, but getting it up there is impossible." Melek said trying several more times.

"Orkan, give me one of your arrows." Without arguing, Orkan handed him one already in the bow. Richard fastened the rope to the arrow and handed it back to his companion and all the time, the scraping sound that they could all now hear, seemed to be getting ever louder and closer.

"Gghhh! What are we trying to do?"

"I want you to try and shoot an arrow into that branch up there. Possibly we can then climb out of here, it's our only chance." Orkan took aim and released the arrow, because of the rope tied now to it; the thing missed its target and fell back into the ash piled floor. Orkan gathered it in and this time, allowing for the extra weight of the golden rope took aim and fired. It struck home with a resounding thud.

"Gghhh! You go first. I can't climb very well so when you're up there you can help me by pulling the rope."

"Bzzz! You're too late; you are never going to get out of here alive." Across the ash pile, peering at them from out of the gloom was an enormous fly; its blue-green body was partially covered with a forest of thick black hair. Its arms ended in sharp claws. A thin tongue licked horribly from the black funnel of its mouth. They immediately recognised that everything about the creature exuded darkness except for its bulbous eyes – they were huge, seemingly sparkling through a myriad of prisms that almost reflected hypnotic light from an uncanny depth. One look and Melek sensed that the eyes staring at them held images not just of this cavern but also of places far away.

"Do not look straight into its eyes, I have a feeling that it might be its most powerful weapon." Melek whispered. "If not, it could be the staff that it carries?" Richard had not really noticed, but now that he had drawn his attention to it, he saw that this fly carried a long staff that was almost like an extension of its own scrawny legs. This elaborate rod was being held firmly by several legs; the rod extended to an elaborate top that was delicately carved, glimmering, with a patterned encrusted pair of eyes that almost replicated its owner's expression.

"Gghhh! Look at those jewels, they are magnificent." Orkan's vision had become entrapped in an almost hypnotised state as the fly slowly, yet deliberately swivelled the rod so that the two orbs glinted, shone and mesmerised the group.

"Oh-oh! Hate flies at the best of times," Richard whispered, noticing that there seemed to be more and more activity happening on the walls flanking the monster fly. He turned to quickly survey the walls of the rest of the cavern, exactly the same was occurring as all around, large moving black masses of flies were appearing as if magically becoming wallpaper markings against the reddish cavern background scene.

"I think they are his soldiers, see how they constantly travel in groups to him? It looks as if they're communicating. It's as if there is a high-pitched buzzing every time a group reaches him." Melek whispered.

"It reminds me of a general receiving report from the battlefront, you have to admit it does look quite imperious sitting there like that. Somehow I don't think we will have to wait very long for it to make its move. We must be ready for anything" Richard whispered back determinedly, then added, "I think you should move slowly to the rope and try escaping, if they try anything, Orkan and I will fend them off for as long as we can?" Still under the watchful gaze of the monstrous fly, Melek moved almost imperceptibly step by small step, knowing that any sudden move would be bound to trigger some form of reaction. He reached the rope and to make sure it was still secure, gave it a slight tug, the quiver of the rope was the attack signal for the giant fly to raise the jewelled sceptre. Instantly, a thick cloud of flies left the walls and descended on Richard and Orkan. The pair fought valiantly against the first onslaught, but it was an almost impossible task as for every few flies they managed to swat, hundreds more immediately took their place.

"Your cape! Make yourself invisible," a confused Melek shouted at Richard. The flies were only attacking the boys and left him alone to escape if he so pleased. As Richard tried to make a grab for his cape Melek saw a barrage of larger horse flies form themselves into the shape of a hand that then shot forward as the hand closed into a clenched fist and struck Richard against the head. He went down under the heavy blow, the flies then retreated to be replaced by sheer numbers of the smaller type soldier flies pinning Richard firmly to the ground, The hand reformed and again metered out the same punishment to Orkan, it was all over as far as Melek could see, there were now just two seething black lumps on the ground where the two had valiantly defended themselves a short time ago.

"Stop! Bring them to me." The giant fly lowered her sceptre and her black arts made the flies part like that of two carpets being rolled back to form a path around the glowing embers and straight to the fly monstrosity. The huge insect raised a claw and beckoned them forward. "Come closer." From behind the large flying hand gave them a couple of nudges to urge them on.

"Who are you?" Richard demanded. "What do you want with us?"

"Fair question. I am Narkum, the Fly Kind and Spy Master, and you are the supposed Chosen One, are you not?"

"Who told you that? I don't know what you're talking about. Huh! Chosen One? What next? Richard lied.

The giant fly raised a claw and pointed it at the two in turn. "You are Golan's minions. Simply feeble pawns who have now been duped to your certain death by his honeyed tongue of one who claims to represent 'good', Ha! Ha!" Narkum's pessimistic laughter swirled like ball bearings bouncing on a kettledrum.

"Golan? Never heard of him," Richard again defended defiantly. We were just crossing the forest when we came under attack by Grapfrits.

"Liar!"

"You have no cause to hold us like this, we've no grudge against you, Richard tried bluffing his way through.

"Oh but, you will have soon, it is now your turn to suffer for the havoc you have wreaked on some of our associates" Narkum snickered. "You think I'm a fool do you?"

"Not at all, you have power; you are the general of your army, why would I be so stupid to even think you were a fool?" Richard hoped that praise might help their position.

"You see, I know everything there is to know about you two and your worthless quest. My spies are everywhere in this realm. They see all and report back to me so that I know everything that happens here." Narkum's eyes flared for a second, "and in other worlds too. Your lives are mine from beginning to end." He paused to let these profound words sink in, his eyes sparkling deeper than ever. "I am fair in my judgements, you see, we will even let the librarian escape if he so wishes but you two? The fire embers grow hotter as we speak and you will become bones upon my favourite alter, of this, there is little doubt."

"He can leave without hindrance? Richard enquired hoping to gain time.

"He is free to leave right now. In fact, I want him to leave before your demise in order that he can get back to Golan to let him know how your mission failed so miserably. I will even send some of my troops ahead to clear a path to the Ancestral City for him. You two however, will have to reach Golan as smoke because as I said before, you're both mine and we are partial to enjoying a bit of crackling."

"No!" Richard cried, letting his temper take over. Drawing Juroot's dagger he had sheathed earlier, he lunged towards the Fly King.

"Throughout these proceedings, Orkan had been nervously fingering his amulet. When his companion dived towards Narkum, he moved to stop him by shooting out a foot tripping Richard and sending him sprawling to the floor and just missing landing among the glowing embers. Narkum laughed triumphantly.

"You cannot kill me with a mere dagger; I am the one that does any killing in here." As if to prove his point he lifted and swung the rod in a short arc above the prone boy's head and the fly hand shot from behind Orkan to dive straight into the ash and embers. There was a little screeching sound followed immediately by what sounded like a large amount of popcorn in a hot pan. "Life to me is cheap and instantly can be replaced. They did not protect me, they died but, your friend did aid me in order to save his own worthless hide, so shall I spare him? The answer is I won't." Again the hollow chuckle rang out.

While their attention had been focused on the unfolding drama being played out the Fly King and his army had for a moment neglected Melek. Even before Narkum's mirth had ceased the librarian flicked his wrist downwards and outwards so fast that the rope became a blur as it wrapped itself around the sceptre and whipping it out of the giant fly's claws. The gleaming rod spun across the room and smashed into the ash and embers, several of the magnificent jewels shattering on impact. Immediately swarms of flies began dropping to floor buzzing helplessly, while those in flight seemed to be like attacking kamikaze pilots diving straight into the embers to create an even larger popping fireworks display.

"That's evened the odds a little," Richard said, trying to get up and locking eyes with Narkum he saw that almost every colour of the spectrum now flashing across the Fly King's all seeing orbs. Visions of eternity clashed and collided, being replaced by deep-seated fires of hatred.

"You will die!" Narkum screeched.

The reflection of the embers expanded into a fierce, ruby light that was directly aimed at Richard. He dived away from the ashes and rolled to avoid the initial laser beam attack, there was no escaping more attacks unless they could kill, destroy or maim Narkum in this slight respite period Melek had managed to obtain for them.

"Get that sceptre," he shouted at Orkan who was nearest the rod's handle. Orkan however, was moving in a daze, his amulet spell still holding him from aiding good and his only thought at that moment was to save himself as he stumbled towards the chimney. Melek realised what was happening as he drew his sword, his trusty rope again snaked out around Orkan's legs sending him crashing to the ground in front of him and letting his sword fall from his grip. He collected it and even still limping shot to the ashes and used the sword to try to break up all the jewels within the now brightly glowing sceptre. All he managed to do was force the bejewelled head of the rod deeper into the gleaming hot cinders.

Narkum's voices cracked into a loud screech as he saw the head of the rod disappear beneath a sea of orange. He left his task of destroying the Chosen One and scuttled towards the flames beginning to lap from the rod. His dark taloned arms stretched out in order to snatch the sceptre back from the embers, one talon closed around the prize, then another but, in that moment of victory, fire snaked up the rod and suddenly the entire room came alight as flames leapt across and attacked Narkum's hairy body. It was fuel to the fire and within seconds Narkum became a huge torch of flame lighting every corner with unaccustomed brightness. Narkum did not move as a starburst radiated straight up his arm to his body. For an instant his eyes fixed on Melek through the flames. The fire and starburst took that away, first cracking then blacking the huge orbs like a pair of convexed windows being blasted out of a burning building.

"It is time to leave this place," Melek released the still prone Orkan. "Fire another arrow with the rope as you did before." An obedient Orkan's aim was true as they heard the thud.

"You will go first then I will follow." Melek pointed towards the slightly dazed Richard who didn't need a second invitation. Because he and friends had often practiced this near his house on a rope tied to an old tree. Hand over hand he quickly pulled himself to the top and was surprised to find that the exit was an old well. He leaned over the wall and looked down in the bright light of Narkum's burning shell he could make out Melek starting to clamber upward, he helped by pulling at the rope until he reached the top and Richard then dropped the rope for Orkan to use.

Looking over the wall he froze as an enormous snail began entering the central area below. Even from this high up position he could that as soon as the thing saw the unsuspecting Orkan struggling on the end of the rope, it opened its mouth and Richard could see multi-rows of white flashing incisors that they were meant for business, and it was moving slowly towards his companion that was so intent with trying to climb that he hadn't seen the thing.

"Orkan! Behind you!"

"Wheeooee!"

As if by magic, the struggling companion seemed to suddenly grasp the idea of rope climbing as he literally flew up the rope and over the top of the well. Richard pulled up the rope while Orkan retrieved his arrows from the branch and thanked the tree for aiding their escape.

"Gghhh! I told you that there are only nasty things under the ground, never again if I can help it."

Suddenly from within the bowls of the earth there was a terrific blast followed by a lesser explosion sending hurricane blast-waves up and through the forest.

"What now?" Richard and his two colleagues moved to the chimney wall and looked over, Narkum had disappeared, all that remained was a massive black hole and the huge snail, now minus its split conical shell, was writhing in all directions across the cavern floor, leaving a wide slimy silvery trail in its wake. The dark patches of dead flies all of a sudden seemed to have been blown into a heap against one wall by Narkum's explosion, the colossal black quantity began to come alive once again, the pile began to slither and slide en masse, wriggling, twisting and breaking out of their husks.

"I thought that they were all dead, but now they seem to be pupating. Dead is supposed to mean dead, not come back to life," Richard said watching thousands of Narkum's army undergoing an extraordinary transformation below. "They are metamorphosing into goodness knows what?"

They all remained transfixed, looking down upon the scuffling fly bodies that moved and jumped like Mexican beans to spread themselves away from the pile that had already survived both fire and blast were also starting to break free of their twisted black body shells to reveal beautiful, multi-coloured insects, which grew larger by the second, unfurling wide wings that shone with a mixture of almost pearly white glow from the little sunlight drifting down the chimney. The sound of their skins being sloughed off filled the air with a steady crackle, as if someone down there were walking across of dead, dying and dried leaves.

"There's your answer, they are not flies, and they are insects." Melek smiled at Richard.

It began with a flutter as the struggling insects started twitching their antennae, stretching limbs spreading their wings to test the air, and then flying short distances, before heading upwards into the vent that brought the dazzling array of colour soaring past the three onlookers and out into forest. The sound grew and grew as the air below filled with more and more joining the cloud of airborne creatures until the roar sounded like a fighter jet about to take off. They poured into the surrounding trees until the whole area looked as if there had been some sort of rainbow snowfall in the immediate vicinity. One of the larger insects came to rest on the wall right in front of the group; it did nothing but seemed to be staring straight at Richard through eyes that reflected all the colours of the rainbow. Strangely Richard no longer felt the slightest bit nervous or afraid standing his ground while the creature before them seemed to complete its inspection of the companions.

"You must be the Chosen One," it said. "What you have just witnessed is all that remains of the insect race that used to inhabit this world. Our numbers were decimated when the Evil One sent Narkum here, we battled long and hard but it was useless. His magical powers given by his master were simply too great and we were overrun by his forces and systematically destroyed, fighting became useless. Those of us that knew of the prophecy decided that we had to live and became his spies. We changed into flies to do his bidding and were his eyes, keeping track of everything that went on. Bit by bit, we watched the Forces of Good being hunted down and destroyed without being able to do much about it. When you arrived, we decided not to reveal your movements or quests to Narkum, not all could keep some of the details from the King Fly but in general, he was not aware of what has happened to many of his evil associates. We hoped that what has happened here today would happen and are deeply in your debt."

Richard thoughtfully absorbed the news, and then asked gently, "Do you have any information that could help us with this mission?"

"Not really. Events move too fast here and in the short time of your arrival anything could have happened because whatever I reveal would probably be out of date, that incorrect information might place you in danger. I can tell you that many of those who you have helped escape the Evil One's power have made their way back to the Ancestral City to await your return."

Richard's mission seemed to take on an even greater urgency. "Will you also be joining forces with other survivors in the Ancestral City? He asked.

"Most definitely," the creature replied. "There's no time to waste, for more recent news I suggest that you talk to Totlo, his forces may be able to help you with any questions."

"Where do we find this Totlo?"

"Don't worry, Totlo will find you." The creature spread its wings, raised one of its claws in salute and barked orders in a language Richard did not understand. From the surrounding trees there was a shout and fluttering of wings as if the army of insects were also saluting the group. We go now. Good luck to you all, may your mission succeed and we meet again at the Ancestral City. We will be keeping watch and reporting to Golan." With that, the insect rose high into the sky, ordering his followers into squadrons and flights, they peeled away, chitting the air with their wings, hovering for a moment over the companions then darted off in orderly fashion.

"Well, well. That was quite something, wasn't it?" Richard said as he waved farewell to the disappearing insect forces and silence again descended on the forest around them.

"We should all be proud of what has so far been achieved," Melek reflected. "The forces of Good grow with your quest, we must believe in each other's capabilities." He looked directly at Orkan, "That includes you."

"Gghhh! Right, what do we do now? "Orkan held a cupped hand to his enormous ear.

"Did you hear that?"

"What?"

"That! It's ahead of us somewhere."

Richard listened carefully; all he could hear was what sounded like the chirruping of crickets coming from the woodlands around them.

"You mean those crickets."

"Those aren't crickets, then it could be the Namatoes. I have read that they sound just like crickets." Melek intelligently offered an explanation.

"Aren't they?" Richard listened careful, they sounded just like crickets to them. "Then they're bound to be something nasty? That's not the sound the Grapfrits make? So what are these Namatoes then?"

"They're supposed to be the smallest spirits in our world. You won't see them but, they're all around us believe me, you can be sure they're watching us and that noise is them talking among themselves. That is what I understand of the texts about their ways."

The high-pitched chirruping around them slowly died until the Namatoes were absolutely quiet once more. "Totlo, if it is you, I am Melek the Seshet and Scribe from the Ancestral City. I introduce you to my friend Richard," he pointed towards Richard. "He is the Chosen One and is helping to find the missing guardians and Pods of Life." The forest became alive with the strange chirruping sounds once again, and then the racket subsided as quickly as it had started.

"The Chosen One requests to meet with you and the Namatoes, because he has instruction from Golan, the keeper of all Ancestral Stories."

Suddenly, as if from a vision, a ghostly grey image started taking shape, Richard watched, thinking that somehow it looked like a photographic negative slowly transforming into a picture. Bit by bit, the figure was changing from its ghostly see-through being, into a solid kindly looking old man. One minute Richard could see through the apparition's body, the next, the creature had become an ordinary man. Richard watched the whole transformation in sheer disbelief.

"Good day to you and Orkan. Good day to you, Master Richard, we welcome you all to our humble forest dwelling." He bowed low and indicated for them to enter the ring of shining leaves that seemed to have appeared from nowhere. Richard felt immediately relaxed and at ease with this person. Totlo's slow speaking voice carried a warm and comforting manner as if, lulling them into a sense of hypnotic state. "So, Master Richard, you have been chosen to advance through the Ancestral Trail and trace the Pods of Life? It is a great honour indeed that's been bestowed on you."

"Why? Since my arrival, nasty things have done nothing but tried to capture, kill or eat us. What's so honourable about that? I would rather be home in bed." Richard studied the man carefully. He had pointed ears and a flat head, his eyes seemed deep and hidden like shallow pools behind a covered mantle and his nose appeared slightly deformed, as if it had be broken. Totlo looked more like a prize-fighter than a creature of the forest, yet, something about his very nature, oozed calmness and knowledge.

"Do not be so alarmed. Any source of learning is always a good thing." It was then that Richard got his first whiff of a strange and pungent smell "Ah, here come my messengers," proclaimed Totlo proudly. Richard almost let out a scream but somehow managed to rein it back as he bit sharply into his tongue.

As far as the eye could see, there were thousands of little bug-like creatures shaped and seemingly replicating pebbles like you would find on a stony beach, except they were very much alive and all making their way from the safety of the forest towards the leafy ring.

"W-W-What are those," Richard stammered.

"They are the Namatoes, my special spiritual messengers and now that you have been allowed to see me, you are also able to observe them for they are everywhere." It was a horrendous experience, mainly because Richard hated any form of creepy-crawly and here he was in the midst of what seemed to him like millions of moving walnut shaped cockroaches or locusts swarming across the ground towards them.

"They look just like moving pebbles. W-Will they harm me?"

"Oh no. Not unless I order them to do so. They're only interested in what we have to say to each other and their camouflage is excellent, nobody notices a pebble? You see, Master Richard, my Namatoes are sent to all corners of the earth to gather knowledge for us. They, like the birds and insects keep us up to date with what's happening out there." Richard noticed that as they reached the circle of leaves, the overpowering smell of a mixture of rose petals and dirty seawater drifted up his nose. The smell was something he had never experienced before; it made him somewhat light-headed and slightly giggly.

"Can they talk?"

"Only to me, they have a language of their own that only I can interpret. They understand everything; words, sounds, musical notes, even all languages. They report back in their own way, it's this form of transmission that lets me understand exactly what is going on out there." Totlo gave Richard a reassuring smile

"Are you able to help us then?" Richard asked hopefully.

"I can help you with only two points relating to your quest. The first being, you must travel upwards to find the source of the rock avalanche then make your way down through and between the fallen boulders. You will have to tread carefully while there."

"Why do we need to go there?" Richard asked hopefully.

"A guardian trapped is hidden there," he turned to Melek. "You bear the book, you need to solve this riddle before entering the slope of stone."

"Is there any more information?"

"Not on this matter, I receive mostly general information and it would take a while for me to fully interpret what the Namatoes have seen, or exactly where they saw it. For instance, before you arrived I already knew roughly about your journey, what brought you to this place and what you had achieved so far and could pass this information on to others. At all times, these little helpers are updating us and this helps fight the Evil One.

"Pity about that, I suppose we should move on and find this rock field?" Richard said.

More importantly, I also know that you should retrace your recent steps to retrieve the amulet you lost when you were punched to the ground by the flies"

"It's gone!" Richard's hands immediately searched for Golan's amulet with mounting desperation. "It's gone! We must find it. Melek we need your rope again."

"Good hunting, we will track your progress." Totlo began fading and the Namatoes turned and headed back towards the forest. The three companions returned to the chimney wall and looked down, nothing seemed to be moving.

"Gghhh! I know the Fly King is dead but, I also have a bad feeling about that place, I don't think it's quite finished with us yet? I'm not going down with you."

The Granite Man Attacks

On the Sixteenth Day...

A treasure burned needs water thrice,
A friend regained will cross it twice,
But water once brings danger near.
The rocks themselves a source of fear.
A rolling stone unlocks the jail,
Flight from there to no avail.
Cunning holds the key to all,
Death comes from a final fall.

"Right! You help Melek pull me up if I get into trouble," Richard was annoyed as he let himself down the chimney again. He moved cautiously around the blasted pit where Narkum had perished, slowly easing his way to a position around the still red hot glowing ash pile, where he felt he and Orkan had been overpowered. Using the tip of the dagger he began scraping and searching in among the dead and dying fly remains but found nothing.

"I can't find it anywhere here!" Richard shouted

"Gghhh! Maybe Narkum found it, search around the area where he was last seen." Orkan shouted back. Richard moved around the darkened pit and searched the whole area, Richard began to despair at the thought of losing it as Golan's threats entered his head. He moved to the highest point in the cavern at the edge of the dark hole and suddenly caught sight of something at the bottom that gave him a lift. He fiddled clumsily and pulled out his torch and shone it at the object.

"Found it! But it's at the bottom of the hole. Any suggestions?" he shouted.

"I could climb down and then use the rope?" Melek replied.

"No! You stay up there with Orkan." Richard's immediate thinking was that with Orkan's strange behaviour he didn't need Melek down in the cavern with no way to rely on Orkan to get them out if trouble struck. "I'll find a way." He decided there was no way than to climb down himself. The sides in the hole was loose sand covered by a sooty black film caused by the blast as he slipped and slid his way to the bottom and then tried to pick up the amulet. "Ouch!" The thing was really burning to the touch and he immediately dropped it. This time he used the knife tip to carefully lift it, then using a corner of his tunic he cleaned it up. It looked different somehow, the sparkle had gone and Richard wondered if the heat or explosion had damaged the amulet. Richard hoped not as he placed it into his pocket and started what was a long and slippery journey upwards again. There were no footholds and for every step he took the loose sand gave way sending him downwards as he scraped, clawed and scrambled his way, it was as if he was trying to run through a lake of treacle.

"Watch out! That huge snail is heading straight for the hole. Get out!" Melek screamed.

Richard was using the dagger as mountaineers use an ice pick to haul himself upwards, but as he was near the top, Melek's warning made him aware of impending danger and he saw the multi-toothed mouth start appearing over the rim. He dug in his footholds and blindly slashed out with the knife into the open mouth situated just above his head.

"Get out of there!" Melek screamed as he saw the snail recoil in pain and start squirting silvery white slime across the floor again. "Watch out for its slime, it's their defence and make sure you don't step in it, otherwise you will get stuck."

Richard clambered over the lip of the pit and skipped, hopped and jumped like a ballerina until he reached the rope. With as much energy as he could muster and his adrenaline pumping like mad, it was a reasonably quick climb to the top and then sat down, totally spent and began to realise what he had just achieved, Golan's amulet was in safe custody once again.

"Thank you Totlo!" Richard shouted towards the quiet forest. "Now we go to find that guardian." The forest suddenly sprang to life with strange chirruping sounds of the communicating Namatoes for a short while, then stopped. "I reckon Totlo already knows what has just happened?" Richard giggled.

The trio moved on towards the direction that Totlo had directed them to take. Soon the forest began to thin, and before too long they arrived at a river that crashed and thundered through a series of rapids.

"This must flow down to the lake where we escaped from Hulkan and his mud men." Melek observed. They looked back down the flow and although the current was fast, it snaked between large, flat-topped boulders that made perfect stepping-stones. The three crossed the rapids. "I think this must be near the place that Totlo indicated? He also said we should consult the Book of Prophecies before going any further so why don't we have a rest and do that first?"

"Gghhh! Good idea. I'm n-not putting a foot in that water." Orkan found himself a comfortable place to sit on a large flat rock and with his back against another then closed his eyes while Melek removed the book from his back, laid it on the flat stone and searched through it for an appropriate riddle. He beckoned Richard over, the two studied several conundrums found in amongst the wording.

> *A treasure burned needs water thrice,*
> *A friend regained will cross it twice,*
> *But water once brings danger near.*
> *The rocks themselves a source of fear.*
> *A rolling stone unlocks the jail,*
> *Flight from there to no avail.*
> *Cunning holds the key to all,*
> *Death comes from a final fall.*

"Hmm," Richard mused as Melek returned the book to his shoulders, "If I'm right, crossing water three times might even bring both my amulet and Orkan back to normal? But that is only guesswork."

"Did you hear that? I thought I heard something or someone shouting, I cannot be sure because of the noise from the rapids." Melek stood up, the wind blowing in from below tugged at his hair. Probably I'm just imagining... No wait! There it is again, it's coming from down there somewhere."

"I might have heard something, what did you hear?" Richard lied innocently.

"It sounded like calling for help." Melek listened more intently then nodded confirmation, "someone's in trouble down there, it could be the guardian Totlo told us about, then again, we've seen many dangerous traps before today?"

"Let's go carefully. Orkan wake up!" Richard kicked the bottom of his foot and the pig-like shot almost bolt upright, sword in hand and a nasty looking gleam flaring in his eyes.

"Whoa! Steady on, it's only me." Richard quickly danced backwards that he almost overbalanced off the end of the huge boulder. The group slowly picked their way down the hill in between the huge and sometimes loose standing rocks. Richard made sure he followed Orkan who kept a reasonable chunk of land between himself and the fast flowing water. After making their way down the grey boulder strewn obstacle course they all heard the plaintive cry of someone in distress, the voice becoming stronger as they continued to move.

"Help me!" the plea came again, "I'm trapped under this rock." It was Melek who was closest to the voice when it cried out a second time. He got down on all fours and peered into a narrow crevice between the base of the rock and the underlying boulders.

"Who are you?" He shouted, just as Richard caught up with his companions.

"I'm Zard, Guardian of the Reptiles," came back the answer. "The Evil One trapped me here. Can you get me out?" Another Guardian, Richard thought with relief, and without a trace of doubt in his mind, he called back, we'll see if we can get the opening unblocked somehow. Together, they pushed and pulled trying to widen the gap without any success; Richard searched the area and found a driftwood log that had once been a tree of the forest and by using another boulder as a fulcrum tried levering the boulder out of its position. The wood simply snapped off at the boulder end as they combined and applied their weight to one end.

They wondered what should be done next, when Melek pointed at some boulders above their current position, "I was examining the terrain and those boulders up there seem different from the rest of the landscaped rocks in this gully. I think it could be the result of a recent rock fall because they seem as if they could be loosened more easily than this big rock that is wedged in tight. If we could create a landslide of sorts, perhaps the power would move this boulder just enough to widen the opening?"

"That's risky. What if they slide down here and stop? It would seal Zard into a stone tomb wouldn't it?"

"Gghhh! Let's do it." Orkan was again fingering his bracelet and the dark thoughts were coming to the fore as he properly called into the narrow crevice, telling Zard of their plan and warning him to move to the very back of his prison.

They approached the strange looking rocks; Richard noticed that there was a main rock that seemed to be acting as the keystone by holding the surrounding boulders from cascading down into the valley.

"Gghhh! Water spilling from under that stone," Orkan pointed out the trickling water washing over another algae covered sloping stone and into a small pool below the keystone.

"Don't worry Orkan, I think that could help us unlock that keystone, the water and slime will make it easier to lever. We need that log." Without any arguments Orkan joined Richard to retrieve the timber while Melek examined the area around the stones. He noticed that on the rear end that the main rock was oddly shaped to look more like some peculiar sort of face of man drinking water. He felt uncomfortable and moved towards the other rocks to see what would be their best method of attack if they were to accurately try and dislodge the big boulder housing Zard. All the while, his eyes kept drifting back towards the strange outline on the backside of the keystone and were relieved when his two companions returned. He pointed out the facial markings, the two jutting out stones that could have been ears and even Orkan said that he could not help noticing that the face's eyes seemed to be following and examining him.

"Orkan, look at that, its solid rock. Don't tell me you think that it's alive?"

"Gghhh! Don't be silly, how can any rock be alive? But I just got the feeling it was watching us. Gghhh! Gghhh!" Orkan snorted in some sort of mocking laughter as Richard using Melek's instructions, began wedging one end of the long log under what looked like the rock face's broad chin.

"One, two, three!" they all added weight to the log when suddenly the ground shook from somewhere deep in the rock face, as if there was an impending earthquake about to hit the valley.

"Get away!" Richard shouted as they heard and felt the danger surrounding them. They raced up the hill and to one side onto one of the flattest and most solid rocks before Richard dared turn to look down at what had just happened. The keystone had now become an enormous figure struggling to free itself as it thrashed and clawed at surrounding boulders with massive limbs to raise itself up until finally, it stood below them and in the open.

"Gghhh! My imagination was it? That gigantic stone man 'was' watching us." Orkan said, "Our weapons will be useless." watching one of his worst nightmares materialising before his very eyes.

"Oh-oh! He's seen us, now what? We cannot fight him?" Richard watched as the giant swivelled, fixed on the trio, then grinned.

From where they now stood, the companions all heard the grating sound as the stone man's cheek creased. He then took a step towards them, then another, every time his monstrous feet struck down, they heard of sound the rubble being disintegrated underfoot.

"There's no way we can fight, our weapons will be useless against that creature. We have to go back to the top of this ravine; it's our only option of escape." Melek declared intelligently.

"What about Zard, we must save him?" Richard declared.

"Without us alive the Guardian would be doomed anyway, with us alive we may find a way." The stone man was slow and laborious but, he was still making headway towards them. They turned and fled towards the top, finding their ascent a lot harder going than their descent had been. In searching for the easiest route for them to take, Richard noticed there was a large round boulder that seemed to be precariously balanced on some much smaller rocks. Their journey to the rock took them in an altogether roundabout route whereas their pursuer, given his heftiness, seemed to be able to move in the straight line by being able to use the sheer weight of his legs to grind the surfaces into footholds. It was now becoming a bit of a race to reach the boulder and the trio got to the rock as the stone man reached a narrow lined plateau not far below this spot. Richard knew he did not have very much time, as the enemy below raised his pebbly eyes and saw his foe moving in and trying to hide themselves behind a large boulder at the top of the outcrop.

"He's coming, get ready," and when the stone man was almost halfway up the slope Richard shouted the command. "One! Two! Three! Heave!" The boulder seemed to rock back and forth twice before it came free and started accelerating with a thunderous roar straight towards the climbing gargantuan. There was no way the stone man could react quickly enough to avoid the hurtling granite boulder from smashing him to rubble. At the very last second, the boulder bounced against a small outcrop of rock and shot slightly off-course. It skimmed just past the stone man's large frame, it continued on its haphazard destructive path downwards bounce, bumping, smashing and loosening other boulders that lay in its path until it disappeared from sight

"Oh-oh! Now we're in trouble!" Unbeknown to the trio that even in failure, Richard's plan had unexpected success, because as the boulder had smashed its way downhill, it had also struck the boulder outside Zard's prison and shattered it into fragments. The stone man hadn't moved as the loud rumbling of a rockslide abated and dust began to clear. That's when Richard first saw the slither of movement further down the rock gully; a large lizard crawled from the debris and bounded uphill towards them.

"Zard," Melek whispered, "he's escaped." He watched as Zard moved effortlessly across stone, and finally up the final hill past the stone man who only understood that the Guardian had now broken free, once the lizard joined the three companions.

"Aarr Gghhh! The stone man's angry bellow shook the place as he once again began to move upwards towards the fugitives. Richard was pleased they had helped save a Guardian but he also somehow realised, that this chase had now started in earnest.

"Follow me, I know this area," Zard led the way leaping nimbly over the plateau. For a while they made very good progress using the advantage of the flattened high ground to lengthen the gap between themselves and their pursuer but, once the huge giant reached the top, and started along the almost level ground and his much longer stride, the tables began to turn. Zard was aware that by himself he would be able to outstrip his hunter but he could not leave his new allies who were battling to keep up with his pace especially Melek who was still hobbling a little. More and more frequently Zard found himself having to stop to let them catch up, giving his chaser an advantage to close the lessening gap, the big lizard knew that at this rate they were bound to be caught eventually.

We are going to have to change the scheme of things because he could probably keep going all day, I'm just sorry that I didn't warn you about him when we first talked. There!" he shouted swerving off towards the gully once more. The others stumbled after Zard and only realised too late, that the lizard must have taken a wrong turn as they had now entered a narrowing rock canyon and were going to be caught in a trap. The Guardian kept moving full tilt towards the steep ravine that formed the sheer walls of the boulder avalanche area where the river flowed and there was no chance of going back to face their giant pursuer.

"Gghhh! It's a dead end?" a panicky Orkan questioned skidding to a halt next to Zard and looking down into the precipice forming the cliff edge. "There's not even water we could jump into, it's almost all solid rock down there. He turned just as Richard and Melek joined them.

"Hide! Get behind some of that rubble and stay hidden." Zard commanded, "Don't worry about him. At this moment his only thought is to come after me first, because he'll be in big trouble if the Evil One finds out that I have escaped, and it won't be long before he does find out." The ground began to shake; small rocks started falling from the sidewalls and into the deep ravine. "I've got some thoughts and a trick or two that I can use to possibly outwit him. Now go quickly. He is coming."

The three barely had time to hide themselves behind the loose rock piles before the stone gargantuan pounded his way up along the ravine. The ground shuddered as he drew closer and closer to Zard who was teetering right on the edge of the long craggy drop. The trio was unable to resist the chance of a ringside view as they peeped from their various positions, only to become puzzled at what they could see happening.

"Zard's become demented." Richard whispered pointing a spinning forefinger at his head. "He's deliberately taunting the stone man. Why?" Richard could not fathom out the lizard's logic as Zard danced to and fro across the edge of the ravine making vile jibes at his adversary. They all stifled any sound or cries when the Guardian suddenly did the unthinkable; Zard flipped onto the giant's craggy face with the dexterity of an Olympic gymnast and stuck his front claws into the two pockets where its eyes were supposed to be. Half blinded, the giant's slower moving brain was battling to entertain even the idea of puzzlement as he slapped and pushed with stony hands at the lizard in an attempt to sweep Zard away.

"Gghhh! Zard's hoping his superior speed will somehow distract the stone man. Do you think we should make a run for it? He does not stand a chance and will die." Orkan shorted as quietly as he could.

"We stay, there are four of us in this together now." Melek castigated softly. Zard jumped back to the ravine edge and again continued doing his strange, almost taunting ritualistic dance along the cliff's border. The boulder giant had moved forward and was now close enough to reach out and catch the lizard, he looked almost fixated at this opportunity of retrieving his prancing prisoner as he stretched out and made a wild grab at Zard.

"I see what he's doing but he's also playing with death." Melek whispered.

Zard evaded the first attempt with an agile back flip, the stone moved in closer and tried again, and again the lizard was able to avoid the craggy grasp. The stone man got in even closer, Richard could see the deep look of concentration on the face as the giant's brow furrowed, he shed a fine powder of ground stone. For a third time, he grabbed out at Zard who for the third time evaded the huge fist. This time however, Zard had miscalculated the giant's slow intellect because when sweeping with his left hand and missing, his right hand had shot out in anticipation of where the lizard might move.

"Gghhh! He's got Zard!" Orkan's soldier brain and excitement immediately recognised what was about to happen. Zard flipped backwards and disappeared over the edge of the cliff leaving the puzzled stone man holding onto the lizard's tail. Orkan gaped, knowing full well that it would be the turn of the trio next.

"Gghhh! I told you we should have run and now it's too late," he was incensed as they looked on at the surprised giant to see what he was about to do. The stone man was horrified, for he had managed to outwit and grab hold of his prisoner and now he had lost the lizard, and had only a bloody tail that slapped and writhed in his closed fist to show for it. He suddenly went into an uproar, stamping and jumping in utter outrage, the ground shook and trembled as he roared his frustration at the heavens as he hurled the tail after the lizard.

"Oh-oh! Now he's really mad, Richard said trying to figure out what to do next. Just then, there was an explosive thundering and cracking as the cliff edge broke away and unbalanced the huge giant, sending him over the edge and into a long downward drop to the bottom of the ravine. There was a mighty crash echoing throughout the gully followed by a rattling hiss, as if a truckload of gravel had been emptied onto the ground. An enormous mushroomed cloud billowed out of the ravine, hung in the air and finally dissipated in the gentle breeze.

"Pity that Zard had to lose his life to save us?" Melek was truly upset at the loss of a Guardian. The three crept out from their hiding places and carefully moved towards the jagged edge of the damaged cliff. Far below at the bottom of the gully, they could make out an outline of rubble that was all that was left of the gigantic stone man. Their eyes searched the grey stone below to see whether they could see what had happened to the Guardian, he was nowhere to be seen.

"Maybe the stone man landed on top of him, we'll never know. I think it's time to move on?" Richard took a last look down into the ravine. "Oh well, I will remember Zard as the most unselfish soldier ever." He gave Orkan a very pointed look.

"That's good to hear," The trio spun to see a red claw hooked over the edge at the one spot that had not been shattered; slowly Zard's head appeared above the parapet. "That was a close thing; luckily us lizards can climb walls, so all I did was move left in order to make Zard think I had fallen all the way down to the bottom." Zard pulled his tail-less body over the edge. "I really did not expect his dramatic reaction but, I'm glad he is out of the way."

"Your tail?" Richard asked

"This is not the first time my tail has been lost, it will soon grow back." Zard said. "The most important thing now is to get my weapon back, I think I know where it has been hidden." He nimbly disappeared over the rim of the cliff again, heading for the valley below.

"We are going to have to move on again," Richard declared. "Melek, let's check the Path Finder to see what direction we need." He handed him the item and it quickly revealed that they should move to a green swathe of forest beyond the edge of the plateau on which they now stood. "It looks as if we must head back to the forest again. Are you comfortable with that Orkan?"

"Gghhh! I suppose." Orkan now seemed to be uninterested in the proceedings as he stared glassily into the distance. He had been acting this way ever since Zard had shown himself to the group, after tricking the stone man. He constantly fumbled with Dragora's amulet; his mind was again being pushed into a far darker place.

"He is still not to be trusted; somehow we must get him to cross water several times. Richard whispered to Melek.

"Perhaps on our journey to that forest, we will be provided with an opportunity?" Melek too was worried about their companion.

"They will never know, do not worry because you're safe with me." These soothing words wafted through Orkan's head. "Do not pay any attention to these people. Their concerns don't belong to you, their mission is not the same as your mission. They lead you to certain destruction if you should be a follower, you must be strong, without fear, as victory will only be given to the Chosen Ones. You are my Chosen One." A rue smile crossed Orkan's countenance as a rhyme kept repeating in his head, the lines now pointing him to the true and rightful path and his destiny. He began to mouth the lines as they replayed through his brain;

> *Blood runs through the thickest lake,*
> *Blood that makes the Gator wake,*
> *Blood that others want to make,*
> *Blood, the thirst that you can slake,*
> *Blood that makes for no mistake,*
> *Blood the prize that you can take.*
> *Blood! The blood of those you hate!*

"I think that somehow, the Evil One has reached Orkan, we must remain wary of any of his motives, we must attempt to break any of the motives he may entertain. Somehow, we must believe the riddle from the Book of Prophecies, we need him to cross that river several times. I think it is the only way we will remain safe?" Melek was keeping a close eye on Orkan; he could even make out several words as he mouthed them. "He has become obsessed with one word …Blood!"

"For the moment, we must keep him on side, not let him think we know something is wrong. Only after whatever it is that's bothering him has been clearly banished, and we can trust him again. Until then, we watch him carefully. Agreed?" All at once they heard a series of squeaks followed by a deep groan that quickly developed into a tumultuous thunder that Richard knew too well. The ground began shaking beneath their feet as yet another avalanche rocked the plateau.

"Back! Get back!" Richard screamed as the noise and tremors grew in intensity around the trio. They raced for all their worth back down the narrow cliff-lined passage. "That should be far enough." Turning, they could clearly see that a large section of the edge of the cliff where Zard had climbed down to valley had now also disappeared. Richard gingerly returned to the newly formed cliff edge and looked down; the outline of the stone man below had been almost entirely covered by this slide. His eyes searched to find Zard, it was as before, no movement and just then his thoughts suddenly returned to the prophecy, 'Death comes with a final fall', perhaps the Book of Prophecies had had really been referring to Zard and not the stone man and possibly, the

Guardian has chanced his luck simply once too often and had not made it this second time around, he thought glumly.

House of Reptilian Giant

On the Seventeenth Day...

In the swamp a hidden danger
Beckons the unwary stranger.
Find the prize in Gator's mound.
Find the friend from good unbound.
Find the craft that saves the day,
Find the swiftly flowing way
That leads you to the land of dreams
Where all is never what it seems.

"What do we do now? Wait awhile or move on?" Melek enquired.

"Gghhh! It would be better to move on," Orkan offered wryly. "The lizard has probably been squashed to death." Richard noticed the grim smile on the pig-like face; it sent a slight chill through his spine.

Richard looked at his bracelet, hoping that somehow Golan would give him guidance but it was not sparkling and there were no clues coming form that quarter, he knew that any decision would now have to be his.

"My ankle still pains me, is it possible that at this point we have a break, the forest is a long walk and now that the stone man is no longer pursuing us, it would be an ideal time to refresh ourselves and give my foot a rest?" Melek purposely gave Richard the opportunity to resolve the question, or at least make a firm compromise.

"Good thinking, we could all do with a short break?" Richard went into his bag and extracted the half-filled water bottle together with the last of the pellets that Covelette had given them. Richard offered them to his comrades. "This will at least give us energy?" Just as he seated himself on the flat rock, he heard the scrabbling sound of something at the cliff edge and was both surprised and happy to see Zard clambering over the rim and pull himself to full height and waving a golden battleaxe.

"How did you escape the avalanche?" Richard was intrigued.

"Luck had a major part to play. When I was imprisoned the stone man spitefully removed my axe and hid it, through that small crack I watched and there was a large rock that I had to roll away to get at my weapon. When I dislodged the rock, it in turn displaced another and another. I only just managed to rescue the axe and scramble away before the landslide took hold. I must admit that it worried me, seeing the avalanche spread up the hill to where you were, but now all is well.

"I still have a little water," Richard offered his plastic bottle to Zard. "Here drink, you must be parched?"

"I had a drink from a small pool in the valley, you have it, we will find more as we travel." Zard said. Richard finished the last of his liquid nectar and placed the bottle into his backpack. He noticed that one of the pods seemed to be blinking as if trying to catch his attention but when he reached out to lift it, it sparked quite violently as if to warn him off. "Strange." He closed the bag then pulled it onto his back, he saw Melek give him a friendly smile as he did the same with the Book of Prophecies. Orkan was still seated staring out across the gully; Richard could not help noticing that he still had that brusque look about him.

"Come on Orkan, next stop, the forest." Richard jibed in an almost friendly way, trying to get his companion to lighten up. It had no effect whatsoever Orkan simply turned and scowled back at his companions.

They made their way up the hill and across the plateau, skirting around the stone valley they made good progress walking in loose formation over the boulder-cluttered ground, heading downhill towards the green outline of the forest. Everyone, except Orkan, concentrating their eyes and ears alert for enemy action. Once within the wooded area, they made their way back towards the trees where they had passed through the small door and met up with Narkum but before they reached the large tree; the recognizable buzz of Grapfrits began filling the air.

"I think they could be heading this way, don't they ever give up?" Zard quickly moved to an enormous old oak tree. `"We've got to find somewhere to hide." The lizard used the golden battle-axe with the deftness of a surgeon with a mighty vertical blow that sliced a long cut deep into the tree. He repeated the motion once again and then with a mighty heave, removed a large slice from the tree.

"Gghhh! We don't have time, let's run." Orkan nervously snorted.

"You go by yourself then," Zard shouted as he quickly removed several large slices from the outside towards the centre of the tree until there was a gap big enough to house all four. Zard herded the three into the gap as he lifted the first slice cut from the tree.

"Quickly inside!" he ordered with the buzzing sound arriving at breakneck speed.

"Wheeeooee! They're almost here."

"Shut up Orkan. I sometimes wonder why you simply don't put up an advertising board to announce this way for a meal." Richard whispered

"I can't help it."

"Stop arguing you two there's no time." Melek said sternly as Zard quickly climbed in behind them and starting with the bark slice skilfully pulled several slices into place in behind him so that they were now camouflaged. The lizard was sure that nobody would be able to tell that there was anything concealed inside the tree and that to anyone on the outside, it would simply just look like another old oak tree.

"Wow! That's some axe. It cut through the wood like a knife through butter." Richard was very impressed.

"Shhh." The Grapfrits arrived in the clearing; it was if they had found direction and were now tracking the group's scent trail, instead of moving straight through the area, they buzzed around the region, Zard held firmly to a single slice of bark separating them from the marauding flying oranges with their knife-like spinning blades and snouts.

"Cloc! Cloc!" There was a rapping sound somewhere higher up the tree. "They're testing the tree to search for us, their smell organs tell them there is something different in this area." whispered Zard in Orkan's ear.

"Whee..." Orkan suddenly grabbed at his snout and blocked the sound. Richard wasn't sure if his legs were going to be able to support him for much longer, his head swam and the palms of his hands seemed to be on fire.

"Cloc! Cloc!" The sound moved further down the tree until the buzzing had now reached a fermented pitch from outside. Richard was sure that the Grapfrits had found their hiding place and were seeking for a way into them. "They know we're here," he whispered to Zard.

"Shhh. Maybe not." The thumping on the old oak tree carried on for a few minutes, then as suddenly as it had started the loud buzzing sound moved away from the area. Zard pushed the slice away and light flooded in the confined space. He stepped out into the open and looked up and slowly shook his head, the old oak had almost been stripped clean of all its bark. "We have been very lucky today."

"Why?"

"You can quite often see where the Grapfrits stop and actually feed, they're messy eaters, sometimes eating even bark from an old tree when they're extremely hungry and they haven't found anyone to attack. Without realising we were inside the tree, I think that they took its bark back to the nest for their queen and that spells danger because the bark means that the queen is about to give birth to a huge number of new Grapfrits. We must find the nest and destroy it."

"What! We've just had a lucky escape. Well, at least they've gone. Now you want to go and find them and then try to destroy them? There's no way?"

"Gghhh! I suppose we better move in case they return for more bark." Orkan snorted sarcastically.

"We have time, I think we should consult the Book of Prophecies before we do anything?" Melek said diplomatically, he could see that there was a possible row about to break out as he removed and then opened the book on the ground. Both Richard and Zard kneeled next to Melek as he began to read the text.

> *In the swamp a hidden danger*
> *Beckons the unwary stranger.*
> *Find the prize in Gator's mound.*
> *Find the friend from good unbound.*
> *Find the craft that saves the day,*
> *Find the swiftly flowing way*
> *That leads you to the land of dreams*
> *Where all is never what it seems.*

"We must find Gator's mound." Richard said when the librarian had finished.

Before long the ground sloped into a gentle incline split by a spring-fed rivulet joining forces with the much slower moving boulder valley stream. The four travellers followed its course downhill and Richard refilled his water bottle once more. Further down the way, they found their path being blocked by a densely packed jungle filled with tall thickets of spiked and thorn encrusted dry bushes. More significantly to Richard, were the abundance of sweet smelling yellow berries that adorned the plants.

"If I'm not mistaken, those look like they could be Killer Sunrise bushes." Richard said, remembering their lethal potency. "There is absolutely no way we can get through that undergrowth without someone being damaged."

"I could carve a way from beginning to end but, would have to be very careful. Alternatively, we might try bypassing this brush?"

"How? It seems to stretch for a long way into the forest."

"The bushes stop at the edge of the water, we could wade past all those shrubs, it would save time?"

"Agreed but first, Orkan you used up the last of your berry ammunition against the three-head serpent didn't you?"

"Gghhh! Yes, let me stock up." Orkan went across to the nearest bush and as before gently lifted the yellow orbs one by one on the end of his sword into the small leather pocket at the side of his quiver. What puzzled Richard was Orkan's immediate readiness to carry out the task, especially after his constant lack of enthusiasm at every previous suggestion. What all of them did not fully realise was, Orkan was now working to a different agenda. "Gghhh! I think it would be better if we tried to cut a pathway, the water route scares me."

"Zard is correct, it won't take us long if we ford the stream, it does not seem very deep. That's the way to go." Entering the water, Richard was reminded of the prophecy and wondered whether this patch of river may perhaps mean that Orkan had, or could be returned to normal. Orkan completed his berry-collecting task and reluctantly fell in behind the group.

The stream turned into a wide flow that wound its way between ever-thicker clumps of vegetation. Soon the clumps turned into islands and the once-fresh water curdled into a much bigger stagnant mass. The whole place had become a seemingly endless swamp and yet the poisonous bushes on both banks prevented them from getting back to the land. Richard checked with Path Finder, it pointed directly ahead towards a large hillock that rose from the quagmire that they were now having trouble navigating because it was also becoming a lot deeper.

"Here, hand me the Book of Prophecies, I will carry it on my head." Richard offered the librarian. His shorter stature meant he was having difficulty in keeping the big book dry and with each step taking him deeper, it was sensible for him to make the offer.

"Gghhh! Hate water." Orkan tried his best to remain dry, using the islands as his path, but it became very unreliable because it was impossible to tell whether each floating island was made up of solid earth or just jumbles of floating debris that had over time, locked together to look like some kind of solid mass. More than once, Orkan was fooled by the camouflaged debris and had fallen through the green mat into algae-covered water with a hefty splash. Eventually they all accepted the inevitable thought of remaining dry, and continued on through the unpleasant swamp with its evil-smelling pockets of methane that occasionally bubbled up from below the now slimy green marsh that was becoming deeper the further they travelled

"If it gets much deeper, I'm going to have to swim." Melek declared as the water reached the level of his neck. "Anyway, it would take the weight off my foot for a while and also, get rid of some of the slimy creatures that I keep feeling are swimming around my legs."

"I've also felt them, but it would also be like swimming through thick pea-soup, I don't think you would make much headway." Richard joked, even though he was becoming worried and disturbed by the slippery underwater swamp creatures, periodically caressing and winding themselves around his legs. They trudged on regardless and after what seemed to them like an endless trek the four finally stopped to grab their breath.

"I hope we don't have to return this way. Melek proclaimed, "I don't think I could have made it much further." Zard helped him onto an island; he then clambered up behind him.

"What's that on your leg?" Richard questioned as he too pulled himself free of the water and now noticing that there were fat slugs clinging to various parts of his companion's legs and bodies. There were traces of oozing blood wherever these creatures had attached themselves to flesh. Richard looked down and gasped, his arms, legs and torso was covered with the monstrosities, he reached out and was about to remove it when Zard stopped him.

"Don't! They are bloodsuckers, if you pull it off, its teeth will remain embedded inside and then you will die a slow and painful death being eaten from the inside. I have come across them before and the only way we can get them to loosen their grip is with fire."

"We need kindling, anything dry," Melek started scratching around and soon located a dried bird's nest and some scraggy brittle reeds, "Like this and a little bigger." Meanwhile Zard searched the little island for any kind of rock, not finding one he swam to the shore, saw one below the bushes, hacked at the tough base several times and retrieved the stone. He returned holding it aloft in order that it remained dry and Richard took it from the lizard.

"Now what?"

"This!" He struck the stone several times to make a spark

With some difficulty, he then got a small blaze going before slowly adding twigs into the spluttering flames. Melek blew into the smouldering kindling until they produced fire and only then did he add some of the larger pieces of driftwood.

"Orkan I need one of your arrows, Zard commanded, he too had already noticed that Orkan didn't fit with the other two. Orkan's whole body seemed to be free of these slug-like invertebrates, not so with the others, they were covered. Reluctantly, Orkan passed Zard one arrow, the lizard immediately placed the metal tip into the embers until it too, was orange with heat.

"Now for the fun part." Richard watched as Zard quickly placed red-hot tip against one of the creatures, it immediately sizzled and dropped away leaving a set of clean but, tiny punctures to show where its fangs had gripped the lizard. "Ladies first." He turned to Melek. Zard worked methodically and quickly working around the single ones before tackling those in clusters. Periodically stopping only long enough to reheat the arrow tip, they all were fascinated as one by one the bloodsuckers were dispatched from Melek, then

Richard and finally Zard tackled those he could reach before handing the arrow to Richard in order to clear his back. Richard was astounded to see just how many there were locked onto the open wound stump where the lizard had lost his tail to the stone man.

"Done? Right find as many of these as you can," Melek bent forward and picking up a clover-shaped leaf from the ground, began to rub it hard across several bite marks. "Make sure you get the leaf to seep out, because the juice will not only seal the wound but prevent those openings from becoming septic.

"Magic, it's a new type of ancient day plaster? What next?" They moved around the place and with Melek's practiced eye, soon had enough leaves to smear themselves. Alone and helping each other Richard felt that this might be his only chance to discuss Orkan. "You also noticed his strange behaviour, haven't you?" Zard nodded, as Richard quickly blurted out the story and when the change had happened.

"I think that I know what is happening, I have seen this before but, we must tread carefully and await our opportunity. Now come, we need to tackle that hillock" As they moved forward towards the large hill ahead Zard suddenly stopped and held up his finger to his mouth. "There is something slithering in among the reeds, my senses tell me that something or someone is tracking our movements." Zard whispered. "You keep moving, I will find out who is interested in us." His camouflage was of such high quality, Richard blinked as Zard simply seemed to disappear in amongst the reed-bed. The three companions kept moving until they reached the base of the very large mound; they waited nervously for a while to see what had happened to the Guardian.

"There's something there," It wasn't long before Melek whispered and suddenly motioned towards the end of the reed-bed. It was as if a slight wind had disturbed the tops of the fronds but there were no airstreams anywhere across the swampy marsh at that moment.

"Come out and show yourself!" Richard shouted as he reassuringly gripped the handle of Juroot's sword. To his surprise it was Zard that rose from the reeds, and then, another smaller and more unkempt rugged lizard whose tattered clothes had once been a uniform, showed himself only to be followed by another, then another until there were a whole troop of them.

"I found some of my army." Zard said proudly, "They bear arms and had to hide from us because there is a sizeable fighting group from the Evil One's forces in the area." Richard could see that among the group there were those that were just as scarred and battered as their leader, but they looked well-armed and all had a defiant look in their eyes.

"A Guardian and the Chosen One! This can only catch us unawares, the chief lizard said, glancing at Richard. "My name is Fengal and this is a very pleasant surprise."

"Why?" Zard interrupted.

"We have been under constant threat since the war and have lost many good soldiers but, have learned much to become an excellent guerrilla task force and battle hardened. We have heard word that other survivors are regrouping at the Ancestral City. We were making our way there to join up with them."

"That's good," Zard broke in, "but right now you could be more help to us. We have to retrieve one of the Ancestral Pods that we believe is hidden up there." Zard pointed towards the hillock."

"If you are going in there, you'll definitely need help. We've battled with a few of the Evil One's forces in the swamp already and it has not been easy. They are tough and ruthless and their leader is extremely powerful. What do you want us to do?"

Richard carefully outlined the task before all, except for two wounded lizards that were left behind as sentries, set off through the low-lying mist to begin the climb up the huge mound. As they moved away Zard and Fengal suddenly motioned for the group to halt, Zard lifted a clawed finger to his mouth. "There is something else in among those reeds," Zard pointed to the last of two reed-beds ahead and Richard saw slight movement. Fengal waved through some of his soldiers who immediately disappeared into the reeds on two sides just as the mist wafted gently away ahead of the group. "It could be a trap, don't move until our friends find out what is lurking ahead." After a brief wait the mist had cleared enough to reveal the first sight of the group's enemy.

"Oh-oh!" Richard's hand went straight for his dagger for now, before them stood a mob of alligators – large, leathery and well armoured, all seemingly jostling impatiently, eager to do battle. They did not attack immediately, not before the largest one of the group slithered out of the reeds and moved across to a rough nest of branches where it settled onto the pile. Richard looked at the deep-set yellow eyes. The long snout, the killer teeth, he felt a gush of terror sweep through his body.

"Welcome to my kingdom!" The creature spoke with cavernous chuckle, "I am Gator... Murmur my name as you die." He turned to his troops and bellowed, "Get them!" The alligators rushed forward on mass thing an easy victory would be a formality and not expecting hardened battle warriors to put up any resistance. Fengal immediately marshalled his troops with a clever counter attack that developed into the traditional horns and chest of the buffalo formation; their aim was to encircle the alligator's position. From out of the reeds, the rest of the lizards that had gone to investigate, joined the conflict by closing the circle, it was the alligator's turn to have walked into a trap. The fighting was fierce as soldiers from both sides fell to the heat of battle, but slowly the lizards began gaining ground and that's when Richard decided to act on his own account. He ducked and dived his way around the field of combat.

Gator's piercing eyes were occupied with the fight. Only Orkan noticed Richard's departure, he knew that Fengal, although limited in numbers, having managed to trick the alligators into a tough vice-like grip, that the final outcome would not be a foregone conclusion, mainly because of the alligator's numerical supremacy. He also knew that the Evil One was the only master, and he knew that this was his opportunity to kill Richard. He, too, found his way around the harsh battle to follow his old friend.

Richard circled round behind Gator with one thought in mind, to take the alligator by surprise by sinking his dagger deep into the soft frontage of Gator's neck. He edged ever closer and was readying his aim, as he raised his arm to deliver the fatal blow Orkan grabbed his hand. Richard lurched back and saw Orkan's raised arm holding his sword when from nowhere, the spiralling whirlwind of Zard leapt from behind and grabbed Orkan's arm, throwing him to the ground in one movement. During the brief tussle, one of Zard's claws accidentally hooked Orkan's amulet and ripped it from his arm as the pig-like boy fell attempting to break free in order to finish what he had set out to do. Kill Richard.

"Gghhh! What happened?" Orkan cried. Richard saw his companion rubbing his eyes in bewilderment, shaking his head and then Orkan looked straight at Richard, all trace of guile had now disappeared.

"I don't know but welcome back Orkan."

"It was this, look it bears the mark of the Evil One," Zard pointed to the inside of the bangle and Richard saw the horned emblem in the pulsating primitive bracelet. "It feels strange, it is cursed." Zard hurled the amulet towards the swampy water, there was a flurry of sparks as it splashed followed by a series of minor detonations and it was gone.

"It was that amulet, Richard said grimly," It must have been a trap set by the Evil One. It changed you completely." Orkan hung his head dejectedly. "If it hadn't been for Zard, you would have killed me."

"He didn't but I will!" Gator boomed, turning towards the group and lunging towards Zard raking iron claws and swung his tail with a vicious swipe that smashed against the head of one of his own soldier's head creating a spew of yellowish brain-matter. Gator whipped back for yet another attack but, the lightning fast Zard was already on him, raising his axe, he swung it with all the force he could muster sinking it deeply into the alligator's broad chest. Gator blinked once in disbelief, then slowly slumped back on his nest. The fighting was done as the few remaining alligators fled past their dead leader running, scuttling and crawling in sheer cowardice.

"We need to reclaim the pod. Let's go." Zard commanded, handing Orkan back his sword as Melek joined them. The four made good time getting to the top of the hillock where they found a circular stoned rim housing a black hole. Looking into the darkness they could hear scuffling but could not see anything below. Richard used his flashlight; he could see this thing impressed the unflappable Zard. The light caught something that looked like a giant lobster, it moved slowly around a large and tightly packed woodchip stack. Richard immediately saw a pod on top of the mass.

"We better be quick, we've stumbled onto a Grapfrit nest, that's the queen and that heap probably houses thousands of unborn Grapfrit's. It is the largest nest I have ever seen, they are the Evil One's flying soldiers and are getting prepared for the next battle by producing a nest as big as this." Zard reflected. "We have to destroy it before the Grapfrits return."

"How?"

"Fire. We set light to all that wood in the nest"

"First, how do we rescue the pod?" Richard asked.

"With this." Melek lessened the rope from his midriff. "I think I can do it." Zard checked the black stones then found the right one.

"Orkan we need kindling," he ordered. Without question, Orkan raced down the hill and began collecting dried reeds and timber from round the area where Gator lay dead. The lizards were busily gathering up alligator prisoners who all seemed to bear dazed expressions on their faces. Orkan hurried back and between the two managed to use their weapons on the stone to create sparks that got a healthy fire going.

"Now what? Richard asked.

"Orkan, you use you arrow tip to spear a flaming branch then shoot it to the edge of that pile, the Grapfrit queen will be distracted and will start calling for help, it depends on how far the rest of the Grapfrit group are at how much time we have so, we must work quickly. Zard was in full soldier battle command mode. "As soon as she becomes preoccupied with the fire, you concentrate on the pod. Only then will I be able to lift the fire and drop it onto the nest. Is all clear? We do not have the luxury of time, we have got to get down there before the Grapfrits arrive back here." He pointed towards the swamp area.

"Gghhh! Arrow gone!" Orkan shouted. Zard held Melek back until he saw the queen Grapfrit start to move towards where the flame had taken hold, what they had not expected was the swiftness at which the flames began to spread up the pile. Melek's wrist flicked with speed, it took a few attempts to get hold of the pod but he somehow managed to loop it, and tighten it before cautiously and very gently hoisted it out of the den. Richard pocketed his torch to help Zard by carrying loose fiery sticks and dropping them onto the now fiercely blazing pyre. There were sounds of ten thousand cracking finger joints that floated up, the fire had fast become an inferno and over the top of all this noise came the distant and familiar whirr of Grapfrits somewhere in the distance.

"Gghhh! Quick! Let's move, the Grapfrits will be here soon." Orkan screamed and the four raced down the hill as fast as their legs and balance would allow. At the bottom Fengal began mustering his remaining forces, fearing another attack; he had them spread out and hide themselves together with their somewhat becalmed prisoners.

"Grapfrit nest on fire! Zard shouted as he reached the bottom of the hillock.

"Ahh, their forces are being reduced?" Fengal smiled.

"Where are we going to hide? We could use those reeds as snorkels, Orkan and I did that before." Richard panted.

"No need to hide ourselves," Fengal pointed as a buzzing dark swarm of angry Grapfrits arrived above the mound, assessed the situation in their own way then dived into the smoking hole to try to rescue their queen from the fire. From their position below it sounded and looked like a chain reaction fireworks display, the kamikaze Grapfrits caught up in the fire began to crackle, pop and boom en masse.

"Gghhh! Stupid Grapfrits? Destructive but very stupid." Orkan reflected idly.

"Not stupid Orkan, they are soldiers trying to save their sovereign and dying in the process. We would all do that if so requested, wouldn't we?" Zard gave a sly wink to Richard.

"I suppose we would, that's exactly what we are doing right now, aren't we?" Orkan dropped his head as everyone had a quiet giggle at his expense.

"You must proceed with your quest." Zard told Richard "It's time for us to part company but, I am certain we shall meet again?" At that moment Richard wished that the gallant Guardian could travel with them a while longer but also knew inwardly, that Zard was sore needed back at Ancestral City. Melek handed him the Path Finder, the arrow indicating they continue through the unfamiliar stretch of the swamp.

"We will have to face those bloodsuckers once more." Melek said distastefully. "Hate them."

"That's the direction we've just come from," Fengal chimed in. "There's nothing that way. The swamp simply runs into the sea."

"All the same that is the way we must travel" Richard replied.

"Then you may take our boat, it is hidden beneath that tree, and it is but a hollowed out log but, also served us well."

Zard moved forward and placed his arm around Orkan's shoulder. "As for you young man, you were duped by the Evil One and came out alive. It is now your duty to safeguard these two very special companions." He pointed to Richard and Melek. "They believed in you when others tried to destroy you, repay that faith by protecting them with your life."

"Gghhh! I will" With that, both Fengal and Zard gave the companions a stiff salute.

"Until we meet again may your fate be all good." Zard, Fengal, the raggle-taggle lizard soldiers and the reformed alligators headed off round the hillock in one direction while the three friends headed off in the opposite way in search of the boat.

"There, that's it." Melek's alert eyes picked it out amid the growing dusk. They checked it over, it was covered in slime and moss except for on the wooden struts that the lizards had used as seating, all seemed in order, even down to several sets of roughly fashioned oars placed in the bottom of the boat. "How did they all fit in here? It's too small?"

"Maybe they made several journeys each time, who knows? It's too late to ask Fengal." Richard reflected idly. "It's getting dark and I don't know about you two but I would not be comfortable spending a night here, especially with those about." He pointed to the sky where vultures had already started gathering high above the battlefield, "They are scavengers and will pick the bones clean, within hours nobody will be able to tell that valiant soldiers died here today." They pushed the boat away from its hiding place, clambered on board. Richard and Orkan began rowing, the channel became wider with less islands, the abundant number of trees with garlands of hanging moss reduced the further they rowed.

"Gghhh! We're still on water, I'm getting used to it, but never ask me to trust water, too many bad things live down there." Orkan spat out. "Water equals trouble and now we're heading towards the sea? That means big trouble awaits us?"

Twin Bodied, Winged Griffin

On the Eighteenth Day...

A treasure now regains its sheen
When past water thrice has been,
Leads them streetwise through a maze
To a hero's captured gaze.
Return with rope to lead him out,
But death of evil is in doubt.
Who once was brave is braver now.
Fight the waves from stern to prow.

Reaching the junction between swamp and the sea, they wearily eased their boat onto a fine sandy beach shore.

"We will rest here for the night and see what tomorrow holds," Richard said authoritatively. It was almost dark as the little band pulled their rickety boat as far up the beach as their strength would allow and then headed towards the sand dunes.

"Gghhh! What do you think that is over there?" Orkan pointed to grey shadowy silhouette in the distance. "It could be a castle of sorts but it's too dark to make it out. Maybe we should head for that?"

"The sand is fine, it makes a good bed." Richard said as he and Melek found themselves bedding down among softer tufts of comfortable and densely packed, grey-green Marram Grass, a familiar feature of most coastal sand dunes, within minutes they were asleep. Orkan stayed awake and kept the first watch.

"I needed that break," Melek said as he arose, his two companions were already on top of a dune scanning the surrounding area, their interest mainly targeted towards a city built onto the sand. "My foot is so much better this morning, in fact, I do not feel any pain whatsoever" Melek rose, strapped the Book of Prophecies to his back and joined his companions.

"What do you make of that? There is something very peculiar about the look of those buildings." Richard mused as they continued to survey the partially hidden city straddling sand dunes further along the beach. "Look at it, it seems a little blurry, do you think it could just be some sort of a mirage?" The morning freshness meant that the whole location was bathed in lucid sunshine and they could see things very clearly in the distance, yet the outline of this large city with its imposing battlements and an ancient lighthouse seemed indistinct and hazy. "I don't like it, let's see what the Path Finder indicates." After several sweeps, the answer always remained the same and now Richard was in no doubt, that this somewhat indistinct shaped city was to be their next step on his quest. "We must follow the pointer." They set off along the beach with Orkan in the lead. It did not take them long to almost reach the outer perimeter walls when something strange occurred, one second Orkan's outline was clearly obvious, the next, he broad frame took on the mantle of being like the city walls, he became unclear in shape.

"Orkan, stop where you are!" An alarmed Richard called. Orkan immediately turned.

"Gghhh! What?"

"Something's happened to you. Walk back towards us." Richard watched as Orkan stepped towards them and at one certain point, it was as if he had stepped through an invisible curtain. His whole frame changed from being an obscure delineated pig-like person, to becoming the real Orkan once again. "Turn around and take three steps towards the wall and stop." Richard commanded. With his second step, he simply again became a blur of a figure. "Look at the city, what do you see?"

"Gghhh! I can see the walls and lighthouse very clearly now."

"Take two steps backwards, keep your eye on the city walls." Richard had a hunch that there was some form of invisible illusion draped between their separate positions.

"Woooeee! The city has completely changed its shape." Orkan stepped forward and backwards several times to ensure that what he was seeing was really happening."

"Keep an eye on this." Richard heaved at a small tuft of dune grass, it came away from the beach quite easily, sandy root-ball included. He swung it in a circular motion several times and then released it in the direction of Orkan, as it passed through the invisible curtain it changed shape and clarity. "What a clever disguise?"

"I remember once having read about just such a city, nobody could describe it clearly," Melek commented. "In all the books, it was simply described as a Mythical or Lost City because of the many conflicting opinions about where or what it really was, or in fact, whether it even really existed. Possibly this could be the land of dreams that the prophecy earlier alluded to?"

"Gghhh! Come, let's see what this city holds." Orkan moved forward slowly, his two companions followed suit, when they were a lot closer they stopped and inspected the place. At first glance, it had the look of a city that had once been a real powerhouse; there was enough evidence in the wall carvings alone to give Richard the thought that long ago this place had housed a very influential and thriving community within its wall.

"Perhaps it only became like this when the sea receded?"

"You could be right. Perhaps the people that lived here moved to the Ancestral City and this place left to deteriorate, it must have been very beautiful once." Melek replied. "I wonder if anyone still lives here.

"Gghhh! Only one way to find out." Orkan moved forward again.

A colossal arch straddled the beach sand entrance, that gave it the look and feel that when coupled with the lighthouse at the far end, meant that this magnificent entry point could have once been a harbour frontage entrance to the city beyond. Now the wind and sands had again reclaimed the entire frontage into, and through the main access. Beyond what would have been a quayside a surrounding band of tight fitting, run down fishermen type abodes separated only by darkened narrow alleyways, lead away towards the city proper in the background.

"You don't have to be a genius to see that this was once an ancient dockside port. Mother Nature can be cruel sometimes? Richard reflected as they passed under the huge archway.

"Whoever said that this destructive work was carried out by nature?" Melek asked simply. Think about it, we have already seen some of the places touched by the Evil One, could this simply not be another?" Melek reflected as they moved into what would previously have constituted a small harbour area. Ahead they aimed for a set of stairs built into the harbour wall that would take them away through the streets to inspect the rest of this seemingly abandoned capital. Richard kept getting the feeling that something was out there as he kept imagining fluid shadows slipping and sliding around the narrow buildings stationed above the quayside.

"Gghhh! There is something about this place, it feels... well, sort of haunted by ghosts of the past." Orkan said nervously, "we can't fight with shadows and that worries me."

The trio strode into a narrow street lined up an incline road with the remains of small houses that became ever larger and more like grand homes the further they travelled upward. As they reached a crossroad, Richard suddenly heard a flapping sound from above and behind him, turning he saw something that unnerved him.

"Oh-oh! What's that?" He screamed in panic.

It was still at some distance but they could see that the thing seemed as surprised by their sudden appearance as they were. Richard took another quick look at the strange looking beast, it seemed to have two interlinked bodies, all supporting two huge, furry dark manes like male lions. When it saw them, it immediately spread its gigantic bat-like wings, each one fixed to one of its outer bodies wide apart to make itself look as big and wide as possible. As he ran for cover, Richard's brain was functioning very well, but this thing was obviously not the sort of thing that one stopped and had a friendly chat with. It had scared his companions so badly that Orkan had taken off like a scalded cat racing for one of the houses and, he was running faster than on any of the other previous occasions.

"Kronis! The winged lion. Follow me!" Melek raced away.

"Gghhh! Run for your life, that thing isn't about to play games. In here!" Orkan shouted from ahead as he ducked into a smaller, but seemingly sturdy house. His disappearing voice made Richard run even faster as he raced down the path in the direction his companions had taken and trying desperately to catch up with the fast fleeing Orkan.

"Orkan! Wait for me."

"No ways, it's everyone for themselves." Richard just made it to safety before a thunderous blow rocked the entire house, sending them sprawling on the floor. A second impact followed the first as the twin lion bodies charged against the outer wall.

"It's trying to break down the outer walls." Melek panted. Luckily the three managed to run to the rear of a hallway leading to the back of the house, the beast tried a different tactic by reaching in with a paw, scrabbling around but not finding its prey.

"Look at that, there is a narrow passage leading somewhere." Richard shone his torch at the dark hole cut into what must have once been a rock face. It led into a wide kitchen that looked as if somebody had recently vacated the place. At the far end was a large open fireplace with its heavy iron coupled andirons to hold up the logs and also an open hearth on which to bake. The house shook again as the beast again threw itself at the outer walls that were beginning to crumble against the continued pressure.

"That fireplace has a large chimney, perhaps we can use it to escape or, perhaps that thing will give up and go away and leave us alone?" Richard asked hopefully.

"Gghhh! No chance of that, he'll be around the entrance somewhere. Kronis never gives up when he's got anything in his sights."

"Both of you know this beast? Who ...or rather what, is this Kronis?"

"Gghhh! He's one of the Evil One's generals, but even worse than any of them and more rotten than the rest because he attacks and kills anything or anybody who isn't working for the Evil One."

"I see why you were scared."

"Scared? ...Me? I wasn't scared, I was petrified, remember, I've already seen Kronis at work during the great battle, he simply rips everything apart with those enormous claws or those terrible fangs of his. The worst part of his attacks are, he unlike others, then always rips and eats flesh while his victim is still alive. That's Kronis for you." There came another thunderous shaking as the front wall of the house crumbled under the heavy attack by Kronis.

"To the back, the chimney is our only chance." Melek being the smallest led the way but a short way up encountered a problem as the hole narrowed and he became stuck. The other two forced themselves higher and higher right up to the point where everyone was huddled together as far up as the opening would allow. The rock opening into the kitchen was far too narrow for Kronis to pass through; even with one of his paws at full stretch he was still unable to reach his victims with his huge talon-like claws. Kronis tried various methods to reach them, knowing that he could not batter down the rock and eventually gave up. With a fearsome roar into their cave hideout the beast turned and flew off into the morning sky. Richard waited for a while just in case Kronis tricked them and returned but all remained quiet.

"He's gone," slowly they pulled themselves down out of the cramped space and very carefully moved to the narrow passage that had been their redeeming saviour from Kronis' onslaught. Looking out, they could see the line of crumpled masonry where the beast had forced it way in. "I suggest we check the Book of Prophecies first, we don't need any more unpleasant surprises like Kronis, do we?" Melek laid out the book in the contracted passageway where there was now enough light to read.

A treasure now regains its sheen
When past water thrice has been,
Leads them streetwise through a maze
To a hero's captured gaze.
Return with rope to lead him out,
But death of evil is in doubt.
Who once was brave is braver now.
Fight the waves from stern to prow.

"Treasure?" Richard said thoughtfully touching his amulet. Its old spark and glow were back once again. "The prophecy is correct this time," he exclaimed. "Regains a treasure its sheen" I think it's because we crossed water three times and the amulet and Orkan are now back to normal?" He danced a little jig and grabbed Orkan to give him a bear hug.

"Gghhh! None of that, I'm a soldier you know? I do not do hugging." The hog-like companion embarrassingly pushed Richard away.

"What about the rest of the riddle?" Melek asked as he again lifted the book onto his shoulders.

"Not quite certain, but it did mention streets, a maze and also, that we may even find someone or something. It looks like we have to go back out there and search through the place. The thought of Kronis doesn't fill me with gladness though. But then again, I trust the book's wording and we must go where the words instruct us to go. No time like the present?" The little group set off from the battered house, darting from door to door, in case they had to again make good their escape. They moved towards the main city centre, traversing street by street and searching for anything that would give them some sort of a clue about a maze.

"Perhaps these streets are the maze?" Richard said.

"No, I do not think so, the book has riddles, but then again, once you understand what the real meaning is, it tends to be very precise. We will know when we find the maze." Melek said. At the end of one street, a high wall in which was set a heavy door blocked their way. It swung open before anybody touched it. It revealed a series of arched corridors. "This is the maze, we have found it, and "Melek crowed triumphantly," Always believe the Book of Prophecies." The corridors began leading them through yet more corridors as Richard firmly gripped his amulet, the unspoken feeling being that somehow, Golan was now directing them to whatever and wherever it was to be found. He strode confidently, turning this way then that, as they walked, the three could feel and occasionally see that the dark shadow shapes fleeing before them and this time the faint whispers, like the echoes of rumoured conversation had once again returned.

"Gghhh! The ghosts are back, I'm not exultant about that." Orkan snorted. The companions moved through the passages continually accompanied by the shadows, one way then another but Richard was confident that he was headed on the right course. Backwards, forwards and sideways until they finally came to a tall, beautifully sculptured wall where the archway at one end, which Richard instinctively knew to be the by means of two enormous green marble dragons mounted on either side of the archway entrance.

"This has to be the maze centre? It possesses a kind of spiritual essence." Richard said reassuringly yet hesitatingly, being totally unsure of what they were about to discover inside this imposing wall. "Be ready, just in case." He automatically placed a comforting hand on Juroot's dagger while Orkan drew his sword as the neared the archway.

"This is the right place. Look!" Melek pointed to the centre of what was a large arena. Firmly tethered to a carved pillar was a unicorn. Its coat gleamed silvery white and iridescent and its single horn shone with a pearly brilliance. Lustrous, turquoise eyes gazed nervously at the three strangers as they crossed the courtyard to the captive beast.

"It's all right," Richard used his most comforting voice as he drew nearer. He then quickly explained his mission, who they were and as proof of his identity, held up Golan's amulet.

I am Cerosomon, Guardian of the Mythical Beasts," the unicorn said with obvious relief. "Kronis, the winged lion, made me his prisoner and also relieved me of my Sacred Spear and Dagger."

"Gghhh! I will cut you free first, then we can try to get your weapons," grunted Orkan. But try as he might, he could not get his trusty sword to sever the bindings around the unicorn."

"Only my weapons will cut me free, the threads used to make up ties for the rope are each treated to differing magical elixirs that make it impossible to sever the strands with anything else but my dagger."

"I understand that. Melek too, has a magical rope and we've already met up with Kronis." Richard said briefly.

"You are still unharmed? You have done well to escape him then. Cerosomon said, "A single scratch from his claws or fangs will deliver enough poison to kill an army. You must stay clear of him, leave the Mythical City now!" The three companions looked at each other without saying a word, their minds each merging as one.

"Where can we find your weapon? That is, if we were fortunate enough to stumble across them?" Melek posed the question.

"Do not be foolhardy and go anywhere near the lighthouse in the old harbour," Cerosomon continued, "That is Kronis' lair, he keeps close guard on his domain and you can be certain he'll be waiting for you. Get beyond the Invisibility Curtain, and you will be safe from his attacks because the Evil One has determined that since the great battle, that Kronis should remain within the confines of this city."

"Why?"

"Kronis was born to be a killer. After the war he went on the rampage, anyone that opposed him was struck down, but when he went too far in trying to dethrone the Evil One, he had a curse placed on him. Unfortunately, the Evil One chose the Mythical City as a prison for Kronis."

"Gghhh! Why did he not kill you?" Orkan questioned.

"A decree by the Evil One prevents that ever happening. Kronis and I am held here as an example to all of those that dare to ever oppose the Evil One. We are both trapped here."

"We must attempt to retrieve your weapons from the lighthouse then? That will free you so that you can help others at the Ancestral City." Richard said pragmatically. They bade their farewells and moved quickly moved back through the archway.

"Did you notice that the shadows are following us again?" Richard asked as they entered the street.

"Yes," Melek answered, "but did you notice that some of the shapes have now taken on more realistic outlines? There are some of them resembling some of the incredible beasts described in Morbane's book?"

"Gghhh! How are going to find our way back here if we don't find Cerosomon's weapons?" Orkan's soldier training sprung into action. Melek whipped the golden rope from around his waist, "with this. You said it was magic, after all, it did somehow miraculously lengthen so that I could help Covelette, maybe if we believe in it again, we could tie one end to the archway and unwind it as we go?"

"Perhaps that might work, let's try it." Richard nodded agreement.

As Melek had suspected, the rope did stretch as it snaked out behind the travelling group. As they began to traverse their way down the hill through the maze of narrow streets, Richard took hold of the amulet in the hope that it would lead them directly to the harbour lighthouse but this time, it seemed to deserted him and except for understanding that they must head downwards through the city streets, they were lost among the many similar looking buildings. All the time, the rope continued to extend behind them as they criss-crossed the area. Richard was about to give up and return along the course of the rope, when a large and familiar shadow swept across their path.

"Kronis! He's found us. Run!" They were now racing for their lives, twisting and turning along strange paths and corridors trying hard to throw off their pursuer but unfortunately for them, because Kronis was able to keep watch on the fleeing group by gliding and swooping down from above. He had the advantage and was using it by pushing them towards his lighthouse through a narrow corridor into a dead-end where he planned to finish them off.

"In there!" Richard was horrified when he saw they had been led into a blocked off street but fortunately there was a small trapdoor to one side, Richard heaved it up and pushed Orkan into the tiny space, Melek followed and Richard dived in at the back and was surprised to see that it widened into what looked like some kind of laundry room. Kronis landed, the trapdoor, because of his twin body bulk, once again prevented his getting at his prey. Again he used his long reach to blindly claw at his unseen trapped victims but this time they were ready with sharpened sword and dagger that flashed out several times, some of the slashes found their mark. Unable to see what had happened, or to manoeuvre within such a concentrated and confined space, Kronis retreated into the air, blood gushing from the pads of his paws.

"Move! We must get away before he returns!" The three fled heedless of direction, switching direction, heading up the hill again. Richard constantly searched each passing area for somewhere safe to hide. A little thought kept nagging at the back of Richard's brain, Kronis never gave up once he had a potential victim in his sights, while another line of thinking persisted, he had to reach a safe place.

"The maze, this is it," he shouted as they reached a corner and saw the magnificent green marble dragons further along the high carved walls. Before they could reach their goal, a roar sounded from somewhere high above. "In here!" Richard shot into a narrow doorway cut into the stone face opposite the wall; his two friends followed him closely. The entrance provided enough light for them to see that it was nothing more than a shallow gravelled cave; there were no doors, no chimney, no back way out and no escape from Kronis. Richard's brain whirled at super-speed, he had made a dreadful mistake and now he felt it his duty to undo the error. "We can't stand around like this indefinitely. We must do something. I have an idea." Richard knelt to the ground and ran his hand over the cobbled floor around his feet. He picked up several three even sized stones about the size of his fist and handed them to Melek. "When I give a nod, throw the stones as close to the entrance as you can." He whispered.

"Gghhh! Why?"

"You'll see, just get your bow and arrow ready, if you can use a couple of those poisonous berries, so much the better Give me your sword." Orkan reluctantly hand it over. In the dim light they watched as he adjusted his grip on the golden long handled sword until the sharp edge was exactly to his liking, then waited. They heard the approaching flapping of Kronis' wings outside, then everything went so quiet that each of them could actually hear their own heartbeats sounding like tribal drums being played behind their own brain. All of sudden there was an almighty crash as Kronis tested the outside wall for strength.

"Wheeeooee!" all three were now expecting to see his claw enter their domain. It went quiet again. Richard took half a step forward to the side of the opening and raised the sword as high as the stone roof would allow, he nodded his head, Melek tossed the three stones, landing them just inside the cave entrance bouncing harmlessly against the outer cave wall.

"Hiss!" Everything happened so quickly that Melek hardly had time to blink as a single head of Kronis shot into block the cave entrance and to see where his victims were placed. Richard dropped the golden sword with his full might which caught Kronis fully I the mouth, there was a tremendous cracking sound followed by a large howl of pain as the beast whipped its head back away from the entrance.

"Got him that time!"

"Are you sure?" Richard pointed to the ground. What looked like a stone lying just inside the entrance was in fact one of Kronis' large fangs, "he won't be able to bite anyone with that missing. I don't think he's going to try again for a while."

"Gghhh! I still don't trust him. Let's try and find another way out of here." Orkan moved slowly to his left, testing every step to find a possible escape route. Nothing that way, so he moved in the opposite direction. "Look!" He had found the smallest of holes hidden beneath what look like a roughly broken up marble slab. Orkan bent down to measure the hole's diameter against his own body, realising it was going to be too tight a squeeze even if they had tried to slide feet first into it. "I don't like the idea of such a narrow tunnel. What if it's the hiding place for other creatures?

"No it's too small for us to use, we could be sliding straight out of Kronis' mouth into a something worse." Richard said sceptically. No Orkan, I don't like it." Suddenly there was the sound of slow flapping from outside the cave,

"Gghhh! I think that could be the sound of our problem being solved?" Sword raised in case of some trickery Richard moved forward, just in time to catch sight of the twin bodied Kronis lifting high into the air.

"He's going." Richard knew that they had won this battle but yet, somehow had to still win the war against Kronis that was, if they were going to ever be able to release Cerosomon by rescuing his weapons.

"Kronis is badly wounded and will head to sanctuary of the lighthouse. He may even have some sort of potion or balm to possibly repair the damage. He will return and try again." Melek said knowingly." The rope has worked its magic once more," he said proudly "We are still able to find our way back to the Ancestral Guard when we need to do so." Richard ran over and hugged the little scribe, unlike Orkan; he accepted his congratulation with a smile written right across his features. "We should act quickly; it will give Kronis less time to react." He whispered.

"Right, it's into the winged lion's den?" Richard looked straight at Orkan.

"You are starting to think like a soldier now, strike while the enemy is at his weakest." Orkan smiled. The small group sneaked back into the streets, moving down the hill and tracked by the golden cord in the secure knowledge, that Melek's rope would once again return them to the Guardian The lighthouse loomed before them, a square tower topped by battlements that had once held signal fires. As they got closer, a telltale trail of fresh blood indicated that Kronis had returned to nurse his wounds.

"Gghhh! A blood trail, he is going to be extra dangerous." Orkan turned to Melek, "You remain here, you do not have weapons and will be in the way as an extra target for Kronis to attack." Orkan ordered. The two pushed open the door and started up the small-width staircase that climbed up the side of the wall. There was no rail, so they hugged the wall keeping away from the central well that reached from the base of the old building right to the top of the tower. Richard drew his dagger while Orkan had already strung an arrow with two poisonous berries into his bow. Once fully prepared the pair moved quickly up the remaining treads, near the top, they burst into Kronis' lair. The lion was in one corner, licking his wounded paws. Among other items lying beside him, were Cerosomon's weapons. Orkan moved like lightning, his arrow striking deep into a hind leg of the huge cat's one body. His second, found its mark between the second body and where its wing joined together. Kronis reared up in pain.

Then Richard showed true valour with his concentrated determination to recover the guardian's weapons, he darted forward, constantly slicing his long dagger back and forth while desperately trying to avoid the lethal claws from finding their mark. A third arrow from Orkan sunk itself into one of the lion's broad chests, Kronis roared in agony and this momentary lapse gave Richard the opportunity he required to snatch up the Guardian's halberd and dagger and then race back towards the stairway amid a hail of arrows that sped from Orkan's bow. One arrow pierced the beast's throat; another found its mark in one of the great head's eye socket.

"Orkan let's go!" Richard took a quick glance at his enemy; Kronis was writhing around pawing at the missiles that had already found their mark. Orkan released a last arrow with purpose as Kronis turned side on to him. It entered the lion's body behind a front leg puncturing the lung. Instead of roaring Kronis began wheezing and coughing blood from one of the huge heads. This was the time to leave, they raced down the narrow stairway, out of the lighthouse where Melek had nervously waited for them He took the lead, continually coiling in his rope as they followed it all the way back to the maze entrance where Richard took over relying on his amulet to guide them back to Cerosomon.

"Hold still," Richard used Cerosomon's dagger to cut through the Guardian's bonds with magical ease. Once the guardian was free, Richard handed him his weapons giving him no time to stretch his stiffened limbs.

"Gghhh! Kronis is still alive and could be a threat again," warned Orkan. They followed the rope back out of the maze into the walled street, Melek gathered it in and as it had magically stretched, so it again shrank back to normal length that he placed around his waist. As they moved between the buildings and down the hill, the shadows now began materialising all around them, the nearer they got to the harbour and lighthouse, the now more pronounced and half formed darkened shapes began revealing themselves.

"Gghhh! The ghosts are changing." Orkan observed. As the four came in sight of the lighthouse, they saw that the badly wounded Kronis had managed to drag himself out of the old building to confront them." What do we have to do to kill Kronis?"

"We do nothing, because he is dying." As Cerosomon pointed out the thickening shadows advancing towards the stricken lion, he barked an order. The shadows seemed to close in to envelop and smother Kronis in a mantle of death,

"Gghhh! Kronis' ghosts are beginning to materialise." Orkan stated, drawing his sword. "We better get ready for their attack." They all watched mesmerised as colour and bizarre shapes flooded into their bodies turning them into an array of unusually weird beasts.

"No wait! These are my forces; they are transferring their Life Force back from Kronis to themselves." The unicorn declared. The shadows were quickly developing into horned beasts and dragons with enormous wings; other creatures were taking on combined structures of several animals, while some bore no resemblance to anything ever seen. "They are mythical beasts, the half-believed figments of mind and legend. This is our city, once Kronis imprisoned me, my forces became mere shadows with no strength, no power because it was these virtues that were absorbed by Kronis. Once they have materialised by taking back what was rightfully theirs, Kronis will be no more."

"Look! The sea is beginning to return to the harbour," an excited Melek pointed out the encroaching waters drifting through the archway, across the sand, heading towards the far side dock wall.

"With the steady demise of Kronis, it would seem that all things he stole from us will return to life as we once knew it." Steadily the shadows came to life changing from wisps to silhouettes, then developing into becoming three dimensional negatives before taking on a coloured hue as they become real once more. As they did so they progressively drifted away back to the city and their homes.

"This process will take time to complete, once we have regained strength we shall join the others at the Ancestral City where hopefully, we will again assemble to win the war. I know that our people thank you for their release, you have excelled in your bravery today."

We must continue with our mission. Richard suggested looking out at the rising waters in the harbour water. "Our boat, we must get back to it before the sea takes it away. How do we get to the beach now that this place is filled with water?"

"Through one of the gates in the wall, come, I will walk with you." Richard knew that there had been no gates anywhere to be seen in the battlement wall when they first arrived, but alongside the harbour there was now a gate. The group made their way onto the beach after bidding their goodbyes to the Guardian. The rising sea was already lapping at the underside of the boat and it was already beginning to float against the incoming waves.

"Run, if we lose the boat its back through the swamp." Richard raced but at that moment it looked very much as if the sea would claim the boat for itself.

Meeting the Immortals of the Deep

On the Nineteenth Day...

Sea falls fast and deep
Ship speeds deeper still,
Down to hidden Coral's Keep
Where Evil wreaks its will.
Merman King locks the spell,
Guardian's magic is the key.
Chosen One must use it well
To set the others free.

Richard was surprised as Melek flew past him making straight for the boat, but were they all too late as they painfully watched the as water reclaimed their boat.

"Gghhh! See what happens when things return to normal, we have lost the boat and now we must face the blood suckers, that is not normal behaviour." Orkan bitterly complained as he resignedly sat down to watch the bobbing craft moving further and further from the shore.

"Does it look as if it is coming back?" Melek suddenly pointed out. The craft became bigger and clearer. Richard noticed movement from behind the craft, as it got nearer he could see that some sort of sea creature was hurrying it along.

"Orkan, don't knock normal, I think the sea creature bringing our boat is one of the Guardian's ghosts that is now normal. Whatever that thing is, I'm glad it is on our side?" Richard teased when the beast, with one last heave, pushed the craft onto the beach, then turned and headed back out to the sea. Melek handed Richard the Path Finder that when swivelled, clearly pointed them directly seawards.

"Gghhh! Water means trouble, I am not happy." Orkan complained.

"We must follow its direction, it has never failed us." Melek countered, rising and heading towards the small craft. "It's our destiny and we must obey?" Orkan dragged his way behind the other two, he knew he spoke the truth and after all, he had promised the Guardian that he would protect his companions.

They rowed on the calm sea for a while until they noticed a full-blown storm heading towards them. Black waves marched from horizon to horizon and began tossing the frail craft brutally across the ocean. Their paddles made little impact as the sea around them grew in intensity, one moment down in a trough, the next balanced on a peak staring down in terror at a near-vertical sheer wall of water.

"Gghhh! Told you, water was trouble!" Orkan screamed in total panic; as the little craft was buffeted, pushed and pulled in all directions by rampant wind and violent seas. They could do nothing against these elemental forces but crouch in the bow, and be blasted by salt-spray until the storm finally blew itself out. The wind slowly calmed, the sea-swell began to subside allowing the thoroughly soaked trio to pull themselves back onto the makeshift seating.

"Land!!" To Richard's astonished delight, he could now see land on three sides, at this distance he thought that it was a becalmed tidal inlet that had formed this shallow looking body of water. At that moment none of them thought about or even cared where the terrific storm had taken them, all their senses simply concentrating on the safety that the not too distant terra firma would now provide for them. Richard and Orkan recovered the makeshift oars that they had been lying on so as not to lose them overboard and immediately began rowing the boat towards the lagoon. After a while, Richard turned to see if they were still on course and noticed that the shore seemed no nearer than when they had started rowing.

"The tide is going out. Row harder!" Richard and Orkan rowed as frantically as possible but the sea current was too strong for them to make any headway. Eventually they found their arms becoming too tired to continue the frenetic pace, both began slowing their stroke rate and the small craft started moving back towards the open ocean once again. Sluggishly at first, the slower their oar drag became, the faster they moved, continually gathering speed at a fearsome rate strong enough to create quite a sizable bow wave.

"Oh-oh! What's that?" Richard questioned, hearing the distant thundering reverberation of what to him sounded like cascading water.

"I cannot see anything, it could be a seafall." Melek answered.

"Gghhh! What is a seafall?"

"It's a great water hole, not like a whirlpool. Apparently something more like a waterfall, except it only happens in the ocean." Melek shouted. The fear and tremor of his answer caused both Richard and Orkan to spin off the seats grabbing the librarian and pulling him back to the bottom of the craft.

"Hold on tight!" Richard screamed as the little boat hurtled towards the edge of the liquid chasm. They held their breath, hanging on tightly to whatever they could grasp on to as the little craft grated against rocks, spun around, then they went over the verge, sliding down a precipitous wall of water.

The impact shattered the small scow tossing the companions deep into the opaque maelstrom and for one awful moment they touched the seabed. Richard stretched out an arm and caught hold of Orkan before swimming towards the light. They broke through to the surface, Richard having a distinct feeling of dizziness, thinking that he had experienced this feeling before. Melek popped up and shook his head sharply as he greedily drank in air with a cough and splutter; Richard found a length of longitudinal timber that had been the keel of their boat

"Grab onto this." Richard pushed Orkan towards the boat's keel. Melek also draped himself over the wooden beam. "Are you both okay?" Richard bellowed, both were too weary to answer immediately and simply nodded. At first glance, in his mind's eye, this place felt more like finding themselves at the eye of some sort of water hurricane; the water remained calm while white saltwater spray drifted right across the becalmed watery region. "A boat," he croaked. "Look!" The followed his pointing finger and saw an old schooner slicing towards them from out of the mist, its sales were in tatters. There was no sign of a crew, nothing to indicate that the companions had been spotted. The dark vessel creamed its way over the sea, a rope ladder trailing from its side. It seemed as if it was going to hit them as it passed by, Richard and his friends instinctively grabbed at the hemp steps and clung on for all their worth. Richard scrambled hand over hand up the first few rungs then helped Melek up and Orkan followed until all cleared the water, the trio moved to the top, one by one they toppled over the ship's gunnels and flopped onto the deck, completely exhausted. It took a short while to recover sufficiently enough to sit up and start taking in their current surroundings. To Richard the ship seemed deserted, a large, very old ball-like brass diving bell stood unattended on the deck.

"Gghhh! This does not feel right?" Orkan drew his sword.

"Wait, let's first check the Book of Prophecies," Melek said, opening the book.

Sea falls fast and deep
Ship speeds deeper still,
Down to hidden Coral's Keep
Where Evil wreaks its will.
Merman King locks the spell,
Guardian's magic is the key.
Chosen One must use it well

To set the others free.

As they pondered the message there was a creaking sound of a hatch being opened, Richard thought he also heard steps and groaning. Turning, he saw nothing moving.

"This is an Evil spooky place," he commented, feeling the telltale chill begin galloping down his backbone.

"I have read of something similar about ghost ships," Melek pulled his book onto his back. "According to ancient legend, the Nemisis is supposed to be a large ghost ship sailing the seas around a small island off our coast. The Nemisis magically appears as a beautiful schooner with tattered white sails," he pointed upwards to the masts. "This ship like the legend has three masts of three sails each and a ferocious beast as the figurehead. It is also said that it always travels with utter silence on board, but the tale relates that it quickly disappears again, leaving no evidence of its presence. The ghost ship is also known to be able to navigate under water." Melek continued explaining. "I somehow think that the Nemisis has found us, don't you?"

"I've heard of a well known ghost ship called the Flying Dutchman." Richard intervened.

"That myth also suggested that the ship is crewed by the drowned, who are brought aboard the ship by its master or captain called Nemis, some sort of mythological merman king, it is said that the dead can resume an existence as if they were alive again, but only once Nemis has claimed them as his crew." Melek's story was suddenly interrupted by timber creaking and footsteps close behind them – the ship was suddenly heaving with activity as real looking beast type sailors began reefing sails, battening hatches, lashing down loose objects, all seemingly in preparation for more approaching stormy weather.

"Gghhh! Where did you come from?" Orkan said, walking to the stern by crossing the deck past sailors, up some stairs to the poop deck he reached the helmsman. "You saved our lives," he said, patting the wheelman's back in thanks. His hand passed through nothingness as Orkan stumbled forward. "Gghhh! It's a ghost," he spluttered. "Melek was right, we're on a ghost ship!" The ghost pilot turned to Orkan, he was lashed to the wheel and no face looked out of his mildew-covered canvas foul-weather hood. Orkan took off down the stairs, across the deck among the ghostly crew to join up with his companions. Suddenly a short, piping trill rang through the air. Instantly the crew dashed below leaving only the tied up helmsman and the companions remaining alone.

"What's happening?" Richard shouted.

"Gghhh! I don't know." Orkan grunted. "No use asking the one steering this boat, he does not say much." They looked towards the poop deck just in time to see the spectre at the helm throw the large wheel one way; the ship seemed to go straight into a nosedive. The trio was immediately hurled against the railings, Richard could see that the ship was heading for the deep as first the bow, and then the foredeck began submerging in a turbulent lather of seawater.

"The diving bell is our only chance!" Melek screamed. They dragged themselves through the rising water to the brass bell; Orkan spun the hatch wheel, yanked open the circular barrier allowing them to scramble through the tight opening. He slammed it shut and instantly spun the hatch wheel again until it sealed tightly against the elements and fast rising sea with only seconds to go. Richard headed straight for one of the round portholes, pressing his nose up to the grimy glass he peered out, through the green sea he could just make out the helmsman, busy battling with his task of guiding the ship to their next destination

"There's nothing but sea water out there." Richard said, turning to companions who were both inspecting their new quarters. He quickly noted that it was a small globular room without much headroom with several circular inspection portholes evenly distributed around the centre bulge. There were also several very old valves and copper piping situated alongside the hatch, these seemed to Richard to be some sort of air control apparatus, he could not be sure.

"Hope we do not have to spend much time here," Melek said. "The air cannot last forever."

"I think it will last for quite a while but somehow, something tells me that we won't have to wait too long to find out what fate awaits us, we've managed to escape a host of nasty things to date. That probably means that the Evil One has not given up trying, we have annoyed him profusely and are not meant to simply suffocate in the sealed world of a diving bell, that's not his way of revenge. We cannot do anything right now, so let's rest and see what this journey might bring." Orkan again took first watch while his two exhausted friends stretched out and immediately fell into deep sleep.

"Wake up!" Orkan shouted. Both he and Melek came awake in a flash, the bell had warmed and the atmosphere seemed stuffy. Orkan had his face pressed to one of the portholes. "I think we are there," he said excitedly. The sleeping pair instantly crawled to see what Orkan was telling them. The ship skimmed through a maze of differing coloured coral along the seafloor. The formations of reef-structured coral were intricately fashioned into houses and streets. The ship began to slow and suddenly came to a shuddering jolt of a stop that caused the round diving bell to dislodge from the moorings on the deck and to roll over the newly opened gunnels to bounce heavily onto the seafloor. The sudden action took the three off guard when the impact threw them sideways and then across the floor as the ship came to rest. Richard immediately jumped up rubbing his back and got to a porthole where he saw crew clambering down rope ladders, they began heaving and dragging the weighty diving bell along the seabed towards an ornately carved coral gateway entrance of the equally opulent palace.

"They are taking us into the palace." Richard stated. They could do nothing except peer through the portholes as the sailors manoeuvred the brass ball past the gateway into a magnificent throne room thronged with some very strange features and an abundance of seashells that added a beautiful iridescent sparkle to the whole place. This sumptuous décor also overflowed with a huge range of peculiar and macabre looking creatures drawn mostly from beneath the ocean depths while dotted among them were others that the trio recognised as being from mythological and humanoid extraction.

"This must be Nemis the Merman King," Melek said as the crowd parted and a vicious-looking merman clutching a coral trident floated towards the diving bell.

"Gghhh! I get the distinct feeling this could be an enemy?" Orkan blurted nervously.

The Merman moving towards them was half-human, half-fish monster with tight blue scaled skin, a huge mouth full of sharp teeth, long, scraggly green-moss hair drifting high behind as it caught the drifting sea, small stickled fins placed over its body and bubbles emanating from what seemed like a blowhole somewhere on its back.

"Orkan for the first time, I think you could be right in your assumption," Melek teased as Nemis swirled to a stop and peered at the trio. His menacing stare held them entranced before he spoke.

"At last!" The Chosen One, I have long waited for such a grand prize." The three were astonished that they could hear underwater, only Richard was more dumbfounded that he could clearly hear everything Nemis had said, while the merman was on the outside of the diving bell. "I intend being rewarded handsomely by delivering you to the Evil One along with the Twin Guardians that have recently come under my care." Nemis cackled cruelly.

"Guardians? Who are these two, I know nothing of any Twin Guardians." Melek bravely tested Nemis.

"Ahh! The librarian speaks for the Chosen One now does he?" Again Nemis cackled cruelly. "As for you two," he pointed at him and Orkan. "You must beg and perhaps, just perhaps, I will allow you to become crew members on my ship. Your days of speaking on his behalf are now numbered."

"I speak up for myself; you say you have captured two guardians? I do not believe that for a moment." Richard interrupted the gloating merman.

"The Guardian of the Fishes, Tishon and Shunta are safely held captive. If you look through the windows on the far side, you will see I speak true. I have heard rumours of your exploits, do not think you can dupe me." Nemis moved around the hull of the diving bell. The trio did as ordered and moved across the floor to the far side portholes. Nemis made a sweeping gesture towards a net in which two figures covered in spines and feathery fins writhed helplessly. "As for you two, for doubting my word, you no longer have the choice of becoming crew members on my ship. I have something 'very special for you' to endure, very special indeed."

"What does he mean?" Richard turned to Melek.

"Mythology indicates that Nemis kills by exsanguinating his victim with his teeth and blowing their blood out of his blowhole. Even though a victim could escape, while Nemis could survive on land, he is incredibly slow and bulky and not effective at finishing off any incapacitated victims. That's all I have read." Melek's voice held terror in his words.

Nemis waved his hand upwards. A huge octopus looking beast rose out of the crowd lurking behind the merman and floated towards the diving bell, where it then disappeared from its occupant's view as it moved above the bell. Nemis watched the huge octopus-like monster spread tentacles fanned out wide beneath a vast black hood, a thin trail of black ink dribbling from its vicious parrot-like beak.

"There are no clues in the prophecy," a frustrated Richard blurted. His hand moved onto his amulet and suddenly he sensed Golan's presence telling him to free the Guardians and he too, would be saved. "That's it; we must somehow save the Guardians in order to save ourselves. We must face Nemis; somehow one of us must distract him while someone tries to free the others. But how? The water will drown us." The clunking hatch wheel spun and water began rushing into the bell as Nemis swung the door wide open.

"Gghhh! Die Nemis!" Orkan with water pouring in flashed his sword directly at the merman but with the pressure forcing against his body, he missed his target although the attempted blow did force Nemis to retreat away from the bell. They all took as deep a breath as their lungs could hold and burst through the opened hatch, Melek and Orkan heading straight for the Guardians. Nemis was heading back to his throne and did not notice their escape. Nor did the octopus looking thing, the spread mantle blocked its vision below. Richard drew Juroot's dagger and stabbed out at the huge beast's tentacles in order to try and distract any attention away from his companions. The pair had reached the Guardians, Orkan slashed at the net when suddenly; a webbed hand snaked out through the hole and grabbed his weapon, while another pulled Melek through the opening and pressed a scaly mask over his face. Orkan was unable to hold his breath any longer, he saw a guardian hack the opening as his brain started spinning from lack of air. In an instant the Guardian had placed a mask over Orkan's face and everything came back into focus as the magical mask began supplying much needed air into his lungs. One of the Guardians headed straight for the bell just as the huge beast was about to strike out a sucker arm at the weakening, fast running out of air Richard. Using Orkan's sword, the Guardian whipped the weapon through the water with the dexterity of a master butcher, slicing off one of the beast's large striking tentacles. The octopus-like animal let out a thundering and alarming cry, which in turn, immediately alerted the merman to the danger happening behind him. He spun to immediately assess the position, and then raced back towards the bell, his lethal trident prepared to strike down his enemies. The Guardian moved in unison to block his attack but he was able to keep them at bay, even succeeding to drive them backwards towards the diving bell. Richard heard another mournful cry from the beast above his head, he glanced upward to see yet again an unfurling tentacle heading directly towards him, when the swift shadow of a great dolphin appeared from nowhere, ramming into the beast with the force of a train smashing over a rabbit. The strike immediately threw the octopus-like beast into a flaying tentacle, inky cart wheeling mass of a sprawling glutinous mess, Richard now completely forgotten, as the dolphin struck the beast again and again. He turned to see that the Guardians were almost back to back with him, Nemis was gaining an upper hand.

Melek whipped his rope belt free of his waist and with a second flick, wrapped it around Nemis' trident, he yanked hard. Nemis' weapon, that had seemed so threatening before, instantly snapped like a brittle stalactite. The immediate effect had an alarming and astonishing upshot. With Nemis having lost the source of his power, he began to literally fall apart, the process took hold at the tip of his tail, working its way steadily up his body, chunks of flesh were beginning to waft away from his internal bony core structure. More and more flesh drifted idly away exposing the lower half of his torso revealing his skeletal bone and there was nothing Nemis could do to prevent the progression. Nemis' unsupported legs wobbled and gave way, sending him crashing down to stir up a flurry of fine brown clouds from the seafloor that slowly peeled away, to uncover a body that consisted of a sharp ended bony framework, Nemis' carcass looked very much like an X-rayed fish. All that remained of the merman was a pile of fetid matter, a spindly skeleton that now nonchalantly rose and fell with each gentle passing swell of ocean tide movement. Richard's fascinated gaze tore away from Nemis' demised fishbone trunk and he saw that the host of marine creatures were curling and whooping in joyous celebration. Richard looked across at his companions knowing that this time everyone had played their difficult parts to perfection and that Melek's quick action had proved the prophecy correct yet again, the spell had been lifted. Richard and the Twin Guardians inspected the ink stained mess that had been the octopus.

"Where did that dolphin come from?" He asked curiously.

"It's Delphost, one of the last large Sea Mammals," one Guardian replied. "Using his sonar to keep out of range, he managed to escape the spell that befell the rest of his people and has been a constant thorn in Nemis' side. We were very lucky he was here today."

"We are also lucky and thankful that you and your friends arrived. Without luck playing a part, things for all of us could have been so very different?" The Guardian's Twin interjected.

"It wasn't all luck. We were guided here by Golan." Richard quickly related the happenings to date.

"Delphost can carry you back to land, where do you need to go next?" The first Guardian enquired.

"I do not know. Let's consult the Path Finder." Richard, Delphost and the Guardians joined Melek and Orkan. The shimmering pointer indicated their next direction of travel; Richard showed it to Delphost and the Guardians.

"That is the direction towards Glaciotor." Delphost said in a highly pitched voice that belied his size and strength. "It's also the coldest place here. I know this, because it's also where my people are being held prisoner, they are entrapped in ice walls. I have sneaked around Glaciotor on many occasions hoping to find a way in to rescue them, it's a hopeless task."

"The Path Finder always directs us that is the direction we must take. Perhaps we could help your people?" Richard replied.

"This may help you," the Guardian handed Richard a small shell like flask. "It contains special fish oil that we use to protect us from the worst cold found in the deep oceans, maybe it will keep your blood from freezing solid as well. Rub it into your skin." Richard pocketed the container as the Twin Guardians acknowledged their deeds in raised salute. "Your work is successfully done here, we go to join our newly freed forces in order to do our duty. Thank you again, may you fare well wherever your path may next lead you. Until we next meet, we take our leave." The twin fish swam towards their waiting companions.

"Ever onwards," Richard said as he helped Melek onto Delphost's back, soon the Coral City was left behind as the dolphin steadily rose through the ocean, finally emerging on the surface. Delphost made good time as he splashed in graceful arcs across the flattened swells, their masks took a while dissolving slowly in the sunlight and air until like Nemis had done, the facemasks disintegrated completely and the three could breathe freely once more. At first, the warm sun on their backs felt good for a while before the sea started to become much colder, the sea thickened into sludge of ice crystals that slopped in the ocean swell, it was as Delphost had predicted it would be. Richard rubbed the Guardian's protective oil into his skin then handed the flask to the others to do the same.

"That must be Glaciotor." Melek said pointing to a ribbon of white growing on the horizon. "That oil hasn't helped much, I am chilled to my very core." He complained. As they drew nearer, the white band expanded until it became a sheer cliff of ice that stretched on either side as far as they could see. Ahead of the steep frozen walls of packed ice lay a no man's land of white islands that heaved together crushing and splintering to form a flattened area with only half-frozen channels closer to the seaward side that they were fast approaching.

"It is almost impossible to cross that lot on foot." Richard shouted.

"Gghhh!" Sure death to fall in or cross the water." Orkan shouted back. Delphost headed for the widest ocean parting in between the tightly gathered ice-packs and began scouting the safest route for a landing point when the channel he had chosen began to quickly narrow. Heavy ice breaking off the cliff ahead and a large iceberg began pushing in from the sea forcing the already narrow watery canal to close in on the little group. They were becoming trapped.

"Hold on tightly!" Delphost screeched as he accelerated towards the falling and breaking ice cliff directly at their forefront. All Richard could see ahead was a closed-in, flat surfaced causeway thin strip of white behind which, there was a mountainous iceberg blocking their path, in turn that was surrounded by freezing cold large waves created by continuous and massive explosions from the gigantic releases of ice mountains breaking away from its core. They reached the end of the channel at full speed and Delphost shot into the air above the flattened ice ribbon with a perfectly timed jump that ended with the dolphin coming down belly first on top of the smooth flow. "Jump! Now!" He squealed, rolling his body sideways and tossing his passengers through the air. Landing fairly softly Richard rolled several times before coming to his feet and watching Delphost, who continued sliding in a long arc and missed hitting the iceberg by the narrowest of margins before plopping into the water beyond.

"Sit tight, it won't be long before this ice breaks apart, it will then drift back towards the cliff. There are many caves and holes along the coast that are naturally caused by melting water finding its way down to the ocean. Use one of these larger cave-pipes to reach the top of the cliff."

"That is, if we don't freeze to death first," Richard countered. "Thanks for the lift."

"Good hunting, I wish I could be with you when and if you find my people." With that, the dolphin disappeared below the cold water line. Richard surveyed the freezing area as he joined his companions.

"This is a very desolate area; we may as well be in the middle of a harsh desert as this. I think we are going to be stranded for a while so let's build ourselves an ice mound. I once saw how they did it on a thing we call a television. It will get us out of the wind and keep us warm, all we need is snow, there's plenty around. Let's do it." For some time they all gather the top layer of soft snow into a mound then scraped out the middle and packed themselves into it. Their warm breath soon began heating the space around their tightly crammed bodies.

"Gghhh! Snow to keep you warm? What next?" Orkan laughed at his own question.

"What next indeed?" Melek was far more serious

The Ice Palace

On the Twentieth Day...

Sear of ice chill best is fled
By cutting that which in a head
Is single, cold and seeing all,
The eye that holds you in its thrall.
A blinding arc destroys the past,
Then they start the trip at last.
Beware at length a fall of snow,
Another city? Far to go.

The trio was rudely awoken by what sounded like a thunderclap followed almost immediately by a heavy juddering. The solid ice was now rocking and moving in the swell.

"The ice must have broken clear as Delphost said it would do. We better get out and see what is happening." They unblocked their entrance to their warm ice mound and squeezed out of the small opening. They were already drifting towards the ice cliff dead ahead when a chunk of ice the size of a small mountain crashed off the sheer face into the sea. It was quite a way to their left but what worried Richard was the giant sea swell heading in their direction.

"Get back into the ice mound!" Richard screamed. "We'll be washed off by that wave." They raced back and once again sealed themselves into the mound, the swell arrived and lifted the floating ice platform, like a surfboard, it drove them along for some distance before moving on. Only once the ride seemed to have subsided, did the trio then dare to come out of hiding. The loose lying snow had been either washed off or had frozen solid leaving all surfaces looking more like an ice rink. Without realising it, the wave swell had carried their ice slab to within almost touching distance of the sheer cliff ice face.

"It's a cave!" Richard shouted. "Delphost said we should use the water caves." Just then, another huge ice block came off the cliff further down. Richard instinctively knew that they had just one chance otherwise they could be forced away from the cliff by the oncoming wave swell. "It's slippery, be careful". He edged his way across the glassy surface towards the cliff, one eye on the cave, the other watching the approaching wave. He waited for the ice slab to nudge the cliff.

"Now!" The trio jumped, Orkan slipped and started sliding back towards the ice slab and freezing sea. Melek instantly whipped his rope towards Orkan, he grabbed the end but his weight was too much, the ice floor friction slowly edged both seawards. Richard smashed Juroot's dagger into the floor, grabbed the rope and twisted it around the handle. Orkan stopped dead, then hand over hand pulled himself to safety.

"We better move, that swell could wash into this part of the cave." Fortunately, Richard led them up a roughly chipped ramp until he considered they were high enough to take a breather. The swell passed by, washing through and filling the area with water that they had only just vacated.

"Gghhh! Thank you my friends, for everything." Orkan placed his arms around his two companion's shoulders. "You have saved me in many, many ways." Melek turned and smiled at Richard, he gave the pig-like boy a gentle hug.

They steadily made their way up the huge steps of the tunnel along this very large and cavernous water drain, in some places where ice had fallen from the sides and broken into smaller chips, they found it easy going using these as a natural stairway. In other parts, the ice was as smooth and glassy as a mirror, but they quickly found a way to overcome the problem. Orkan shot arrows with Melek's rope attached to it into the ice higher up, then using their daggers like ice picks, they slowly hauled themselves ever upwards until they finally emerged triumphantly out of the huge hole at the top of the cliff. They found themselves on a plateau, to one side they could look out towards the sea and floating icebergs, the view in the opposite direction, rising before them like a ship from the flatness, was Glaciotor, an ice city.

"Against all odds we've made it this far." Richard looked at the shimmering walls of ice glinting in the sunlight, the place had an abundance of spires rising skywards into the blue beyond. It was like looking into a fairy tale land.

"How can such beauty and the presence of the Evil One fit so well together?" Melek said softly. They all instantly remembered the ominous warning that they had been given. "I feel our reception is bound to be warmer in there," he pointed at the city, "than the freezing wastes are out here, don't you?"

"I suspect you are correct, we have to tread carefully." Richard could not but help noting that there was a monumental arch a little way to their right. "Again, we have to pass through an arch into the unknown?" He said with a touch of regret tingeing his voice.

"Gghhh! In the mound I was warm. Climbing, I was warm. Standing here, I am cold and I do not think the oil that the Guardians gave us is doing anything for me. Let's get inside; at least a good fight will warm me up again." Orkan drew his sword as they all moved towards the colossal archway entrance of Glaciotor. As the three got closer to the mammoth arch built of gritty ice they saw vague, twisted lumps that they recognised as distinguishable creatures. Here they made out a tail, there an eye. Cold mouths gaped wide in silent fear. Either side of the arch, dolphins were frozen in agony, their grey faces showing masks of fear and terror. In silence, the trio tramped through the arch into the city of ice to see that streets stretched in every direction, straight and extremely empty.

"It looks like a ghost town, something does not feel right." Richard's hand moved to the shaft of the dagger. "We must find a way to release those poor souls."

"Gghhh! The way to do it is to confront the source of their confinement. We cannot do this on our own there's not enough time." Orkan reflected.

They could see that where once rooftops had shone in the sunlight, the pristine avenues were now cold, dark and unwelcoming. Stalactites hung menacingly like rows of swords in uneven rows along the lines of now frozen houses. Icy slabs of pavement led away like blue slides of gloom as the three stepped forward towards the stark environment. Richard felt that each of the vacant houses they passed seemed to somehow ooze fright or hostility towards the group, there was nothing to substantiate this feeling; it was probably the fact that no matter where they searched it revealed the same outcome, one of complete barrenness. Nothing moved, the only sounds were the crunching of their footsteps on ice or an occasional spitting of cracking stalactite. They were all becoming frozen, the cold seeped into their bones and Melek began stumbling with fatigue. Richard and Orkan were both weary and about ready to give up when Melek suddenly slumped down to the ground. Orkan grabbed the girl and lifted him into his arms.

"Gghhh! You must not go to sleep; you'll die from hypothermia if you do. We need to find a warm place." Richard began vigorously rubbing the scribe's arms to try warming him so that his blood circulation would speed up. They were so intent on rescuing their companion that they did not see or notice the large shadow approaching until it was too late. The obliteration of disturbed light bearing down on the little group in that lifeless street quickly proceeded to envelope the trio who were now all too cold and exhausted to move away. Richard was the first to see the looming giant. He was thickly bearded, and clad in a mixture of fur and rough woollen clothes to insulate himself against the freezing cold. In the middle of his forehead sat a single, blue-grey eye that stared expressionlessly straight at Richard. "Whooeee! Ogre!" A terrified Orkan screamed loudly.

"Welcome to Glaciotor," the creature boomed as he advanced towards the shivering companions. In a single manoeuvre, he managed to scoop all three into his huge arms, Richard and Orkan tried struggling against this force but it was useless, they were simply too cold and weak. The giant then tucked them into its clothes behind his wide red beard, his body smell was overpoweringly potent and numbing to the little group's senses, they all drifted into unconsciousness.

"Orkan, wake up," Melek was the first to revive, he found himself in a vast chamber of ice. Orkan was to his left, he snorted as the librarian pulled his hand out of the roughly stitched woollen blanket and gave him a gentle push against his head. "Wake up, where are we?"

"Gghhh! Giant, I dreamed of a giant." Orkan instantly sat bolt upright, his keen soldiering eye hurriedly surveying their neighbouring surroundings. At the far end of the huge grotto and seated in some sort of pretentious throne made up from jagged silvery ice sat the relaxed hulking giant. "No! I did not have a dream, he is very real, and if I'm not very mistaken, that is the Chosen One lying in front of him." Orkan had also spotted the crumpled pile of material on the floor before the immensely large creature and not seeing Richard anywhere, had automatically made the assumption that they had been separated from each other.

"What do we do?" Melek whispered

"Gghhh! We wait to see what happens next," the pig-like boy lay back, almost casually extracting his weapons as he slowly rolled onto his side so that he could keep an eye on the giant.

"Ahhh, my prisoners are awake I see. I am Spector, Keeper of the Ice Kingdom." His deep gravelled voice echoed through the cavernous area. "This is my citadel. I will allow you freedom enough to move about and take pleasure in it for the moment. Later, I will hand you over to the Evil One, I do not think the Chosen One will enjoy his hospitality." The giant let out a resounding chortle that woke Richard. "You will not be able to escape from here, if you do, your blood will freeze first. You are my special guests, so relax and enjoy yourselves because like the others in my keep, your postponed journey is bound to be a long cold one after I have had a rest." Spector raised a hand to his forehead. There was a muffled squelch as he removed his large single eye, leaving a large, unrefined gaping pink hollow situated in his brow, and situated just above his equally pink bulbous nose. "Do not try anything, I will be watching you." The ogre carefully placed his eyeball into a glass jar filled with green liquid on top of the ice table handily positioned at his left side. Within seconds the whole place rang to the tunes of Spector's heavy snoring, Richard pulled himself from the warmth of the tattered woollen blanket, the cold hit him forcibly, the temptation to climb back into the warmth was almost overpowering but this was too good an opportunity to hatch a plan. Instead, he began running on the spot, his gaze never leaving the solitary giant's eyeball even when he slipped twice on the icy surface, He then turned and ran backwards in a zigzag pattern towards his two companions.

"Did you see what the eye did?" He asked in a whisper.

"No," the librarian answered.

"That eyeball followed my every movement, up, down, left and right, I think it could be the giant's brain housed inside that all seeing orb." Richard said, turning his back towards the eye so that it would not be able to lip-read any planned escape discussions. "We must find a way to block its view, let's look at the Book of Prophecies; perhaps it could give us a clue as to what we should do next?"

"Spector was correct, if we try to run, this place is so cold that we will simply expend energy and will not get very far." Melek laid the large book on the woollen blanket and then said "Found the correct riddle, this means it is day twenty, there are but six more days left before the pods and Guardians all need to be found?" Richard nodded agreement. Melek made sure that he too faced away from the eye and began reading the text in whispered tones.

> *Sear of ice chill best is fled*
> *By cutting that which in a head*
> *Is single, cold and seeing all,*
> *The eye that holds you in its thrall.*
> *A blinding arc destroys the past,*
> *Then they start the trip at last.*
> *Beware at length a fall of snow,*
> *Another city? Far to go.*

"How?" Melek enquired as he closed the book and began strapping it onto his back... "It sees our every movement, if we try to even approach it, it will alert the giant and we don't need that to happen, do we?"

"The book mentions something about blinding, that's what we must do, we must somehow achieve that and I have a plan." Richard sounded confident. "We need to huddle, you stand between the eye and me so that it cannot see what I am about to do." His two companions linked together to hide him from

Spector's single eye. Richard dipped into his shoulder bag and extracted his invisibility cape that he drew over himself." Let's hope this works. Can you see me?"

"That is great, you've now completely disappeared." Melek whispered. Richard moved towards the jar very carefully. The first steps were nerve-racking mainly because he was unsure if the magical eye could somehow override the spell and see him beneath his cloak. He was half expecting Spector to jump forward at any moment, he concentrated on the eyeball, it stayed fixed upon his companions and did not waiver as he started moving to one side, it was only then that he thought that his plan might be working. Richard had worked out that in order to give himself a split second advantage, he needed to be behind the table, so he stealthily worked his way step by small step in order that he did not slip or slide on the glassy surface. He positioned himself, the eye was still concentrated on his two companions but there was something wrong, from his hidden viewpoint so close to his goal he could see that the eye was beginning to twitch, it was searching for the third companion and as it did so, Spector's hand also began to go into spasm. Richard knew he had to act fast, he threw back the cape and grabbed out at the green filled jar holding the eye, his intention was to race to his friend but that never happened. Grabbing the jar, the deepest of pains seared right through his hands and up his arms, the jar was freezing to the point that the blood in his hands started to congeal into a solid, it was if he had dipped his arms straight into liquid nitrogen.

"Arrghh!" Richard threw it forward and away from himself. The jar rose in a long semicircle upwards before crashing down onto the solid ice floor and smashing into thousands of glassy splinters. The thick green contents began fanning out across the ice and started to bubble up as the eye kept rolling towards Orkan and Melek, only to be met with a hail of arrows coming from the opposite direction. Spector bent forward in agony, both hands clutching and tearing at the hole in his forehead. The eyeball with three arrows in it stopped rolling, without its shielding liquid the evil eye instantly began to dry up causing it to shrivel and like a snail having salt poured on it, it started foaming violently until it disappeared into its own disarrayed gunge.

"Bring your blankets," Richard shouted. "This way." He raced around the ice table, collected the blanket he had used in front of the screaming giant and headed straight for the only door he had seen. The others had followed suit and were racing, slipping and sliding in the same direction. "Look out! He's coming." At the door Richard turned to see where his companions were and also saw the blinded giant begin stumbling in their direction.

"Gghhh! Go! Go!" Orkan urged as they caught up to Richard. They burst through the door and found themselves in yet another gigantic hall; the walls, floor and ceiling were made up of polished ice-sheets that reflected their forms a thousand-fold. It reminded Richard of a fairground hall of mirrors. Richard's mind was confused as he searched for an escape, within seconds; the rebounding mirrored reflections bounced back and caused them to lose all sense of their bearings. It was impossible to tell where they had come from or where they should be going. The trio's scourge suddenly smashed straight through the door behind them, they stood dead still as the giant stumbled about then Spector, still holding one hand to his forehead stopped to listen for any tell-tale sounds of the companion's whereabouts. It remained as a stalemate situation for a couple of very long seconds, the only sound filtering through the great hall being that of the giant's very heavy breathing. It was Melek that broke the tense deadlock, he carefully removed his rope and handed one end to his companions, his wrist flicked out, the gold rope snaked out and wrapped itself around the giant's heavy leg.

"Pull!" The trio yanked together their combined strength and the ice floor was enough to upend the surprised leviathan, he crashed to the floor and cracked his head against the solid ice,

"Keep behind me," Richard ordered as Melek whipped the golden coil back and around his slim waist. "The only way out is along the wall. Do not separate from each other." With Orkan and Melek close on his heels Richard shuffled wearily away from the centre of the hall. As they, and the giant moved, so too did the mass of reflections from all sides and angles, each one feeling as if they were now somehow trapped within this enormous kaleidoscope. With a sigh of relief, Richard's outstretched hand then encountered the burning chill of ice.

"It's the outer wall," The three fumbled along as quickly as they could, all the while Spector was beginning to recover and his intimidating reflections were bouncing across the walls and ceiling. They were all wondering how much longer they could keep this up, their pace was slowing as the cold began taking hold and the giant was now starting to move. Suddenly Richard's hand met empty space, it was the doorway, he held out his hand to Melek, he in turn did the same to Orkan and then Richard led them through a short narrow passage until they reached a darkened patch of rough-hewn rock, using fingertips the three followed it until that opened up onto a street. For the moment, they had managed to escape Spector, none of them knowing for how long.

"The blankets, wrap it around you." Richard ordered. Whatever the woollen contained within its fibres made a substantial difference to their well-being, it prevented penetrating cold from reaching their bodies and even started warming them. The three darted into the lonely city, skidding and sliding along the icy pavements until they accidentally came upon another huge archway that contained more trapped sea mammals in abundance just like the arch they had first encountered when entering the Ice Kingdom.

"We have to save them somehow." Melek implored just as they heard a terrifying roar of anger heading their way. What they still had not realised was that the giant over time, had also developed exceptional hearing and smell abilities and each time any of the three spoke, Spector could simply track them by their sounds, or even their smell. Now he was on their trail yet once again, his driving thought being that nobody had ever escaped him, he was going to make this lot pay dearly for what they had done to him.

"Gghhh! He's coming. I have an idea, it's risky but it could work. I have to move quickly, Melek I need you to fix your rope around the top of that archway." Melek flicked his rope in a high loop so that it wrapped around the central portion of the arch then handed the other end across to Orkan. "You carry on that way, go to the other side of the archway." Orkan quickly began struggling to climb up the rope, knowing that he had to reach the top of the arch before Spector arrived. It was now a race for time, as well as their lives.

"It's one of those water drains to the ocean; it's just like the one we climbed through when we arrived here." Richard said. Now, standing just outside the city perimeter, they had spotted what looked like a large circular but low retaining wall. They looked over the ice wall down into the depths of a massive great smooth sided hole that seemed to go on forever. "Let's get to the other side." Richard followed the line of the wall to lead Melek around the humongous hole. They placed themselves on the far side of the hole away from the arch, Richard desperately hoped it would give them an edge or at the very least, would give them an alternative escape route. They saw Orkan reach the top of the arch, he adjusted the rope so that it was fixed dead centre, drew his sword, waved at his two companions before he turned and quietly squatted on his haunches to await the giant's arrival. They did not have very long to wait before a monstrously large shadow appeared in the street beyond the archway.

"He's here. Doesn't he ever know when he's beaten?" Richard whispered, not knowing that this one statement had now given the giant both speed and direction of his enemy.

"All of the Evil One's people have the same trait; they would rather die before giving in." Melek replied in a whisper. Richard had already worked out what Orkan's plan was going to be, he looked towards his valiant companion, then crossed his fingers.

Spector strode purposefully towards the archway, both hands outstretched. As he reached the archway the courageous pig-like Orkan with one end looped round the battlement, and the other tied around his waist launched himself into space. Just then Spector made contact with the ice-archway and began pounding the upright with both fists, his frustration very evident to the watching pair. Orkan flew in a perfect arc up until that moment; his intention being to use his sword to spear Spector's vulnerable eyehole and hopefully kill the giant but, the shockwaves being transmitted through the arch changed his course of direction. He was about to miss the giant.

"Hey Spector! We are here, you hairy slob!" Richard immediately realised what was happening and screamed as loud as he could. Hands in front of him, the giant hurtled straight out past the archway towards the sound just as Orkan flew past Spector at the bottom of the rope's wide arc.

"Whoooeee!" Orkan could not control himself as he missed his target by completing the long curve. He started down again, the confused giant pulled up just before reaching the low wall outside the city gate. Shouting ahead, shouting from behind, he was unsure of which way to go so stopped to listen. That was Spector's big mistake as Orkan hurtled towards him and violently kicked the giant who then lost balance and crashed over the wall into deep nothingness below. The relieved trio heard thunderous crashing and his screams as he fell and bounced down the pipe and suddenly all was very quiet and still by the time Orkan had stopped swinging.

"Wow! That was a stroke of luck?" Richard and Melek joined their companion.

"Gghhh! Luck? Luck? I promised that I would protect you, that is what I did." Orkan laughingly bragged as Melek collected his rope. "See what is happening to the ice? It is starting to melt."

"Another of the Evil One's spells has been broken and our forces continue to expand?" Melek said tying the rope belt around his waist. With Spector's death, Glaciotor started returning to its former glory, it was as if his demise had suddenly created a furnace to be lit under the ice city. It did not take long for the meltdown to reach the citadel walls and archways where tall spines dissolved into shapeless lumps freeing the imprisoned mammals. "I wonder how these mammals will reach the sea?"

Richard, Orkan and Melek watched in bliss as the animals plunged in and out of pools created by the melting ice. Whale song and tail slapping mixed with the chattering dolphin squeaks; penguins had a lot of fun using the flowing water into and down the water pipe as their escape route.

"If I'm right," Richard offered, "This melt-down could soon travel right through the ice-cap, the sea mammals will be able to get back to the ocean and join up with Delphost who will guide them to open water so that they connect with the rest of Golan's forces." The three relaxed and took time to have something to eat; the sudden warmth soon had Richard removing the woollen blanket "I wonder if I should keep this?"

"Gghhh! Something struck me as I kicked out at Spector, I think that these blankets are made up from his beard trimmings." Orkan also removed the blanket.

"That would not surprise me at all, there are very few fibres that could have withstood that cold. I am going to hold onto mine, just in case." Melek had suffered more than his two friends and wasn't yet ready to shed the lightweight blanket. Richard thought he was being sensible and rolled his blanket before popping it into his shoulder bag.

Sure enough a little while later Richard's prediction started materialising as, after some boisterous leaps and water-jetting, the larger mammals started disappearing from view as they began moving seawards in the rapidly forming flowing rivers which were now sufficiently large to carry them away to join their groups in the oceans. The city was returning to normal as ice melted to water and flowed away leaving behind a series of pitched-roofed dwellings and clean bright streets.

"Time for us to move on?" Richard said, taking the Path Finder from Melek. "Where next?" The pointer was guiding them to head up the hills and into the mountains. "Nice day for a walk in the hills?" Richard said jovially feeling very pleased with what they had recently achieved. The sun was warm, there was very little wind and they were refreshed once again. At first the ground was hard and flat, the air was so clear that they could see the ocean below and they were moving very easily. It did not take very long before they spotted the blue, white capped mountain range ahead some way in the distance. Climbing steadily they began encountering small shade protected snow clumps pushed up against overhanging rocks the higher they moved. Chilliness overtook the warmth they had been feeling as heavily laden clouds started sweeping across the peaks above.

"I thought it would be prudent for us to hang on to these blankets." Melek stated, stopping only long enough to draw his woollen protector around his small frame. "That looks like ominous storm weather, I suggest you two do the same." Reluctantly Richard had to agree with him as he and Orkan donned their blankets as well.

The little band of hikers were completely unprepared when the blizzard struck them. They had watched its progress but had not realised how ferocious the freezing darkness would become until it enveloped them with howling winds that passed through with lightning strikes driven on by a fearsome gale. Blinding darkness, rain, ice particles, plunging temperatures and snow simultaneously lashed wildly at the three trying to knock them off the mountainside.

"Keep close! Richard shouted. His voice almost drowned out by the sheer ferocity of the snowstorm and gale force winds now battering their bodies. He turned towards his companions to ensure that they had heard his message. They were not there, his eyes tried searching through the blinding darkness but he saw nothing of his two friends. He was alone, covering his face the best he could he decided to sit down, back to the storm and wait for the tempest to blow by, or at least until he could see far enough ahead to avoid any mishaps.

"Orkan! Melek!" Richard screamed over and over again, his words simply became swallowed up by the savage winds churning down the mountain. This was his lowest point of the mission to date; somehow he had lost his only friends.

Ice Cold Grave

On the Twenty-First Day...

Tread lightly on the rocky heights,
A sudden fall, a triple plight.
An evil comes, an evil goes
Buried under sliding snows.
Remember though, when far ahead,
Trapped is not the same as dead.
Nor is haste the same as speed
Nor the led the one to lead.

The wind slowed for a moment and Richard saw two snowy lumps a little down the slope, his heart leapt for joy as he pulled himself up and made his way back to his two companions.

"I thought I had lost you," he shouted above the squalling tempest

"Gghhh! You don't get rid of us that easily." Orkan returned. He stood up and the two helped Melek. The wind was now beating down and snow was drifting as they started off ever upwards. The trio battled, barely able to see anything in front of them. "I have never been in a blizzard as fierce as this; we have got to get into the mountains and then try to find shelter. Orkan shouted during a minor lull in the ferocious wind speed. He licked his lips; they were numbed from wintry icicles dripping from his broad snout. "We cannot remain in the open for much longer, woollen blankets or no blankets we are dead."

They stumbled on with renewed intention. Reaching the upper portions of the mountain did not help them; their paths were interrupted with bottomless flurried snowdrifts and valleys that were blocked by loose snow that had avalanched. All the while their journey slowed. They were travelling blind; one wrong step could be a fatal step.

"I think we better rope up just in case. Cannot see anything ahead in this whiteout and I'm afraid that sometime I will take a step and just disappear." The three used Melek's rope to tie themselves together before carrying on. The higher they went the more intense the snowstorm became, redoubling in intensity, it now constantly thundered around them like some sort of elemental beast, pressing down with the full weight of mass airborne snow and ice. Richard was seriously thinking of giving up and returning to the valleys below. Each time the thought crossed his mind; he felt a throbbing and even saw the flashing light from his amulet. It was as if Golan was there by their side and egging them on. They reached a particularly narrow and treacherous slope when Richard decided that enough was enough but the amulet would not let him stop there. They slowly and very gingerly moved across it, Orkan slipped once and the rope held until they got him back and continued moving step by slow step around a long mountain bend where Richard saw what looked like a vast horizontal crack with windswept snow piling at the base, it was not too far ahead.

"That could be a place where we find shelter," Richard shouted against the next passing squall as they stumbled and stuttered their way through the large snow pile in front of the massive crack in the mountainside.

"Gghhh! We must be careful? We are not the only ones to be seeking shelter from this type of storm. I'll lead the way, stay close." Orkan drew his sword as he led the small group between two ice-covered rocks into the fractured cliff face, past the largest boulder and around a cornice. They were surprised to find themselves in a narrow corridor that soon opened up out to a stark toothed domed hall. The walls and floor of the fissure blinked under a thinly layered coating of snow and ice lit up by a narrow beam of light appearing to come from somewhere high in the centre of the dome that seemed to stretch upwards to infinity.

"Somebody has been using this place for a storage facility," Melek shuddered as he noticed several partly devoured remains lying around on natural stone shelves dotted around the place. "Whatever or, whoever lives or uses this place, is a likely killer, we better keep our wits about us. Perhaps we should leave right now?"

"Gghhh! In order to face that killer on the outside? I think it would be preferable to meet this one in here. Look at those carcasses, they are small, whatever killed them is certainly not as big as Spector and look how he finished up. I will protect you. We need rest; as usual I will take first watch."

"All the same, this place does not feel comfortable; it is time to check the Book of Prophecies is it not?" Melek stripped the big book from his back and set it on the floor directly beneath the light beam. He read out the text to their next conundrum.

> *Tread lightly on the rocky heights,*
> *A sudden fall, a triple plight.*
> *An evil comes, an evil goes*
> *Buried under sliding snows.*
> *Remember though, when far ahead,*

Trapped is not the same as dead.
Nor is haste the same as speed
Nor the led the one to lead.

"The triple plight makes sense but the rest? It's a warning that trapped is not dead and that bothers me a little. What do you think?" Richard looked solemnly at his companions.

"Gghhh! If you are asking my opinion, it means we must kill the killer or be killed by the killer. I am happy to do that because I don't like the idea of being dead. Gghhh! Gghhh!" Orkan chortled at his own absurdity.

"Then let's rest, the book says we have evil coming, we must be rested and strong enough to make sure evil goes as the book also says." Richard smiled at the pig-like boy. "It was a good thing you made us bring along these woollen blankets that Spector gave us, or rather we took, without them, we would not have made it through that storm." Richard found himself a spot without ice and was soon asleep. Melek found an empty natural stone shelf and as always used his book as a pillow but somehow could not simply drop off as Richard had done. This was the type of uncomfortable place that in his childhood days, he used to have nightmares about. Except his dreams used to have ghostly figures coming to life in them and for a while, he could not get those thoughts out of his head. Eventually tiredness got the better of the librarian and he fell into a deep but disturbing sleep.

"Come on lazy bones, rise and shine. The storm has passed and it's a sunny day outside. We must continue our journey." Richard gently shook Melek. They stepped outside and found Orkan surveying the mountain.

"I did some thinking before I went to sleep and thought about anything that could be a killer and can also live at these heights. The first thing I remember reading about was a snow leopard; it is a natural predator and part of the same group that belongs to the Leopardmen clans as was Maerkat but, they are on our side and do not kill randomly. However, the other one I have heard of has a terrible reputation and could be far worse than any snow leopard. It is called Maquac and lives above the snow line, it is said that he guards the route to the Forgotten City. Not much is known of him or his followers except that he has a ferocious temper and could be very dangerous."

They moved off up the slopes of virgin snow that shone brightly in weak sunlight and everything was still and calm. After the raging blizzard, their journey over peaks and down through valleys was unreal giving the impression that they were alone in a new and pristine world. Moving over a small rise they were surprised by what lay below.

"Look! There's a group of apes having a hot bath. How cute is that?" Richard said pointing to a natural rock hot spring tub fashioned into the side of the hill. Dense white steam clouds surrounded the entire pond, wisping at the edges before drifting skywards and disappearing into the morning crispness. The chocolate box scene beneath their position fascinated the trio as they excitedly watched the gingery troop of extremely happy looking large primates romping about, splashing and teasing each other far below them.

"Hot water like that can only mean one thing." Melek declared, "There is some form of volcanic structure inside this mountain. Bear that in mind."

"Do you think they could be friendly?" Richard questioned.

"Gghhh! If they are not..." Orkan's reply was rudely interrupted by a booming cry that filtered from somewhere lower down the valley. "There's your answer." A second howl, plaintive and cold, scoured the hillside. "Look at the size of that one." A gigantic looking burgundy coloured orang-utan like beast was heading upwards from the lower valley.

"That must be Maquac, those in the water, his soldiers." Melek said as they watched the hefty ape like creatures bundling themselves out of their hot tub. Their relaxed mood instantly changed, orders were passed around between themselves as rubbery red faces began scanning the mountainside, once the three companions had been targeted, the area below filled with chatter and various calls. Another booming bark from the ape leader further down the hillside filtered up to the troop who immediately and with purposeful intent, set off from their poolside as a fighting troop, their body language showed they were now in fierce attack mode as they began racing up the steep incline towards the three. Richard watched as the red carpet spilt out like blood against the white snow background.

"Oh-oh! These guys are not playing anymore and there will be too many for us to take on." Richard was horrified at the speed of the mass of red coming up the hill led by an alpha male that had already outstripped the rest of the group.

"Gghhh! They have no weapons." Orkan loaded his bow and waited to face the large ape leading the troop. The full-size male ape was well ahead of the rest, when it reached their position, it pulled itself up by rising onto two legs, then it bared its great fangs at the companions. Orkan's bow whipped up, the arrow found its mark straight into the menacing blue and red mouth of their tormentor. The primate grabbed at its throat as another arrow found its target in the belly of the beast and it fell back to begin rolling down the hill towards the oncoming troop. The rolling ball gathered soft fresh snow as it bounced downwards gathering pace, it triggered a small avalanche that poured down the hillside gathering everything in its path, ape troop included. The group were stunned by the speed and wildness of snow now pouring down into the valley below, this white descending mass grew substantially as it hurtled further downhill collecting up everything else that lay in its path, small bushes, boulders, animals became a jumbled heap of moving destruction. At the bottom of the valley the white surge ran out of steam and piled up into a very large looking snowball precariously perched at the head of the valley below.

"Gghhh!" Orkan snorted, replacing his bow he turned to his companions. "That's how to deal with those pompous primates." He bragged. "We better move before their leader gets here. He is going to be pretty upset with us." Orkan looked downwards towards where he had last seen Maquac, there was no sign of the huge primate below as they moved away, following the ridgeline of the hill. The crest slowly began dropping into a small basin skirted by a sharp rising incline on the hill side, before it then continued upwards again on the far side of the shallow gorge. The small group made their way down and were about halfway across the small flattened valley when they came upon the freshly killed carcass of a large deer, telltale signs showed massive foot trails, leading up the valley, a struggle, then footprints leading away and up to the next ridge.

"Gghhh! Maquac has been here and is now up there somewhere. He has the advantage of commanding the higher ground." Orkan's military brain was now working overtime. "Check the Path Finder." Melek handed the instrument to Richard.

"Bogooom!" The booming sound reverberated right above the trio. In unison the three looked towards the ridge ahead to see Maquac, like a possessed racing devil retracing his footsteps, a plume of white snow flushing out in his wake. Orkan immediately went for his sword. " Bogooom!" the huge primate boomed out again.

"It's the Yeti." Richard whispered nervously. As it got nearer they could clearly see that the creature's face was strikingly human, rubbery and wrinkled into dark, clean-edged segments.

"Gghhh! This is good, he is stupidly coming down to kill us, we are all on the same level." Orkan whispered. "Let him come to us, I will deal with him." Richard pushed forward until he stood shoulder to shoulder with Orkan to face the fast moving Maquac. "This is his territory, he is in his element, see how he moves through the thick snow, it is with ease. Wait for him to make the first move." Orkan commanded.

When it stopped in front of the pair, its eyes seemed concentrated on Richard as the beast surveyed the newcomers to its territory.

"I am Maquac Guard to the Forgotten City, you have destroyed some of my forces and for that, I will take my revenge." The ape-like creature opened its wide mouth to show his four massive pointed teeth-like fangs then took one deliberate but intentionally intimidating step forward. Neither companion moved a muscle, neither did they demonstrate any fear. "You are the Chosen One and I will not hand you over to my master, you are to die right here." Maquac took another step forward. Inside Richard was quaking like a leaf, he knew from experience that if he tried to run, Maquac would be all over him like a rash.

"Many have attempted that before, many now lie dead. Did your master also tell you that?" Richard pointed the Path Finder at Maquac, the pale sunlight caught the golden glassy surface suddenly and with a dreadful groan Maquac dived forward knocking Richard off balance and seizing the instrument from Richard's clenched fist with ease. Orkan leapt into action, this was no time for fear or calculation, he brought his sword down in an arc, but the beast was too quick reversing backwards, it roared deafeningly and beat a hasty retreat, turning and fleeing back up the ridge.

"He's got the Path Finder, We will be lost without it! Richard screamed in utter panic.

"I think he's also badly injured, there's a wide trail of blood leading up the ridge and Maquac began slowing and limping." Melek pointed out. "He won't get very far with a large wound."

"Gghhh! We have to follow his trail. Keep on your guard, there is nothing more dangerous that a desperate or wounded enemy." Orkan immediately started off up the ridge with reason. They followed the trail for a long way, noticing that the left footmark was quickly showing signs of being dragged through the snow. Every now and then there were back and forth distressed sounds echoing back and forth until the mountains rang out like a tuning fork.

"Gghhh! We are getting close, Maquac is in a lot of pain and has slowed to a walk." Orkan pointed to dragging heel marks in the snow. "Right now, he will be either searching for a hiding place or somewhere that can trick us into his clutches." Richard was pleased that Orkan was back on their side. The blood trail led them up the mountain to a small-levelled plateau that had an oblong shaped cave entrance situated to one end. "This is an almost perfect lookout point, look behind you." Richard turned, the panoramic view almost took his breath away, he could make out everything right down to the brown valley floor way below. A sudden bellow from the cave brought Richard's attention right back to the task in hand as they climbed onto the snow covered table in front of the cave entrance.

"Gghhh! More apes!" Orkan shouted drawing his sword. "It's a trick." Four large ape-like beasts exited the cave. "They will taste my blade as did Maquac." That's when Richard noticed that the biggest one now carried the Path Finder.

"He has my Path Finder" Richard drew his sword, "he's mine, you deal with the others." The four moved towards them, three then stopped about halfway to the cave entrance, the one carrying the Path Finder kept moving towards the trio. It raised the golden blade in a gesture of offering it back to them.

"Gghhh! More trickery, I will not fall for it" Orkan whispered. He need not have worried, the large primate laid it on the snow and took several steps back before indicating to them to pick it up. Richard and Orkan moved forward slowly and suspectingly to retrieve the Path Finder, their eyes continuously darting around in search of any traps Maquac had possibly set for them. Having retrieved it safely, Richard checked to see if it still worked properly by sweeping the area, it showed him the way back to the brown valley floor. Richard handed it back to Melek for safekeeping.

"Now leave! I am mortally wounded and would like to die in peace." Maquac's booming voice came flooding from the cave. Richard was uncertain, the beast had done the honourable thing, he felt that he should now at least offer to help the stricken primate. Orkan and Melek turned to leave then realised what Richard was feeling.

"Do not do anything rashly, Maquac has asked us to leave, we must respect that request?" Melek requested, he took his arm and tried to lead him away but Richard stopped and faced the cave.

"You said you were Maquac, Guard to the Forgotten City?" Richard shouted.

"That is so, I am."

"Do we have your permission to enter that city?" He shouted.

"You have my permission," came the loud reply.

"Where is the Forgotten City?" Richard asked.

"You need to follow the trail straight down the mountain, it lies in a valley at the bottom of the foothills." Richard was now sure that Maquac was not tricking them, the Path Finder had also pointed the same way. Richard thanked then apologised for hurting him as they started their journey downwards to the Forgotten City. A short way down the broad snowfield reduced in width when Maquac's booming voice barked something from high above. They turned just in time to see several apes rolling boulders down from above, these in turn broke into the smooth snow pattern starting an avalanche that was gathering speed and heading directly for them. Behind that, Richard saw Maquac lording the group's demise from the plateau.

"Die! Die you fools!" His voice boomed down the valley.

Snow cascaded towards them at immense speed in a wide trough, before squeezing itself into the tapered gully where the trio were desperately trying gain the sidewalls before it struck. Richard, Orkan and Melek were swept off their feet and away like twigs in a fast flowing stream. Tumbling, dipping, dropping and sinking they careered helplessly down the mountainside until the massive force slowed and spread itself across the valley floor. Richard was fortunate enough to be the only one lucky enough when the avalanche slowed and was spat out of its hold to the surface, he rode the last trace of the dying rush like a surfer. His nostrils and eyes were clogged with snow but suddenly everything was hushed and calm, he began peering around for his companions and saw a shoe sticking out from the very white surroundings. He dragged himself to it and pulled with all the strength he could muster at that moment. The shoe was attached to Melek, heaving, hauling and manipulating soon extracted the spluttering librarian from his snowy burial place. Both began scanning the area, there was still no sign of Orkan, no shoes, no bow, no nothing they shouted his name and carried on searching even though both of them began to fear the worst. Unexpectedly a sword blade popped through the snow, Orkan cut his way to freedom.

"Gghhh! You have got to hand it to Maquac, now that was one a great bit of trickery. If I ever meet up with him again I shall shake him by the hand, then I will kill him." Orkan snorted indignantly,

"At least we got the Path Finder back?" Melek parried. "There has to be respect for the way he tricked us?" He checked the Book of Prophecies to make sure that no harm had befallen it then handed the Path Finder to Richard. After all that rough and tumble you too have probably lost your bearings?"

"We had better keep moving, our time is running out." Richard checked the direction of travel. "That way." He pointed to a spot beyond the snowy mountains where the ochre slabs and the more hospitable hills stretched out before them,

"There was that bit of the riddle that said trapped is not dead, maybe Maquac knew that as well. He was trapped, was he not?" Melek smiled reassuringly at the other two. "We must learn from this experience."

The companions fell into line and made their way down the long valley, all three remaining on full alert and ready in case Maquac or any of his soldiers put in an appearance. All eyes, especially Orkan's, constantly strayed upwards toward the mountain heights, each was thinking that the tricky primate might well have something else arranged or even be on their trail. None of them felt completely safe until they had reached the far end of the valley. Stretched out below made a quite pleasant change for the trio, the area was changing to brown and yellows of a world not immersed in constant winter and cold. Beyond the rocky outcrops and Snowy Mountains lay a series of jagged hills, in places small green and yellowing pastures intruded on the distant woodlands.

"There's an old fallen down bridge spanning a canyon, pity though, would save us time if it were still standing?" Richard thoughtfully mused. Further away, clustering below some of the several hillocks dotted across a wide plain they could only just make out the shapes of what they all agreed could be a string of buildings. They trudged on down the slopes, crossed the gorge that bordered the snowline and entered the plains and pastureland with improved hope. Along the way they noticed that this area had probably once been prosperous farmland but now, the grass was long and unkempt and fenced off by a disintegrating line of wooden stakes. The whole location had the feeling of being well heeled, efficient and tidy but no longer inhabited.

"I get the feeling that this all used to belong to a thriving community, but now, it is so run down. What turns a place as vibrant as this into a down-at-heel zone?"

"Gghhh! We will soon find out." Orkan answered "Between those two hills ahead, there is a city that I can see."

"I think we have at last found the Forgotten City." Melek said casually as they moved forward to see what lay within the hidden place and why it had been forgotten.

"In its heyday, this may have been unbelievably beautiful." Richard stated.

Buildings were made of finely chiselled blocks of stone that fitted together without mortar, with such artistry that it would be impossible to slip a blade between the joints. Nothing except spiders and geckos moved as they walked through the deserted streets, nowhere could they find any signs of life.

"If it was icy here, I would be expecting Spector to appear around the next corner." Melek recalled. The doors that they opened led either to empty rooms, or revealed heaped piles of skulls.

"This whole place has an underlying feeling of death. I feel the hand of the Evil One has been at play here." Richard checked for his dagger.

"Gghhh! This city has no external walls to defend the people, this demonstrates that the people here were welcoming and used to living in peace, they were not expecting to be attacked. It must have been an easy target for an assault." Orkan added.

"There's nothing for us here." Richard said after moving through a few more houses and finding nothing changed. "Let's check whether the Path Finder can add anything?" The instrument lit up when pointed at one of the peaks rising high above the deserted city.

"There could be a pod hidden somewhere up there." Melek suggested dreading another haul up yet another big hill.

As they moved away from the city Richard felt some anxiety because when passing by several pastures there were cattle skeletons with their tightly drawn hides over white bones dotted about the fields. This was not what he had expected; that the Evil One's influence had not only targeted busy areas, it also besieged remote locations. The trio were feeling exhausted as they continued away from the flatlands upwards to rockier slippery shale surfaces and scattered with the odd leaning windswept tree. The thinner air, harsher sun and slippery slopes were not helping the tired companions but they pushed on regardless. They were within touching distance of the top when there was a prolonged but distanced howl that each of them immediately recognised as that made by Maquac.

"Gghhh! This is good, I want to meet him again, we have some settling to be done." Orkan snorted with glee. They turned and even from this far away they could make out against the white background the speck moving down the distance mountain. "Keep coming this way my friend." Orkan rubbed his hands, but mentally was working out how a deep wound that the primate had suffered still allowed him to move. There was plenty of time before he found out he wisely decided. Reaching the summit, their hearts dropped as they saw that there was yet another deep valley stretching out before them brown and dust filled with a glowing pyramid at its centre.

"Wonder what that could be." An exhausted Melek removed the book and handed Richard the Path Finder. He pointed it at the structure and it glowed.

"That's where we have to be next." Richard said. "I think we better take a break, our energy levels need to be restored if we are to stand a chance?"

"Gghhh! " What worries me is that there is an enemy chasing from behind, there also could be an enemy ahead, that is not a comfortable position to be in." Orkan's military brain was working again in overdrive.

Early dawn light was beginning to break through to introduce a new day; there was still blackness with the slightest hint of an orange border edging. Melek was the first to wake, Orkan as usual, had remained awake watching over his companions, he rested comfortably against a boulder, his eyes remained closed but yet he was fully alert especially when the librarian rose to strap the big book onto his back. Curiosity mixed with the feeling of spectacular promise to what this day could bring and that sunrise was about to break the cool weather made him more than a little restless. He ambled across the flat smoothly worn shale plates, took a long look towards the distant snowy mountains that were just beginning to show their white lined caps. He then moved to the other end of this tiny plateau and looked down into the valley that was still very dark and black except for the tall edifice that glowed a soft yellow in a central position. The building was like some sort of beacon for outsiders to find, the positioning of a glazed building in that particular location tickled his ever-curious intellect. The pyramid styled structure was more modern than he had ever encountered, it raised the question in his mind as to whether this building and the death and destruction of the Forgotten City were linked. Standing close to the edge, Melek leaned forward a little to try and get a clearer view when there was a snapping noise from a shale plate below his feet. He could not do anything to stop himself sliding down the slate filled hillside. Melek gave a cry of surprise as he cannoned down the incline. Orkan raced to the edge, there was nothing he could do at that moment; he turned and shouted for Richard to wake up.

"What?" Richard was immediately aware that something bad had happened.

Death from Within a Tomb

On the Twenty-Second Day...

Deep in geometric gloom
Do not open long-sealed tomb.
The curse of Evil then will fall,
Not on one, but surely all.
Seek instead the golden prize
That evil guards with six-fold eyes.
Follow where alone he goes.
Above, the prize. Below? Who knows?

"Gghhh! Melek's fallen into the valley." Orkan said, frustration tingeing his voice.

Numbed by Melek's sudden disappearance, Richard and Orkan gaped open-mouthed over the edge where the librarian had stood, trying to locate any movement of their companion. They saw nothing except the brown eroded hillside strata leading into the valley below.

"We cannot leave him down there on his own." Richard said taking the first cautious step. Reluctantly the two slid, traversed and made their way down the long hillside until they reached the valley floor. They searched around the immediate area where Melek would have come to a halt, inspecting every nook and cranny trying to find traces and clues that he had at least reached the bottom. There was nothing, it was as if the ground had simply swallowed up the scribe together with his books.

"Without all the books and especially the Path Finder we are going to be in trouble." Richard pointed out." We must try to find him."

"Gghhh! I agree, but our main priority is still the pods and the Guardians. I think we need to head for that pyramid thing first, Melek is very sensible and level headed, if he can, he too, will find his way there." Orkan stated psychologically, "If we are able to come out alive from whatever is in there, and we still have not located him, then we search right through the valley?"

"I suppose you are right. Oh well, it's into the Evil One's den." Richard said as he moved onto a well-trodden path.

"Gghhh! What makes you think that this has something to do with the Evil One?" Orkan said as he fell in behind Richard.

"All that death we came across back at the Lost City is one good reason, when last did we find anything that had nothing to do with evil? His hand has somehow touched everywhere we have been; I don't think that this pyramid will be any different. Do you?" Richard reflected. They trudged along the path through the brownish valley basin; the morning sun rising higher seemed to cause broad plants yellowing leaves to droop under increased heat. At closer quarters they noticed that the landscape surrounding the large obelisk-like building was dotted with clumps of strange looking trees and plants. From either side of the two, now came eerie rustlings, Orkan gently eased his sword from its sheath, for all the two knew, Melek might even be lost in among those same trees and bushes, surrounded by whatever unseen creatures were stalking them and creating these crackling and swishing sounds.

"There is something out there but I cannot see anything." Richard said nervously. "What about you?"

"Ghhhh! Keep moving, maybe they are probably assessing our strength, if we stop they could try an attack. I saw something a little while back that almost blended perfectly into the background. Its outline was lizard shaped but I do not think it was a lizard, then it just seemed to melt away." The building turned out to be made from a glassy type of polished amber of stone and not glass as Richard had suspected when they were at a distance. Along the base of the translucent structure, the blocks were covered with a series of angular motifs and hieroglyphic designs similar to those dotted around the helmet he had first found when his adventure started. Also scribed into the almost seamless inclined walls were massive evil masks depicting what Richard felt could be a celebration of the Evil One's previous victories.

"This is where we really need Melek's experience; I think that he would have been able to interpret what all this represents. We have to find him somehow," Richard wishfully said. "I am sure that something on here would give us an indication what lies ahead." The couple steadily worked their way around the whole base searching for an entrance, there was none to be found.

"Gghhh! I have a gut feeling that a place like this will house a stolen pod or even another Guardian; we have to get inside, there must be a hidden entrance in this wall somewhere. Let's go around again, look out for anything out of the ordinary, especially around those strange carvings. They set off along the first section of the pyramid, this time their eyes searched for anything that could look even remotely out of context with its surroundings, found nothing. In the middle of the second wall they came across a carved impression of a huge facial mask that by its very appearance portrayed nothing but evil, especially the scythe-like horns, the wicked and lustrous mouth and severely penetrating eyes.

"Brrr! Would not like to meet him on a dark night." Richard commented.

"Gghhh! Something tells be we could even be looking at the shape of the Evil One. I have never seen him myself, nor do I know anyone that has but, during the great battle, I did see a few shields that bore similar features to this mask."

"If there is an entrance, this is where we will find it." Richard said with confidence. The mask was many times larger in height then two companions. Their trained eyes hunted everywhere crossways, top to bottom, left to right but nothing seemed out of place or without purpose and they were just about to move on when Orkan stopped while checking through some of the strange hieroglyphic writing at the base of the mask below the central portion of the mask's chin. There was something not right, above and slightly aside a narrow white flash in the centre of the macabre chin was a curved shadow that matched the rest of the carving. Orkan ran his finger lightly across the flash to the curve; the white portion was flat yet the curve took the form of a seamless but slightly raised area.

"Gghhh! I think this is what we are looking for." He pushed down on the bump, nothing happened. Richard then ran his hand slowly over the bump and found the inner part of the moon shaped curvature was indented at the base against the smooth wall surface.

"You're right; this is some form of handle." He pulled at the imperceptible finger grip, there was a soft click and the dark frame of the chin slid sideways revealing an opening where the concealed white flash had been situated.

"Stairs leading downwards." Richard could see the first few stretching down into the dark below. Orkan drew his sword.

"Gghhh! That's where we must go; here I will lead the way." They moved carefully down the constricted inclined stairway that eventually led them through a solid doorway into a carved stone lobby. The whole of the internal of the building that confronted them seemed to be bathed in soft and subtle amber lighting. Richard could see that the floor they now stood upon was covered in a fine film of perfectly even dust, there were no footprints whatsoever to be seen, it was as if this place had been shut to the outside world since the building had come into existence. On the far side of the entrance hall was another square arch with more peculiar writing scrolled around its framework. "Nothing here, we go though those doors, we might find something there." The couple took three steps when suddenly there was a deep rumbling sound and they felt the whole floor base begin to move beneath their feet, then came the coarse clank from some underground mechanism kicking into action as the entire solid block of the floor suddenly dropped downwards. For a moment both Richard and Orkan felt as if their feet were losing contact with the floor and their stomachs lurched violently as they plummeted downwards into the unknown. It was like being on the inside some kind of gigantic high-speed fairground drop except there were no safety harnesses to cling onto.

"Aargghh!" Orkan cried in pain, there was no telling how far they had travelled when the welcome heaviness upon their bodies signalled that the floor was losing its speed and reaching its destination.

"Prepare yourself, this could be painful." Richard shouted. Steady crunching of rock grinding upon rock brought them to a sudden jarring halt. Standing up, Richard could see that the finely covered dust was disturbed almost right across the vicinity where they had trodden or rolled while attempting to protect themselves from being hurt. The floor had ground to a halt at one end of a cavernous chamber that was also covered with the same fine but untouched dust throughout.

"Gghhh! Move! This floor may suddenly drop or even rise again." As one, both Orkan and Richard stepped off the slightly elevated floor into the great amber lit filled grotto. As they moved off the raised floor, the familiar rumble started up again, the floor disappeared rapidly up the shaft, returning itself back to its original station high above. "You see, Orkan knows best?"

"Only sometimes, unless I am sorely mistaken, I do not think this was one of the times." Richard said nervously. The outsized space that now stretched out before the two contained nothing within its towering crafted walls, except for a squat slope-sided block of carved stone topped off by what looked like a flat slab lid that was highlighted by a powerful stream of light emanating from somewhere far above. The stone box was placed centrally at the far side of this great room. As far as Richard could tell, there were no doors anywhere and their only means of escape seemed to be the way they had entered this hall, but even that way was now barred to them, they were trapped like fish in a barrel down here. "I think we have been delivered to the heart of this place because that stone thing over there," Richard pointed to the stone crypt, "looks vaguely like some kind of tomb or alter?"

"Gghhh! Maybe it only houses another pod." Orkan hopefully reflected, "Perhaps it could even be our way out of here?"

"With our luck so far, I doubt it very much." Richard drew Juroot's dagger and with Orkan by his side slowly crossed the room to the tomb-like sarcophagus. Its surface was covered with iconographic figures and pictorial symbols which meant nothing to the companions.

"This looks similar to the writing in the Book of Prophecies." Richard murmured. "Perhaps there is another hidden catch somewhere?" They began feeling their way bit by bit around and over the carvings. Orkan suddenly gripped Richard's arm tightly.

"Gghhh! What was that?" The fighter's keen sense of hearing picked up a dry rustling shuffling reverberation from somewhere behind him but Richard saw nothing. All they could both hear was the sound of their own breathing "I thought I heard something."

"Your nerves are twitchy." Richard tried to make light of their situation. "Let's keep checking. They continued and out of the blue there was the definite sound of a hollow click from somewhere across the hall, they both stopped searching and listened.

"Gghhh! You heard it as well that time, didn't you?" Orkan drew his sword. "You carry on, I'm going to investigate." As Orkan turned there came the familiar rumble noise followed by the swishing resonance that immediately blew the loose sand outwards across the floor. The floor from above came hurtling to a grinding stop and a rather harassed Melek picked himself up from the floor, he stepped down onto the main hallway floor, the upper floor disappeared upwards into its dark hole once again. Richard mentally noted as the travelling floor had settled then retreated back into the darkness, that the force of its two-way movement had first blown then sucked the fine dust one way then another covering all traces of any footprints or, disturbance in the antechamber where they now found themselves reunited.

"Am I glad I found you?" Melek declared triumphantly. "I opened a door on one side of the outer building and got trapped inside a maze; it took me ages to find my way out. I managed to follow your tracks and found the door you so conveniently left open for me. It was not too hard to see where you had stopped and that is how I got here. Just what has happened so far and what is this place?" Orkan and Richard looked at each other in utter dismay at what had just occurred.

"Gghhh! Melek, it's great that you are safe, we were worried about you." Orkan walked over to the librarian and placed a hand on his shoulder. "Please do not get lost again."

"I managed to decipher some of the words on the outside, this place was the Evil One's first home here, perhaps he is still to be found at this time."

"You can decipher those symbols? If the Evil One is around we must get out quickly, we are no match against his power on our own." Suddenly Orkan spun around, his intense hearing again picking up on something moving.

"Gghhh! There is something there, Melek you help him, I am going to investigate."

"I think you better see whether the Book of Prophecies can help us." Richard declared with authority. "I will continue searching." Melek unstrapped the large book and laid it on the floor while Orkan, sword at the ready moved away. "Found it!" Richard said triumphantly as Orkan saw two panels slither apart at the far end of the room.

"Gghhh! No need, There is an open doorway here." Orkan's worst nightmare appeared to shuffle into, and fill the entrance frame. "What does your book say?"

Melek read out the puzzled words as quickly as he could.

Deep in geometric gloom
Do not open long-sealed tomb.
The curse of Evil then will fall,
Not on one, but surely all.
Seek instead the golden prize
That evil guards with six-fold eyes.
Follow where alone he goes.
Above, the prize. Below? Who knows?

The thing Orkan faced then began to shuffle forward towards him. The creature was half-bird and half-reptile with its lower frame resembling an iguana, but with a pair of powerful wings that sprouted from its broad shoulders, upon which three scaly long swan-like necks curved up to feather covered heads equipped with a curvilinear toothy beak and glittering gimlet eyes. Its expression when it spotted the companions in the hall was one of pure viciousness as it moved forward with purpose and menace.

"Six-fold eyes, this is the beast." Knowing the horrific beast blocked their immediate path, Richard in fear mixed with panic, yanked hard at the bulbous tomb's lever. There came a gentle click sound, as the flat rock surface on top of the crypt slowly began to creep lengthways with a grinding noise of rock scraping against rock. "The tomb is opening!"

"Nooo!" Melek's piercing scream echoed around the entire chamber. "That is the Tomb of Zolteen and that," he pointed at the three-headed beast jerking its entire group of heads backwards and about to strike out at Orkan, "is Kylaton, the beast that guards this place. You do not know what you have done."

"Oh-oh! The words of the riddle, *Do not open long-sealed tomb*, now rings a bell." Richard said, realising his big mistake. "Help me. We must stop it from opening." Orkan shot across the room, as did Melek. The beast at the far end saw the opening cover, all six eyes widened in horror as it backed away, turning tail and unseen by the trio trying in vain to hold back the slowly moving stone hatch, Kylaton disappeared as if by magic through the far wall opening. The heavy closure continued to scrape and grind its way open releasing an overpowering forceful smell of rotting flesh and death that was beyond description. It was so bad that the companions had no alternative but to retreat away from the crypt.

"What's buried inside that tomb?" Richard nervously enquired.

"From what I could make out, this place is a trap meant for Guardians by the Evil One. Opening the tomb sets off a chain of events that will destroy the pyramid, taking all within its walls to their death. Melek broke the news that chilled Richard's blood to ice.

"Let's get out of here!" He shouted almost hysterically. "We'll try to use the entrance that the creature used." Looking across the hall his heart sank, the beast had vanished and there was no longer an open doorway for them to escape through. They quickly made their way across the cavernous hall; and comfortably picked out the shuffling footprints in the dust of Kylaton leading back to the wall but, could not find any joints to show that there was indeed any sort of entrance built into the wall. They knew that the whole building contained hidden latches and immediately ran their hands over the carvings.

"There is a hole in the wall here, but there is nothing inside it." Melek claimed pointing at one eye of a carved primate that reminded them of an evil looking Maquac. The hole was cleverly disguised in the eyes, both seemed to be black but one was carved and painted, the other a deep hole.

"Gghhh! Maybe some force is required." Orkan used his sword, pushing it handle first into the hole then using the sword's guard to force it inwards and the wall panels separated evenly and they moved as one to the opening. Just as they entered the opening there was a wailing groan from inside the hall, Richard turned only to see a clawed hand reaching out of the half opened tomb before the twin doors swished closed. The trio raced up the narrow, slippery stairway in a headlong rush to try to vacate the building when suddenly there was a swishing sound of the doors and Zolteen's vile stench of death floated up from below and began permeating the whole building. The group reached a small landing on the stairway when from around a corner much higher up, Kylaton shuffled into view again to block their path.

"Gghhh! No way out." Orkan loaded his bow and at high speed sent off a spray of arrows at the three-headed beast, several finding their mark. Kylaton let out a screeching wail, but this did not stop the beast from continuing its now slower momentum downwards shuffle towards the group. Richard kept a wary eye on the stairway below realising that their path ahead and behind was sealed.

"Zolteen's coming!" Richard shouted as he saw the spectre appear at the bottom of the stairway. The stench was becoming so overpowering that all three were finding it almost impossible to take in breath. Both ends of the stair were completely blocked off to the companions. "I think the book is correct this time and we could die right here." Richard took hold of the amulet hoping that somehow Golan would magically whisk them away from their dilemma.

Melek looked upward, there was a narrow airshaft above their heads, and he could only just make out the outline of what looked like a grille blocking the way out. He flicked the rope from his waist and in a single movement the rope snaked its way through the slim tube and around the stone grate.

"Come on, follow me, we have a chance." Melek scampered up the rope like a monkey up a pole; Orkan followed him with Richard bringing up the rear. At the top, and to and make sure Melek coiled the end of the rope around the end stone bar. "Pull the rope hard, we need the centre bars to break." In unison they began using their combined weight to bounce and one by one the stone bars started snapping leaving a hole just big enough for them to scramble through. The stench from below had filtered up and all three were breathless as they found themselves half way up the narrow shaft and into a tiny room. Before continuing, they stopped for two reasons, the first was to draw breath, the other was to have a quick check of the room's contents in case there was something they could use.

"We have found another pod by accident." Melek said while pointing. The room had several pocket type square holes sunk into the surrounding walls, each contained an artefact of sorts but Richard only had eyes for the pod. He stroked the amulet against the pod and the bangle flashed several vivid colours, Richard immediately started the ball rolling when he pocketed the pod, their main aim being to escape the building before the predicted destruction. It suddenly dawned on him that he could almost recognise the enveloping stink seeping right through the building because he had momentarily come across a similar rotten egg foul stench just once before in a science class when one of his friends opened an experimental cabinet, the whole class suffered from the overwhelming stench. That was small, this was not an experiment and this, was massive. Removing the prized item seemed to somehow set the curse in motion.

"We must leave now!" Richard shouted urgently. Melek try the next part, hopefully it will lead out of this death trap." Richard watched as Melek expertly flipped the rope to the next grille in one single movement and began scrambling upwards.

"Gghhh! These look like my arrows. I wonder why they are here." Orkan had found several arrows placed into one of the holes dotted around the tiny room and grabbed them taking second position behind Melek, Richard took up the final position behind the struggling Orkan who was now holding him up. "Move Orkan!" Richard's head was now forced tight against Orkan's underside."

"Gghhh! Stop, I cannot climb any faster and these arrows I've just rescued are not helping." He dropped one arm and Richard saw the fist full of arrows.

"Put them in your quiver," Richard ordered sharply.

"Gghhh! No! I'm almost out of these special arrows and must first check that they are mine otherwise, like your pods, if they turn out to be fake, you two will die when I next use it in my bow." Orkan parried. "Let me do it right now." He tightened his legs around the rope enough to hold his weight and in order to leave his hands free. He then extracted an arrow and began striking one of the arrow tips against the wall to test that they were indeed from his special stock that the Guardians had presented to him. To Orkan, the arrows seemed like the real thing as red coloured sparks spattered off the blade.

"Gghhh! They are mine!" The pig-like boy was not to know that his action was to trigger a chain reaction with devastating consequences for everyone still within the building.

"Nooo Orkan!" Richard screamed, the warning came too late as the sparks ignited the gas inside the chamber that sizzled past Richard. "Melek cover your head. Now!" Richard screamed. Melek was almost at the grating and without question, whipped out the Book of Morbane and held it against the top of his head as there was a thumping explosion from the small room that they had recently vacated. The pressure from below was enough to force the two upward until all three were crammed tightly together.

"What was that?" Melek demanded fiercely, his head and the book now firmly pressed against the stone grille.

"Get ready! There is going to be a massive explosion when the flame reaches the lower levels." The gigantic detonation from below forced hurricane strength winds churning throughout the building which in turn set off a string of mammoth blasts that gathered in intensity.

"Gghhh! The curse! It's happening!" Orkan shouted. Already the pyramid was growling its way into the ground with tremendous sounding blasts, creaking and snarling collapse. The noise grew and grew as the structure began to crumble and heave below. Unlike Richard knowing what to expect, Orkan and Melek yelled in terror. Richard released his shoulder pack and awkwardly tied one strap to his belt and the second to the rope below. That's when his heart froze with the chill of ice, he saw the shadowy figure of Zolteen enter the lower section of the shaft below.

"Zolteen is coming, the blast missed him!" Richard tried shouting over the pandemonium and noise. He could now clearly see the wrinkled face of incalculable antiquity staring fixedly with hatred. The pyramid lurched again hurling Zolteen off balance so that he slipped downwards back onto the stairs and he disappeared from sight. "He's gone for the moment, but he will keep coming after us!" Richard screamed. Suddenly from below the whole place shook so violently that the shaft tilted at an angle, Richard looked down and saw a fireball heading up the lower shaft. "Hold onto the rope!" He shrieked as loudly as his lungs would allow.

Richard was the first to feel the extremely forceful blast of oncoming rushing hot wind barrelling up the shaft from below as it forged its upwards path against the three and drove them so hard against the stone grate that it shattered. The tremendously forceful energy from behind was so devastatingly powerful, that it hurled them like three bullets being fired from a rifle, right out of the top of the narrow barrelled shaft, high into the sunlit sky.

Richard, Melek and Orkan spun helplessly out of control upwards on the current of hot air. They all saw the earth flashing past them on all sides as they tumbled upward in a long arc away from the pyramid until the hot jet dissipated enough to send them falling downwards at great speed again. The trio thudded straight into the surrounding foliage that broke their fall. Orkan was hooked up into a tree while Richard and Melek found themselves tangled up in some of the bristly bushes. Richard checked across to where the pyramid continued collapsing in on itself with great ferocity, his brain was unable to comprehend the unfolding devastation happening right in front of them. The whole building simply seemed to be swallowed into the harsh brown ground in minutes; the only trace left was what looked like a wide expanse of freshly turned soil. Richard and Melek carefully extracted themselves from the bushes and onto firm ground before checking that all was in order and nothing broken.

"Gghhh! Help me!" Orkan was not as lucky as his two companions; his bow had hooked itself to a thick branch leaving him dangling precariously high in a tree. Both Melek and Richard laughed at Orkan. "It will not be funny if the bow strings breaks, who will do your fighting if I should fall and injure myself?" The two companions giggled as they made their way to help the frustrated Orkan.

"Look! Is that a bird stuck in that tree?" Melek joked.

"No, I don't think so but it could be a flying pig. I suppose we should help him?" The two companions burst out laughing loudly much to the annoyance of their stranded companion. Melek flicked the rope behind the bow and over the branch supporting Orkan. "Hold onto the rope and lift your bow off the branch and slide down to us." Richard shouted taking hold of the end with Melek. Orkan found it an easy matter to get down, but was somewhat unforgiving at the jibes they had made. Suddenly there was movement from in among the trees and bushes surrounding the companions, Orkan and Richard immediately drew their weapons.

"Gghhh! There was something following us when we arrived." Orkan whispered. A single thorn bush rattled, then another. Two large primate figures stepped into the open, both looked almost identical to Maquac but then again, there were differences.

"I am Ackquak, leader of the Forgotten City. There are not many of us left, the Evil One has destroyed a lot of our kind because we would not side with him. We followed your arrival but were not sure whether you were friendly or not so, we waited to see. Somehow you have managed to destroy the Evil One's great temple, that proves you are friendly. The Evil One will seek revenge for your deed but it is good it has been obliterated and we can again return to our city instead of hiding away as we have done for so long."

"What about your kind in the Snowy Mountains?" Richard enquired.

"With their leader now dead, his followers will return and hopefully we will become a thriving community again."

"Dead? You are speaking of the one called Maquac I presume?" Richard was surprised.

"We are, he was in league with the Evil One and another called Kylaton, today we had the opportunity to revenge ourselves when a badly injured Maquac stormed through the Forgotten City on his way to the pyramid. We stoned him to death using the skulls of some of his victims, it was a fitting death don't you think?" We have you to thank." Richard quickly explained what their mission was to Ackquak.

" Bogooom!" The large primate boomed. As if by magic hundreds of Ape-like people appeared from nowhere. "If you need us to fight the Evil One's forces, we are ready even though we are not a warring nation. You have saved our City and given us back our dignity and for that, we are prepared to help in whatever way we can." I have been to the Ancestral City and now I will lead my people there."

"Gghhh! We too are now about to return to the Ancestral City and must leave at once for our mission is not quite over but, be sure we will meet again." Orkan gave the people a smart salute.

Melek handed Richard the Path Finder and he checked for direction. It had pointed to the distant range of stony mountains at the far end of the valley.

They bid their farewells to the Primate People and trudged past the area where a short time ago the monumental pyramid had reached skywards.

"This is how it should be, calm and serene. Another evil has been dispatched." Melek said quietly as he pushed his way between his two companions and grabbed their hands as they strode briskly towards their next task.

The Fiend of Combustion

On the Twenty-Third Day...

Beware the fire from demon sprung
By the bridge so weakly slung.
From the danger bravely run
The fight has only just begun.
Remember well what legends say,
There is a green hill far away.
The path you seek as hard you may,
But evil 'tis that rules the day.

It was a good journey across the smooth basin for the companions; the sun was shining, easy movement across level terrain and the valley dotted with trees and bushes, all things that gave them time to reflect on just how close they had come to death. It also gave them stages of silent self-contemplation to realise just how much they had achieved on their short expedition. It even gave Richard and Melek the opportunity to raise teasing jibes at Orkan being caught up hanging in a tree. This was the first period of real and relaxed bonding time where all things were well with them as a group so they made the most of these precious moments. The happy, frivolity mood began to change to one of concentration as they neared the rock-strewn foothills of the stony yellow mountains.

"The sides of these hills are steep, so the most obvious path would seem to be through that foothill chasm?" Richard pointed to sudden interruption of continuity; it was a multi-layered scar of an angled gap in the otherwise boulder strewn high mountain battlements. "That looks like it could contain a natural pathway leading into the hills." Richard was correct in his assumption. When they entered, the whole area opened up to give them a panoramic view, there was a widening furrow that dropped down steeply from centuries of erosion to form into a deep chasm skirted by steep yellow stone cliff faces. Hugging along one side of the precipice was a man made narrow boulder strewn trail cut into the side of the canyon wall.

"Gghhh! If I am a flying pig, then which one of you two is going to be a mountain goat?" Orkan joked as he surveyed what was going to be a tricky path with various hidden dangers. "That mountain trail does not look very safe to me. One loose footing could send us to our deaths, I don't think it has been used for some time."

"The Path Finder pointed us this way so let's at least try" Richard commanded.

"I'm the lightest, so let me lead the way." Melek set off along the trail. For a while they managed because the path had remained intact in most places, even though split slithers of mountainside debris had crashed down and loosely piled up in several places along the unstable trail. Before long the three found that the deep gorge had to be traversed by means of an old rope bridge spanning across to the upwards-continuing trail on the other side. The thick rope cords supported a series of wooden slats that on first inspection seemed sound enough, some showed signs of cracks but in general all three felt the bridge was in passable condition.

"Do you think we should rope up together, just in case?" Melek asked.

"That bridge looks a little rickety, but I think we'll be all right. If you want to rope up then let's do it." Melek tied a loop around his waist then Orkan and finally Richard's waist before stepping out onto the swinging bridge. Orkan took a few cautious steps forward as the bridge bounced slightly under his weight.

"I think it is sound enough, let's hope it's the same all the way across." Richard commented apprehensively as he gazed down into the long elongated ravine, "That's a long way down."

Looking down, they saw a white torrent swirling and foaming over blackened rocks far below. The bridge rocked and swayed gently as the three made their way across, then, their worst terror occurred without warning. The ropes holding the timber planks in place seemed to turn to dust and the slats began hurtling down into the abyss below. Then, with a deafening shot, the rope cables holding the crossing behind them broke loose from the rock face and swung in a long, slow semicircle down into the gorge.

"Gghhh! Grab onto the bridge rope." Orkan yelled as he dived out and wrapped his arms around the main cord and in turn, dragging both companions towards the soft swinging pendulum of hope. They held on tightly as the thick cord crossed the abyss, timber falling all around, heading towards the far side cliff face at speed. The other rope also broke free and slithered down the cliff like some enormous snake. With everything happening at lightning speed, Richard instantly presumed that their ongoing luck might still be on their side. The three clung to the roughly cabled cord like limpets to a rock as it bounced against the rock face, the large breadth shielding them from the full force of the impact, they still felt the jolting shocks. Painfully slowly but steadily the rope linked trio pulled themselves upwards towards the edge. At any second, they expected the big rope to break its mooring and hurl them down into the yawning canyon, but it held fast until they were within reach of the lip and of safely surviving. Orkan stretched out an arm to lever himself over the edge but before he could do so, a jet of fire shot out of the sky, splattering against the far side cliff rock face.

"Wha..." Richard swung around and caught sight of a serrated red shaped outline flashing through the canyon. The crimson blur looped and swooped upwards in a long lazy vertical steep turn enabling Richard to now see the beast more clearly. Its whole body was covered with ruby coloured scales; its eyes were two deep pools of emerald green, above that a pair of backward-sloping almost circular horns jutted out of its head. There was a continuous gust of flames shooting out from its sharp-toothed snout. One thing that stood out against the red scales were the several rows of carbon black jagged teeth.

"What the heck is that thing?" Richard shouted in alarm as it levelled out and headed past them at speed releasing another searing ball of flame that smacked against the cliff edge extremely close to the three fellow travellers. Several positions dotted down the length of the large twine started smouldering, smoke and steam leaking from out of the bulky cable. The large Draco-like beast hurtled high into the sunlit sky above in a lazy returning curve preparing itself for yet another sprint attack through the deep gorge.

"Orkan! Climb, it's coming back. I don't think that this rope will hold much longer." Richard bellowed as he braced himself for the worst-case scenario. Orkan heaved himself over the rim of the stony ledge and immediately started levering Melek's thin golden cord upwards hand over hand until the librarian scrambled across the path's lip. He didn't have to be asked to help Orkan, he grabbed the rope and the two steadily dragged Richard towards safety. As he clawed at the ledge, they heard a shrill battle-cry from above their heads ring throughout the valley, Richard did not even look upwards, expecting one more attack and preferring to take his chances from the security of the narrow pathway. As his two friends yanked him over the last hurdle, the high-pitched cry was replaced by a sharp screech, they retreated away from the valley rim towards the relative safety of the cliff face and scattered rocks before checking what was happening in the sky. Looking up they saw that there were now two creatures locked in a battle of flame burst exchanges,

"Gghhh! Try to find sheltered spot behind those loose boulders." Orkan instantly directed the group towards a large pile of cliff rubble. High above, the trio's sharp-winged attacker was ducking this way and that, desperately attempting to evade the attention of an immense, autumn-plumed bird. Manoeuvring themselves into looping arcs before spitting streaks of differing coloured flame at each other. Their attacker's hot breath bursts of broad, red streams, the newcomer in contrast, with sharp spurts of radiantly brilliant blue propulsions. Richard was so fascinated by the overhead battle, and the astonishing combat that it held his attention, and he did not move to immediate safety along with his two companions, preferring to hold his position on the cliff path for a ringside view. Richard knew that their fortunate luck remained on track with the timely intervention of this newcomer; he was now rooting loudly for this unknown champion that had definitely saved them from a horrible death.

"Go on! You can do it!" Richard shrieked at the top of his voice. At times the sky became filled with multi-coloured flashes of fire, then becoming pinpricked with scorching starbursts of light. To the onlookers it was like observing a massive fireworks display amid a roaring dogfight with no quarter being given by the raging combatants.

"Gghhh! Kill, kill, and kill the assassin!" Orkan joined in his encouragement. When the fighting reached its zenith, the aerial display condensed into a tight fist of smoke and steam mixed in with loud detonation cracks of explosive fire being launched between the two flying fighters. When they broke apart, it did so with volcanic pillars of flaming combustion. At the centre of the flame and smoke, the two warring warriors were endeavouring to blast each other into absolute extinction. "You are winning! Finish him off!" Orkan hollered their support for the newcomer as the creature that had attacked them was the first to break off from the battle line, pinning its wings back, shot away like a bullet over the high mountain range horizon, leaving the victorious combatant to wheel and swoop into a victory roll of triumph. It glided down towards the group, Richard suddenly realised that he was still in the open; he raced to join his fellow travellers who had found themselves a protective position behind a large boulder. The trio watched in awe as the bird gently landed on the edge of the path then shuffled itself forward towards the trio's hiding place.

"Thank goodness I got here in time. You can come out for the moment," said a soft, feminine voice. "I am Valgote the Firebird." She looked over to the black charred rope that hung limply into the gorge. "You have all had a very narrow escape, I apologise for your stressed discomfort, I should have been here sooner but at least, you are safe for now." The massive bird showed signs of its battle, various feathered tufts charred and twisted nestled among the lovely autumn colouring red and yellow plumage.

"How did you even know we were in danger?" Melek questioned.

"When you entered the pyramid Golan lost all contact with you. He was distraught with worry; he initially thought that you had not survived your arduous mission until you again appeared to get out of that building. Knowing your direction of travel, it was Oganga that sent me to help you with your search."

"So who or rather, what was that thing you chased away?" Richard enquired eagerly. He suddenly had a million questions he needed to ask.

"Drahog, the Evil One's demon of fire," Valgote replied. "He is both powerful and vicious and seeks to kill you all, especially for the extensive damage you have already created to his forces and to his beloved pyramid shrine of evil. Your battle has become personal to the Evil One, his forces have been severely weakened through your efforts and he is now stalking you with some of his deadliest warriors." Her voice carried stern warning.

"What news of Golan?" Richard asked excitedly, relieved to hear that Oganga had survived the battle with Boltor.

"Many of out lost forces have arrived at the gates of the Ancestral City and many more are on route thanks to your efforts," Valgote said, "Juroot is back in command of his forces and countless others that have survived keep arriving. What about your mission? Much rests on your success."

"Unfortunately, we have not been able to save all Guardians and there is still one remaining pod to be found and not much time to do that." Richard said with some feeling of gratification.

"Ahhh! One of the lizards informed us that there was a pod seen at Magus's Well, it is a long journey and you will have to pass through the Illusionist Falls. That will not be simple, we must move on..." Before Valgote could complete the sentence, she was interrupted by the sound of heavy wings pouring through the gorge. "Drahog's returning. Remain out of sight behind those boulders; I will try to draw him away from you." Valcote soared high into the sunlit sky. Melek and Orkan ducked low behind the large rocks, Richard curiosity got the better of him, he lifted himself just sufficiently enough to peer over the brim of a boulder at the same time that the crimson Drahog appeared out of the gorge and above the line of the cliff, for the briefest of moments Richard and Drahog's eyes locked on each other. It gave Richard just enough time to drop flat before a globe of red flame lurched out of the beast's beak smashing against the cliff face behind the three. For a short while nothing moved, the surrounding tension in the air was so conspicuous that it could be cut with a knife.

"I didn't hear him fly away, did you?" Richard whispered. Both companions shook their heads. "Stay down, I will take a look." Orkan grabbed out at

Richard's tunic to stop the crawling boy, but it was just too far to reach. Richard eased up into a different spot to where he had previously been, his hope being that if Drahog was still about, he would be targeting that previous area and would not immediately be expecting to see Richard much further down the line of the protective boulder. He found a small opening between two locked rocks that could be used as a spy hole, very slowly, he moved his head across the nearside corner and was surprised to see the Evil One's fire demon hunched over like some giant vulture on a nearby crag, just waiting and watching with malicious purpose for any sign of movement from appearing from behind the boulder. It was stalemate for the moment, Richard indicated with his hand for the other two to remain where they were and not to move. The large beast knew it had the upper hand and was fully aware of their exact location, so attempted to scare them out by beginning to let out a raucous, cackling laughter, before it picked up several boulders as if they were mere playthings, and began tossing them around in several directions. Richard froze when the beast unfortunately uncovered the lair of some mountain creature. It scuttled away, a ball of stripy fur that resembled a cross between a red rock hare and a baboon. Drahog pulled his beak into an ugly look of scorn, then struck out with one of its talon claws at the smaller beast. Richard thought that the foothill rock creature had escaped with nothing more than a slight scrape but very soon learned a valuable lesson and that Drahog's talons were loaded with venom. The less significant creature began wobbling and skidding on the rocks, then it let out a high-pitched cry of pain, lifted itself as tall as it could off the stones, gave one last pitiful shriek then fell to the ground in unqualified agony, it gave one last kick, then simply lay still. All of this was too much for Richard, he drew Juroot's dagger, Orkan was watching him closely and although unsure of Richard's intentions, loaded an arrow into his bow in preparation. In order to save anything else beneath the boulders from being harmed, Richard calculated that he had the valiant Valgote as his backup and he was safe for the moment behind the large stones. He bravely decided it was worth taking a gamble and drawing Drahog's attention toward himself.

"Can't you pick on someone your own size you bully?" He shouted loudly and watched the beast's head whip around, flame streaks already becoming visible from its pointed beak; Richard dived away from the small gap just in time to miss being struck by a searing fireball that hit the opening and sprayed outward against the back wall. Orkan stood up and started firing a volley of arrows in a rapid machine gun type burst, every single missile found a mark and stuck into the large beast's scaly body, as Orkan ducked down to retrieve more arrows Richard crept forward over scorching rock to see what damage had been done when he heard the now familiar crack of fire smashing into stone behind him. Drahog had turned and let off a fireball in Orkan's direction but it gave Richard the opportunity to quickly peek through the opening.

"Your arrows have had no effect," Richard shouted nervously as he hastily turned away from the opening, he was relieved to find that the fireball had been too far away from his companions to do any real harm to them. Another barrage of fireballs in Richard's direction were sprayed through the opening, against the back cliff wall and even below the protective boulder in a concerted effort to reach him but he rapidly moved closer towards his friends and also remained unharmed. This was now becoming a very dangerous cat and mouse competition, and the mice were starting to run out of options.

"This is now a battle between Drahog and me." Valgote shrieked. The recognisable sound of splattering fireballs instantly lifted the spirits of the trio. Orkan hastily rose up and sent another rapid volley of missiles straight into Drahog as he lifted off the edge trailing smoke in his wake. "Finish your quest Chosen One; I will hold Drahog back for as long as I can." As Valgote plunged down into the gorge after her adversary, the three raced up the rock-strewn path. Reaching the top of the sloped trail, they found that the unsafe track hugging the cliff face contour, then swung around a long bend before continuing downwards following the gully line to the back of the mountain range. They stopped for a short breather, behind them the sky continued to ring with the sound of brutal battle. Richard hoped that their saviour would again come out on top as he tried to see what was happening to the evenly matched combating warriors through the thick haze of smoke filled sky.

"Valgote has put his own life on the line and given us the opportunity to possibly track down the last remaining pod. We must find it and honour his bravery." Richard said with true conviction. Following Volgote's directions the three cohorts battled their way along the land slipped trail for some time, they made slow progress, even now and out of earshot, a distant glow indicated that the huge air battle was still in full swing. On several occasions they came across areas of the path that had been so badly smashed by falling stone it sometimes left large voids of nothingness to cross. With the aid of Melek's golden rope, the little group became quite expert at tackling each precarious emptiness in turn by roping together like mountaineers and then with the help of their companions, individually swung themselves across the yawning voids. Finally the high stone cliffs and insecure pathway began to peter out as the mountain range became foothills once again that then changed to flattened fields of yellow stone, interspersed with carefully tended areas of green and brown grasslands as far as the eye could see. The rushing waters barrelling in from the deep valley slowly spread itself out below them forming a swamp artery system that unhurriedly disappeared into the ground. At the centre of this whole area and in the distance, stood an outsized craggy outcrop with a tall flat-topped central peak.

"That's where we will find Illusionist Falls but first, we'll stop and take a short break over there." Richard felt he had an intimate knowledge of the land ahead and pointed to a shaded spot beneath an overhanging wedged flat keystone that stuck out from between heavier boulders. Seated in the shaded spot, they discussed Valgote and their forthcoming tasks,

I think it might be a bit late but now that we have the time to rest, we better see what the Book of Prophecies has to tell us, don't you think?" He released the book and laid it on the ground,

Beware the fire from demon sprung
By the bridge so weakly slung.
From the danger bravely run
The fight has only just begun.
Remember well what legends say,
There is a green hill far away.
The path you seek as hard you may,
But evil 'tis that rules the day.

"The first few lines make perfect sense, they refer to Drahog but the green hill could be anything, couldn't it?" Richard asked.

"As we already know, some words in here are never meant to be literal, so the green hill could mean a hill with something green contained within the hill." We will just have to wait and see?" Melek reflected when suddenly a pig-like grunt sound came from behind the rock at their backs. Orkan shot onto his feet, sword in hand.

"Gghhh! That was not me." Orkan said, "There is something behind that large stone. Richard and Melek were at his side in a flash, the librarian fixed the big book onto his back again. Orkan moved to the rock and examined it carefully; he turned and beckoned Richard forward.

"This is well camouflaged," Richard whispered. What looked like the edge of the large upright boulder on the left side was in fact a neat split in the rock that leaned at a slightly jauntier angle to that of its larger twin boulder. This angled stone provided a very small opening at its base but big enough to slide through this entrance that they could all now see on close inspection, had been used extensively.

"Gghhh! There's something hiding behind this main rock but I do not like the idea of crawling through that tiny gap head first." Orkan stated softly. "It could be a trap." Orkan moved away and indicated for the others to do the same. A couple of steps back and the entrance was completely hidden from view. "Gghhh! What do we do? It's an almost perfect bolt hole."

"Melek, your rope please." Melek looked confused stripping the belt from his waist and handing it to Richard. He extracted his modern day torch and tied it tightly to one end, checked it was still working then gathered the loose end and handed it back to Melek. "Orkan I need plenty of small pebbles, the smaller the better." Orkan walked away grumbling but was not away long before returning with a lot of pebbles in the fold of lined jacket, he placed the pile in front of them. Richard searched his bag and found a cleaning cloth that he had used for his bike. "Just the ticket," he explained, as he took a handful of the chipped nuggets Orkan had collected and placed them inside the cloth before tying to the rope just behind the torch. "Right! Let's scare them out." He said explaining his plan to the two. Richard placed the stone filled bag on the ground in front of him then dragged it along, the rattling pebbles rubbing together inside the bag hissed like a snake as the bag traversed behind him.

"Gghhh! That will never work" Orkan grunted disdainfully.

"Oh ye of little faith. In the dark of the cave with the flashing torch and that sound, they will think it's a monster of some sort and that, will divert their attention. At least let's give it a try" Richard scoffed as all three moved to the hidden entrance and got ready to enter the diminutive opening. Richard turned the torch on then switched it to flash rapidly. Right, it's your turn Melek." The librarian flicked the rope and it shot a long way through the hole, he then began dragging it back towards him. What happened next was totally unexpected, suddenly there was a lot of snorting and squealing sounds originating from behind the upright stones as several bodies fought madly to clamber out through the narrow gap. Panic, pandemonium and terror ruled the day, and it was clear to Orkan that Richard's plan was working as he drew his sword and lifted the first one into an upright position by the scruff of the neck.

"Gghhh! Please do not let that Reptile harm us." The petrified person screamed, his feet were still in running mode but were off the ground. Orkan almost did a double take, this terrified pig-like creature was smaller than him but was almost his exact double, he could have been looking straight into a mirror. Another four had already forced their way out through the tiny hole and clambered to the sunlit safety.

"Gghhh! Stop! We are friends." Orkan shouted the command as loudly as he could. Taken aback, they all froze exactly where they were and realisation struck them forcibly as they stared at this new stranger in total disbelief. "I am Orkan and have spent long days trying to uncover your whereabouts. Do not be afraid, you are my brethren and we will save you." There were now seven pig-like beings, all smaller versions of Orkan outside the entrance as Melek pulled the hissing blinking rope back through the small opening. All of them cowered at the snake like sound made by the pebbles being dragged along the ground. "It is no snake, you were tricked into thinking it was." Orkan continued, "There were many more captured by Sundra so where are all the rest of our community?" One of their prisoners pointed towards the large craggy rock formation.

"Gghhh! They are all held captive in that stone castle. I am Nakan, if you remember we trained together back home." He explained. "I escaped from there, found this place of safety and have rescued six more. Sundra is extremely dangerous; he has captured most of the Landsmen as well."

"Landsmen?" Richard enquired.

"Gghhh! Those fields provide food for the Evil One's forces, the Landsmen tend the fields while our people are made to turn the crops into food in the large manufacturing works within that complex."

"Gghhh! Why do they not all escape?" Orkan asked.

"Gghhh! Nobody escapes Sundra; once he captures somebody you become his for life. I was lucky, our training helped and I got away. I kidnapped each one of these people, it takes days before the Sundra's spell leaves them." Nakan replied abjectly.

"Spell?" Melek asked,

"Gghhh! Our own people and the Landsmen will fight for him. I have never been inside Sundra's castle; it would be too dangerous to try. Instead, I have had to sneak the kidnapped away when they are in the plantations. If I were to be seen by our own people, they would attack and kill me because they are all under some kind of spell. It takes days to get them to think logically again, they cannot remember anything or even being Sundra's servants." Nakan replied. Orkan got them to sit together as he explained the mission and listened to the information they could give him about Sundra and the Illusionist Falls. "Can we join you, we want to save our people and would like the opportunity to take some revenge against Sundra for what was done to us all."

"Gghhh! That is not possible; you must remain hidden here in case our mission fails. If we succeed then you and the rest will then be needed to look after them and guide them back to the Ancestral City." Orkan commanded as he prepared to leave with his companions. "So far this has been a really good day for me, we will try our best to get the rest of our people back to you." Orkan gave Nakan and his pig-like associates a soldier's salute, turned and set off at pace towards the rocky outcrop and Sundra. They fell into a steady marching rhythm for a short while as the foothills began to flatten to the pastured lands. Melek was the first to hear the heavy beat of wings; he looked up to see a dark shape coming out of the sun.

"Back to cave. Run!" he shouted." Drahog's back."

Their pursuer came down right next to them with a heavy thud; the large wing spread wide enveloped the three with an acrid stench of burning. Richard wriggled from under the feathers and drew Juroot's dagger to face their attacker. It was not Drahog as they had supposed. It was Valcote, and not quite the flamboyant Valcote that had saved them back at the bridge. Her brilliant feathers were scorched. In places they had burned off altogether, leaving dark ruby coloured patches of weeping skin. Her face was a dishevelled mask, out of which peered bloodshot eyes.

"You have really been in the wars, are you going to be all right?" Richard asked in dismay as Melek and Orkan pulled themselves free.

"I will live to fight another day, Valcote replied with a smile in her eyes."Drahog is dead, he nearly finished me off, but the longer the fight lasted the weaker he became. I think that all those arrows in his body helped to weaken him." Richard could see she had given her all. Richard quickly explained what had happened so far. "I will rest here for a while in case you should require help, before getting back to Ancestral City to get my wounds seen to."

"Good and I hope you recover soon, we all owe you our lives. Thank you and now we must go." Richard said. "You are a great warrior."

"Be continuously on your guard." Valcote warned, "and the best of luck to you."

The three bade farewell to the stricken firebird fire and headed off towards Sundra's rocky fortress and the distant sound of falling water. It did not take very long reaching the craggy outcrop and Richard fathomed that they circle it until they met with the water that fed into Illusionist Falls and the one that seemed to scare everyone. It was time to face the grim reality called Sundra.

The Ghostly Apparition

On the Twenty-Fourth Day...

When risen from enchanted blight
A slender hope across the height
Takes them to the torrent's door.
Swept by spirit off the floor
Then in evil's clutches bound.
Break with thrice the backwards sound
Of names of those so tightly held
The genie's magic rudely spelled.

The river when it came, ran deep and raucous out of the ground from within the rocky outcrop, spewing from the rocky slices that had carved it over many centuries into rocky soil. They followed its course until around a corner and down into a dip they came face to face with the Illusionist Falls.

From high above their heads, water sluiced down in a torrential downpour to splatter against a mishmash stack of rocks and stones at the cascading water's foundations. The spray-filled space was filled with shifting dancing rainbow patterns and the noise became ever more thunderous the closer they got to the falls.

"Gghhh! How do we get through that?" Orkan tried competing with the fluid's din as the stared up at the wet, bubbling sheer drop of water. Richard's mind raced as he stared at the waterfall's upper rim, where the waterway plummeted into thin air creating such heavy spray that it was like standing in a tropical rainstorm. He touched his amulet to see whether there was any form of guidance coming from Golan, there was not even a flicker on the bangle, his ever present concentration and optimism quickly changed to despairing contemplation that perhaps the prophecy was correct and that Evil perhaps had ruled the day. With the constant water salvo he was finding it extremely difficult, to think, then he recounted Golan's wise words so he turned and moved back a short distance until he was a short way from the falling water. Surprised by his retreat, Orkan and Melek followed him.

"What are you doing?" Melek enquired.

"Taking a think break, may I have the Path Finder please?" The librarian lifted the slightly sodden book from his shoulder then handed him their pointed guiding rod.

"Gghhh! It's pointing upwards to the falls, there is no chance that we could climb to the top. Is there?" Orkan asked with some trepidation.

"Perhaps it we can get to the other side of the falls there could be something to help us reach the top? Orkan's people surely do not use this route to get to the fields?" Melek suggested.

"I think that would possibly be a waste of time and the Path Finder has never let us down. No, we need some form of inspiration, what does the Book of Prophesies tell us?" Melek opened the book and found the riddle.

> *When risen from enchanted blight*
> *A slender hope across the height*
> *Takes them to the torrent's door.*
> *Swept by spirit off the floor*
> *Then in evil's clutches bound.*
> *Break with thrice the backwards sound*
> *Of names of those so tightly held*
> *The genie's magic rudely spelled.*

"A slender hope across the height? The height, the height?" Richard repeated. "The height can only mean that cliff face can't it?" Richard moved towards it, his eyes covering almost every inch until he found what he was looking for. Looking at it intently for several minutes he could just make out what looked like the rock fault line, possibly the result of subsidence in bygone time and as a result, where the rock had shifted there was now a slight protrusion that rose crossways to a point somewhere partially up the falling mass of water. "That's the way to go, there's a very slim chance that we will make it but words like it takes them to the torrent's door fit perfectly. What do you think?"

"Makes sense to me." Melek finished tying the straps that held the big book. "I am ready."

"Gghhh! I hate water with a passion but the good thing is we do not have to go swimming in this water." Orkan joked, with a touch of serious humour attached to his voice. "Unless one of us happens to fall off that ledge and into that swirl pool that lies below us."

When he approached the ledge, Richard had second thoughts when he saw that it was a lot narrower than first thought. He weighed up his options as to whether they could do this, he was sure that under dry conditions they might just make it, but the plumes of wet spray and very limited visibility once they started climbing would now reduce their chances quite considerably.

"Let's rope up," he suggested. Richard took the lead, everything played against the trio ever making it up the inclined ledge, slippery surfaces, and smoother rock meant limited handgrips as they pressed their bodies against the upright wall and slowly moved along the tiny outcrop. It was a very scary and nerve-racking journey, as the downpour pressure became heavier and the outward slanting rock face bent their bodies into ever more painful positions while attempting to stay locked on the tiny toeholds. The higher they moved, the more terrifying their ordeal became with every pebble underfoot, every bump becoming the source of possible disaster. Once they reached the cascading water, conditions eased. The narrow ledge widened, the rock face began straightening out, and then they soon found themselves on a widening rim of stone. The widened ledge gently curved heading straight into and through the tumbling waters. Richard took a deep breath and ducked into the burgeoning downward irrigation only to find that it was thin, being more a curtain of water than a walled torrent. Richard took a few steps and was surprised when he emerged through the back of the waterfall to find himself staring at a dry yawning cave. Melek and Orkan scrambled through the tormenting downpour into the warmth and dryness of the welcoming cavern.

"Gghhh! Now you know why I hate the wet, if it's not riddled with nasty beasts then somehow it tries to kill you." He shook himself vigorously; a pool of liquid began forming around his feet. "There, that is more comfortable." Ahead of them, yet another pathway tunnel sloped gently upward towards the heart of the craggy stone castle, soft fluorescent, eerie lighting glowed against various wall locations and seemed to be beckoning their way up to the next level. They began their walk up the path and into the iridescently lit tunnel; it sounded like their footsteps had suddenly began to ring with an unnatural juicy reverberation the deeper they penetrated into the rocky subway.

"What's that?" Richard pointed as an insignificant wisp of coloured smouldering began to twist out of the ground ahead of them. Orkan immediately charged his bow with an arrow, as the flimsy corkscrew of smoke seemed to briskly materialise in size and strength, twisting upward to become a wheeling, swirling column that almost filled the entire passageway ahead of them. The white smoke then instantly changed as it initiated itself with a series of glittering minute colourful sparks that fizzed and popped as it started to materialise into a recognisable shape.

"Gghhh! Sundra," Orkan released his arrow, it passed straight through the stacking formation of a fast emerging ghostly vision. The smouldering feature began forming itself into a fully-fashioned figure starting at the head, representing some human features except for the looping goat-like horns protruding around its ears. Then came the broad shoulders, set above a waist-coated muscled torso that glistened and sparkled as if twinkling fairy lights were attached to this beast. The lower half of the phantom appeared to have signs of being a caprine-like hairy creature, including a goat-tail that drifted back and forth into the hazy smoke that made up the rest of the Beelzebub-like ghostly spectre. The creature was a scary mixture of a satyr mixed with a genie.

"Who even dares to try and enter the empire of Sundra, spirit of the atmosphere? The large manifestation challenged. "As for you," It pointed a long hooked finger at Orkan. "You dared to assail me with your measly missile, were you not informed that I cannot be harmed?" Sundra's voice boomed through the confined tunnel. Richard's mind worked overtime as he tried placating the creature blocking their path.

"We mean no harm we became lost, there is nothing else in the valley and this place seemed our only opportunity," he lied consciously feeling that they were too near their objective to jeopardise matters with an unnecessary clash. "We seek only to continue our way to Magus's Well and apologise for entering your realm uninvited. If you so please, we would like to proceed," Sundra's features squirmed in defiant contempt at Richard's feeble excuse.

"You cannot make a fool of me with untruth and then expect a favour in return," he smirked wickedly. I am not an idiot, I know why you three seek out Magus's Well." He crowed with delight

"But..." Richard didn't have time to make an objection, as Sundra unexpectedly jabbed out his long-nailed crooked finger at the group, a gush of blue and white sparkle shot from the tip, freezing all three in mid-progress. The three never knew what hit them; they were frozen in a trance. When they came around, to their surprise, they found themselves in a plushly decorated room with a stream flowing through the centre of it. All around the slowly drifting water various coloured smokes gently wafted and intermingled low to the ground like a morning mist across a field. Sundra floated above the trio on a high-adorned pedestal placed in the centre of the opulently decorated room, with its beautifully delicate and imaginative carvings of beasts and strange figurines wherever they looked. One wall was entirely devoted to satyrs, nymphs and goblins all containing some sort of creature-like features and fronted by gold chairs with luxurious padded seats. This was obviously Sundra's pleasure palace.

"Gghhh! What was that?" Orkan gave a slight skip to one side. "There's something moving in the smoke." Richard too felt something brush lightly against his leg.

"You have come to steal my crystal and I cannot allow anyone to do that." Sundra's face drew back scornfully into a mask of hate. "It's your insolence and lies that have now condemned you for all time. You have not yet met my personal pets but you will do so shortly." His eyes took on the ranting look of a mad dictator as his voice got higher and faster. "This place will be your final objective, you will serve me and nobody but me forever." His distorted hand shot out as it had before. This time there was a fine confetti-like spray spurting from it but the finger was not pointed at them this time. "Here my lovelies, meet your new detainees." He swept his hand in their direction; Richard thought that the pink coloured ice felt like falling snow. "It is time that you learned not to take us for fools, we are not that," Sundra stormed. "For that mistake you must pay the ultimate price, from now on you are mine." Suddenly appearing from below the rainbow smoke there were the largest worm like creatures popping up everywhere to meet the falling pink snow. Substantially huge sized bubbles foaming from their wide open basking shark type mouths." Come on girls, dinner time," Sundra cackled like an old witch as he swept his deadly finger over the area above the three companions to make more and more pink snow to rain down upon them. The massive worms were like starving beggar kids being thrown candy as it became a free for all to reach the pink snow, jostling bumping and knocking the three helpless friends one way and the other. Their saliva bubbling orifices gobbled up the frozen cerise in a diminishing circle around the trio.

"Oh-oh! I think we are going to be the desert," Richard stammered nervously.

There was an abrupt bellow that stopped the entire fracas dead in its tracks, the giant worm-like creatures seemed to simply melt away below the smoke, Sundra's screeching ceased and from out of the multihued smoke appeared the daddy of all worms, it was gargantuan in size. It moved quickly towards the small group, its mouth opening and shutting to expel huge foaming salivating effervesce bubbling around the non-existent face of the creature,

"We're dead," Richard declared almost mournfully. The beast's serrated tongue skilfully lapped up everything pink, all the while the bubbling froth grew in size and structure leaving some of them in its wake, it didn't seem to be interested in the three, as it consumed the reddish ice, licking them until all traces of the pink stuff was gone. Then it burped loudly, a massive bubble shot out and enveloped the three in one go, the huge beast, finding no more disappeared like the others had done. The trio were encased in a large slimy, slippery bubble.

"Gghhh! Sundra's vanished, this is our chance to escape." Orkan drew his sword and struck out at the globed wall expecting it to part; instead it simply moved with the blow. Touching the material, it felt exactly like softened rubber, Richard was the first to realise that they were now cocooned inside a large rubberised ball and the wording of 'he cannot punch his way out of a paper bag' came straight to mind. The other two pushed, pulled and stabbed at the vulcanised interior, it had no effect.

"We can only burst this from the outside," Richard conceded. "Bubbles are round because there is equal pressure from the centre outward, we push the wall here and the pressure automatically balances itself elsewhere. We need a sharp rock or something to hit the outside, then like a balloon, this bubble will pop."

"There is a large opening over there," the librarian pointed to the far side of the room. "Perhaps we can roll this bubble through that because there is nothing in here that we can use, is there?" The three all moved to one side of the ball and used their combined weight to start moving it towards the opening, as they got into a rhythm the bubble moved relatively easily and even picked up speed. The opening loomed ahead; Richard could not help but think that Sundra had missed a trick by leaving them the freedom of an opening large enough to get their captive ball through. Passing the doorway into a large room, the ball suddenly gained momentum of its own as it rolled down a slight incline into what Richard thought looked like an outsized shallow empty swimming pool, filled with masses of similar bubbles. There was a lot of banging bumping and bouncing as the rubberised ball collided with more of the comparable assortment of rainbow flecked orbs, it was something like being inside a ball on a pool table. Once everything stopped moving and everybody had picked themselves up off the floor, it was Melek that first noticed that each of the bubbles contained a shadowed body inside them.

"Let's move this thing across to one of those and see who's inside them." The three manoeuvred their bubble in between several neighbouring balls.

"Gghhh! They are my people and Landsmen," Orkan exclaimed gleefully, peering through the grey membrane.

"Ask them what's going on, try to get information," Richard said. "Perhaps we can help each other get out of here." Orkan began trying to make conversation with his countrymen but none of them even knew he was talking to them, they all seemed somehow to have become like zombies. The trio moved their bubble around until they found one lone one away from the others against the side; the shadow inside was actively attempting to roll his ball up the slight incline. They bumped their bubble against the moving ball and the shadowy figure turned to face them, his mouth brown, stained with what looked like beetle juice.

"Hey easy, you have not been changed yet but you too will become like the rest of the souls in here." The shadow announced. "Now leave me to try and get out.

"I am Orkan, can you give me any information?" The shadow moved against its rubber wall.

"I have heard of you. You were a legend back home. What happened to you?" The pig-like man asked. "My name is Lokan, I found that eating the brown plants kept me from becoming like them, I couldn't tell any of them because they would have informed Sundra." Orkan struck up a long exchange with Lokan about his adventures and their imprisonment under Sundra, questioning him on every aspect in order to gain a clear understanding of what they all now faced. It appeared that Sundra was holding them until the Evil One arrived. At first they had all tried to break out of the bubbles with power and force, nothing seemed to work and slowly they had all drifted into their own little worlds of singularity. The bubbles were almost magical in design and strength, no matter how hard they had tried, the outer skin just did not break. "I think that Sundra is the only one who knows how to burst the bubbles, he uses that twisted finger of his and they just pop."

"When does he let our people out of these balls?" Melek enquired.

"Gghhh! This chamber fills with water and he floats these over the falls and then opens them so that the Landsmen and us can work the plantations outside. Those large worms act as guards, nobody escapes and when we are through, they herd us back and we are again placed in new balls and put back in here." Lokan explained.

"How do you get back from the falls? We battled through the waterfall to get here." Melek said.

"There is a hidden door in the rock, Sundra is the only one that opens it with magic words, stairs to his chamber lead up through the floor then that huge worm bubbles us again. That's all I know." Lokan reflected quietly.

"Magic," Richard pondered. Didn't the prophecy say something about spells?"

"Break with thrice the backwards sound, of names of those so tightly held, the genie's magic rudely spelled." Melek repeated aloud." Perhaps there is nothing to it but I think that Sundra's spell must be broken by magic, not force?" Melek suggested. "We three are tightly held in this bubble ball? But what does the backward sound mean?"

"That's it! Our names spelled backwards three times. That's it, let's try it. Melek, Orkan, Richard in that order.

"Alkin! Nakro! Draheir!" They first tried the chant together three times. Nothing happened, then they tried it individually, still nothing, then they tried saying a single name together. Nothing seemed to work

"I'm sure that this is what the prophecy is about, what are we doing that's not right?" Richard said glumly. "It must be something about the names that are not right."

"Perhaps, this is only a suggestion but you are Richard, I am Melek and Orkan could also be known as Orkan. He has two names, let's try that." Melek offered. They tried all the combinations all over again using the name Orkan but still nothing happened.

"Lokan, say your name backward three times. Trust me." Richard urged the hog-like man in the next balloon.

"Nokal! Nokal! Nokal!" His rubberised cell burst releasing oily smoke that floated upward, Lokan was free. "Thank you! Thank you! It worked, it worked! Now how can I help you?"

"Chosen One! That is your correct name, that is what you are known by here and he is Orkan, let's give it one more try?" Melek urged.

"Alkin! Namgyp! Eno Nesohc!" They repeated three times and their balloon did exactly what Lokan's had done.

"Gghhh! How do we get the others to do that without setting off the alarm?" Lokan enquired.

"You said Sundra floated you over the falls didn't you? How does the water get into this part, that's not by magic, there is a sluice gate around here somewhere that redirects the water. So where does it come in from?"

"Of course, he always floats in and seats himself on that large chair then the water starts to flow into the chamber." Lokan excitedly replied.

"Gghhh! I will find the lever" Orkan raced away and sat on the throne but nothing happened, He began pushing and pulling at several protrusions and still nothing then, on closer inspection found that both armrests were shaped dragon type carvings, one had its tongue sticking out, the other did not. He pushed the beast's tongue down and the sound of flowing water filled the room.

"Let's get out of this pit," shouted Richard. They raced up the gentle incline just in time to prevent the tidal wave from washing them towards the falls. "Now what?" Richard had not thought the whole plan through.

"Gghhh! The balls will float over the edge, down into the waterfall pool below, the people inside the bubbles will be safe for a while." Lokan shouted over the noise of rushing water.

"No! I mean how do we get back down? We jump into the pool."

"Oh-oh! Who's going to tell Orkan?" Richard laughed.

"My advice is for us to say nothing then push him so that he has no say in the matter." Melek giggled.

"Good thinking." Joined by Orkan the four headed for the lip of the falls as the first of the bubbles began to drop. Melek moved onto the ledge and pretended to be losing his balance. Orkan shot to his aid with Richard close behind, as Orkan grabbed at Melek Richard by accident, on purpose did not stop his forward momentum sending all three over the side for a long drop into the pool below, Lokan simply shut his eyes and jumped. As usual, Richard while dodging the floating bubbles, then helped the highly vocal Orkan swim to the edge of the pool and Melek did the same for Lokan.

"Melek go and see if Valgote the Firebird is still where we left her, we need her down here, then go on to the cave and get the rest of Lokan's people, we need them here as well. Their kinsfolk are going to require looking after." Melek raced off and soon located Valgote still resting at the same spot but now looking much stronger and cleaner than when he had last seen her. He quickly explained the situation and moved on to locate the hidden cave.

"Gghhh! I need to show you something." Lokan confessed, "Stay close and follow me." He raced in under the waterfall where Richard had earlier retreated from, the others followed and could only just keep track of Lokan's shadowy figure under the deluge of falling water "In here!" They turned into a narrow passageway that opened into a large room filled with bottles of pills and potions for Sundra's use. In one corner piled up was a jumble of weapons and armour. "That all belongs to my people, they will be glad to get it all back." Several items immediately grabbed Orkan's trained soldier's eye, the main one being a highly polished spear that was much longer in length than any of the other weapons. "Ahhh! That belonged to one of our illustrious leaders but alas, we fear he has been killed. So it is yours if you wish to claim it."

"What's in the bottles?" Richard asked.

"Gghhh! I do not know other than Sundra spends a lot of time in here, I suspect it may be that this is his laboratory and where he mixes his potions." Richard immediately grabbed bottles from the shelves, smashing some, mixing others, pouring yet more onto the floor; until he was satisfied that Sundra would not be able to easily use them again. They retreated back to the falls, Orkan found the long spear difficult in the confined space until he left the narrow passageway, then he dashed away to catch up to the others who were already clear of the falls. Just as they got to the dry part Valcote swooped in and landed gently near them, Lokan got such a fright at seeing the large Firebird that he fell cowering to the ground until Richard assured him that Valcote was friend not enemy,

"Ahhh, you look so much better, the old sparkle is back even though you are wounded," Richard declared. "We need some of our own sparkle to match Sundra's magic. Are you up to help us this once?"

"Naturally, my fire has started returning, what is it I can do?" Valcote asked.

"Those people in the bubbles cannot think for themselves, Lokan here will break the spell of the balls, we have to stop them returning to Sundra because I think they have been hypnotised and programmed to obey only him, if you can terrorise them as you did to Lokan, perhaps we can get them away from here?" Richard explained.

"I understand. I will do what I can." Valcote flew up to the top of the falls and hovered, while Richard and Lokan began pushing several balls to the edge of the pool.

Lokan peered into each ball, recognised the people inside and called their names out backwards, the balloons deflated and the zombie army soon began to grow, many of the released simply stood around while others started walking away aimlessly. Suddenly Valcote dived with a massive roar released a ball of flame that smashed against a wet wall that burst into flame, smoke and steam. It was as if somebody had suddenly shaken them all from their drunken stupor, most ran towards the sunlight, the odd one cowered but all had instantly come alive again. Orkan herded them to safety and away from the river and the falls; some even began chatting among themselves trying to figure out what was happening. In the distance he could clearly see Melek and Nakan heading towards them across the stony valley. Again and again they went through the same routine, break several bubbles, let people out, scare them back to reality then shepherd them to safety, it was all going so well and there were not many balls to go. Out of the blue there were mysterious splashing and plopping sounds ringing from around the Illusionist Falls water area, Valcote swooped down and shouted for Richard and Lokan to quickly leave the water as there was danger arriving. The two no sooner clambered onto the stone surface than a number of green heads popped up above the water line, as Richard watched, more and more heads began appearing, it was the gathering of Sundra's guard worms. Their powerful tooth filled jaws now snapping their defiance at having lost most of Sundra's prisoners while several worms formed a tight circular ring around the remaining balls,

"Gghhh! We cannot leave them at Sundra's mercy, we must do something," Orkan pleaded with Richard as the horde of massive worms swam to the edge of the pool together, growling and barking like a pack of rabid crazed green Rottweilers on the attack. All of them foaming large rainbow coloured bubbles from their mouths.

"Back, they're going to attack," shouted Richard. As the two moved towards the sunlight, Orkan used the newly acquired spear to slash out at one of the lead worms, it pierced several bubbles at once and the violence of a substantial explosion inside the beast's mouth was horrific, blowing the head right off the creature, the wriggling headless body spilling greasy, slippery yellow glop that floated on top of the water.

"Gghhh! You help others, I will keep them in the water." Orkan ordered just as Melek appeared. Richard hustled him away from the pool to where a happy Nakan and his six countrymen were busily ushering their countrymen into some form of order. Back at the pool, there was a huge splash into the pool; it created very large waves that Orkan saw arriving and forced him to race away to safety. Just then the gigantic worm that had created the trio's bubble surfaced from the pool, it discharged such an ear-splitting bellow that reverberated through the whole place, and even momentarily drowned out all sound made by the deafeningly noisy Illusionist Falls. "The big bubble beast's back!" Orkan screamed at his two companions.

"Oh-oh! Look who's also arrived to join the party? I think we could be in big trouble, Sundra doesn't look at all happy." The Beezlebub-like Sundra seemed to appear from nowhere as he drifted towards the giant worm now reaching the side of the pool, huge bubbles frothing from its enormous crater of a mouth.

"So you managed to escape? Very clever, I underestimated the Chosen One the first time, but let me assure you it will not happen again. I will never let the Evil One down," Sundra raised his crooked finger and a blurring jet of blue and white spark shot from the tip but before it could reach the trio there was a resounding crack like thunder exploding. A vast magical fireworks display thundered out midway between Sundra and the three companions, it erupted right over the head of the oversized worm that took fright and sank quickly below the blue pool waters. Valcote swooped in past the three just as Sundra released a second volley towards them, again the magical display of fire meeting ice erupted in a violent explosive exhibition over the pool sending a shower of sparks in all directions. Sundra's confident mask slipped, his goat haired face pulled into one of rage as he turned to concentrate on his overhead battle with the still injured Valcote. Richard was not sure that the already wounded Valcote would survive a second major battle. Just then, the gigantic worm started pulling itself from the pool, Richard could see that it was in full attack mode and it was being followed by the masses of large worm-like beasts.

"We are starting to lose our advantage, we must draw back." Richard shouted in desperation.

Prowler from the Oasis

On the Twenty-Fifth Day...

Walking underneath the sun,
Do not fear the vision double.
Do not waver! Do not run!
Falsehood now is not a trouble.
Shifting shapes amid the sand
Travail the three by Wizard's Well.
A toothy welcome is at hand
To chink ajar the gates of hell.

"Gghhh! You go, I am staying to try and hold back more of the smaller worms, "the defiant Orkan shouted.

"We need another lance." Richard raced along the pathway, under the falling water, into the room that was now prodigiously filled with toxic smoke from Sundra's mixed up concoctions. He grabbed two javelin type spears and quickly made a fast retreat back to his friend. He poked out a point at one caterpillar and missed but it still left the creature with a deflating face, Richard only just made it past the advancing army of hostile smaller worms leading the strike. He handed one of the weapons to Nakan who had now joined them. Together they became a formidable team, stabbing, piercing and slaughtering the worms as they slowly worked their way down the long line leaving beheaded, screeching worm bodies in their wake as they moved closer toward their main adversary, the gigantic slug.

Valcote too was gaining ground, her constant barrage of fireballs had weakened Sundra's magical powers and his ice strikes were becoming weaker and less efficient, the Firebird steadily forced Sundra down towards the pool and backwards until he was almost touching the back of the great caterpillar. Valcote fired another fast volley of rainbow coloured projectiles towards Sundra who was thrown backward and over the head of the great maggot that in confusion of being attacked from above, instantaneously blew a large bubble that enveloped the hairy goat-like floating beast.

"Gghhh! Now see how you like being stuck inside a ball?" Orkan snorted triumphantly. The rest of the slug type beasts very swiftly retreated back under the water and disappeared somehow knowing that without Sundra; they were no match for the courageous squad that had confronted them.

"Sundra knows how to break the spell; he will release himself just as soon as we leave. Won't he?" Richard enquired, as they inspected the carnage and disarray left behind. Worm heads jiggled and popped, white slime covered the once blue waters of the pool, decapitated green bodies in their death throes jerked and floated around aimlessly in the water. Valcote completed her victory roll and swooped down to join the three.

"He could do that but when the Evil One gets here and finds that Sundra has failed miserably, he will devise something far worse for him to endure. No, I think we have seen the last of Sundra for a while because that coward will fear reprisals being metered out by the Evil One, with his powers destroyed Sundra will simply melt into hiding for some time.

"Valcote, you have saved us yet once again, we cannot thank you enough," Richard saluted the Fire Bird. "Do you know anything about Magus's Well?"

"You can thank me by completing your mission. Time is short, I will stay back here until you are safely away and everyone else has left for the Ancestral City. The only thing I have heard of Magus's Well is it is a desert and well guarded by several beasts. Should I try to meet up with you there?"

"No, you have already done enough, you need rest." Just then Lokan and several others began retrieving their weapons and handed them to their owners, Nakam presented Richard with an impressive suit of armour.

"Gghhh! It belonged to one of our greatest warriors when trying to escape from Sundra, it is now yours." Without wanting to offend the pig-like countrymen, Richard gratefully accepted the gift and strapped the foreign sections of metal on to and around his body with Orkan's assistance. The armour fitted perfectly, Richard was surprised by its lightness and flexibility, he could hardly feel that he had it on as he moved and pirouetted like a model on a catwalk. There was much backslapping, saluting and cheering as Lokan and Nakan led the Landsmen and Orkan's countrymen away and across the stony valley.

"It's time for us to move on." For the second time that day they bid their firebird friend their parting farewell. Lokan said we should pass under the falls, there is a passageway that will take us onto the path that leads to Magus's Well." With a last wave, the trio raced through the long and wet assault course beneath Illusionist Falls and finally burst out into the fresh air again. They quickly found the door and stairway that Lokan had mentioned, the group climbed a long way past Sundra's throne room to the top of the stairs where they found they were once again back on a mountainside. Before them in a wide natural bowl, lay the lake that fed the Illusionist Falls.

"There are many ways we can go, let's consult the Path Finder first." Richard said. Melek removed the book from his shoulders and handed it to him, it showed them that the way forward was down the mountain, between two smaller hills of Yellow Stone Peaks beyond which, the lengthening shadows from their high position, looked very much like a flat desert. "Right again Valcote, that certainly looks like desert in the distance. We are all tired, I think that it would be wise to rest somewhere and I need to fill my water bottle, the sun won't be up much longer. What do you recommend Orkan?"

"Gghhh! Let's get your water and there is enough time to reach those foothills. We rest there and we can make an early start while it is still cool in the morning." Orkan suggested. After filling their containers they made their way to the bottom of the mountain and found some boulders with overhanging rocks as their shelter for the night. As usual two fell into deep sleep while Orkan took the first watch.

"Gghhh! Time to move." Orkan woke Richard. He looked up; the faintest shimmer of orange on the horizon only broke the dark sky. "If we move now we will cover much distance before it heats up and becomes unbearable. Richard trusted Orkan's judgement. Melek also pulled himself up and the trio set off out of the hills and into the sand filled desert that seemed to stretch as far as the eye could see, it looked like the early morning sky and rolling carpet of sand met along the distant horizon. Every dune looked identical, as did the deep drift valleys that connected the constant sandbanks. Their early start meant that nothing stirred and all that could be heard was the sound of the companion's own breathing as they forced themselves onward. For the moment air remained temperate so they made good progress for a while following the Path Finder directions but each knew that the blistering hot air would arrive in time.

"Orkan, your countrymen all had similar names to you, Lokan, Nakan, Orkan, is there a reason that almost all have the same endings to their names?" Melek questioned. "I am simply curious."

"Gghhh! All the names that end with K-A-N mean it is the eldest son. My name means I am the eldest son of Or, and Nakan is the eldest son of Na. The females all end in K-E-S so my sister would be called Orkes. Each family has no more than two children, one to replace one parent and the second to replace the other parent. That way, we maintain the balance." Orkan carefully explained. The trio's pace began to slow to a snail's pace as the morning sun rose higher in the sky making it unbearably hot. The sands became unstable, their hardened sun-baked surfaces covering slippery depths of sand. More than once they scrambled up a slope only for the yielding sand to give way under them, sending them skidding back the way that they came. As they strained against the desert, the sun's intensity rapidly became more severe on their backs and shoulders. Richard felt the soft leather straps of the newly acquired armour bite into his soft tissue. Yet at the same time he found it surprisingly light to wear because it did not seem to confine the high temperature within the metal at all. In a strange way he was pleased to have it on because danger could lie in wait behind any of the large dunes. Richard's fears were confirmed when the rolling sand hills suddenly ended, revealing a parched expanse of flat ground. In the middle distance he could make out three figures moving towards them. From this distance they seemed sluggishly exhausted but had, nevertheless an erect purposeful air.

"Look!" Richard grabbed Orkan by the arm. "So who do you think they are?"

"How should I know?" The soldier looked fiercely at his companion. "This heat haze makes it difficult to make them out we cannot be sure whether they are friend or foe so we must be careful."

"It's flat, if we can see them, then it's a good bet that they can see us as well." Melek intervened.

"Gghhh! All the same, we shouldn't take any chances until we find out who they are. We will walk in single file towards them, that way we reduce our outline so that they only view a single person moving towards them." Orkan's military brain had come into play once again. "We could possibly be unnoticed if we move in a semi-circle." The two bunched up and into line behind Richard but to his surprise to note that the silhouetted figures in the distance had mirrored their movement.

"They have the same thoughts as us, this could be trickier than we first thought it would be," he told the other two. "Get down!" he whispered to his two companions. They did so and instantly their foe copied their movement.

"This is not funny, they copy our every movement," still keeping an eye on the enemy ahead, Richard rolled onto one side to draw Juroot's dagger from his pocket. From across the plain he saw that whoever their antagonists were, they were mirroring his every movement. A thought suddenly struck into his head, he raised an arm. So too did one of the antagonists, he thrust up a foot, so did the misty outline ahead. Richard stood up, so too did one of his opponents. At that moment Richard felt rather stupid as he sighed and sheathed the dagger, as did the person on the opposite side.

"Sometimes I can be so dim-witted," he scratched at his head. "Those so-called people in the distance are quite literally we three. Therefore, they're not our enemies."

"Gghhh! I think that the sun has fried his brains," Orkan said to Melek.

"No, what he means is, that it is a mirage" Melek explained. The light winds kick up fine specks of dust, so when the sun hits them at a certain angle, it becomes a natural desert mirror. We have been worried by our own reflection. Do any kind of movement and watch those figures in the distance." Orkan did a short dance. He was amazed as the supposed enemy followed his every move. The three laughed.

"Come on, this sun is killing us. Let's try to make it to Magus's Well before we all go a bit crazy." The three continued to trudge on, the ghostly figures of themselves faded and slowly evaporated away. Several times Richard referred back to the Path Finder, each time it showed they were still on the correct course. A little while later another set of shapes emerged in the distance ahead of them.

"Look, the mirage is back, an excited Melek pointed to the distant fuzzy silhouettes. The trio were not alarmed but as they got closer the outlines became more defined.

"Those aren't people, they look more like palm trees. It could be that it is an oasis. I even think we might have reached Magus's Well after all." Richard was right, as they got nearer; they could make out the distinct vision of gently waving palms surrounding what looked like a crystal blue small waterhole. This was a sight to behold for the exhausted travellers; it stood out like a turquoise jewel of productive fruitfulness against the vast surroundings of unproductive desert. The three began jogging; the lure of refreshing themselves together with finding the final pod giving them renewed optimism and hope.

"Isn't that one of the Apeptas' army lizards?" Richard asked as the huge beast appeared across their path. Orkan immediately unsheathed his trusty sword.

"Gghhh! I am not taking any risks; all lizards look the same to me and they can be very dangerous soldiers." Orkan said. However, this reptile was a lot darker in skin tone than Richard had committed to memory, this creature was as large as those found in Dragora's cave but somehow, there was something different, this living thing was not quite the same as those in the cave. This one had more of a Komodo dragon type feel about it, the way it stopped and sized up its chances against the trio, the way its tongue constantly flicked in and out testing the smell of the newcomers. It was not hostile nor was it welcoming. Deciding that the three were too heavily armed just at that moment it sloped off towards and behind an uneven windbreak made up of half buried stacked stones and desert sand built to one side of the oasis perimeter. The first thing each did to restore themselves was taking a long large drink of the cool elixir of life. Richard then extracted the Path Finder to consult their next move; the coloured flashes circulated the central ring indicating that they had reached their destination for the moment.

"The pod is here somewhere, we must locate it." Richard stated. "We could fan out and search individually, but that lizard worries me so I think we should stick together?" The others agreed. They moved from the pool outwards in a large circular sweep, checking around the palm trees, it took time to cover the inner area but nothing. The only place left to search was around that sand windbreak.

"Gghhh! That's where that lizard vanished, it could be lying in wait." Orkan withdrew his sword again, they moved purposefully round the whole area and the only thing they could find was a neat round hole slipping down under the rock pile.

"I think that is your lizard's lair," suggested Melek.

"If the pod is down there we are in real trouble." Richard extracted the torch from his bag; the tunnel angled down and turned a corner. To get a better view, Richard moved closer to the entrance, suddenly a hiss shot out of the hole as it unexpectedly filled with a bulky head of an anaconda sized snake. Richard whipped backwards, Orkan instantly had his bow loaded with an arrow but as he drew back the cord to fire the huge reptile retreated back around the bend to safety.

"Wha... What was that?" Richard asked, "That definitely wasn't the lizard."

"Gghhh! It was still a reptile; this place is crawling with dangerous things. To me, that looked like a very big snake." They continued around the whole perimeter and found nothing. Returning to the pool they sat down.

"We've searched everywhere, nothing. We must find it today, our time is almost up." Richard sighed.

"Not everywhere," Melek said. The pod could be lodged somewhere at the bottom of the pool. Let me first check the Book of Prophecies, maybe there will be a clue.

Walking underneath the sun,
Do not fear the vision double.
Do not waver! Do not run!
Falsehood now is not a trouble.
Shifting shapes amid the sand
Travail the three by Wizard's Well.
A toothy welcome is at hand
To chink ajar the gates of hell.

"Part of this riddle makes sense, part does not," he said as Melek quickly stripped down to his very skimpy underwear. For the first time since their arduous journey had begun, both Richard and Orkan observed that Melek's slim body was beautifully tiger striped across his entire torso. He moved to the pool and that was when his companions also first saw the unwinding banded long tail that ended with a ginger coloured fluffy ball of cheeky fur. The two astonished men looked at each other then turned to see the attractive librarian gingerly enter the cool water, he began refreshingly splashing around. Orkan jumped up sword drawn, his water splattering alerting him that he could be in trouble. Melek ducked under the water and came up right where Orkan was standing, he teasingly splashed his soldiering companion "It is lovely and invigorating, why not join me or, are you still so scared of all water? Come on Orkan, you are no longer a baby." Richard noticed that Orkan was rather reticent in taking up his offer. To reassure the pig-like boy, Richard didn't need any invitations; he quickly stripped down to his boxer shorts and raced his very white body straight at the pool to unceremoniously bomb into the water beside Melek. The two friends romped and played, their hidden agenda all the while, was to entice the third member of their group to join in. Finally, Orkan relented. He stripped down to his pants revealing a muscular upper torso and unlike Richard carefully made his way into the rejuvenating blue waters. Both Melek and Richard splashed water at him and he suddenly joined in the frolicking game, they were relaxed, having fun and not on their guard.

What none of them saw as they enjoyed their horsing around was the evil slatted red eyes of Faswong the Wendigo-like beast who lurked behind the stone windbreak. While they were fully occupied, the spirits of a beast stealthily slunk forward using palm trees for cover, carefully the animal monstrosity furtively collected up the trio's belongings and weapons. The large alien-like canine beast rapidly whisked what he could carry away to his hole built into the stone and sand windbreak. The group playing in the water were completely unaware of the danger they could be facing as Faswong returned a second time and skilfully pilfered the rest of the trio's items that he also deposited in the stone gap.

In amongst their frolics the three hunted the bottom of the pool searching for the pod that they knew was somewhere in this area. Melek came up for breath and out of the corner of his eye caught an unexpected movement near some of the palm trees. Some sixth sense made him glance across and what he saw almost rooted him to the spot. It was Faswong changing shape. His long thin legs were becoming shorter, he was developing a long bushy tail. Ears pricked on the head and his sharpened jaw line was developing large fangs of a canine muzzle. Dark bristly brown hairs the full length of his sinewy body were replacing their silvery feathered strips. The complete transformation took place within seconds. In pace of the frightening Wendigo-like beast was now a powerful looking wolf.

"We better get out of here quickly and arm ourselves. Don't turn quickly but there is a shape-shifter behind you near the palm trees." Melek whispered. Richard tried to turn around casually, but Orkan spun and seeing the dominant and ravenous looking lupine, headed straight for the spot where he had left his weapons. "First a lizard, then a Wendigo and I saw it materialise into that wolf, now the shifting shapes of the prophecy makes sense, it was not meaning shifting sand, it was warning us of the shape-shifter." Faswong raised his head and gave a ferocious howl. Richard and Melek scurried out of the pool.

"Gghhh! Whatever that is, it has stolen everything," said the very frustrated Orkan. "We cannot defend ourselves against something as powerful as that, get to the rocks, that's our only chance." The three raced for all their worth to the sand filled wind break. Aswong took his time stalking after them; he was in no great hurry knowing full well that with his speed, he could easily outpace them if he wished to do so.

"What is a Wendigo? Richard asked as the trio gathered several smaller stones that they could hurl at the beast. "I've never heard of it before."

"It is reputed to be a mixture of a beast much like the vampire, werewolf, or zombie. Another problem is that they are never satisfied with killing and consuming just one person." Melek said passing another collected stone to Orkan. "They are gluttonous and if the tales are true, people attacked and eaten by it, will also become possessed by the demonic spirit of the beast."

"Gghhh! We have to separate slightly, if it attacks one of us the other two need to try to stone it," Orkan commanded. Handing them each an armful of sharp edged rocks rapidly picked from his pile. Move!"

Aswong got close enough to smell their fear and showing a wolfish sneer stopped the stalking to survey the three sodden figures with relish.

"Who are you, what do you want?" I am Aswong the Desert Stalker put here by my master, the Evil One to prevent you from going any further. News travels fast here, I have heard of some of your heroics but your time has come. I have outwitted all three of you and now you will die. I made certain that you have no defence, you are now the weaklings and will not be able to resist me." Long loops of saliva drooled down from his open jaws; his eyes were shimmering red slits. "I will take you first," he said, pouncing at Melek. Aswong moved like lightning, Richard and Orkan hurled rocks at the beast, one second the librarian was standing there, the next he was gripped in Aswong's arms as the wolf backed away from the barrage of stoning material hitting him, mainly about his head.

"Run! Save yourselves!" Melek shouted, squirming as the large wolf looked as if it was about to attack and eat him. Richard and Orkan had but one thought in mind and gathered up more stones and raced straight at Aswong hurling the last of their ammunition as they drew closer to the wolf. The beast concentrated on the two, his momentary feast forgotten, the writhing Melek instantly broke free falling to the sand before Aswong could react. But, he knew that time was on his side against the now desperate little band and that this was going to be a great feast shortly so he backed further away to avoid the last of their missiles. What nobody in this melee had heard was the beat of heavy wings flying in towards the oasis. As Richard discharged his last stone at the wolf he glimpsed the beauty of two great winged creatures dropping from the blue sky.

"Valcote! Help us!" Richard shouted

Flying in towards them low over the water creating whirlpools of turbulence with their strong wings was their old saviour, the firebird this time accompanied by a magnificent looking white winged horse. Its mane flowed back in the wind, and its galloping hooves kicked up little plumes of spray as they caught the water's surface.

Aswong, too, had now seen the two apparitions. He bared his teeth in a snarl, and then let out a ragged howl. Melek, ignoring his cuts and bruises sustained by the rough handling, wisely crawled towards his two companions who raced to help him away from further danger. Valcote released one of her fire shots towards the feet of Aswong, the beast saw it coming and jumped away, his full attention towards the small explosion and the dipping flight of the firebird, he did not even know what hit him. The white horse lunged at Aswong by way of striking him with both strong hooves carrying such force that it the wolf lost his balance. Then with a torrent of heavy blows the white horse smashed Aswong to the ground.

"Gghhh! Yes! Yes! Kill him!" Orkan shouted loudly. The trio watched in disbelief as Aswong's inert body changed into a myriad of different shapes before disappearing completely. The white horse cantered across to the companions.

"My name is Slepnor," the horse said gently. "I am glad that Valcote and I reached you in time. Golan's Forces are almost ready. I was sent to assist the firebird, when we understood that she had been injured. My orders were to also collect you in order that you could complete your quest. Thankfully Valcote knew where you were headed and was worried about you, so on her way to the Ancestral City we diverted to Magus's Well.

"Thank goodness you did, that thing was about to eat Melek." Richard placed an arm around the librarian shoulder. "We must first find our weapons, that creature stole all our things and hidden them."

"The hole! That shape-shifter changed itself into a large snake and scared us away. It has to be down there?" Melek said excitedly, the ginger fur at the end of his tail quivering exaggeratedly. Just then Valcote swooped in and landed gently.

"We meet again Chosen One," the large firebird said quietly. The nasty red welts had disappeared and her feathers had miraculously healed up since they had seen her at the Illusionist Falls. The gleam was again back in her eyes.

"You keep saving us and I don't understand how you are almost back to normal?" Richard said enthusiastically. "Not that I'm complaining."

"You had a quest to save the pods and hence bring balance to the universe, it is my duty to help make that happen, if that required my life to save you, I would gladly have given it up. Fortunately, we soldiers have so far managed to protect you from harm." Valcote looked pointedly at Orkan. "Now we must return you to Golan's safe keeping."

"Not before I find the last pod, it's got to be here somewhere. First we must find our things." Richard led the way around the windbreak to the hole where they had seen the snake. Stuffed tightly into the entrance were all their missing items. Hauling everything out of the hole, the three rapidly got dressed into the lightweight armour, the happiest person being Orkan who was back in his guise as a soldier. Melek completed his dressing, his rope waistband finalising his attire, he took a long look at the hole.

"The one place we have not searched is down the hole?" He said quietly. "I am small enough to fit through that space." Valcote awkwardly waddled forward and looked down into the dark abyss.

"Here, take this, it is probably dark down there." Richard handed him his torch.

"Gghhh! It can be dangerous; we still do not know if Aswong is still around, he could be lying in wait down there." Orkan said protectively. Suddenly Valcote blasted all types of flame balls straight into the hole. There was a huge shriek as the smell of burning flesh wafted out of the hole. Valcote blasted more fire down the deep opening, a black burning and singed Aswong pulled himself out of his pit, flopped down on the sand in front of them, he kicked out one last time as his body burst into flames and expired at their feet.

"The Evil One has now lost one of his most treacherous allies." Valcote reflected without any passion in his voice. "The beast's lair is safe to enter.

They waited a short time for the heat below to dissipate. Melek scrambled down headfirst, after a few short moments his hand reappeared gripping the pod, Richard took it from him and quickly held it against his amulet, and it glowed brightly. The group whooped with joy and Richard held the glowing pod in his palm.

"We have all six pods, my quest is over, I can go back home now." Richard smiled at the others.

"Not quite, we must get you to Golan, he will explain all." Slepnor intervened. Now, all of you get on my back and I will take you back to the Ancestral City.

"I will accompany you just in case the Evil One should possibly try to prevent you from reaching the Ancestral City." Valcote opened her wings and lifted from the sand. Richard, Orkan and Melek clambered onto Slepnor's back. Seconds later they were in the air circling Magus's Well.

"Please bring us right up to date about everything that is happening." Richard enquired. As they flew high above the ground, Slepnor brought them up to date with news of Golan's challenge to the Evil One. The Guardians believed that it was finally the time to confront and put this malevolent, plotting, wicked and malicious evil to flight. Golan had now rallied the forces for good and was waiting for Richard's return with the pods. Also the bad news was that Sarkel, Broon's bear-like lieutenant and a few soldiers had been attacked and killed by Cozards before he could rejoin his leader and the rest of his troops. Even with the damage inflicted on his forces by the trio, the Evil One had managed to build up his following over a period of time and had summoned his violent troops to the Ancestral City. Slepnor was in no doubt that they still faced an army that would be numerically superior to anything that Golan's Forces had encountered so far. The companions asked various questions that the white horse answered, Richard now knew that his task was not yet complete and that he faced the stiffest battle on this long journey. For a while as the sped their way back to the Ancestral City, the three managed occasional discussion, they then fell silent, gathering their individual thoughts about their own frailness and possible death in the Final Battle.

Golan and the Final Story

On the Twenty-Sixth Day...

Night arrives with Evil force.
Terror, bloodshed run their course.
Doom awaits on either hand
But victory in sea, on land,
Brings at last the light of day.
Yet to not turn so fast away.
For even in the final scene
All is still not what it seems.

For hours Richard, Orkan and Melek flew the air on Slepnor's back occasionally one of them would start dozing off. Valcote maintained pace with the large flying horse and suggested that the three tie themselves together with Melek's waistband rope, just in case of accidents. The trio took her advice and then either Richard or the librarian regularly nodded off while Orkan excitedly droned on giving a running commentary about places he could recognise way down.

"Gghhh! That is where those man-eating plants almost swallowed Melek and the Grapfrits and Cozards waged battle," he eagerly pointed out the landscape as they passed over the volcano with its sloping hills that were now black charred and crater pitted from top to bottom and all the way to the cliff and lakeside.

After some time had passed the large horse suddenly tilted his wings and started a long descent, Richard could see the battlements of a city in the distance.

"The Ancestral City," he shouted excitedly. The fortress was easily recognisable standing among several hills with its grey fortified turrets free of the dark unnatural light of day that made him certain was of the Evil One's doing. As they drew closer to the imposing stronghold wafting black smoke began drifting below so that only in patches could they glimpse the forests beneath their flight path. As they began descending lower towards the ridge of hills and the dappled grouping of campfires, Richard caught sight of the citadel at the heart of the Ancestral City. Above the city the sky was strangely bright. Valcote went ahead to ensure that there was no danger and Slepnor flew in a long arc before spreading his wings widely and gliding down into a gentle landing among the forest trees.

"We are home, there seems to be a welcoming party awaiting our arrival." Slepnor folded back his powerful wings against his body with the elegance of an aircraft entering a hanger that allowed the three to use them as a stairway off the big white horse.

"Thank you for the lift and your help at the oasis, we would never have completed the mission without you and Valcote," Melek made a regal curtsy before the two, Richard and Orkan gave the two a stout salute. All three turned and shook their stiffened limbs until life returned before crossing to meet Juroot who was patiently awaiting them. The Guardian greeted all three enthusiastically gripping each in turn with a lovely bear hug.

"You have done well," Juroot announced after Richard had given him a bullet pointed account of their adventure at both Illusionist Falls and Magus's Well. Juroot specifically then concentrated on Richard. "Your task is almost done, but the Evil One's forces now hold the city. Not until they have been destroyed can the pods that have been retrieved be returned to the Tree of Life and the Guardians, like me, will then be reinstated. Only once evil has been rooted out and destroyed will this world be secure once again." Juroot's face was harsh. "Come, you will attend the Council of War."

"Juroot led the companions through the forest. Everywhere they looked, there were processions of soldiers with unwavering faces showing harsh determination for the task that was about to confront them. Juroot ushered the trio into a large clearing packed with an array of differing creatures seated on felled trees or on the ground. Among them were many that the three immediately recognised Oganga, Covelette, Broon and others.

"Where's Golan?" Richard felt sure that the old Guardian would be at a war meeting or at the very least be there to welcome them back.

"Golan is with us in spirit," Juroot calmly replied. "Not until we reach the Tree of Life will he show himself.

"Why?" Richard asked.

"Golan is the Great Elder, his presence is continually with us Guardians. Should he bodily show himself, the Evil One would soon find out and target him, if he somehow fell into the grip of the Evil One, then it would truly be a disaster worse than losing all other Guardians. Therefore, he must remain hidden at this time, but believe me he is here."

Immediately an opening appeared for the group of newcomers, it was not presumptuous in any way; it was as if the trio had earned every right to be seated on this important council. The talking began; it flowed in several directions as various arguments poured forward as everyone sought the most opportune way to get into the city. Many favoured a concerted frontal attack believing that the forces for good were strong enough to break through; others disagreed believing that the best method would be to tunnel beneath the outer walls. The opinions ebbed and flowed in several directions but always returned to the two main ideas. As the deafening clamour grew in intensity Juroot drew himself to his full height and held up both hands.

"We have now thrashed out all the potential options; we have to make a decision. From experience, a frontal attack would possibly cost too many lives; we do not have the numerical strength so we must try to use stealth and surprise. Those dwarf forces previously commanded by Zock are natural tunnel makers, The twins, Metie and Mockie will lead the way to excavate under the main wall, smaller groups will draw attention away from them by pretending to be getting ready for a frontal attack. Once through, they will give us the signal then Oganga and his airborne troops will cause a diversion from above. Hopefully that will give several lizard soldiers the opportunity to slip through and concentrate on the gates. The insect brigade will keep us informed of the enemy's activities while the main body of troops are to be split into groups in order to attack various weak points at first. Timing will be everything, if that is done correctly we could substantially reduce their forces so our first attack once the signal is given, must be simultaneous." Juroot fell silent and surveyed the gathered council with a steely gaze before continuing. "Zard, you take your troops through the main gate on the west side when your lizard troops open them. Broon, take the east, Covelette your company will have to take on the southern gate. The initial internal assault will come from the dwarves, it will throw their forces into disarray and hopefully the overhead invasion will add to that strike. My garrison will attack from the north side where the main concentrations of their hostile heavyweights are based and Richard, Orkan and Melek will accompany me. Remember that the Evil One's forces are expecting a gate attack and hopefully the first charge will reduce their overwhelming odds. Be vigilant and good luck to all."

Juroot's carefully worked out scheme was greeted with passionate approval and cheers, it had satisfied both main plans. The Guardians nodded their approval, mainly because the shock strategy meant the possibility of less threat and danger to their own forces. Juroot began to draw up the full battle plan, the Guardians enthusiastically added their own knowledge and ideas until everyone was secure in their own minds that their forces now would stand a chance against the statistical larger number of foes pitted against them. With everything committed to memory the Guardians marshalled their troops and then melted away into the smoke filled forests.

"It is time to find out the future of our land, we were not expecting the last battle, this time is different but the Evil One has also had time to amalgamate his troop's numbers into a larger and more sizable collection. Thanks to your mission, the destruction of those main leaders has considerably diminished his strength. This gives us the chance to take back what was once good and peaceful." Juroot said quietly as they each prepared themselves for the battle that was going to be won or lost before the day was out.

"Come we must organise our armed forces, the whole plan is totally dependent on the surprise and timing of the first launch, we must act as one unit, we cannot let the others down." Darkness filled the skies right around the citadel, the overhead dimness of drifting clouds gave the dwarf forces an extra cover they needed to get close to the battlement walls and to start tunnelling.

"Let us look at the Book of Prophesies; perhaps it will reveal the outcome of this battle?" Melek advised quietly

Night arrives with Evil force.
Terror, bloodshed run their course.
Doom awaits on either hand
But victory in sea, on land,
Brings at last the light of day.
Yet to not turn so fast away.
For even in the final scene
All is still not what it seems.

"It seems as if it will be a hard fought night, I do not like the final line, it forebodes a warning." Melek closed the book and began walking away, he stopped and turned to his two companions. "I will be back shortly; I am going to make sure the Book of Prophecies is well hidden just in case the battle does not go well for us."

Meanwhile Juroot's bogus attack plans on placing the Evil One's forces inside the DEFENSE area out of position went smoothly. With their combined expertise and numbers Mockie was soon able to report back that the first tunnels had already breached the outer walls. Except for sporadic and simulated attacks at the gates, the main body of forces for Good waited in silence on the plains surrounding the stronghold. The message from Zard came through that the subways were completed and the lizards ready to make their attempt at opening the gates. The trio joined Juroot at the head of the column of diverse forces as it moved forward into position. Richard watched the first wave of Oganga's bird forces fly over their heads to start attacking and distracting the enemy. He was both horrified and fascinated when many were struck down in mid-air and went plummeting to the ground inside and outside the battlement. The faint sound of droning wing beats signalled an incoming scout to update progress from within the city, it did not look very good as massed troops were now gathering at the north gate preparing themselves to attack Juroot's assorted collection of soldiers.

"Somehow they have found out which is to be the strongest of our network forces and on concentrating their superior numbers on us. The plan could still work, but it requires a few adjustments to it," Juroot gave the scout instructions for the rest of the Guardians before urging the main body of forces forward towards the north gate that were being opened by the lizards.

"Gghhh! Here we go, good luck to both of you," Orkan indicated for his two companions to fall in behind him. "Your duty is to stop anyone attacking my flanks."

Soon the military of Evil could be seen packed and shoving through the wide opened gate, a combination joining in a tight forefront of poison aimed directly at Juroot's incoming armed forces. The torches they carried radiated a lurid glow that carried the impression of multiplied shadows to make the numbers seem even greater than they actually were. Juroot's brave army moved forward with a steady but unfaltering rhythmic beating of steel against steel, while at the same time from the midst of those pouring through the gates, came hoarse shouts and cries of torment. Juroot's main force continued their sturdy forward advance, the balance of his group quietly skirted around to the outer edge of the high walls in order to form a pincer attack by driving into the Evil One's advance from both sides. Muffled cries came from the darkness where the skirmishing Landsmen had now met the leading Cozards face to face. The battle had begun; others took tighter grip on their weapons steeling themselves for the offensive. Flaming arrows and pointed iron darts rained into the centre of the Evil One's forces with such ferocity that the large group of scorpions covered in blaze, raced about in frenzy among their fellow attackers, igniting all that they brushed against. As the Grapfrits prepared to assail Juroot's forces, another and another volley of flaring barbs arrived out of the blacked sky to halt their ferocious onslaught sending them bursting against each other like overripe tomatoes in mid flight. Giant earwigs, worm-like creatures and killer bees that all convulsed and spasmed weakly under the constant barrage of the incoming fiery tempest. All manner of deformed creatures of the night ballooned and frenzied in anguish, spreading further fear, confusion and chaos behind them as they sought relief by moving among their warring colleagues in helpless fashion.

Steadily but slowly, the enemy were being pressed back toward the now closed gate, the Evil One had simply left the troops to die. A scout arrived to inform Juroot that both north and south gates remained shut and that their enemy was now preparing catapults for some sort of attack on the successful forces that had already entered through the west gate. Zard had already been forewarned of the possible assault and had instantly begun moving his troops in among some of the houses instead of being caught out on masse. Despite the warning, Richard was taken aback by what he saw next. A volley of fireballs lit up the sky above the citadel as they soared through the air towards Zard and his troop's last known position. The Evil One had realised the advantage of using fire when his own troops were decimated so quickly outside the north gate, now he brought the full weight of his war machine into play. A second shower of fireballs rose into the sky. They burst on impact, cascading burning pitch-like acid substance that saturated all material it came into contact with, demolishing armour in a sizzling, smoking and foul smelling vapour. It did not seem to have bothered the Evil One that these vicious fireballs were destroying his own troops together with some of Zard's forces.

"They keep on coming." Juroot shouted as he spotted another squadron of Grapfrits heading over the wall and towards them. Again, a bombardment of flaming arrows from the forest met them before they could cause any damage. "The gates are open once again," Juroot urged his army forward and unbeknown to him, Zard had already directed many troops away from the fireballs into side streets for him to head the soldiers towards the north and south gates. Broon and Covelette's forces had not met with extreme opposition so had managed to meet up their forces at the centre. Zard's troops linked up with the formidable fighting group of tunnelling dwarves who explained that the north gates had been shut. Moving in behind the enemy, they surprised them with an all out attack while several lizards managed to open the north gate for Juroot's forces. When at last Richard managed to enter the city, he saw that it was in worse shape than he had formerly thought. Some of the previously beautiful buildings had been reduced to heaps of rubble while several towers lurched perilously on the point of collapse. The battle once inside the walls raged brutally, Scorpions, Cozards, killer bees, giant worms and earwigs together with a host of unfamiliar creatures teemed through the streets. On a narrow staircase to the battlements a group of dwarves and lizards were fighting for their lives against a compact formation of pressing Cozards in full flow. The dwarves however, although no physical match on a person to person basis with the powerful Cozards, were allowing the lizard force to match the domineering troops in hand to hand combat, while using their shortness to slip beneath the battling lizard's guard and constantly strike powerful blows into their opponent's torso.

"Gghhh! We must help Zard." Orkan shouted and moved towards the large lizard, several outsized earwigs that used their sickle-shaped horns to slash out at the Guardian as he sliced vigorously at the enemy with his battleaxe were attacking him. The trio set about slashing at them, green blood spurted heavenwards on several beasts before they retreated to safety behind a band of worms and snakes that had swept in from one of the side streets.

"Thank you but, I could have dealt with them myself." Zard nodded at the three appreciatively. The fighting was fast and ferocious when Juroot came under attack by several Cozards when Mockie and Metie managed to join him in the fray

"The forces of the Evil One are a lot stronger than we had predicted, it is as if there is a never ending line of bodies before us to tackle." Juroot admitted to the twins

"Do not fear, Broon and Covelette have gained ground on the foe and already closed the back door on their forces as we speak. I think that they are steadily pushing the rest of the Evil One's enemy towards us," Metie offered hopefully. Have you heard anything about the sea battle? How does that progress?" Metie struck out at a large rising worm, decapitating it with a single blow.

"From all accounts their battle is as furious as ours; the last report was that our forces had been trapped near the sandbank and that the two Guardians Tishon and Shunta are also struggling for their lives. We await news from the scouts but it is far more difficult for them to gain a clear picture as most of the battle takes place underwater." Juroot explained.

The sea folded into a large bay that served as a harbour for the Ancestral City, two enemies drew battle lines across the wide expanse of water. The fireballs at the fortress had heralded the beginning of the fierce underwater battle between the forces of Good and Evil. The first strike came about immediately by Nemis' ghost sailors that were no match for Delphost's dolphins. The sea mammals inaugurated their bottle-like snouts like forceful battering rams against the far weaker seamen, the contest became very one sided and the sailors fled away. Sumar was disappointed at their performance as the great dragon-like beast accompanied by a giant squid and a school of stingrays dragged itself through the sand. The forces of Good were driven back into the shallows towards the eagerly awaiting Tolosh after quite a few attacks were made on the huge beast without much affect. Tishon and Shunta kept urging their forces forward, alert to the trap in which most of them were now caught. Some sea creatures tried swimming to the side and out of the trap but the stingrays quickly herded them back into the pincer entrapment and the waiting Tolosh that used their scissor like teeth to inflict damage. Suddenly the sea became a boiling mass of bodies being ripped apart and thrashed about on the surface as the brigade of alligators and crocodiles moved into the fray. They had circled around the deadly Tolosh and were now attacking them in turn with such speed and ferociousness that the doll-like beasts stood little or no chance of evading the incoming reptiles. Claws ripped along spongy underbellies, hard teeth crunched into heads of fragile skull bone with accuracy and spinning motion that each attacked Tolosh died instantly and never even knowing what had happened. The reptiles continued until the few Tolosh that had managed to escape, simply disappeared into the sandbanks and all that remained behind were clumps of brown fuzzy hair that floated along the tidal surface like seaweed. The sea had by now turned a pinkish red with the surface remaining frothy white by the dancing sea-horses above the waves blown in by the southerly winds.

Heartened by this sudden victory; Tishon and Shunta powered up speed towards the slower moving Sumar, staying well away from the powerful jaws and massive teeth that could split them in half in an instant, the two dived and circled around the green Moss Beast. It was then that Sumar made the mistake of raising her huge front end off the sea floor and before the great reptilian knew what had happened, the two Guardians were at her throat. A swift knife stroke opened her neck to the bone. The gigantic squid and stingrays were powerless prey to constant onslaughts by Delphost's sea mammals. Several made it to shore or were picked off and devoured by the cruising alligators and crocodiles while a few battered individuals were lucky enough to get out into the deeper sea and escape the carnage .The lone scout headed for the citadel with the news that the battle for supremacy of the seas was now well and truly over.

"Look! Covelette and Broon's forces have broken through," Richard shouted excitedly back at the Ancestral City. "The Evil One's forces are beginning to scatter." Completely surrounded by the forces of Good; Oganga, Valcote and a few other firebirds sailed into the sphere of battle, trying to finish off the defeat by spraying massed fireballs that consumed the surviving enemy. The Evil One's army that was still alive fell into absolute disarray and began melting away into the side streets in order to save themselves.

"We have won! The Evil One's forces are on the run," Juroot raised his battleaxe and shouted jubilantly. The forces for Good raised their weapons and cheered in reply. When the insect scout arrived bringing news of the victory at sea, a rolling cheer swept throughout the city walls at the information that the powers of the Evil One had been further weakened by the massacre at sea.

"We might have won a battle, but the war is still not yet over, we still have much to do," Juroot exclaimed. "We must not rest on our laurels and steel ourselves for one final onslaught." Richard understood that the Evil One's forces had now been disadvantaged having earlier relied on sheer weight of numbers to win the day. In the narrow streets, against the original inhabitants of the Ancestral City the tables were turned. The trio was sent to the safety of the forest camps while the forces for Good fought their way into houses, up the towers and battlements, into secret tunnels and through the surrounding hills. From every available opening in the city, missiles hurtled into the now panicking enemy as they attempted to hide or escape. The fallen were piled up in small heaps and then set alight creating large pyres that sent dark smoke spiralling skywards. The final clean up of the enemy was swift, precise and merciless as the sky began to lighten with the arrival of early dawn. Juroot and several Guardians began picking their way through the mass of debris and bodies, occasionally stopping when recognising the mutilated and battered bodies of some of their lost comrades. The air around the city was black, grainy and smelling of death, the scene of destruction that greeted the eye was horrific as the slow process of sorting the bodies started the clean up process. Personal weapons and artillery were placed in piles on street corners, smouldering wreckage moved into city squares to await removal. Much hard work was going to be needed to clear the battlefield debris as two major piles of the remaining bodies were stacked up, one for the Evil forces, another for Good. The solemn duty of lighting the two huge pyres fell to Juroot, twin black columns rose in a straight but twisting line heavenwards. Troops lined the battlement walls and were even hanging out of windows watching silently as the gathering flames consumed their comrades. The only sound for some time was the popping and crackling of the soaring fires licking upwards and once the twin bonfires had died to embers did Juroot hold up his hands and turn to the crowded area.

"It is now finished," he said wearily. "Our lives can begin once again, there is much to do before it will return to the place we all once knew and loved. Such evil must never be allowed to take root again." The silent respecting crowd did not cheer, but instead slowly dispersed and moved away to quietly contemplate with a sense of pride what had been achieved over the last hours.

Juroot motioned Richard, Orkan and Melek to follow him as he passed through the large north gate. The little band passed by the busy hill camps that had been collection points for the Good forces; these were steadily being packed up and cleared away, they moved on down and into the dark forest. For a short time the path twisted and turned in various directions and led them to a place that Richard immediately recognised. In front of him was the great Tree of Life and Golan's pebbled pedestal, this was the sacred place where his entire mission had begun.

"But where's Golan?" Richard anxiously enquired.

"He is here in spirit," Juroot replied. "Patience is bitter, but its fruit is sweet, Golan chooses the time and place." They seated themselves comfortably, each person visibly exhausted. Orkan was seated in front of Juroot while Melek and Richard sat together back to back on a broad tree stump.

"The Book of Prophecies has been proved correct, this adventure has taught me much," the librarian said philosophically. "I have learned that hate, disgust and revulsion can live comfortably beside camaraderie, familiarity and especially the feeling of affection for one's companion. All these things were totally foreign to me; my books have always been my life. " Melek mused, placing his hand on his back and gently squeezing the soft skin above Richard's hip."Indeed, I will deeply miss your company when you have to leave us." Richard placed his hand over his and the two locked fingers.

"Wonder where the Evil One is hiding right now?" Richard said. A sudden beam exploded down through an open canopy in the trees, straight onto a sparkling centre circle. "It's Golan!" Richard laughed and jumped to his feet and pulling Melek with him. This was a very different Golan to the one that had just disappeared all that time back, he was considerably changed, instead of the chameleon face ogre there was a kindly looking old man with a flowing white beard wearing a golden monk's habit and his head covered by a beautifully gold braided cowl.

"Well done!" he beamed. "Your path has been long and dangerous but you have succeeded as I knew you would." He moved across to Richard and for a moment the red pinpricked laser stare searched the boy's innermost thoughts.

"The last time we met you had the gruesome look of a beast, why?" Richard asked.

"You arrived as a boy with a head filled with idiotic thoughts, when what was really needed was for you to be concentrated on the task that lay ahead. I simply frightened you and that, determined your future thinking." Golan explained gently. "You have learned much." As Golan spoke Richard realised just how accurate this was. He felt stronger, braver, wiser, better able to cope with the unknown. He wondered if it had anything to do with the pods he carried and if the newfound knowledge would disappear once they left his possession.

"Do not fret," Golan had read his thoughts. "The pods have played their part and taught you much, their true wealth lies in the manner in which you gained each one. The value of that experience will forever remain with you." Richard had a sudden thought.

"You said Orkan was to be my guide but I had two," he lifted Melek's hand. "Together they were with me all the way and are the ones that brought me through this mission."

"Yes." Golan smiled and stretched out a hand for the pods. Richard opened his satchel and carefully unwrapped each one that was then returned to their proper place on the Tree of Life. Once all seven were in position they began to exude a warm, golden light. "I said there would be a guide." Golan continued. "But it was neither Orkan nor Melek that was your true guide, was it? It was your inner self and your belief in yourself that was your true guide. Now, we must prepare for the Great Ceremony of Aght, you will be part of that, Juroot will help you." Juroot took Richard by the arm and led him away from the sacred area into the forest where they found a cave. Inside Juroot handed Richard the sacred Helmet of Roshta with its seven golden glowing decals.

"You must wear this helmet and also be dressed in the habit and cape that brought you to us. I must also change and will return shortly to collect you for the ceremony." Juroot left and Richard found himself alone for the first time in a long while. He was tired, yet was unable to relax. As his mind travelled back through his long mission the truth of what they had achieved in twenty-six days made him swell with pride. He drew Juroot's dagger and sparred with his shadow.

"Still practicing I see." Juroot was at the cave entrance and wearing a fantastic suit of gold armour.

"This is your dagger and I must return it to you." Richard said sheepishly offering the weapon to Juroot.

"No, I gave it to you to use, it is yours, keep it. Perhaps you will have need of it again. Come, we must return to the Tree of Life." The two made their way through the forest, the Guardians were gathered together. What Richard saw left him a little speechless; all the Guardians were now wearing ceremonial armour of gold. In their midst, complete with his own golden armour and weapons, was Orkan.

"Broon, Guardian of the Common Beasts, was captured and killed by the Evil One sometime during the Final Battle. Golan explained. "Orkan's destiny was to join the Guardians. He takes Broon's place."

"What about Melek?" Richard asked.

Golan smiled and beckoned with his hand. From behind the Guardians stepped the petite figure dressed in fiery vermilion robes. It took Richard a second or two to realise that this was the ragged librarian who had accompanied him on his adventures.

"You are so beautiful," Richard exclaimed.

"Melek of the Sauge has been made the official Keeper of the Sacred Runes," Golan said. "As such he will also be the new leader of his people."

"That is how it should be," Richard said quietly.

"Say your farewells too," Golan said, "For the time has come for you to return to your own world." It was hard for Richard to believe that it was all over, but suddenly he experienced a strong yearning for home, his family and friends. He had so much to tell them, that is, if they believed him. As he said his goodbyes Richard felt a deep sense of regret in knowing that he was also losing true friends.

"You have saved our world. Your name will be revered and go down in our history. You will never be forgotten." Just then a whirring of wings brought a scout into the clearing. It announced that the Evil One had fled this land via the sacred red pool below the mountain with its zigzag waterfall. Golan turned immediately to Richard.

"The amulet must remain in the Ancestral World as must the helmet." Golan held out his hand and Richard handed him the two items. "You are in danger and must enter the water immediately. The Evil One has somehow located the 'Tranverse Intensifier' it was that, that brought you to us, hopefully it is still open back to your home." The whole group moved through the forest arriving at the point where Richard had found himself when he first met Golan and Orkan.

"Quickly! You must enter the water, walk to that small whirlpool, that is your way back home Go!" Golan demanded. Richard did what he was told. As he reached the small vortex there was a blinding flash of white and red that seared his eyes. He shut them tight and when he opened them to the black darkness in which swam two slanted red eyes. For a second the eyes became pinpricks of concentrated malevolence then they disappeared leaving a faint impression of the Evil One. Before Richard passed out his last sane thought was the question; had the Evil One really been vanquished?

FINIS

The Ancestral Trail Trilogy

1)   Long Ago & Far Away
2)   NewTime & Time Again
3)   Once Upon & Time Again

Frank Graves Copyright 1990

ABOUT THE AUTHOR

Frank Graves is an author and film producer raised in South Africa and is the great grandson of Sir Thomas Maclear named as one of the foremost royal astronomers at the Cape of Good Hope. He is also distantly related to Robert Graves the renowned writer and poet who was a large inspiration for Frank to eventually take up writing. Robert Graves encouraged Frank to start writing with several correspondence letters and stories while still a boy at school.

His first published work was published in 1989 was a fictional political thriller named African Chess (Now revamped, updated and republished in March 2014). African Chess was loosely based on his South African upbringing and the then apartheid system in place before Nelson Mandela's release from prison or his death.

His next major work published by Marshall Cavendish in 1992 was an epic 832 page "The Ancestral Trail" was 'split' into two halves of 26 issues each, making a total of 52 issues in total, all contained consecutive page and issue numbers. The first half, published fortnightly throughout 1993, takes place within a mythological 'Ancestral World' that describes a boy's struggle to restore good to these worlds. After the initial international run that sold over 30 million copies worldwide, the second half of that series was then created and was published in 1994 and took place in the totally different 'Cyber Dimension' all about the same boy's attempt to find a way back to his own world. Graves has now updated and re-written the full "Ancestral Trail Trilogy" in the form of three major novels. In January 2014, the first section covering a journey through an 'Ancient World' within "The Ancestral Trail Trilogy" named "Long Ago & Far Away" in a 450-page novel was published. The next novel is the second continuing section of the trilogy that covers a 'Cyber World' published in November 2014 and the third section of the trilogy, covering our 'Exponential World' published in mid 2017.

African Chess by Frank Graves is a newly updated and revamped conspiracy, adventure thriller originally published in 1990. Recent events in South Africa such as Nelson Mandela's Death, Oscar Pistorius's Trial, Shrien Dewani's Extradition for Murder, 16,259 Murders in 2012/13 and Epidemic Corruption have all helped to heighten attention and draw in a lot of focus on that country.

African Chess - The Story - Michael and Robert born at exactly same time and place at a remote hotel in one of South Africa's most beautiful regions are treated as equals until they grow up. Robert demands equality and falls foul of the dreaded South African police when he joins the African National Congress (ANC) as a freedom fighter. Both flee to England to escape and at Oxford Robert find more racism. When the security chief Dirk tries to kill them, Robert is helped by his white brother Michael and beautiful cousin Sharon. Their family business empire gives him certain protection. He learns to wheel and deal on London's commodity markets and uses this financial strength to fight back at the apartheid system. African Chess is relentless suspense, with move upon counter move until final checkmate.

The Culling novel is his third published work during 2014 and the story is that Western Governments use scientific evidence that within a few years, their world faces disaster from uncontrolled population explosion; especially by burgeoning third-world countries probably creating extra desert regions to ruin the industrialised world. No government could openly admit that it intends killing tens of millions of unwanted people worldwide. A number of major international conglomerates collectively called

"The Affiliation" are enlisted to conceal this man-made earthquake programme without any awkward questions being raised... It is a human survival war!

The Kixing is his fourth publication in 2014

Using hardened trained human fighters with lightweight gladiatorial designer armour, these very private illegal bouts are always held amid sumptuous black-tie dinner events especially laid on for the extremely rich and titled. In every vicious contest, the loser always being smashed to a pulp, critically maimed or better still and mercifully ...killed in full view of the sophisticated audience and is known as "THE KIXING". The reason for protection of this sport is the massive illegal gambling side with ensuing high stakes. There are never any other winners in commerce or sport when the conglomerate chairman promotes his beloved Kixing fights.

A major conglomerate attempts a hostile take-over of a small family company using dirty methods including professional and underhanded industrial espionage methods. However, the large group meets their match as the owners of the small firm that is Mafia connected resists the attempt. The chairman of the major group is also a well-known boxing promoter, who when acquiring a bookmaking business using similar type tactics creates his own total undoing of his business empire.